Photo courtesy of News Ltd

HARRY GORDON has been a columnist, sportswriter and foreign correspondent, editor of Melbourne's *Sun News-Pictorial*, editor-in-chief of the Herald and Weekly Times group and the Queensland Newspapers group, and chairman of Australian Associated Press. In 2003 the Melbourne Press Club honoured him with its Lifetime Achievement in Journalism Award.

He has written 10 previous books. One of them, *An Eyewitness History of Australia*, won the National Book Council first prize and the Barbara Ramsden Award.

His Olympic involvement began at the Helsinki Games in 1952. He was the only journalist accredited to cover both Australian Olympics — in Melbourne (1956) and Sydney (2000) — and is the official historian of the Australian Olympic Committee. He helped plan the Sydney torch relay, and named the streets at Olympic Park and in the Olympic Village. In 2001 the International Olympic Committee awarded him the Olympic Order, and in 2002 he received the Australian Sports Commission's inaugural award for Lifetime Achievement in Sports Journalism.

For his service to journalism, sport and history, he has been honoured with a CMG (Companion of the Order of St Michael and St George), membership of the Order of Australia, and induction into the Sport Australia Hall of Fame and the MCG Media Hall of Fame.

for

SARAH and SCOTT

SYDNEY and OLYMPIA

HARRISON and MATTHEW

THE TIME OF OUR LIVES

Inside the Sydney Olympics

Australia and the Olympic Games 1994–2002

HARRY GORDON

First published 2003 by University of Queensland Press
Box 6042, St Lucia, Queensland 4067 Australia

www.uqp.edu.au

Design and layout by Peter Evans
Printed in China by Everbest Printing Co. Ltd

Cataloguing in Publication Data
National Library of Australia

Gordon, Harry.
  The time of our lives: inside the Sydney Olympics.

  ISBN 0 7022 3412 5.

  ISBN 0 7022 3417 6 (pbk).

  1. Olympic Games (27th : 2000 : Sydney, NSW). 2.
  Olympics. I. Title.

  796.48

Foreword

By JOHN COATES
President, Australian Olympic Committee

When Harry Gordon's *Australia and the Olympic Games* was published in 1994, it made a big contribution to this nation's heritage. We needed a full, authoritative account of Australia's involvement over one hundred years in the Olympic movement, and that book provided one. It told us about the triumphs (as in Melbourne's 'Friendly Games' of 1956), the low points (as in the gold-less expedition to Montreal in 1976), and the challenges (as in the government's interference during the lead-up to the Moscow 1980 Olympics). It told us all about our heroes, people as disparate in time and style as Edwin Flack and Fanny Durack, as Betty Cuthbert and the lads of the Oarsome Foursome. It covered all this territory, and so much more, and it did so accurately, fairly and eloquently.

Now, nine years on, we need to know more. All that has happened since the Olympic Games of Barcelona (1992) and Lillehammer (1994) demands to be similarly documented: the extraordinary dramas behind Australia's participation in the 1996 Atlanta Olympics, when our team recorded its best-ever performance at an overseas Games; the trials and tribulations that dogged the organisation of the Sydney Olympics, and the ultimate triumph of those Games; the inspirational story of Cathy Freeman — Harry Gordon calls her 'a creature of destiny' — who lit the cauldron at the opening ceremony and went on the run the race of her life in the 400 metres final; the Australian team's capture of 58 medals (16 of them gold), spread across 20 different sports, to finish fourth among nations at the Sydney Games; the history-making breakthrough that brought us two gold medals at the Salt Lake City winter Olympics. It is timely, on the eve of the return of the Games to their original home in Greece, that all this be told. Harry Gordon has done so, in this companion volume to his earlier work.

If any history of the Australian Olympic movement was to be

written, there was always clearly only one person to do it. Harry knows it better than anyone else. He knows the athletes and the administrators well, and they in return have confidence in him — along with trust and respect. It would be foolish for any of us who were involved in the travails of the organisation of the Sydney Games to expect special favours from him. He has been very critical at times in his chronicle of what was and wasn't done, and that is how it should be. He decided to write this book only after receiving assurances from the Australian Olympic Committee that there would be no attempt to influence his account — just as he did before he embarked on *Australia and the Olympic Games*. Objectivity has always been a hallmark of the man. He sees it as a necessity in any search for truth.

For myself, those Sydney Olympic Games represented a unique experience. I consider myself privileged to have occupied several roles: to have been president of our national Olympic Committee during the period of bidding for, then winning, the Games; to have been part of the organisation of the Games; and to have had the immense honour of leading Australia's most successful Olympic team ever. It was gratifying that the whole adventure of the Games — and that's what it was — took place at Homebush Bay, just across the railway track from where I spent all my schooldays.

After the Games ended, the Australian team attended parades and celebrations in every capital city, and more than one million people paid tribute to them. That was as it should have been, because those Olympics were never just Sydney's They were Australia's, and the Australian team comprised athletes from the length and breadth of Australia.

During the lead-up to the Games, Juan Antonio Samaranch, then president of the International Olympic Committee, impressed on me that the success of Sydney 2000 would be judged by the Australian public — not on the size of the crowds, not on the number of tourists who came, not on SOCOG's financial results, but ultimately on the performance of the Australian team. He cited the cases of Barcelona in 1992 and Lillehammer in 1994, where host-country teams did very well indeed. It was a valuable observation, and one I quoted when I visited Paul Keating, then prime minister, in 1994 to solicit $135 million in funding, delivered through the Australian Sports Commission, for our athletes and coaches. It was in our minds when we at the AOC set some very difficult targets for Australia's 2000 team. We aimed at finishing fifth among nations; we finished fourth. We nominated a target of 60 medals, 19 more than we had ever won before; we finished with 58.

That our athletes achieved so much serves to remind us of the huge debt we owe to federal and state governments. Surely the most significant government decision affecting sport in this country related to the establishment of the Australian Institute of Sport in 1981. It was a visionary judgment, and remains the subject of respect and some envy among rival nations. The AIS, along with all state institutes and academies of sport, has made a huge contribution to the performance of our athletes. It is important in this context to state that since 1992 the AOC has neither sought nor received any direct federal government funding for the participation of our Australian team in any Olympic Games. The relationship we have with government in Australia is, I believe, unique. I'm proud that the AOC happens to be one of the very few national Olympic committees that provide direct support to athletes and coaches, as well as other sports-funding assistance to its member national federations. And I'm very pleased we've remained independent.

The Sydney Games, remembered so lucidly in this book, have given Australian sport, and the country itself, extraordinary momentum. As we look forward to Athens and beyond, we need to resolve not to allow that momentum to slow. The Melbourne Games of 1956 — so perfectly organised and (foreshadowing the Samaranch dictum) so successful for the host nation — left Australia with a legacy. Sydney's Games, which emulated the spirit of 1956 and took Olympic competition to a new level, have provided another legacy of goodwill and success.

Even as we savour the warm memories evoked here of the recent past, we need to be building on what has been achieved. To fulfil our obligations both to our athletes and to the Australian public on whom those Games had such a positive impact, we need to be planning for the challenges ahead. The truth is that it's a continuing effort, and we simply cannot afford to stop. If we did, the athletes, and the public, would not forgive us.

Contents

An Olympic reflection

By CATHY FREEMAN

The title of the book says it all for me — the Sydney Olympic Games *were* the most exciting time of my life. As a young girl running around a park in Mackay I dreamed of winning a gold medal in the Olympics — and in the year 2000 it all came true.

I was stunned to be given the honour of lighting the Olympic cauldron. I almost had to pinch myself to make sure I wasn't dreaming. I thought others deserved the honour more than me, especially legends such as Dawn Fraser, Betty Cuthbert, Herb Elliott and Marjorie Jackson. But as an indigenous person I was proud to light the flame on behalf of all Australians. They say it helped unite the country behind the Games. I am very happy if that was the case.

People have asked me since whether my task with the cauldron inflicted extra stress on me before my big race in the 400 metres. I know some officials were a bit concerned about that. The truth is that it didn't. I tend to thrive on pressure.

I knew the whole country was behind me in that final. The noise in the Stadium that night was deafening. I had nerves, fears and doubts and it was a great weight off my shoulders when I crossed the line and that gold medal was finally mine.

My story is just one of many in this magnificent book by the doyen of sports journalism and one of nature's gentlemen, Harry Gordon. Harry has talked to champion athletes, to those involved in the bid to win the Games for Sydney and to the organisers of this huge event. He reveals what went on behind the scenes at the 'greatest Games ever'. I know you will love it.

Congratulations Harry, you deserve a gold for this effort.

An Olympic reflection

By IAN THORPE

What does an Olympic Games mean to me? When people are asked this question the answer often focuses on the enormity of the event, the competition itself. They think about the athletes and the preparation that is needed to reach Olympic standard.

For me, I look much further back. I look back to when I wasn't a competitive swimmer, to when I was just a kid knocking about in the pool with my friends. I looked up to the champions, the athletes who competed at the Olympic Games. These people inspired me. As I watched them achieve their dreams, they inspired me to train hard, to achieve at a level within my sport so that I too would one day be able to represent my country at this four-yearly event.

The meaning of the Games is still the same to me as it was when I was a kid. It is about being inspired, about setting goals to follow dreams. But I guess the role has been reversed a little. I am now an Olympian, a participant, and I know that kids from around the world watch and draw inspiration from those of us lucky enough to be Olympic competitors. Many are dreaming that one day they too will have the opportunity to participate.

In the world we live in there is so much negativity, but sport can still give us joy and can help us to conquer the setbacks that we all face. The Olympic Games provide a platform where people can express themselves and achieve on an equal playing field. There is no bias, no judgment in an Olympic competition. It doesn't matter what country you are from, what colour your skin is or what religion you practise. It is the best of the best coming together and competing as one world. In a world that is so divided, the Games have the power to unite us ... and we respond as humanity, rather than as people of different nations.

I have experienced just one Olympic Games as a competitor and when I think about what was most important to me it wasn't about being successful but about having the opportunity to be there. It really was a privilege to take part, to feel the extraordinary warmth from spectators, and to feel the excitement throughout the Olympic Village. I am very grateful that I have had that opportunity.

I hope that I am able to compete in future Olympic Games. And I'd like to think that I could inspire young people to follow their dreams so that one day they too might experience what it means to be part of the Olympic family.

Author's note

A couple of years ago I started to work on an update of my earlier Olympic history, *Australia and the Olympic Games*. The idea was simply to expand that book, to embrace events that had occurred since it was published in 1994 — most notably the 1996 Centennial Olympic Games in Atlanta, the Sydney Olympics of 2000, and the winter Games of 1998 (Nagano) and 2002 (Salt Lake City). But the more research I did and the more I began to write, the more I realised that this wasn't the way to go. I felt I couldn't do justice to the subject just by adding a few chapters that would inevitably make a fairly weighty book even more so.

The Sydney Olympics, particularly, demanded better treatment than that. They were, after all, the best ever. They really did give most of us the time of our lives. They provided us not just with memories that we'll treasure always, but with a period of sheer, enduring happiness, possibly unmatched in Australian history. And their organisation, which coincided with the greatest scandal the Olympic movement has ever known, involved considerable drama that needed to be chronicled.

It became obvious that there should be a separate book, a companion volume to the 1994 history. This one would continue the story that began with the first meeting of the International Olympic Committee, in Paris in 1894, and the first Olympics of the modern era, in Athens in 1896, but it would have an identity of its own. What follows, then, is a book in three parts: one on Atlanta, one on Sydney, one on the Australian winter history that reached its high point in Salt Lake City. The largest part, of course, is about Sydney, and is buffered at either end by summaries … one that gives a brief history and background to those Games, one that explains what happened to many key players afterwards.

To tell this story fully I needed the cooperation of a number of people, some of them athletes, some administrators and planners. I have to thank John Coates, president of the Australian Olympic Committee, for entrusting me with access to all kinds of papers, letters, plans and other documents — even the contents of his precious endorsement contract, which caused more than a little angst on the way to Sydney's Games. As with this book's predecessor, the AOC had a healthy arrangement with me: one that amounted to total cooperation and access, without a sliver of editorial control. A number of judgments are made along the way in this narrative, and all of them are mine alone.

I conducted a large number of interviews with such people as John Coates, Michael Knight, David Richmond, Kevan Gosper, Sandy Hollway, Gary Pemberton, Phil Coles, Rod McGeoch, Simon Balderstone, Mike McKay, Jamie Tomkins, Kieren Perkins, Susan O'Neill, Alisa Camplin, Stephen Bradbury, Wendy Schaeffer, John Carew, Daniel Kowalski, Marjorie Jackson Nelson, Raelene Boyle and Bill Roycroft. They were all frank and helpful, and I thank them for it.

I am also grateful to the AOC for supplying statistics and giving much assistance with the task of assembling photographs. In this context, special thanks are due to Anne Vanden Hogen, Dominique Tremblay and Clare Rogers (statistics) and Julie Dunstan (photographs). Apart from helpful general data, the results section at the back of this book gives a thorough rundown on the performances of all Australians who competed at the Games of Atlanta, Nagano, Sydney and Salt Lake City. The efforts of Dominique, Anne and Clare, in documenting and formatting, have resulted in the separate publication of a compendium that offers a complete record of every Australian athlete at all the summer and winter Olympics in which our teams have competed. It is the most comprehensive such document ever assembled.

Bob Elphington, secretary general of the AOC, was unfailingly helpful with information and advice from the birth of this project. Laurie Muller, who announced his retirement as general manager of University of Queensland Press just before the book was completed, has been my friend and publisher through other similar adventures. His enthusiasm and involvement have been much appreciated. To the team at UQP, and particularly to the book's editor, Felicity Shea, and the designer, Peter Evans, I give thanks. And to my wife Joy, for her extreme patience, I am especially grateful.

Harry Gordon
Main Beach, Queensland

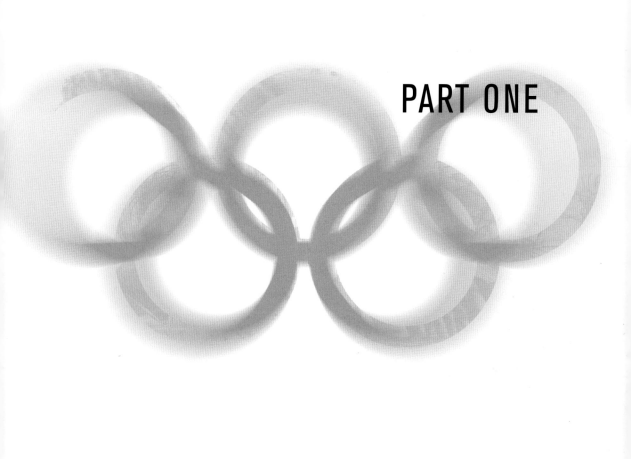

PART ONE

CHAPTER ONE

Stumbling towards Atlanta

Kieren Perkins couldn't understand what was going wrong. Whatever it was, though, the timing was terrible. There he was, demonstrably the fastest distance swimmer in the world, and suddenly he was battling even to squeeze into a place on the Australian team. He was the presiding Olympic champion over 1500 metres and possessor of the world records for the two events that mattered most to him: the 400 metres and the 1500 metres. Over the past four years he had in fact created 11 world freestyle records, and all the portents indicated that he would soon become the first Australian swimmer in a generation — since Dawn Fraser, in fact, in Tokyo in 1964 — to defend an Olympic title successfully. And now: now the very rhythm of his performance had become unpredictable, his normally fluid stroke was prone to breaking up, and he was finding himself inexplicably fatigued at inappropriate moments. Worst of all, he was being outpaced by swimmers with modest reputations. Frustration had become a constant, unwelcome companion.

It was April 1996, three months before he was due to defend his title at the Atlanta Olympic Games and also to attack the 400 metres freestyle, the event in which he had destroyed the world record at the most recent world championships in Rome. The International Olympic Committee's handbook for those Games, the *IOC Official Olympic Companion*, at that stage being printed, expressed little doubt about his prospects. The big question, it suggested, was not so much whether Perkins would win both races, but how much faster he could go (than his world records). 'Bet your bottom dollar he can win golds in the 400 metres and 1500 metres freestyle,' it stated, 'but the trickier guess is whether he can win them in world record times.'[1] Perkins' own view was that, while the 1500 event was his major target, he had a very good

Kieren Perkins
with his coach
John Carew.
(News Ltd)

chance of winning over 400 metres. He had set that world record in Rome just 10 days after the 1994 Commonwealth Games in Victoria, Canada, where he had won gold medals in the 200 metres, 400 metres, 1500 metres and 4 × 200 metres relay, and comfortably created two world records in one race (by slicing the 800-metre mark en route in the 1500 metres). Perkins always cherished the memory of that 400 metres performance in Rome, recorded during the 1994 world titles: it was, he felt, 'the closest I ever got to the perfect race ... everything went just right'.[2]

The first indication that the Olympic trials of April 1996 would be a troubling meet for Perkins came during training in the weeks beforehand. He had not swum well in the Queensland championships, but neither he nor his coach John Carew worried too much about that at the time. He had, after all, taken a long break from serious work in the pool, and had had a virus or two. But gradually, as the trials approached, it became clear that he had a considerable way to go before he was anywhere near his best race form. The break, Carew concluded, had been a little too long. He just wasn't prepared for these crucial races. Just how unprepared he was, was demonstrated in the 200 metres freestyle, where he failed to reach the finals. Then, in the morning heats of the 400 metres, he finished slowest of the eight qualifiers, and was consequently relegated to the unfamiliar waters of an outside lane. In the final Daniel Kowalski, then Pan Pacific champion over the distance, was virtually unchallenged to win in 3 minutes 50.60 seconds. Perkins swam strongly enough over the first 300 metres, then seemed to lose control and faded into third placing, behind the unfancied Malcolm Allen. Allen, generally regarded as a 200 metres swimmer, finished nearly a second ahead of Perkins, whose time was almost nine seconds outside his own world record of 3 minutes 48.80 seconds. Under the strict, sudden-death selection policy of the head coach, Don Talbot, that meant Perkins had missed a berth in the team for the race in which he had been favourite. It also meant that the man who had dominated world swimming for four years had just one chance left to make the team for Atlanta: in the 1500 metres. His entire career was on the line.

It was a harsh prospect, one that stunned the sporting world. 'Mr Invincible faces unthinkable,' a banner headline streamed across a full page of the *Australian*. Briefly there was speculation that Allen might forfeit his unexpected place in the 400 metres to Perkins, particularly since Perkins was, as the swimming writer Nicole Jeffery noted in the *Australian*, 'still regarded as Australia's best chance of a gold medal in this event'. Allen had qualified for the Games separately as a member of the 4 × 200 metres relay squad, and was not seen as a serious contender over 400 metres. But no such deal was ever really contemplated, as Perkins made clear six years later:

> There was pressure, sure, but he never offered, and I never asked. I would never have accepted it, not if I thought he was doing it just to let me in…I always strongly believed in the selection policy of Australian swimming. You have to perform on the day, if you don't you're not in…You don't get a second chance at the Olympics, so if you can't get yourself ready for the day, that's that. Getting through the

disappointment of missing the 400 was a little hard... it was an event I wanted to be involved in in Atlanta, and I really thought I had a good chance to win it. But I missed the opportunity, and I have nobody but myself to blame. I was still confident, though, that I would make the team in the 15 [hundred], because other than Daniel [Kowalski] there wasn't any really strong competition in the 15 at that time.[3]

Apart from Kowalski, Perkins' major opponent in the 1500 metres trial was Glen Housman, who had won a silver medal behind him in Barcelona in 1992. This time he dropped off the early pace set by Kowalski and Perkins, and after the first 200 metres it was obvious that those two would fill the available places for Atlanta. Perkins attacked early and led from the middle stages until the 1200-metre mark, then weakened, to be overpowered by Kowalski. 'Tonight was mentally tough,' Perkins told journalists afterwards. 'When Daniel came back at me I had nothing left, and I thought, "This guy is playing with me".' Perkins struggled over the last few hundred metres, but still managed to finish one second behind Kowalski. He was too relieved at salvaging a place in the team even to notice that a 15-year-old lad called Grant Hackett had finished fifth in 15 minutes 30.63 seconds, swimming an astonishing nine seconds faster than Perkins had at the same age.

For Kieren Perkins and the man he has always called Mister Carew, it was a time for serious reappraisal. For the media and the wider public, it was a time for conjecture. Carew, a gruffly sentimental man who had been Perkins' mentor since the swimmer was nine years old, took him aside and suggested that maybe they ought to break up the partnership. That initiative — the generous, reluctant act of a frankly bewildered man — demonstrated more than anything else the depth of the crisis that afflicted the Perkins camp. The close relationship of these two had begun soon after a shocking accident 14 years earlier in which young Kieren, horsing around his Chapel Hill (Brisbane) home with his young brother Jared, had run headlong through a glass door, managing among other injuries to sever his left calf muscle. The awful wound had required 86 stitches and a couple of hours in microsurgery. Later Kieren had needed muscle-strengthening therapy in a heated pool, which led his parents to the John Carew Swim School, two kilometres away in the suburb of Indooroopilly. So had begun one of the most notable swimmer–coach alliances of modern times, one that would last 18 years, through three Olympic Games.

In April 1996, though, John Carew felt he didn't have quite the understanding he had always had with Perkins in the past. Something was very wrong. He was concerned not just about the slump in form but also about what seemed like a reduction in commitment, and to some degree he blamed himself. He had always been able to coax the best out of his swimmers, but that wasn't happening now. 'He maybe had an idea what the problem was, but I wasn't quite aware of it at the time,' Carew later recalled. 'He wasn't shirking or anything, he'd still come to his training, but things were somehow different. He seemed to be going through the motions. I said to him, "Look, do you think you should get another coach? I mean it. Do you think you should go to somebody else now … like maybe you've had your time with me, and you might be better with somebody else you know? It might be me [who's to blame]." Part of the reason was I felt he wasn't doing what he should have been doing.'[4]

Perkins' response was blunt. 'No, no. It's not your fault, and I certainly don't want to go to another coach.'[5]

Speculation concerning the champion's inability to find anything like his best form dominated many sports pages. Theories about what some newspapers called 'The Perkins Mystery' abounded: he had spent too much time on personal and sponsorship activities, as well as a new job as a television sports reporter; he was increasingly susceptible to illness, particularly a flu-type virus; he was carrying a shoulder injury; he had an iron deficiency; conversely, he had very high level of iron stores that weren't being used, causing loss of energy and strength; his taper (the cutdown in training before a big meet) had been wrongly timed. When Perkins' management company, IMG, issued a statement acknowledging his 'below par performances' and attributing them to an imbalance in iron stores, nutritional and medical experts professed to be bewildered. One said forthrightly that the explanation didn't make sense. And when a reporter asked the swimmer point-blank what the difference was between the Kieren Perkins of April 1996 and the Kieren Perkins of September 1994, he replied deadpan: 'I've really got no idea.'

The truth, which Perkins later came to accept, was simply that he was paying a penalty for distraction. His capacity for total, undiverted focus, normally one of his great weapons, had been affected on several fronts. He had met the girl he was to marry. He had been identified corporately as an exciting sponsorship talent, and become involved in product endorsement and advertising. He was making money in television, and learning as he did so. Against all that, though, his innate sense of self-belief had not deserted him. Six years afterwards he looked back with candour at this fragile period of his swimming career. The passage of time had made dispassionate assessment a little easier. 'I was a little bit rundown and had gotten sick a few times, picked up a couple of injuries as well. I just hadn't been looking after my body well enough. There were periods of time away from the water. My fitness wasn't there and my stroke wasn't grooved in, so when I got into race situations and I'd get tired, things would fall apart.'[6] He expanded:

> The biggest mistake I made was that I was focusing on the Olympics themselves, and probably just didn't ... didn't recognise enough how important it was to be ready for the trials. I just assumed I'd be there. The 400 was a missed opportunity, because Daniel Loader won it in 3.47 and I held the world record of 3.43. Even though I probably wasn't 100 per cent fit, I still think I could have gone that quick and made a race of it, which would have given me a good opportunity to win. But I have nobody but myself to blame ... It is easy to get distracted. Really it came down to the fact that I just wasn't giving 100 per cent in all areas, and I needed to make a decision ... I either wanted to go to the Olympics and win, or I didn't. Once that decision was made it was easy to make sure the diet was right, the rest was good, and you know, I was starting to do all the right preventative stuff for swimming — physio and things like that to prevent the injuries. I had a two-month block there between the trials and the Olympics, where in training everything went really well. It all just fell into place.[7]

Soon after his offer to split, John Carew had come to understand the problem:

> For a world-record class swimmer, he had too much on his plate.

Swimming was just a different part of his life. There were other things in his life and he was starting to find them. He was getting older and discovering things. He wasn't doing things like he was before. He'd go flying to Sydney for corporate talks, and he was earning money. He had found the girl he eventually married. He was doing too many things. He wasn't getting the cross-training he should have. It was just a case of too much outside work and change in lifestyle. You've got to expect that. It was all part of growing up. You can't expect them to be a monk all their life.'[8]

Perkins wasn't the only gold-medal candidate to stumble on the way to Atlanta. In early 1996 the fabled Oarsome Foursome were having serious problems. After their magnificent victory in the coxless fours at the Barcelona Olympics, the quartet — Mike McKay, James Tomkins, Nick Green and Andrew Cooper — had taken a break for nearly two years, then returned to international racing in mid-1995. They had finished ninth at the European championships at Lucerne, then fifth at the world championships at Tampere, Finland, which for an underdone crew, after less then eight months' preparation, seemed a reasonable result. Those events took place against a wider background of disharmony among rowers on tour that led to the recall of the Australian Rowing Council's head coach, Simon Gillett, and the ultimate departure of its CEO, David Schier. Morale among the Australian rowers was low, and it worsened when the rowers found themselves booked into a youth hostel as a cost-cutting measure. They were allocated to large dormitories, among fellow-rowers and foreign backpackers. McKay, as representative of the ARC Athletes' Commission, led the revolt that culminated with the rowers voting for the replacement of Schier, Gillett and the high-performance manager, Samantha Stewart.

The next drama came when Cooper, after much agonising, decided to quit the crew. He had lost some of his passion, and felt he could not in all honesty commit himself 100 per cent to the crew. It was a heartfelt judgment that Tomkins called 'incredibly unselfish'.[9] Green summed it up: 'Andrew didn't want to feel responsible for us winning silver, not gold.'[10] It was a huge blow: some might have seen it as rowing's version of the loss of a Beatle. A measure of the regard in which the rower was held was the ultimate naming of the boat Australia used in the 1996 Olympics as the *Andrew Cooper*.

Candidates auditioned for the role of replacement included Bo Hanson, Richard Roach, Rob Jahrling and Drew Ginn. Ginn, 21, a gifted athlete who had won school colours in four different disciplines — athletics, basketball, football and rowing — at Melbourne's Scotch College, finally got the gig. Before the first Olympic trials at Penrith came another significant change, one that strained relationships within the crew. Tomkins, who had stroked the boat through all its previous success and was regarded by many as Australia's greatest oarsman ever, was pressured to give up the stroke seat to McKay, swapping places at No. 2. Reluctantly he agreed, after coaxing by the fiercely competitive McKay and coach Noel Donaldson. McKay, who effectively drove the four's campaign for Atlanta, convinced Donaldson that the boat simply wasn't going fast enough, and the one–two seating needed to be changed. After the new arrangement was tried in the first Olympic trial, and the four won comfortably, the swap became permanent. 'We all knew it was the right thing,' McKay recalled later, 'but James was hurt. His ego was bruised.'[11] That change was based mainly on McKay's sheer strength as a rower, but it also symbolised his leadership role in the boat. At times afterwards, though, there was jousting between himself and Tomkins, who continued to believe he should be stroke.

After that, the troubles just continued. During a team-selection process that McKay, Green and Tomkins found highly frustrating, the crew was broken up and tried with different combinations. At one stage Green and Tomkins were sharing a boat with Richard Wearne and Rob Walker, and Ginn and McKay were teaming with the Stewart twins, James and Geoff. It was after another such experiment in combination — when Ginn, McKay and Tomkins were joined in a trial by the South Australian Jaime Fernandez, and were beaten — that a clearly exhausted McKay (who was suffering from a virus) dug his oar too deeply and was pulled out of the boat. That undignified exit was an appropriate enough metaphor for the Foursome's collective state of mind. Their understanding had been that if they won their first Olympic trial at Penrith that February — which they did — they would be automatically selected for Atlanta. When that didn't happen, they felt cheated.

The Oarsome Foursome break into grins as they win the coxless fours in Atlanta. They finished a length in front of the Italian crew to win back-to-back gold.

'It got to a stage where there was a lot of self-doubt, even among us,' Nick Green recalled in 2002.[12] 'I felt I was under real threat of being axed until the very last trial.' (It was after this race, during which Green teamed with Ron Scott, Dave Weightman and Jaime Fernandez against his old comrades — and won — that McKay took his tumble.) 'I needed that win to shut up all the critics, particularly within the Foursome. I think out of adversity people sometimes dig a little deeper. The selectors weren't showing a great deal of faith in us, and it rattled us a bit. There seemed to be a few hidden agendas about, even inside the crew. For a

Wendy Schaeffer
on Sunburst
during the show-
jumping phase
of the three-day
event in Atlanta.
(News Ltd /
Brett Faulkner)

while there Mike didn't even know which boat he wanted to crew in — the four, the two or the eight. The whole selection business was a huge ordeal, and we felt an unnecessary one.' McKay, who described the process as 'a complete joke', explained later: 'It's true my sole aim was to win gold, and I wanted to be in the boat with the best chance of winning. Nick was under the pump. He was underdone, and the selectors wanted to replace him with James Stewart. My feeling was that nobody's indispensable. But after that whole affair, my feeling was that I'd never doubt quality people again.'[13]

After two weeks of trials, the selectors finally announced that the Melbourne-based four of Ginn, Green, McKay and Tomkins would be representing Australia in Atlanta. 'We have taken into account the outstanding international record of three of the crew members,' said the panel's statement. And about time, was the view of that trio. Green said later: 'The last three races were a waste of time. We'd had the philosophy all along that we wanted to go as a team.' Just before the waiting ended, they had indeed pledged to stick together.

For the talented young horsewoman Wendy Schaeffer, the prospects for Atlanta were looking bright until May 1996. At 21, after impressive riding at Badminton, England, and apparently assured of a place in the Australian Olympic equestrian team, she had returned home for a short break to Hahndorf, South Australia, leaving her horse Sunburst in England. Then, while competing in a minor event at Narracorte, her inexperienced mount, Whimsical Son, crashed heavily on a bank, breaking Schaeffer's right leg just above the ankle. The Royal Flying Doctor Service immediately evacuated her to Adelaide, and she was operated on the same day by the orthopaedic surgeon Tony Pohl, director of trauma at the Royal Adelaide Hospital. The conventional treatment would have been to encase the leg in a plaster cast, but that would have meant up to four months in plaster and a total recovery period of up to eight months. There were then exactly 63 days to go before the three-day team event was due to begin in Atlanta. With some persuasion from Wendy's mother, Di Schaeffer, a physiotherapist as well as a passionate rider, Pohl opted instead to insert a rigid compression plate, with screws. He then surrounded the leg with a light fibreglass cast, complete with zippers.

Three weeks after breaking her leg Wendy Schaeffer was riding again in Australia, with help from a light leather splint that fitted around her boots. After receiving a clearance from the Australian team's medical director, the Adelaide-based Brian Sando, she left for England to join the Australian squad. Five weeks after the accident, she was astride Sunburst (aka Tommy) again, taking part in a selection gallop, and able to stand in the stirrups. 'I wanted to believe from that point that nothing would stop me,' she said later, 'but I was by no means sure. I was pretty lame, and there was this dead, dull ache in the leg. Also, I didn't know whether the selectors would be prepared to take a risk on me.'[14] In Atlanta two weeks later, ten days before the Games were due to begin, she took Sunburst over jumps for the first time since the fall.

Another pre-Atlanta setback came with a drug scandal in February 1996, involving swim coach Scott Volkers and Samantha Riley, then regarded as the dominant female breaststroker in the world. Riley tested positive for dextropropozyphene, a banned analgesic, at the world short-course titles in December 1995 in Rio de Janiero, where she had won two world titles and broken two world records. Volkers took full responsibility, conceding that he had thoughtlessly given Riley a pain-killing tablet for a headache, without consulting the team doctor. The International Swimming Federation (FINA) initially banned him for two years, but after appeals the sentence was reduced to seven months, which enabled him — at virtually the last moment, and after six months of drama and doubt — to accompany his squad of six to Atlanta. Riley, who had been with Volkers for eight years, escaped with a warning, but the stress of the whole affair affected her considerably. Like Perkins, she failed to produce her best form at the Olympic trials, and was beaten in both the 100 metres and 50 metres breaststroke events by Helen Denman.

Also in the Volkers squad were Susan O'Neill, Ellie Overton, Angela Kennedy, Lise Mackie and Jade Winter. For all of them the agonising drama, and the insecurity that inevitably accompanied it, proved unsettling. O'Neill, who had moved to Volkers from her early mentor Bernie Wakefield 18 months previously, felt certain during the last few weeks that she would be training in Atlanta under another coach, Brian Sutton. She was at the time ranked second in the world

Samantha Riley, obviously unhappy, after failing to win a medal in the 200 metres breaststroke in Atlanta.

in the 200 metres butterfly. Riley obviously had by far the more trying time of it, but for both herself and O'Neill, as gold-medal prospects, the pathway to Atlanta was difficult indeed. O'Neill had one advantage: her capacity for self-containment:

> As an athlete you just have to be really selfish, and I basically tried to ignore [the doubt over Volkers] and did what I had to do. I did my training sessions. I never like to be too dependent on anyone … then, if it gets taken away, it can be hard. I feel I can do my own warm-ups, I could plan my own races in my head, and just go out there. Scott talked about Sam a lot, and at one stage — this was later — I had to tell him I didn't want to hear her name again, especially around competition.[15]

Australia sent a team of 424 athletes to those 1996 Centennial Olympic Games. It was the largest ever to represent the nation, and the third biggest (behind the United States and Germany) of the 197 at the Games. John Coates was chef de mission for the third consecutive time, assisted by Peter Montgomery, Keith Murton and John Devitt. A total of 220 officials accompanied the team, with the medical section alone comprising 10 doctors, 20 physiotherapists, 18 masseurs, a dietician and a clinic administrator/nurse. Incentives for athletes to do well are naturally always high, but this time they were bolstered by an Olympic Dream Medal Reward Scheme — under which $1.695 million was allocated for distribution to all medallists (individuals and

Turkey's weight-lifter Naim Suleymanoglu, who won three gold medals and broke five world records in Atlanta.

teams), on the basis of $25,000 for gold, $15,000 for silver and $7500 for bronze. Along with useful information about the attractions of Atlanta, Australian team members each received a potted guide to the language of the Deep South. Sample extracts: FAR — If it gets out of control, call the Far Department; COLD — What you did on the telephone; FAINTS — What you put around the yard to keep the dog in.

The Atlanta Olympic Games celebrated the 100th anniversary of the first modern Olympics in Athens in 1896, and there was about the opening ceremony a proud sense of occasion. The Deep South collided gently for a while with the Temple of Zeus in ancient Olympia, and somehow the union of those two spirits worked. It was a ceremony that linked unforgettably two great black Americans, the assassinated civil rights leader Martin Luther King jnr and Muhammad Ali — one reciting his dream in mellifluous tones, one looking somehow both noble and vulnerable as he unsteadily lowered the torch to ignite the flame. A nostalgic highlight came when tribute was paid to the greatest champions of the past; and those of them who were living, including such people as Dawn Fraser, Nadia Comaneci and Greg Louganis, were introduced. So was the remarkably spry Yugoslav gymnast Leon Stukelj, gold medallist from 1924 and at 97 the oldest champion of them all.

The Games produced a harvest of historic performances. When Michael Johnson, of the United States, won the 200 metres in world-record time, he became the first man ever to win the 400–200 double at the Olympics. Until the preceding US Olympic trials, the 200 metres world record had sat unsullied for 19 years — and suddenly this man, charging along in his oddly stiff-backed style, had slashed it twice in five weeks. Marie-Jose Perec, of France, also completed the 400–200 double, emulating the feat of the American Valerie Briscoe in the (boycotted) Games of 1984. When Carl Lewis, of the United States, won the long jump, he became only the fourth athlete in any sport to have won nine gold medals, and the third to have won the same individual event four times. Donovan Bailey set a new world record for the 100 metres and was a member of the winning Canadian relay team. When Britain's Steve Redgrave won the coxless pairs, he became the first rower to win a gold medal in four consecutive Games. Turkey's Naim Suleymanoglu became the first weightlifter to win three Olympic gold medals, and he

Russian double gold medallist Alex Popov, who duplicated his Barcelona feat.

broke five world records in five minutes. The Spaniard Miguel Indurain, five times winner of the Tour de France, celebrated the opening of the Olympics to cycling professionals by winning the road time trial. The sprint swimmer Alex Popov, of Russia, completed the 100–50 double, duplicating his feat in Barcelona four years earlier. Hungary's Krisztina Egerszegi equalled Dawn Fraser's three-in-a-row swimming record (for the 100 metres freestyle) when she won the 200 metres backstroke for the third successive time.

The most astonishing results in the pool, though, came from the Irish swimmer Michelle Smith, 26, who collected three individual gold medals — more than any other athlete at the Games — and a bronze. She had had a mediocre record at the two previous Olympics, and in 1993 she was ranked 90th in the world in the 400 metres women's medley. Then her form improved dramatically, and — to many swimming insiders — suspiciously. The doubts were related in part to the fact that her coach (and later husband) Erik de Bruin had himself been disqualified for four years in 1993 on doping charges. Suspicions deepened after the respected American triple gold medallist Janet Evans told a reporter that questions about a certain swimmer were 'a topic of conversation on the pool deck'. In Smith's first event she won the 400 metres medley gold medal easily, in a time that represented a 17.34-second improvement over three years. She then won the 400 metres freestyle — after qualifying in a time 17.54 seconds faster than her previous recorded best — and completed the treble with the 200 metres individual medley. After finishing third in the 200 metres butterfly (won by Australia's Susie O'Neill), Smith said she had had 'the best week of my life', and she was feted on her return to Ireland. Allegations of drug use continued, but none was proved in Atlanta. (In 1998 Smith was suspended for four years by FINA for having tampered with a drug test. In 1999 the Court of Arbitration for Sport rejected her appeal.)

For all the splendid performances and glittering spectacle, the Atlanta Games were far from successful. They were in a sense saved by the 10,301 athletes. From the start it was obvious that major organisational problems existed. The transport system was distressed, and at times chaotic, the computer system was besieged by glitches, the security and crowd control were too often inadequate, and the commercialism that surrounded the Games was tacky and exploitative. In these areas, and others, Australian planning observers in Atlanta learned valuable lessons in what not to do in Sydney. The volunteers were unfailingly polite, but not well trained. Centennial Park, where thousands of visitors gathered in a carnival-like atmosphere among the fast-food outlets and souvenir booths, was not covered by the Olympic security system. This meant that there were no metal-detector precautions or bag searches. Soon after 1 am on 27 July a home-made bomb exploded in the park, killing one person and injuring 111. Hasty, high-level talks were held throughout the night, and at dawn the director-general of the IOC, Francois Carrard, announced that the Games would go on. The competition schedule was uninterrupted. The crime remained unsolved.

That blast, in an area which had been promoted as a safe haven, provoked chilling memories of the last act of terrorism at an Olympics — in Munich in 1972, when Palestinians took Israeli hostages in an incident which cost 17 lives. US president Bill Clinton, who had spent some days at the Atlanta Games, condemned the bombing as 'an act of vicious terror…clearly directed at the spirit of our democracy', and added: 'We cannot let terrorism win, that is not the American way. We cannot be intimidated by acts of terror.' Just days before the Olympics began a suspicious explosion had occurred aboard a TWA airliner outside New York, killing all 230 passengers aboard. Early evidence, though, suggested that the crude Centennial Park bomb — a combination of metal piping, gunpowder, nails, glass and a timed detonator — might have been the work of a local anti-government group, or a disgruntled ratbag, rather than the calculated action of an international terrorist organisation.

A phone call, described as belonging to a white male with a southern accent, gave warning minutes before the bomb was detonated. Similar concoctions had been used in attacks in the region on a civil rights lawyer and a federal judge. Around 30 Australian athletes, mainly swimmers celebrating the end of their program, had been in the park until half an hour before the blast, prompting some worried phone calls and a dawn head-count by officials in the Olympic village.

For Australia, the Games were bountiful. The team won a total of 41 medals — 9 gold, 9 silver and 23 bronze — spread across an unprecedented range of 14 sports. This was the largest-ever haul for a team competing outside Australia. (In Melbourne in 1956, Australia had won 13 gold medals in a total of 35.) In the medal tallies Australia finished fifth for total medals, and equal seventh for gold medals. In Barcelona in 1992 the figures had been 7 gold and 27 overall, and in Seoul in 1988 3 gold and 14 overall. The Atlanta gold medals were shared among the disciplines of swimming, rowing, equestrian, shooting, hockey and tennis.

For the 171 women (35 per cent of the team total), the results were gratifying. They won 4 of their country's 9 gold medals (44 per cent), 5 of the 9 silvers (56 per cent) and nine of the 23 bronze medals (39 per cent). Overall, they contributed 18 of the total 41 medals, or 44 per cent.

CHAPTER TWO

Still the same water

Gold-medal performances inevitably offer inspiration, but few of them could do so more than that of Kieren Perkins in the 1500 metres freestyle. He overcame adversity, he was courageous in the face of apparent defeat, and he demonstrated — at a time when most around him felt his lustrous career was crashing — an unflinching belief in himself and his destiny. After his miserable time at the Olympic trials, both his training form and his sense of commitment improved. 'I was doing what I should have been doing through the year beforehand,' he said later. 'Everything was right and by the time I got to the Olympics, certainly when the meet started, I had the background and everything I needed to perform well.'[1]

The morning before the final, Perkins swam dreadfully in the last heat. His plan had been to win what he thought would be a comfortable race and qualify in a middle lane. Instead, he recalled later:

> I got to about the middle of the race, and there were guys all over me at a time when I expected to be in front cruising. There was a time for part of that race when I didn't think I was going to make the final. I was cramping and having difficulty turning. When I hit the wall and looked up, I knew [from the times] that I'd made the final. But I was disappointed. What was meant to be an easy heat swim had turned out to be a very hard heat swim. I'd qualified in lane eight for the final — which is not where I wanted to be. When you're struggling, the pain hurts more, and I was hurting. That swim created a lot of doubt, that maybe I wasn't ready after all. I really had to shut it out, which was the main thing I tried to do in that 36-hour period before the final … pretend it didn't happen.[2]

Daniel Kowalski qualified fastest with 15 minutes 12.55 seconds, and Perkins slowest with 15 minutes 21.42 seconds, almost 40 seconds outside his best. He had touched out Steffen Zesner, of Germany, by two-tenths of a second, a fingernail really, to survive. He consoled himself about the outside lane: 'After all, it's still the same water.'

For the first six days of swimming competition, Australia's performance did not match expectation. Before the Games, predictions had ranged as high as five gold medals. But with one day to go, there hadn't been a glint of gold. Samantha Riley, world champion over both the 100 metres and 200 metres breaststroke, finished with bronze in the 100 metres but was a well-beaten fourth in the 200 metres. After the longer race, the one she had yearned for years to win, she was in tears, comforted by coach Scott Volkers. He attributed her disappointing performance to the pain-killer drug furore, for which he rightly accepted absolute blame. 'She hasn't been the same since,' he said. 'Something in her head has stopped her doing what she has to do.' A bigger factor in Riley's defeats than the drug-charge aftermath, though, was probably the arrival of a new force in breaststroke swimming. The South African Penny Heyns won both events impressively, setting a world record in her 100 metres heat.

After those six days, Daniel Kowalski had finished with bronze in the 200 metres and 400 metres freestyle finals, but was a raging favourite to win the 1500 metres on the final day. Malcolm Allen, Perkins' conqueror in the 400 metres Olympic trials, had failed to qualify for the final in that event, and had finished fifth in the consolation final. Scott Miller had won silver in the 100 metres butterfly, Scott Goodman bronze in the 200 metres butterfly, and there were relay medals in the women's 4 × 100 metres medley (silver), the men's 4 × 100 metres medley (bronze) and the women's 4 × 200 metres freestyle (bronze). The lack of gold prompted a chorus of criticism from various commentators, including some uninvolved former champions. The head coach, Don Talbot, dismissed them as 'armchair critics', but section manager Terry Buck observed in his post-Games report: 'This [criticism] placed a huge burden on the coaches and athletes…any performances that were less than gold medal standard appeared to be not acceptable to those outside the swim team.'

Kieren Perkins on the way to his gold medal in the 1500 metres.

The final night of swimming restored a sense of pride to a team that seemed under siege by critics. Australia won two gold medals, two silver and a bronze — the best result it had achieved in a single day since the home Games of 1956. In the men's 1500 metres freestyle (with Perkins and Kowalski) and the women's 200 metres butterfly (with O'Neill and Petria Thomas), the team recorded one–two quinella wins. And the 4 x 100 metres medley relay team swam above all expectations to win bronze.

After he warmed up for the final that night, Perkins was more nervous than he had ever been before a race. Lying on his stomach on a massage table, he found himself trying to control an emotion that was quite a stranger. 'The nervousness just took over, to a degree that I felt my heart was going to explode out of my chest,' he said much later. 'It was probably the hardest part of those Olympics. It went on for nearly an hour.'[3] He continued:

> I'd spent most of my life teaching myself not to get really nervous — just excited so you get the adrenalin, but never nervous. And now it

was a freaking-out kind of nervous … Oh my God, what am I going to do? … If I don't win I won't be able to go back home, everyone's going to be disappointed in me … all that silly stuff your brain conjures up in times of crisis. I recognised that my heart rate was really quite elevated, I was really nervous and I got angry with myself for wasting energy. I was committing the cardinal sin of sports performance, which is to put yourself in a position where you've lost it before you've even started. I told myself to be rational … Don't be ridiculous, this is just sport, it's not life and death. You are fit, yesterday was just a bad day, you know how to win, you've done it before. Just bloody get in there and do it. Stop being so silly. After an hour, that's what brought the heart rate down. I calmed myself down in that way.[4]

Carew and Perkins had worked out a game plan, a bluff really. They were aware that if the race came down to a sprint over the last 50 metres against Kowalski, Kowalski would overpower him. The strategy was to go out hard, get in front, and stay there. They wanted the rest of the field to think Perkins was somehow back to his best, and fight it out for silver. Perkins has a clear memory of the race:

After I'd given myself this caning, I got to the other side of it and said to myself: 'Right, let's just go out and do it.' On the blocks I couldn't hear the crowd, all I could see was the water in front of me, my 50 metres of space. Being in lane eight, I couldn't see the other athletes until I turned at the start/finish end — because I always pushed off on my left side and the lane ropes are so big you can't see over them. I could see them at that turn under the water, when pushing off. The guy in lane seven was off the pace, so I could see right across. After the first 100 I had about a quarter of a body length, the second 100 I had about a half, the third 100 about three-quarters, and then when I turned at the fourth I had about a body length and a half. That was really when I knew I'd won it, because I hadn't changed my pace and the guys in the middle of the pool had obviously sort of given up on me and decided to concentrate on racing each other. That was the bluff we planned for, and it worked. After that first 400 metres, I think the guys in the middle did believe 'Perkins is gone, he's back, let's fight it out for the silver'. That enabled me to get away a bit more. I guess after I got about 10 to 15 metres out, I just maintained that lead and struggled home. I hit the wall, checked the scoreboard just to make sure, and that moment was the ultimate release. I had spent so long having people tell me I couldn't do it.[5]

Daniel Kowalski, 21, showed abundant courage in fighting back to overcome Britain's Graeme Smith for second place. Three strokes from home he looked beaten, but he found some reserve that enabled him to finish a touch ahead. He had much to be proud of: he had become the first man in 92 years (since the American Francis Galley in 1904) to win medals at 200 metres, 400 metres and 1500 metres in a single Olympic Games.

Kieren Perkins on the winners podium.

In 2003 he said of Perkins' bluff:

No question it worked. If it came down to a race between us, with the speed I had then, I would have been able to swim over the top of him. I was a good racer, and if he'd been beside me, I think I'd have had a big chance of swimming him down. But I was in the centre and he was over on the outside. Mentally I just didn't handle that race. I stood there at the start and I was really, really scared. I knew I had the opportunity to win it, but I was putting the cart before the horse. I'm thinking I'm going to win, and I'm thinking already about the consequences. I'm thinking what is the country going to think of me for beating Kieren Perkins. That was all that was going through my mind. Mentally I wasn't tough enough to be swimming for an Olympic gold medal.[6]

The victory made Perkins, after a preparation that one sports writer said 'had catastrophe written all over it', one of only three champions to defend a title successfully in the Atlanta pool. The others: the sprinter Alex Popov and the backstroker Krisztina Egerszegi. It also made him the first Australian since Dawn Fraser to win back-to-back gold. More than that: the simple truth was that no greater comeback from the edge of humiliation had ever been made in the history of Australian sport. Like Debbie Flintoff-King in Seoul eight years previously, he had refused to be stared down by defeat.

Earlier the same evening Susan O'Neill broke Australia's gold-medal duck in the pool, becoming the first Australian ever to win the women's 200 metres butterfly. She also inflicted the sole defeat suffered by the Irish triple gold medallist Michelle Smith. Before the final Smith caused something of a stir by failing to assemble with the other swimmers in the marshalling area. O'Neill recalled later:

Every day she [Michelle] seemed to win a gold medal and every night there was rumour she'd be disqualified tomorrow. In my event, no one really liked her, and when she didn't turn up [in the marshalling area] everyone was just bitching about her. She ended up running late. We were all lined up to walk out and she ran in and said, 'My goggles are broken. Can you hold up the race?' The officials said they couldn't do that, so she ran out of the room again, and we all marched out to the

Susie O'Neill became the first Australian ever to win the women's 200 metres butterfly.

start. She didn't go to the blocks with the rest of us, but came running out a bit later. I remember thinking as I walked out, 'Okay, just forget about that. I'm sure she'll turn up.' I don't know if it was a ploy, or if her goggles did break.[7]

Competing in her sixth event in six days, O'Neill had rehearsed that final in her mind repeatedly, particularly the final lap. Volkers had impressed on her the need to concentrate on her stroke, to stay loose and relaxed. The plan was to go out very fast early, then swim three evenly paced laps. In her rehearsals, there were always rivals turning with her for the last lap. As it turned out, she led from the start and there was no one with her at the final turn. Her team-mate Petria Thomas, 20, from the little town of Mullumbimby in northern New South Wales, showed strength and courage to power through the final lap and snatch second placing from Smith.

Volkers had told O'Neill, a young woman noted for her imperturbability, that if she won she ought to display some excitement — so she obliged as she climbed out of the pool and again on the victory dais, throwing her arms in the air. In the stand she could see her support crew — her brother John, his wife Bronwyn and her doctor boyfriend Cliff Fairlie — with faces painted green and gold, all wearing t-shirts with her picture on the front. 'They were behaving like idiots, dancing around and being stupid. It made me feel so good.' O'Neill and Perkins were among the large group of Australian swimmers who later celebrated at Centennial Park in downtown Atlanta, leaving the site less than half an hour before a bomb exploded.

Drew Ginn, the newcomer to the Oarsome Foursome, had some difficulty adjusting to the mood of a confident group that had won two world championships and an Olympic gold medal. At 21, although he had plenty of enthusiasm and confidence, he felt something of an unproven outsider among his older, more experienced comrades, McKay, 32, Tomkins, 32, and Green, 29. In Lucerne, early in the European tour that preceded the Games, he reacted to the self-imposed pressure by going on a drinking binge that led to an angry censure from chief coach Reinhold Batschi. Realising that Ginn was having trouble fitting in, Batschi urged the others to be more considerate with him, to ensure that he didn't feel he was 'the spare wheel'. McKay conceded later that the three senior crew members might have unwittingly treated Ginn too harshly. He added:

> Sure, Drew was headstrong, moody and in-your-face at times. He was much younger, and wanted to run around with his peers. He let his feelings show. He was chasing his dream. He certainly had some arguments. There was one big blue in Amsterdam after which he and James didn't speak for three days. And there was one time when he and I didn't speak for a while because I got preferential treatment from the masseur, Luke 'The Skunk' Atwell. I came close to whacking him then. But he added so much value: youth and experience, a desire to be the best, a really good understanding of what's required. His presence in

the boat was a constant reminder of what was needed. He was a good motivating force, and intensely competitive. After the binge, he rocked up to training early next morning, rowed himself into the ground and spewed during the trip back. We set a golden rule then: 'Don't go out and drink on your own. Do it with us.' He took over the calling role in the boat, and that gave him a greater sense of involvement.[8]

After a European tour in which they came closer to achieving harmony inside and outside the boat, and experimented successfully with tactics, the crew moved with other rowers and kayak paddlers to North Georgia College, near the old mining town of Dahlonega. They were half an hour from the competition site at Lake Lanier and 90 minutes from Atlanta. In their opening race they narrowly beat Slovenia, but were disappointingly beaten into third place, behind Italy and France, in the semi-final. They had failed to lift for the final 500 metres, and it was obvious that someone hadn't given enough. At an emotional team inquest next morning, McKay admitted that he was the culprit. 'From early 1995 the only race I wanted to win was the Olympic final,' he said later. 'In the semi-final I was only in third gear out of five. I was comfortable, I had two more gears to go. I felt if they [the Italians] can just beat us going flat out, it wasn't worth busting our guts just to prove a point. Others saw it differently. Drew took the view: if we can't win the semi, how can we win the final? It was bad communication, really. I thought I was doing it right. We finished with the outside lane, but that didn't matter, on a course out in the middle of a lake.'[9]

If the four needed inspiration for the final, it was provided by Perkins' marvellous swim the night before. They could identify with him: the hassles, the selection struggles, the defence of a Barcelona crown, even the outside lane. That same night they slept unaware of the bomb explosion that had occurred in Centennial Park around 1 am. Suddenly, just after 5 o'clock, they bounded out of bed after a security guard advised of a warning that a bomb had been placed in the grounds of the North Georgia College. 'Grab your gear and get out,' someone yelled. They bolted downstairs, in the confusion leaving behind some 'Seinfeld' videos they'd intended to relax with at the team's halfway house near the course.

Their race plan for the final was to make their surge from the 1250-metre mark. After a warm-up row McKay pasted a note in the boat carrying what to him were key words, 'YES, NOW and BRAVE'. When he returned to the house to await the start he found the others, including Donaldson, in a highly emotional state, close to tears. Donaldson quoted to the crew the words from Herb Elliott that had inspired Debbie Flintoff-King in 1988: 'There is a point of no return … You must reach your goal and trample on anyone who tries to stop you.' As they paddled out for the start, they realised that the boat was wrongly geared. It had been tightened because a tailwind had been blowing over the course, but moments before the start the wind changed to a headwind. 'It's like riding a bike with the wrong gears,' McKay recalled. 'The heavier gear meant a harder pull, and that meant it would be a longer, harder row. Nobody went crook.'[10] At the halfway mark, a third of a length behind the leading Italians, the Australians were rowing easily and already confident they would win. They knew they had rowed the Italians down before. At 1250 metres, they were ready for what they called their gold-medal push. Ginn called: 'Get ready … Get ready … Away we go!' Again, with 100 metres to go, he shouted 'Up!' for a final effort. They finished three-quarters of a length in front. For the *Andrew Cooper*, and its exuberant cargo of disparate egos, mostly unrestrained passion and huge competitive spirit, the punishing haul to this moment had all been worthwhile. They had battled their way to a special place in history. Theirs was the first Australian back-to-back rowing win since Bobby Pearce's sculling triumphs in 1928 and 1932.

That first day of the finals, the most successful that Australian rowers had ever had, the team won two gold medals and a silver. Kate Slatter and Megan Still, who in 1995 became the first Australians to win a gold medal at the world championships, powered away to defeat the Americans Missy Schwen and Karen Kraft and take gold in the women's coxless pairs. The US pair, who had dominated all pre-Games regattas, were widely expected to win, but Slatter and Still scooted from the start and were never headed, despite an ominous late surge by the Americans. So close was the winning margin — .39 of a second — that the Australians thought they had finished with silver. Some indication of their resolve and absolute effort is offered by the fact that they

Megan Still (left) and Kate Slatter, who defeated the Americans by .39 of a second to take gold in the Atlanta women's coxless pairs.

broke their best time by eight seconds. In the men's coxless pairs David Weightman and Robert Scott won silver behind Britain's Matthew Pinsent and Stephen Redgrave, the latter at 34 becoming the only oarsman to win four successive gold medals. Later bronze medals were won in the men's quadruple sculls (Duncan Free, Bo Hanson, Janusz Hooker and Ron Snook), the lightweight double sculls (Anthony Edwards and Bruce Hick) and the women's lightweight double sculls (Rebecca Joyce and Virginia Lee).

What is it about Australian equestrian performers? Bad falls and a few broken bones seem to give them extra incentives, even help them shape legends. The bar for this get-back-on-again brand of courage was set in Rome in 1960 by Bill Roycroft — after he checked himself out of hospital following an awful fall, then rode trussed in the saddle, without power in his right arm, to help his three-day team win gold. In Atlanta the female half of the team that won the three-day event echoed the Roycroft spirit. Afterwards, as they took their places beside Andrew Hoy and Phillip Dutton on the dais, Wendy Schaeffer and Gillian Rolton looked like a couple of nattily-attired crocks: Schaeffer was hobbling on her broken leg, and Rolton was treading gingerly, with her broken collarbone in a sling and broken ribs strapped and padded.

A couple of days before the event, Schaeffer's leg was so painful that she was unable to make the traditional reconnaissance walk through the steeplechase course. Someone tried to solve the problem by giving her a lift in a golf buggy, but officials of another team protested. She finally had one slow, stop-start walk, fortified (as she often was in Atlanta) by sanctioned pain-killers. There was still plenty of pain during all three stages of the event — the dressage, endurance and show-jumping — but the sheer adrenalin in her system sustained her: that and her close relationship with her mount Sunburst, a gift from her mother ten years earlier. Sixth after the dressage test, she, Dutton (on True Blue Girdwood) and Hoy (on Darien Powers) built a massive lead of more than 60 points during the endurance section. That meant that for Australia to lose, the team would have to hit a dozen fences in the final (jumping) phase, with the second-placed US riders having perfect rounds. In fact Schaeffer rode faultlessly, while Dutton and Hoy each hit two fences. At the end of the event Schaeffer led the overall table, and under the rules that had existed in Barcelona — when the individual and team events were held concurrently — she would have won two gold medals (as Matt Ryan in fact did in 1992). In Atlanta the two events were separated. With Dutton finishing second on the points count and Hoy fourth, the Australians ended with a 57-point margin over the United States. For Hoy, who had been given the honour of carrying the Australian flag in the opening ceremony, the victory meant back-to-back gold: he and Rolton (also awarded gold, although her performance was not required on the third day) had both been members of Australia's winning three-day team in Barcelona.

Rolton's problems began on a bend during the cross-country phase of the endurance section. Her beloved mount Peppermint Grove (aka Freddy) came down after treading on a tree root, then skidded along the gravel, taking Rolton with him. She didn't know it then, but she had broken her left collarbone and two ribs. A spectator grabbed the horse and she remounted. As she began galloping again she became aware that it was difficult to breathe, and her left arm wasn't working. At the next obstacle, a water jump, horse and rider came down again after the useless arm prevented her from guiding Freddy through a clean jump. She somersaulted into the water, then waded out and boarded the waiting horse again. She galloped one-handed for another three kilometres, clearing 15 more fences, to finish the course. An ambulance took her to hospital, where she refused pain-killing drugs because she felt she might be needed for the final show-jumping round the next day. She wasn't — but Rolton's gallantry and perseverance served as an inspiration to her fellow riders, and the entire team.

As the Games began, shooting was a sport with an image problem in Australia. Thirty-five people had been killed in a rifle massacre in April, at Port Arthur, Tasmania, and a bitter national debate was raging over projected gun-control legislation. Sporting shooters felt they were being discriminated against, more so after public calls for the removal of shooting from the 2000 Sydney Olympic program. What the sport needed most just then was some encouraging news from Atlanta — and it came in the form of gold-medal victories for two laid-back and like-able marksmen who shared a room in the Olympic Village. Until then Australia had not won an Olympic shooting contest since Donald Mackintosh potted more live pigeons than any rival in Paris in 1900. The first Atlanta winner was Michael Diamond, 24, a third-generation Greek-Australian from Goulburn, who hit 149 clay targets out of a possible 150 to win the trap shoot. With nerveless poise he broke 25 targets out of 25 in the final, unaffected by the encouragement of a patriotic crowd for his American opponents, Joshua Lakatos and Lance Bade. Afterwards the laconic Diamond, who had begun shooting at clay targets when he was eight, stuffed his gold medal into the pocket of a pair

of jeans and folded them into his bag. Next morning he left Atlanta on the air journey home.

Before he checked out, Diamond gave some advice to his roommate Russell Mark, of Ballarat, about the stress associated with going into a final at the head of a field. Mark, eight years older, had entered the sport almost accidentally at the age of 17; he had injured an ankle in his preferred sport of Australian football, and had taken up shooting as a diversion while he recovered. From that time he'd been hooked. Diamond's advice: 'He emphasised how essential it was to have courage to go through the pain for victory,' Mark said after winning the double trap. 'It's gut-wrenching to be in that situation [in front] because it's a once-in-a-lifetime opportunity and the nerves are just incredible. The pain goes away if you miss, but if you keep yourself in a winning position it stays. You have to go for broke. I decided that if I were to miss, I'd miss aggressively.' Mark did not miss much. At the end of the prelim-

Michael Diamond shooting for gold in Atlanta … 149 out of a possible 150.

inary round he and Huang I-Chien, of Taiwan, were tied at 141 points. In the final Mark hit 48 out of 50 targets to win by six points from his nearest rivals. Afterwards, still a little shell-shocked, he reverted to the language of his old sport: 'That's a bit like winning a grand final by 20 goals.'

Other gold medals were won by the women's hockey team, which included three players from the triumphant team at the Seoul Olympics, and the men's tennis doubles pair, Mark Woodforde and Todd Woodbridge. The Hockeyroos' 1996 campaign was character- ised all the way by coolness under immense pressure and a quite pas- sionate sense of togetherness. All 16 members had adhered rigidly to

Russell Mark, gold medallist in the double trap event.

the principles of a mission statement laid down by their coach, Ric Charlesworth … one that emphasised bonding, tolerance and collective sacrifice. The Australians entered the final match against South Korea from a 38-game unbeaten streak, and dominated the second half to win 3–1. The heroine of the side was Alyson Annan, who scored two goals and explained tearfully afterwards that the key to success had been the two 'b's — belief and bonding. 'We're great friends, and we have a belief in each other,' she said simply. Annan had terrific support from captain Rechelle Hawkes, defender Liane Tooth and forward Jackie Periera (all of whom received second gold medals), Katrina Powell and Nova Peris. Others in the championship team were Michelle Andrews, Louise Dobson, Renita Farrell, Juliet Haslam, Clover Maitland, Karen Marsden, Jenny Morris, Lisa Powell, Danielle Roche and Kate Starre.

The Hockeyroos believed that the key to their gold-medal success was 'belief and bonding'.

For Peris, 25, whose presence among the exuberant 16 on the victory dais signalled the arrival of Australia's first Aboriginal gold medallist ever, the journey had been remarkable. She came from Darwin, a city which had never produced an Olympic hockey player, and when she became pregnant at the age of 19, it seemed that any aspirations about becoming an elite athlete might have to be abandoned. In 1992, as a single mother with her two-year-old daughter Jessie, she moved to Perth, Australia's hockey stronghold. Coach Ric Charlesworth saw her play, was impressed with her speed and persistence, and drafted her into the national squad the following year. The Atlanta victory made her the first Australian mother to win an Olympic championship since Shirley Strickland de la Hunty 40 years earlier. After the final, watched in Darwin

Nova Peris, a member of the Atlanta Hockeyroos and the first Aboriginal gold medallist ever.

by her mother, daughter and partner Sean Kneebone, Peris spoke with pride about her hopes that she might inspire other children to achieve their dreams. For her part, the inspiration came from her friend Cathy Freeman, who five days earlier had become the first Aboriginal medallist by winning silver behind Marie-Jose Perec, of France.

Perec, 28, a long-limbed former model who had been born on the island of Guadaloupe in the Caribbean, completed a couple of magnificent doubles in Atlanta. She became the first athlete of either sex to win the 400 metres twice, and she upstaged Michael Johnson just a little by winning both the 200 metres and the 400 metres. (His much-heralded double was completed 15 minutes after Perec had won the 200 metres.) At 23, Freeman was the youngest woman in the final, and she ran the finest race of her career, pushing Perec to the limit. Her time of 48.63 seconds, an improvement of almost a full second on her previous best, would have won any other Olympic final in history. As it was, Perec's time of 48.25 seconds was the fastest in a decade, one that only two women, both from a highly suspect Eastern Bloc training regime, had ever beaten.

At a media conference afterwards Perec reflected: 'After the semi-finals, I knew it was my race. Cathy's in form, but I said, "She's young, she has time".' Then she turned to the young Australian sitting beside her and asked: 'So in four years, okay?' Freeman ran a well-paced race, moving comfortably through the first lap, and was ahead at the final bend. 'At about 80 metres to go I thought, "I can win this", and I lost my concentration. I was thinking, "Where is she? … she's going to come up any minute." With about 40 or 50 to go I felt like someone was tugging at my legs from behind to try to stop me.' Afterwards the girl who had just made history for her people listened to the cheers around her and remarked unbelievingly: 'You'd think I won the bloody thing. I just ran my little black butt off. I can't believe I could push her so hard — that was little ol' me.'

The Woodies — Mark Woodforde and Todd Woodbridge — caused no great surprise by defeating a scratch pair of British players, Tim Henman and Neil Broad, in the doubles tennis final in straight sets. They were, after all, the No. 1–ranked combination in the world, fresh from winning the Wimbledon title for the third consecutive year.

Marie-Jose Perec's win in the 400 metres gave her the Atlanta 200 metres–400 metres double.

But along the way they had their problems. At one stage Woodbridge somehow became involved in an altercation with a security guard and was arrested and fined. Then, in their semi-final, the Australian pair were down two match points against their old Dutch foes Jacco Eltingh and Paul Haarhuis. That three-setter lasted nearly three hours, with the Woodies winning the final set 18–16.

From Australia's point of view, the Atlanta Games will always be remembered for inspirational performances like those of Perkins, O'Neill, Hoy, Schaeffer, Rolton, the Oarsome Foursome, Diamond, Mark, the Hockeyroos, Peris and Freeman. But sometimes a devastating result can yield a moment that offers a shining example of the Olympic spirit. Such a moment came as Shane Kelly launched himself in the 1000 metres cycling time trial at Stone Mountain. He was the last of 20 riders in this brutal race against the clock; he held the world record of 60.613 seconds, and none of the 19 riders who preceded him had broken 62 seconds. There seemed little doubt that he was on the brink of gold. As he pushed down on the pedal, his foot slipped out. That was it. No getaway. No gold. Before it had even started, the race of his life was over. Afterwards there were no tantrums, no hints of the desolation that must have come with the death of the dream that had sustained him for four years. The gold medal went to the 19th rider, France's Florian Rousseau. Kelly took a big breath, walked out to face the media, accepted all responsibility for what had been a human error, stayed for the medal ceremony and congratulated Rousseau, who felt very fortunate. It was an essay in dignity, and sport was better for it.

When Mike McKay was summoned back from an unofficial trip to Savannah for an audience with John Coates, he thought he was in trouble. He was in fact invited to carry the Australian flag at the closing ceremony. McKay asked if the whole coxless fours team could do the job. Coates, a man with much sentimental attachment to rowers, told him the IOC had already ruled that there could be just one bearer for one flag. But, with a nod and something of a wink, he suggested it might be nice to try. For the next couple of hours McKay, Tomkins, Green and Ginn (three of whom didn't carry the requisite identity band on their wrists) bluffed, pleaded and cajoled their way past security men, through check-points, onto a bus. Some official tempers were lost. Finally McKay faced off with the opening ceremony organiser, Eric Rock, who said flatly that there was no way the Oarsome Foursome could carry the flag between them. McKay continued to hound and harass the man. Finally Rock put up his hands and said: 'Give me a break... I'll try and work out something.'

When the flag-carriers of all nations made their entrance to the stadium, they were marching four abreast. Except for the Australians, who were four abreast carrying one flag. 'It was the only way,' said McKay later. 'We came in as team. We won as a team. We had to go out as a team.'[11]

PART TWO

And so to Sydney ...

The link is strong and unbroken. Since the day the visionary French baron Pierre de Coubertin founded the international Olympic movement at the Sorbonne, University of Paris, in June 1894, Australia has been part of it. And since the first Olympic Games of the modern era were held in Athens in 1896, Australians have competed at every one of them. It is an extremely rare distinction, that one, and it's no wonder that Australia guards it jealously. The record owes much to the vision of early administrators, and the preparedness of athletes in the first half of the 20th century to submit themselves to vast absences, embarking on ocean journeys that lasted a long time. It is worth remembering, in this age of the Boeing 747, that the athletes who won three gold medals at the 1920 Paris Olympics — Andrew 'Boy' Charlton, Richmond Eve and Nick Winter — arrived back in Sydney Harbour just over five months after they had sailed for the Games.

Since the Games began in 1896, they have been held in the southern hemisphere just twice — both times in Australia. The first was in Melbourne, in 1956, and it is often forgotten that those Games were preceded by an enormous amount of quarrelling. The organisers and the powers that existed in Melbourne squabbled constantly, almost from the day in Rome in 1949 when the city nosed out Buenos Aires by one vote for the right to stage the Games. The bid campaign committee had handed out bottles of Australian wine to IOC members, hosted a lavish dinner in London at a time when the city was strapped for food, and shown a film that was ... well, interestingly edited. It showed a robust surf breaking onto beaches which simply didn't exist in Melbourne's Port Phillip Bay, and lauded Melbourne's fine dining and wining scene — without mentioning the city's notorious six-o'clock closing-time swill. Melbourne squeaked through the last ballot, and for the next four years the IOC wondered why it had let that happen.

The squabbles that preoccupied the organisers (and nearly caused the IOC to confiscate the Games and award them elsewhere) concerned such basic matters as the site of the main stadium. Although the Melbourne Cricket Ground was then (as it remains) clearly one of the most significant sports arenas in the world, seven different sites were argued about for four years. A problem was that too many vested interests had stakes in the MCG — among them the MCG trustees, the Melbourne Cricket Club, the Victorian Football League and the Victorian Cricket Association. None of them wanted to see an arena that was the historic heartland of cricket and football torn up, resurfaced, adorned with a cinder track and rendered unusable for two cricket seasons — just for an Olympic invasion lasting 17 days.

On 18 February 1952 Lewis Luxton, one of Australia's two members of the IOC (with Hugh Weir), wrote a desperate letter from London to the chairman of Melbourne's organising committee, Sir Wilfrid Kent Hughes, advising that he had been given until 15 May to show some proof that Melbourne was capable of hosting the Games. 'I wish to reiterate that this is Melbourne's last chance to stage the Olympic Games in the next 100 years,' he pleaded. He wanted three guarantees: that a decision had been made on a main stadium, that a realistic estimate of costs was available, and that the trade union movement would cooperate with the Games building plan. 'If I do not receive [them] by 10 May (the few days between that and the 15th are necessary in order that I convey the information to Lausanne), I must tell the IOC that Melbourne cannot do the job.'[1]

The guarantees did not arrive, and from that time the pugnacious president of the IOC, Avery Brundage, made it clear that he believed the Melbourne bid committee had perpetrated a confidence trick. The bickering in the host city continued undisturbed, seemingly oblivious to IOC concern, and it did not involve only the ongoing tussle over the main stadium. Egos jostled throughout, and there was much crossfire between various amateur sports bodies — as well as civic, state and federal politicians — over matters of finance, key appointments and the siting of other venues. The rowing venue was changed three times: from

Lewis Luxton, one of Australia's two IOC members in the 1950s. (IOC Archives, Lausanne)

Far right: Sir Wilfrid Kent Hughes, chairman of Melbourne's Olympic organising committee.

Avery Brundage, IOC president and harsh critic of Melbourne's preparations for the 1956 Games. (IOC Archives, Lausanne)

45

Betty Cuthbert, the 'Golden Girl' of the Melbourne Games.

Carrum, Melbourne, to Lake Learmouth, and finally (just a year before the Games) to Lake Wendouree, near Ballarat.

In April 1955 Brundage, all out of patience, came out to see for himself — just at a time when the construction of Olympic sites was threatened by trade-union-driven rolling strikes, black bans and go-slows. He told the press: 'A group of pretty smart Melbourne citizens attended the Rome meeting six years ago, at which the Games were

Dawn Fraser (left) and Lorraine Crapp (right) won two gold medals each in Melbourne. Sylvia Ruuska (United States) is the third swimmer in the picture.

awarded to Melbourne. I don't know how they did it. There were a dozen cities after the Games. Some were prepared to spend up to $US 20 million to stage the Games, but your delegation was successful. For six years we have had nothing but squabbling, changes of management and bickering. Melbourne has a deplorable record in its preparations for the Games — promises and promises.'[2] He let it be known, rather pointedly, that there were still three or four cities willing to rescue the Games.

Later, in Paris, he regaled IOC executive committee members with his account of what he had told the Australian Olympic officials: 'Your projects have been changed several times. Your sites, even including the

Athletes of all nations enter the arena together at the Melbourne closing ceremony, which changed the pattern forever. (IOC Archives, Lausanne)

main stadium, have been changed several times. I discover that you are contemplating changing the rowing site to a place I've never heard of. Even today you haven't fixed the dimensions of the velodrome, or decided on the shooting site. You have changed the head of your organisation several times, and there seems much confusion.'[3]

Swerving easily among explosive metaphors, Brundage summed up: 'My observations caused a grenade of sensation in the world press, and had the effect of an atom bomb. The reaction to all this ... has been excellent. I just regret I didn't say it earlier ... I think our Australian friends have (at last) taken seriously their award of the Games, and realise that they will profit from their last chance to make a good impression on the world.'[4]

He was right. From that time the arguments and delays ceased, and the machinery of Games organisation moved smoothly and precisely. Even the outbreak of war on two fronts (with Soviet troops invading Hungary and the armed forces of Israel, Britain and France moving into Egypt for conflict over the Suez Canal), intolerable tension between Taiwan and mainland China, and consequential boycotts from the Netherlands, Spain, Switzerland, Egypt, Lebanon and Iraq, did not deflect the planning. The Games proceeded without hitch (well, there was one bloody altercation in the pool when the Soviets and Hungary met at water polo), and a mood descended on Melbourne that it had never known before. Years later this writer was prompted to observe:

> When the Olympic Games moved into Melbourne, from 22 November to 8 December 1956, it was as if the city had been brushed by a certain magic. Nothing before or since — no football final or Test cricket match or Melbourne Cup, neither the departure of Burke and Wills nor the arrival of the Beatles — has evoked such sheer emotional involvement from the whole community. It was not just the huge success of the Australian team, with thirteen gold medals, eight silver and thirteen bronze, that made the Games so sublimely memorable; nor was it the arrival of a whole new contingent of national heroes and heroines, with names like Cuthbert, Fraser, Crapp, Henricks and Rose. These things contributed significantly, of course, but there was also a dimension that seemed almost transcendental. Certainly there was about those Games, at a time of fierce international tension, a reassuring innocence.[5]

Those Games set a benchmark of hospitality and generosity. They ended on a huge tide of goodwill, after a closing parade in which athletes of all nations mingled — not marching, but strolling, laughing, waving, even weeping. This departure from the usual formal closing procession was the brainchild of a Chinese-Australian boy, much later identified (through this writer) as John Ian Wing. So successful was this parade of amiable disorder that it changed the pattern of the closing ceremony forever: ever since, that ceremony has been characterised by its mood of sheer unbridled fun. The Melbourne Games became known as the Friendly Games — not just because of their unusual ending, but also because of the mood that permeated them. Afterwards, even Avery Brundage praised the organisers.

Decades later, further bids were made to bring the Games back to Australia. A very healthy-looking attempt by Melbourne to win the

Games of 1988, initiated by Victoria's minister for sport, Brian Dixon, capsized in 1981 after the prime minister, Malcolm Fraser, refused to support it. A Brisbane bid took off for the 1992 Games, mainly fuelled by the personality of its leader, former Brisbane lord mayor Sallyanne Atkinson — but it never really had a chance against Barcelona. It finished third, behind Barcelona and Paris. Melbourne won a contest (against Brisbane and Sydney) to bid for the 1996 centennial Olympics; its team, led by John Ralph, made an impressive case, but Melbourne finished fourth, behind Atlanta, Athens and Toronto.

Afterwards there were many recriminations; it was suggested darkly that Phil Coles — one of Australia's two IOC members, with Kevan Gosper — had favoured Atlanta, given the organisers advice, and even voted for that city. Coles, John Coates and Gosper had certainly argued for Sydney against Melbourne, but had been outvoted in that ballot; afterwards they had all supported the Melbourne bid. Coles said later that he had been aware of rumours branding him as 'some sort of traitor', and had taken precautions during the IOC vote on the hosting of the Games: 'I made a carbon copy of my vote during each round. I also showed my voting paper each time to the member sitting beside me, Franco Carraro from Italy. Mary Glen-Haig of Great Britain, sitting on the other side, also saw each of my votes. I voted for Melbourne, and made sure I had proof of the fact.'[6] He admitted, though, that he had 'known from the start that Melbourne wouldn't get up ... everyone did'.[7]

Sydney's bid campaign was launched in May 1991, with the Sydney lawyer Rod McGeoch as chief executive of the company formed for the carriage of the bid. Chairing the bid team was the New South Wales premier, Nick Greiner, who had accepted the AOC's judgment that Sydney was the best equipped city to give Australia one more try for the Games. Bruce Baird, Greiner's transport minister, was appointed minister responsible for the bid. Bob Elphinston was general manager. For John Coates, who had recently taken over the presidency of the AOC from Kevan Gosper, it really was a case of just one more shot. '[This] was to be our last bid, win or lose,' he said later. 'I say that because in a country of only seventeen million people, it was unlikely that we could ever again have gained the support of our national and state governments, a city, the corporate sector and the public for another bid cost-ing $18 million. At the risk of appearing arrogant, we also felt there was very little more we could offer the Olympic movement ...'[8]

Coates wrote the first strategy document, which amounted to a battle plan for the bid. In it, as well as setting out an exhaustive lobbying plan, he made a terse assessment of Sydney's strengths and weaknesses. The strengths were the compactness of Sydney's Olympic geography, with minimal travel between venues for athletes; the state government's commitment to sport, evidenced by the construction of $300 million worth of sports facilities during the candidacy; the fact that 80 per cent of the sports facilities would be built by the time the IOC made its deci-sion in September 1993; security and political stability; community and government support at every level; good climate; Australia's Olympic record, and the fact that the nation was making its third successive bid.

The major weaknesses, which needed to be addressed aggressively, were distances involved in travel to an isolated country, and interna-tional concerns that had long existed about the problems of holding equestrian events in Australia. These concerns were a legacy of the 1956 Games, when the nation's quarantine laws prevented the import of horses, and caused equestrian events to be held in Stockholm.

In November 1992 the bid committee announced that it would pay the round-trip air fares of all athletes and officials to the Sydney Games. In March 1993 came the advice that Sydney would also be paying for the round-trip transportation of all equipment — like kayaks, rowing shells, yachts and horses — to the Games. The equine aspect was doubly important. Australian quarantine authorities were now much more sympathetic to the importation of competing horses. Now the world was being told that not only was it okay to bring the steeds; this time they were so darned welcome that the hosts would be paying their fares. Later it was also made clear that Sydney was prepared to bear all expenses for board and lodgings of competitors and officials in the Sydney Olympics village. All this represented a total up-front contribution of US$30.14 million.

Sydney's rival cities were Beijing, Berlin, Istanbul and Manchester. (Brasilia and Tashkent dropped out along the way.) Although China's human rights record was criticised often by commentators, particularly after Amnesty International accused it of lying to bodies such as the United Nations Committee Against Torture, Beijing was always considered Sydney's main opponent. The Sydney bid team prudently refused to involve itself with criticism of China's record in human rights. It relied instead on one consistent, positive theme: that Sydney's Games, more than any other, would be the Athletes' Games.

The international lobbying for votes began with the conference of GAISF (the General Assembly of International Sports Federations) in Sydney in October 1991, but in the final year before the deciding vote in Monte Carlo in September 1993 it was frantic. Coles, in company with his partner Patricia Rosenbrock and AOC colleague Doug Donoghue, was based in Paris, and between them they chased votes from western Europe. McGeoch was everywhere, but most importantly in South America with Kevan Gosper and in Asia with Graham Lovett, a respected international sports promoter. Baird headed for Scandinavia, and Greiner worked his way through central Europe with a Budapest-based consultant, Gabor Komyathy. Another consultant, Mahmoud Elfarnawani, concentrated on the Arab IOC members.

Maybe the most challenging mission was that embarked on in Africa by Coates, AOC secretary general Perry Crosswhite and the redoubtable double act of Gough Whitlam, the former prime minister, and his wife Margaret. Coates decided to follow a strategy devised by Andrew Young, former United States ambassador to the United Nations, to help Atlanta's prospects four years earlier. A strong perception existed that Beijing had already tied up most of the sixteen votes in Africa, on the strength of favours dispensed and promises of new stadiums and sports equipment. The Australian quartet visited eleven countries: South Africa, Swaziland, Kenya, Cameroon, Nigeria, Togo, Ivory Coast, Mali, Uganda, Zimbabwe and Mauritius. Gough Whitlam's presence proved invaluable. Coates observed later: 'He was revered everywhere he went. They knew that this was the man who, six days after he became prime minister in 1972, said that no more racially selected teams would be coming to Australia, or even allowed passage through Australia to New Zealand. As ambassador to UNESCO in 1986 he had chaired the second Conference Against Apartheid in Sport. Many leaders of African sport knew him.'[9]

Signing the host-city agreement after Sydney had won the bid. Seated, from left: John Coates (president of the AOC), Frank Sartor (lord mayor of Sydney), Juan Antonio Samaranch, Marc Hodler (IOC member). At back, from left: Francois Carrard (IOC director), Kevan Gosper (IOC member), Paul Keating (prime minister of Australia), John Fahey (premier of New South Wales). (IOC/Olympic Museum Collection)

Some aspects of this journey — including arrangements later made by Coates with IOC members Charles Mukora (Kenya) and Major General Francis Nyangweso (Uganda) — became the subject of allegations during the IOC corruption scandals of 1998–99, and were investigated during the 1999 Sheridan inquiry into the conduct of the Sydney bid. (These matters are dealt with in Chapter 5.) By Coates' reckoning, the entire African safari was worth five or six votes to Sydney.

Australia's bid team at a press conference in Monaco after Sydney was named as the 2000 Olympics city. From left: Annita Keating, Paul Keating, Kevan Gosper, John Fahey, John Coates, Bruce Baird (MP). (IOC/ Olympic Museum Collection)

Sydney's final presentation, made on the morning of the final vote in Monte Carlo on 23 September 1993, involved John Fahey (who had become NSW premier and bid chairman following the retirement of Nick Greiner), Gosper, Coates, McGeoch, Paul and Annita Keating, Kieren Perkins and an unknown 11-year-old Sydney schoolgirl, Tanya Blencowe. Unfazed by a pride of prime ministers, princes and princesses, Tanya offered a simple message: 'Sydney is a friendly city where it doesn't matter where you come from...' Annita Keating, born in the Netherlands and wife of the prime minister, was sincere and informative: 'I am part of the 25 per cent of all Australians who were born overseas. And mine is now one of over 140 cultures found in Sydney alone.' She finished with an impressive burst of French and Italian. Gosper, as

Australia's senior IOC member, reminded his colleagues that Australia had been part of the movement since its inception in 1894.

Eighty-nine IOC members took part in the voting, although one of them, from Swaziland, made a strange exit after two rounds, heading for the airport and an election back home. Beijing led the first round, as expected, with 32 votes, from Sydney (30). When Istanbul dropped out, five of its seven votes went to Beijing and none to Sydney, giving the Chinese capital a daunting seven-vote buffer. Next to fall away was Berlin, and seven of its nine votes went to Sydney. At the end of round three, Beijing still led the voting with 40, Sydney was on 37, and Manchester had 11. When Manchester dropped out, eight of its votes went to Sydney, enabling that city to win the sudden-death contest with Beijing by just two votes, 45 to 43.

In Sydney it was 4.27 am when the IOC president, Juan Antonio Samaranch, began fiddling with an upside-down envelope that contained the winning name. At Circular Quay, where 50,000 people had been roistering as they waited, an uneven hush descended. Samaranch thanked all the bidding cities in alphabetical order (causing some misplaced joy in a Chinese television studio when he named Beijing first), offered regrets that there could be only one winner, and then uttered the words Australia wanted to hear: 'And the winner is Syd-er-ney.' If he had some trouble traversing the consonants, nobody cared. In truth, his failure to get a stranglehold on the city's name helped only to enshrine the moment.

And what a moment. An ecstatic John Fahey bounded high, in a fashion reminiscent of Toyota advertisements, then began bear-hugging all within reach. Coates, who had briefed the Australian Embassy in Paris (for the prime minister, Keating, and the minister for sport, Ros Kelly) that Australia would win by two votes in the fourth round, just grinned widely, then even more widely. In Sydney the Opera House glowed gaudily, its curves daubed with glowing, fluorescent colours, and ferries, yachts and launches beetled crazily around the harbour with horns and hooters blasting. Across the water and in the streets, people were bound by a raucous camaraderie.

Such was the degree of sheer elation that morning in Sydney, and during the tickertape parade that followed, that it seemed almost as if the city's task was over. Two years of sustained planning and dedicated campaigning had yielded a wonderful result. After 44 years, Australia was to stage its second Olympic Games. For many, as Rod McGeoch wrote soon after, it was 'a great moment in our history'.[10]

In fact, the true challenge was just beginning. During the next seven years, Sydney would have some testing moments on its way to delivering the Games of the 27th Olympiad — and its special pledge to make them the Athletes' Games. There would be controversies, criticism and a fair degree of internal squabbling — some of it just a bit reminiscent of Melbourne's experience on the pathway to 1956. The only real test, though, as with Melbourne so long before, would be in the quality of the Games.

CHAPTER THREE

The Knight of the Long Prawns

The House of Guang Zhou, deep in Sydney's Chinatown, is known as a restaurant where deals are made. The décor may be a little bleak, dominated mostly by tanks containing very glum fish and gently restless lobsters, but the food is excellent. It is a favourite haunt of journalists, broadcasters and politicians (many of them from the NSW Labor Right), and once in a while their huddles look conspiratorial. If the place radiates any mood at all, it is a sense of empty inclusion. There's the knowledge that it's a special place, even if it doesn't look like one.

On a Sunday night in March 1996, John Coates, the president of the Australian Olympic Committee, sat down to dinner in The House of Guang Zhou with Michael Knight, who had become Minister for the Olympics after the Labor Party won government in New South Wales the previous year, and Graham Richardson, former federal minister, Labor Party power-broker, radio personality and lobbyist for the media tycoon Kerry Packer. Coates and Knight, the two most prominent planners for the Sydney Olympics, had been feuding publicly and acrimoniously about the destination of potential profits from the Games.

These two men, who represented separate and clearly conflicting interests, had much in common. They were both realists, tough-minded politicians (although only one did the job for a living) who could fight hard and didn't much like taking a backward step. Coates had always been resistant to the notion of government intrusion in Olympic planning, and when the bid began had even forced a situation by which the Games would be run by a private company wholly dominated by the AOC. It was not hard to trace his desire for independence from government to his (and the Australian Olympic Federation's) difficult experience during the 1980 Moscow boycott. For his part, Knight favoured control by the public sector, on the simple basis that since the government was picking up the tab for the Olympics it ought to have a very big say in running them. They had not known each other long, and didn't trust each other much. What bound them was a resolve, a passion really, to make the Sydney Olympics work, and a shared realisation that if that was going to happen, each would need the other.

Coates, then 46, was the only lawyer ever to have led the Australian Olympic movement. He had had a long and testing apprenticeship in sports administration and the law, a background that equipped him admirably to tackle the defining goals of his career: the winning of the Olympic Games for Sydney, the successful prosecution of those Games, and the forging of a legacy from them that would guarantee the long-term future of Australian sport. The first of these missions had been efficiently accomplished. Coates had been the architect of the bid strategy plan — a comprehensive document that identified the strengths and weaknesses of the candidacy, and suggested appropriate initiatives for what Coates called 'an intensive international political campaign' — that had delivered the Games to Sydney.

The sporting career of Knight, 44, had peaked when he won the St Mary's (Sydney) district primary school breaststroke title at the age of 11. Although he played football, hockey and basketball afterwards, he liked to joke that it had all been downhill since that swimming triumph. But he had always been a sports nut. As a politician, his progress had been unpredictable but sure-footed. He entered parliament in 1981 as a left-wing member of the Labor Party, defected to the right under the patronage of his friend Graham Richardson in 1991, and became shadow minister for the Olympics in September 1994. That early journey, from the ideological left to the right-wing pragmatism epitomised by Richardson and his 'whatever it takes' philosophy, was seen by many as evidence of ruthless ambition. He was loathed at the time by former hard-line colleagues, but vituperation didn't seem to bother him, then or later. One of those ex-comrades once recalled him saying: 'It doesn't matter if they hate me, as long as they fear me.'

Comparing Knight with other politicians who were more concerned about their image, Mike Steketee, the *Australian*'s national affairs editor, wrote of him: 'He wears hatred as a badge of honour — [his]

Michael Knight,
Minister for the
Olympics.

strengths are different, the stuff of pure politics — intrigue, political strategy and kicking heads.' In a sense, he navigated his own course towards the Sydney Olympics. Weeks after Sydney won the Games in September 1993, he had flown to Atlanta, because he 'wanted to be part of it... to know how it all works'. He became a formal part of it, as the responsible minister, after the government changed in March 1995.

The causes of the running feud between Coates and Knight were two provisions in early, interlocking contracts for the Games. One of these had the effect of barring New South Wales from receiving any share of the profits, even though the state and its taxpayers were taking all the risks by underwriting any potential loss. Instead it directed that 90 per cent of any surplus would go to the AOC, with the remaining 10 per cent destined for the International Olympic Committee. The other gave the AOC control over every item in the budget of the Sydney Organising Committee for the Olympic Games (SOCOG). Knight saw both arrangements as not only undesirable and unfair, because they were strongly weighted in favour of the AOC, but also unworkable. He was not alone in this view. Gary Pemberton, the inaugural chairman of SOCOG, had found himself baffled, at times quite frustrated, by the AOC's overpowering control over the organisation's financial arrangements.

Often, because Coates had the board convinced that it had a fiduciary duty to the AOC — that, because of its promised share of the profits, the AOC had a pecuniary interest in every spending decision that SOCOG made — Pemberton had trouble getting meetings off the ground. At one particularly low moment before a board meeting he had told Coates, with conviction but no animosity: 'If you want to run the Games, you run the bloody Games. But what I do object to is that you are not going to run the Games in my name. I'm not going to be the one who is publicly accountable while you're making the decisions. If you want to make the decisions, you become publicly accountable. I don't give a damn. I'll go back to the good life I was having...'[1]

Around this time the government had even threatened to introduce legislation to break the contracts (entered into by a previous government and both national and international Olympic organisations) and force a profit handover. The AOC had counter-punched by declaring that the original arrangements were untouchable — enshrined in law, and Swiss law at that. This issue of the financial and legal control of the Games organising committee was overshadowing almost everything else, to a degree that SOCOG had lost all momentum. Increasingly it had become apparent to Knight and his premier, Bob Carr, that the government needed to extricate itself from a situation it had inherited, one they felt should never have been allowed to happen in the first place. The only realistic way to do that, they knew, was to buy their way out of it.

With the slanging match between Coates and Knight intensifying each day through the media, and SOCOG heading unhappily towards a state of paralysis, Richardson had intervened as peacemaker. 'You blokes are in opposing corners, you're supposed to be on the same side, and this can't go on,' he had told Coates, whom he had known since 1987. 'You've got to sort it out.'[2] His next move had been to do what he had done many times before to settle arguments inside the Labor Party: he had arranged a Chinese dinner in his favourite restaurant, booking a

Incoming AOC president, John Coates, is congratulated by his predecessor, Kevan Gosper, 1990. It was in May 1990 that the AOF (Australian Olympic Federation) became the AOC (Australian Olympic Committee). (IOC/Olympic Museum Collection)

table for 7.30 pm on the otherwise-deserted second floor. The sniping between Coates and Knight had continued as recently as that Sunday morning, via television.

When Coates arrived at The House of Guang Zhou, Knight was already seated at a table, looking morose. Richardson, driving from Bowral, turned up late. Over Richardson's choice of menu — prawn cutlets, spring rolls, crispy chicken, lobster and black bean sauce, salt and pepper prawns, washed down with a Rothbury semillon — the edgily amiable process of bargaining and buy-out ensued. Knight's opening offer was a payment of $24 million, in exchange for which the government would expect the AOC to relinquish its right of veto over the budget, plus its 90 per cent share of Olympic profits (80 per cent of which were due to be held in trust for the benefit of Australian sport). Coates rejected this out of hand.

Over the next couple of hours there was much talk about such matters as the expected profits from the Games (the AOC estimate was close to $300 million), the importance of trust and harmony, the sanctity of contracts, and the likely dire consequences of a continuing, unseemly fight between the two main stakeholders — not to mention the inevitable question of raising the stakes. Before the last course there was a final offer of $75 million from Knight on the table, along with a whole lot of food. Coates accepted. In return for this amount, which would help athletes of the future and go some way to making the AOC independent of government influence — a situation the AOC had yearned for ever since the face-off with Malcolm Fraser over the Moscow boycott — the AOC would surrender its profit entitlements and its budget control. The pair shook hands and Knight said he would make the announcement the next day.

It was a deal of massive proportions, quite pivotal to the efficient working of SOCOG and the planning of the Games. But it wasn't the only significant agreement achieved during that memorable dinner. Coates, sensing that the brawling was about to end, felt the appropriate moment had arrived to argue the case for the introduction of a new, important component inside the SOCOG organisation: a sports commission. 'I was concerned that the SOCOG board wasn't giving any attention to sport,' he explained later. 'The sporting side wasn't being reported on, there was no direction, people running the Games at that stage didn't come from a sporting background.' He went on:

> So I said I wanted a sports commission of SOCOG established under my chairmanship, with AOC majority representation, and for it to be delegated the responsibilities for running sport, within the budget. He [Knight] understood that made good sense, and his first reaction was to say, 'I want someone on the committee'. I said, 'Well, Graham's been Minister for Sport.' Richardson became the Knight nominee.[3]

In fact, while he agreed whole-heartedly with the initiative and said he would do everything he could to make it become a reality, Knight pointed out that he couldn't guarantee it. He was not yet a member of SOCOG, and only SOCOG could create the sports commission that would be its agent. 'Don't worry,' he said. 'I don't have a vote myself, but

Graham Richardson, a SOCOG board member and former federal minister. (News Ltd / Pip Blackwood)

I'll urge the government nominees on the SOCOG board to vote for it.'[4] (Given the Olympic representation on the board, this pledge amounted to a guarantee that the sports commission would quickly be approved. And it was.)

Late that night, after he arrived home from the dinner, Coates wrote out a full summary of his understanding of what had been agreed at the dinner. Next morning he telephoned Knight, who was planning to call a press conference. Coates wanted to ensure that there were no ambiguities. Specifically he wanted to emphasise to the Minister that the dollars the pair had been talking about, from the original contract, had been 1992 dollars. Translated with inflation factors to the scheduled handover date, ten days after the Olympic closing ceremony in October 2000, $75 million would convert over eight years to just short of $100 million. Coates wanted to lock them in, to turn the implicit into the explicit. 'Yeah, yeah, yeah,' Knight told Coates. 'But we can just call it $75 million for now.'

After it became public, the *Sydney Morning Herald* lauded the agreement, calling it a win–win outcome. Coates described it 'an outstanding result for the Olympic movement in this country', and later labelled the day of its signing 'this most significant day in the history of the AOC'. The *Daily Telegraph* later welcomed the establishment of the sports commission, calling it 'an important milestone in the stages of preparation for our moment of Olympic destiny'. But not everyone was happy, according to Coates:

> The board, the rest of the SOCOG board, were a bit aghast with what Michael had done. The government wore it. He obviously had the authority to go out and sort this whole thing out. But they were also very upset with this new sports commission that had snuck in and would be delegating really everything to the AOC, all control over the sports-related and sports-specific matters. And they tried to bog it down. Their lawyers, SOCOG lawyers, in-house lawyers drafted some terms that we fiddled with...the charter I negotiated that night even gave us, the sports commission, the right to appoint the mayor of the village, which further enraged them down the track.[5]

Without any doubt, the accord reached at that Chinatown dinner

— which has passed into insider folklore as the Knight of the Long Prawns — represented a crucial moment on the way to the Sydney Olympic Games. For a start it enabled an organising committee that had become crippled to start functioning cohesively. It allowed the government to take financial control of a great adventure: the largest peacetime undertaking the world had ever known. It ensured that the Games would yield an enduring legacy for the nation's athletes of the future. It was directly responsible for a ground-breaking innovation, a sports commission — one that contributed heavily to the success of the Sydney Olympics and their ultimate acceptance as the Athletes' Games.

Apart from all that, it signalled a shift in philosophies, and a new mood of unity and realism. From the early days of the bid there had been a jostling, a sense of mistrust really, between two sides: the Olympic administrators and the politicians. The Olympic people, particularly John Coates, had never forgotten the experience of the Moscow boycott, when Malcolm Fraser had attempted to strongarm the Olympic movement. During earlier bids involving Brisbane and Melbourne, they had framed contracts and agreements which had been protective — some might have said over-protective — of the rights of the national Olympic committee. For the Sydney Games the original contracts had demanded much from the government and conceded little. The politicians, obviously less experienced in such dealings, inevitably began their negotiations from a position well behind scratch. As Knight later came to admit, they had largely been outsmarted by Coates. Now, though, there was reason — for them, at least — to believe that they had just about caught up.

Reporting to the AOC's annual general meeting on 18 May 1996, Coates summed up the tension between the two protagonists: 'Michael [Knight] and I enjoyed some quite robust debate, some through the media, which was all about whether, in the end, my constituency of athletes is more important than his of taxpayers. To his credit, Michael insisted we keep talking.' Having secured a massive war-chest for sport, Coates was ready now to give Knight solid support to make the Olympics work. The two men were finally, firmly, on the same side.

To appreciate the importance of the Knight of the Long Prawns, and to set it into the context of the history of the Sydney Games, it is necessary to explore the legal paper-chase that was followed in the early years of the bid. Many of the complex contractual arrangements that cluttered the route to the Games had originated from the desk of Coates, working in association with the AOC's legal counsel, Simon Rofe.

Michael Knight once summed up the Coates style: 'The difficulty in negotiating with the man is not only that he's thinking the next step ahead but he's always got one document to pull out of his pocket that you didn't know existed before — and then you find out that it's been signed by someone in authority.'[6] Certainly it seemed that Coates often had recourse to a surprise document; and it was not unknown for such a document to contain a clause or two that had been agreed to while other parties had been preoccupied with other matters. Usually it came out of a bottom drawer rather than a pocket.

One document that became a fearsome weapon was the endorsement contract, a 31-page arrangement Coates had helped design with Rofe. From the moment it had been signed in May 1991 between the AOC, the city of Sydney (whose lord mayor was then Jeremy Bingham) and the NSW government (then led by Nick Greiner), Coates had been in an incredibly strong bargaining position. This contract, whose purpose it was to sanction Sydney's candidature for the right to organise and conduct the 2000 Olympic Games, effectively rendered the state and to a lesser extent the city responsible for the full cost of staging the Olympic Games, committed both to enter another contract (the host city contract) on terms dictated by the IOC, and left the AOC in effective control of the body charged with running the Games. Specifically it required the NSW government to commit itself to building a main athletics stadium and aquatic centre, costing $300 million, before the bid got off the ground. That way it was guaranteed that even a losing bid would deliver real and lasting benefits to the city of Sydney and athletes of the future.

The evolution process of the Sydney endorsement contract began during Brisbane's bid to stage the 1992 Olympics. Kevan Gosper became president of the AOF at the time, and Coates was chief executive of the Brisbane bid. Gosper later recalled: 'John told me he thought we should do something to ensure that the politicians didn't hijack the responsibility for the Games. I said, "You're absolutely right", and I suggested he try to put together a document that would give us security against that proposition. That's where it all started.'[7] No actual contract was framed then, but Coates worked on the drafting of a memorandum and articles of association for the company that would become the organising committee if the Games were won. The effect of this document would have been to give full power over a Brisbane organising committee to the AOF, which would also have been assured a 90 per cent share of profits from the Games. It never had the chance to flex its muscles, or to have them tested, because the Brisbane bid failed. But, in essence, it was the grandfather of the contract that would later test so many tempers.

In 1988, when three Australian cities — Melbourne, Sydney and Brisbane — were putting their hands up to host the 1996 Olympics, Coates presented the premiers of each of the would-be host states with an agreement guaranteeing the terms and conditions under which the AOF would allow their bids to proceed. He called it an endorsement contract. It stipulated AOF control of the bid and later organisation of the Games, plus a payment of $40 million by the successful state to help prepare and fund the 1996 team. John Cain, the former Victorian premier, later recalled signing it: 'It was like a bank guarantee; all for the bank and nothing for the partner.'[8] Melbourne won the right to bid that time, but Atlanta won the right to host those Games. In May 1990 the AOF formally became the AOC. When it was decided to make a Sydney bid during the last month of Gosper's presidency, November 1990, Coates went to work with Rofe on another, much more demanding version, the Sydney endorsement contract. Its purpose was to set out the conditions governing the bid, and the rules that were to apply if it were successful.

Coates later wrote rather proudly in the University of New South Wales *Law Journal* about that contract: 'Much has been written and spoken in the media about the power and influence of the AOC in the organisation and staging of the Games. Without doubt, that power and influence is founded in the endorsement contract. Everything that has developed between the AOC, the state of NSW and SOCOG has its roots in that contract.'[9]

The endorsement contract did not provide for distribution of profits from the Games (the host city contract, signed between the city, the state and the IOC amid much euphoria in Monte Carlo on 23 September 1993, did that job), but its terms were hugely loaded in favour of the AOC, which had the added comfort of knowing that the government would be paying all the bills. The contract gave the AOC effective control of the Sydney 2000 Bid Committee, which got up and running — also in May 1991 — with the appointment of Rod McGeoch as its chief executive. Explicitly, it was conditional on the AOC approving the structure and personnel of the committee. Moreover, if the candidature succeeded, the AOC was to appoint as the organising committee of the Games a company that the AOC had owned and controlled since the failed bid to win the 1992 Games for Brisbane. In what was called a joint marketing agreement, the government would also pay the AOC $60 million for team preparation and funding over the four years 1997–2000. This enabled the AOC to make direct payments of $18 million to individual athletes and coaches under what became known as the AOC Medal Incentive Scheme.

There were several in the Greiner team who could sense dangers for the government in being locked into such a contract. Someone among them suggested in those early days that at least there was consolation in the knowledge that, even if the contract was signed, 'governments can always legislate out of agreements'. Not this one, warned the AOC: it would be subject to agreement with the IOC (through the host-city contract), and Swiss law wouldn't sanction the breaking of contract commitments.

An impasse existed until both sides, the AOC and the government, agreed after much argument that there might be merit in agreeing to revisit the endorsement contract in about six months' time, before it became law. The government claimed it had legitimate reservations about the financial arrangements and the power structure that would emerge from the contract. Its attitude was: 'We're prepared to sign the contract now to get things moving, but we reserve the right to come back and negotiate some amendments.' It was finally agreed that the AOC would be prepared to consider alterations to aspects of the structure and membership of the original company, 2000 Olympic Organising Committee Ltd, if the city or the state made 'reasonable request' by 31 December 1991.

Michael Knight, Juan Antonio Samaranch and Kevan Gosper tour the main Olympic Stadium, September 2000. (Andrew Taylor / *Sydney Morning Herald*)

Astonishingly, that date came and went without any word from the government. It had apparently been forgotten, possibly drowned inside the bureaucracy. Any chance of a softer compromise for the government — and particularly a significant representation on the board of the organising committee — was lost as the big day came and went. Coates could not believe his good fortune. 'I can remember sweating on that date,' he said later. 'It was the date when the government could come and tell us, "Look, we want you to tidy this up. It's time for the amendments. We want you to give us a bit more say, reflecting the financial outlay we're undertaking." The date just went past. It had been a very acrimonious negotiation to get that date in there, and it was missed by the government. I can remember the joy Simon Rofe and I felt when they missed the date. We went out and had a good lunch.'[10]

The host-city contract, signed by John Fahey on behalf of the government within minutes of his return to earth after his triumphant leap in Monte Carlo, dictated the share of any profits from the Games: 10 per cent to the AOC, 80 per cent 'for the general benefit of sport in the host country' on terms to be decided by the AOC, and 10 per cent to the IOC.

Fahey, who had succeeded Greiner as premier, acted quickly to convert the private company that had existed when the bid began (and had been under the control of the AOC) into a statutory authority, which became SOCOG. He wanted to amend the endorsement contract to reduce the AOC's domination of the organisation. He felt it was reasonable that since the government was underwriting the Games it should have some representation on the board that was running them; he also argued that the federal government, the city of Sydney (whose lord mayor was now Frank Sartor) and the community should be represented. He conveyed these views to Coates through Richard Humphry, then Fahey's chief of staff, later chairman of the Australian Stock Exchange. Coates agreed, subject to the inclusion of a series of 'balancing provisions', which he later explained this way:

> Our position was, well...look, that's okay. We understand all that. However, we don't want anyone on the board who might not respect the principles of the Olympic movement...they must be there for the right reasons. So we would like a veto over the people you may appoint. As well, we want certain people on the board, so the two IOC members have to be there, the president and the secretary-general of the national Olympic committee have to be there. We juggled with the numbers, but were essentially left with a right of veto. We made it clear we didn't want to lose control over the budget. Look, we said, if we lose control over this it would be a simple matter for the government to throw in a bridge or a road and eat up any profit...if they are able to do that there won't be any profit. And one of the things we are fighting for is a legacy for Australian sport. There had to be an agreement that the AOC

effectively had line-item control over the spending and the budget of SOCOG. We agreed there should be a statutory authority, but we were in the box seat when it came to negotiating that. The government still had to agree to underwrite the Games, still give us an indemnity, give us a side letter saying we could object to certain people on the board ... So all that happened.[11]

Thus the dreaded endorsement contract lived on, in amended form. The amendment was signed in November 1993 to provide for the creation of SOCOG, with the AOC still very much in what Coates had called the box seat. It had relinquished its total control over the authority, but retained the right of veto over membership and acquired a formidable new power over spending. The all-Olympic carve-up of profits was not affected.

Around this time Coates had another financial win. Inspired by an observation made to him by IOC chief Juan Antonio Samaranch — that the true success of the Sydney Games would be measured not by profits or attendances but only by the performance of the home team — he convened a forum of sports federations in January 1993 to calculate medal targets for 2000. With a realistic objective of 60 medals in mind, he and AOC vice-president Peter Montgomery visited Canberra in May 1994, talked with the prime minister, Paul Keating, and managed to extract $135 million from the federal government's expenditure review committee. Its purpose was to provide more funding for athletes through the Australian Sports Commission, various institutes of sport and national federations, under what became known as the Olympic Athlete Program. A major selling point Coates and Montgomery used with Keating was that his government would 'own' the national team. There may be some irony in the fact that the Keating government lost office in 1996, and it was John Howard as prime minister who stood to become a beneficiary of identification with Australia's Sydney Olympic team.

When the first 15-person governing board of SOCOG was appointed in November 1993, automatic inclusions were the IOC members Kevan Gosper and Phil Coles, Coates as president of the AOC and Perry Crosswhite as secretary-general of that organisation, and the lord mayor of Sydney, Frank Sartor. Others included the first president, Gary Pemberton, who — the legislation provided — was to be independent; two representatives of the premier of New South Wales, Robert Maher and Sallyanne Atkinson; two nominees of the prime minister (then Paul Keating), Simon Balderstone and John Brown; and four representatives of community, sporting, business and commercial interests recommended by the premier, Kerry Packer, Nick Greiner, Graham Lovett and Rod McGeoch. The 15th place would go to the chief executive officer of SOCOG, not then appointed. Until Dr Malcolm Hemmerling began that job in September 1995, Pemberton doubled up as president and chief executive.

Along the road to the Games, 31 people served on the SOCOG board, and only four survived the whole distance: Coates, Gosper, Greiner and Sartor. Three men held the post of president: Gary Pemberton (November 1993 – March 1996), John Iliffe (March 1996 – September 1996) and Michael Knight (September 1996 – October 2000). When it first assembled, the board was not a body with an abundant sense of teamwork. Its early members were well qualified individually, but their agendas were often diverse, sometimes uncertain. Gosper and Coates sat at opposite ends of the elliptical board table, and Gosper later recalled: 'I don't think any of them trusted me, even John. I was seen very suspiciously by most [of them]. They didn't know whether I was a spy for the IOC or whether I was genuinely wanting to participate and get the Games off the ground.'[12]

Gosper had some hearing problems, unknown to most people, which caused him to position himself at one end of the table. Coates simply felt that the geography of the table reflected their relationship: 'There were problems between us in the early days of SOCOG, and it seemed appropriate that we were at opposite ends. I didn't pay much attention to Kevan, and that was obvious and visible.'[13] Coates was much closer to his old mate and mentor Coles. Traces of the old Sydney–Melbourne rivalry still existed, and Gosper's absence in England for two years before he joined the SOCOG board had reinforced his sense of separateness.

CHAPTER FOUR

'What have I got here?'

Gary Pemberton, SOCOG's first president, had an impressive business record as chairman of Qantas and Brambles and a director of CSR, the Commonwealth Bank and John Fairfax Holdings. Another attribute was that he carried no baggage — political, Olympic or otherwise; he was untainted by any previous associations, commitments or debts. He had never even met Coates, Gosper or McGeoch — in fact any member of the board except Greiner, whom he had sometimes encountered formally and briefly at government functions. After he was asked to take on the job by NSW premier John Fahey, he thought about it long and hard. He had never been a high-profile type, and this would be a hugely public role. At Brambles, the company he had joined in 1972 and led separately as chief executive and chairman since 1982, Pemberton had in fact been famous for not being famous: 'It was almost a standing joke ... I didn't make speeches, didn't go to functions, kept out of the newspapers, kept out of the media.'[1] He was not initially enthusiastic, but Fahey assured him that he would need to do the job for only four years.

After he agreed, Pemberton restructured his workload, leaving several boards and stepping back from the chairmanship of Brambles to become a director. For him, the move from corporate life involved some culture shock:

> The Act effectively provided for a series of commissions, which meant that individual directors would be responsible for delivery of some part of the Games. And, even though that was built into the Act, to me it was completely inconsistent with the way you run anything. You can't have board members running bits and pieces and things, because nobody's accountable, and if they don't perform you can't sack them. So my model

was the corporate model, where the chief executive is responsible, and the board oversees the performance of the chief executive and the senior management. But obviously that system wasn't very attractive to a lot of people. In fact when I was first appointed I started to get approaches from people saying, 'I think I'd like to run the cultural program,' or, 'I'd like to run the sport.' And I thought, 'What have I got here? This is going to be like herding cats.' So I think my view of that was to some extent unpopular.[2]

Gosper, who had been chairman and chief executive of Shell Australia, had an early conversation with Pemberton about media relations, one that demonstrated their very different styles. He told him: 'Look, Gary, the one thing I've got in common with you is that I am a corporate chief executive. I think I understand how you think in commerce. One piece of advice I'd like to give you ... is that I think you should, about every two weeks, get a group of responsible journalists

Gary Pemberton, first president of SOCOG.

around you and keep them informed of what we are doing, even with our difficulties, even with our uncertainties, what our priorities are — because we've got seven years to go, and if we don't provide them with the ups and downs of where we are, they will invent stories.'[3]

Pemberton looked at him hard, and responded, 'Are you mad?'

'What do you mean?' said Gosper. 'I just think this is a sensible way of going about things.'

Pemberton: 'Listen, I am only going to talk to those people in the media when I've really got something to say. I think what you're advising is fraught with danger, and I'm not going to do it.'

Recalling the dialogue, which was not disputed by Pemberton in a later interview, Gosper reflected: 'He was absolutely against it, and I think that was very silly.' His own belief was that much of the difficulty experienced by SOCOG over the ensuing seven years was caused by the mistrust of it by Australia's media. 'We didn't take them into our confidence, and that was a very serious mistake,' he summed up. 'I think the weakest performance from the entire SOCOG organisation was in media relations. I think Pemberton should have taken my advice. It could have made a difference — and a number of us would have helped him.'[4]

Pemberton believed he'd made the right decision. 'It wasn't just that I didn't want to take the media into my confidence,' he said later. 'It was more a question of spending your time, spending your time talking when there's nothing to talk about. What are you going to spend time talking about?'[5]

A more serious difference between the two men related to the vital negotiations over the most significant area of profit for any modern-day Olympic Games: the sale of television rights. 'In the early days Pemberton was suspicious of me, because of my IOC role,' said Gosper later. 'And his suspicion grew when the TV rights were being negotiated, which under the host-city contract were the responsibility of the IOC. Pemberton, as a commercial person, believed Sydney should run those negotiations, and get the best possible deal.' Gosper went on:

> He went beyond his remit. He acted privately. He worked very closely with the Murdoch group. He believed he could get a better deal for Sydney than the IOC could with its traditional broadcasters like the

EBU [European Broadcasting Union] in Europe and NBC in the States. He didn't do it without board approval. But he still ignored the basis of the agreement with the IOC under the host-city contract. I had to bail him out a couple of times. At the same time I'd be saying to him, 'Look, we are not a commercial organisation. We do a lot of commercial business, but we make judgments which are not always commercial. We make judgments on the history of relationships, on the people we feel most comfortable dealing with, and on the basis of knowing that they can deliver.' I'd say, 'Don't get too far away from the IOC on this.' Now, he did. Samaranch really held me to account as to why Pemberton was so keen to negotiate these very important contracts, which were a substantial part of the cash-flow for the IOC. Pemberton did some good work. I liked him, and I think he is an outstanding commercial person. But he never really understood how we operated. He only wanted to see it through commercial eyes.[6]

Pemberton later defended his refusal to take Gosper, or the IOC, in fact anyone other than Michael Knight, into his confidence during the television negotiations. 'We needed absolute security,' he said later.

This was 50 per cent of our budget, from the European and American TV rights. There was no way I would take a risk by telling the board what was going on. There were personalities on that board who would not have been able to resist making big fellows of themselves, about what they knew. I didn't trust the IOC, didn't trust any of them. I didn't trust the board. There was too much money involved. That board leaked like a sieve during that period. Some of these little interest groups were planting stories in the newspapers. Even the premier's department wasn't aware of the details of the negotiations. I wouldn't talk to Gosper [about the negotiations] because — nothing could be stupider. The history of the IOC was that the television rights for Europe always went to the EBU. They always got the European rights at a rate, which in relation to any reasonable measure of exposure — number of TV sets, population, whatever — amounted to chicken feed. And the others always, always, went to the NBC in America.[7]

Pemberton's basic approach to the television negotiations had two major prongs. He first involved Joe Bankoff, a contract lawyer who was a crucial member of the Atlanta organising team. And he broke up the traditional, rather cosy relationship between the IOC and the NBC and EBU networks by bringing into the bidding process a very wild card named Rupert Murdoch. Neither Gosper nor the IOC welcomed this intrusion.

On Bankoff, this was the Pemberton reasoning:

> I felt it was very unusual for two Games in sequence to be conducted by countries with the same language and very similar culture. So I figured that I can get on with the Yanks, we do business the same way, we've got similar commercial operating systems and values. Rather than re-invent the wheel I got hold of Bankoff, who quickly confirmed his worth. The way the system works is that you've got these regular players ... you've got the IOC, the nationals, national groups like the AOC. They do Games after Games, for major international sponsors like Coca-Cola and so on. They're all there year after year. Every four years a new group of innocent pigeons come to the table, and they [the regular players] are already sitting at the table. Every other bugger has done this three or four times, knows all the tricks. So I figured that Joe's been through it, and we worked together. We conspired early that we could join two Games together, Atlanta and Sydney, for the Australian TV rights. Nobody had ever done that.[8]

Murdoch was interested in securing world rights to the Sydney Olympics. At the time his organisation and NBC were battling in the US television market over football and other rights, and Pemberton was convinced that 'this made it a perfect time for us to be going to the market'. His purpose was to unsettle the conventional Olympic players — the IOC, NBC and the EBU — and thus disrupt the traditional market. 'The real game was to precipitate some uncertainty,' he later explained, 'having the Americans say, "What's going on here? ... This bloke's a bit different".'[9] From dealings in his previous corporate life, Pemberton had good contacts inside the Murdoch organisation, with Ken Cowley in Australia, Sam Chisholm in the United Kingdom and Murdoch himself in the United States — and he used them, causing some frustration to the IOC.

It was a difficult situation for the IOC to handle. They couldn't manage the information. They were dealing with an Australian (Murdoch) who was one of the major bidders, who had the capacity to ring me and say, 'Look, this is what's going on.' The head of the network being able to talk directly to the head of SOCOG was an unusual circumstance. That sort of thing happened not just with American rights, but with the European rights too.[10]

At one stage, when it seemed that an auction between NBC and the Murdoch network would take place in New York for the US rights to the 2000 Sydney summer Games and the 2002 Salt Lake City winter Games, Murdoch suddenly made a pre-emptive bid. NBC topped the Murdoch figure, and secured the rights. Pemberton was summoned to New York in a hurry: 'The NBC deal was to be announced in New York as soon as I could get there. And the secrecy and security on all this were so tight that I actually booked my flight to New York through [Qantas managing director] James Strong's credit cards, because I was chairman of Qantas at the time.'

Joe Bankoff had told Pemberton that it was traditional on such occasions to take Olympic paraphernalia as gifts. Pemberton recalled what he did: 'I went to a shop in Manly that sold all this stuff, bought hundreds and hundreds of dollars worth of it, took it over [to New York], dished it out to everybody. They all had their caps and pens and t-shirts. I later learned that this was the largest-ever purchase of illegal Olympic souvenir products. As it turned out, what I'd bought and presented as official gifts was all counterfeit stuff … unauthorised, illegal.'[11]

Although the TV rights ultimately went to NBC and the EBU, as Samaranch and the IOC had desired from the start, the involvement of Murdoch in the bidding process had the effect of dramatically pumping up the amounts paid. The US rights cost a record $US750 million, and the European $US200 million. Coates said later: 'Gary Pemberton did a wonderful job in terms of the negotiations with NBC. In both TV and marketing sales he achieved greater than we'd budgeted for … without him any debate about a budget surplus would have been academic.'[12]

Pemberton summed up the situation dryly:

There is no question that if I had taken the board into my confidence, if I had kept them aware of my discussions with Murdoch and others, it would have leaked. And had any information got out, my gut feeling is that it would have cost in the order of $400 million. It just wasn't worth it. Put it another way. If Rupert Murdoch hadn't participated in the bidding process, I genuinely believe Sydney's income would have been $400 million lower. I'm sure there was some resentment on the board about the fact that they weren't made aware of everything, but the stakes were so high, and their track record was so abysmal.[13]

An early example of board leaking came after a discussion around the SOCOG table on Kerry Packer's lack of attendance at meetings. Packer, an original member of the board, had missed a number of early meetings, and some directors argued that because of this he should be asked to resign. 'I wasn't attracted to that idea,' Pemberton said later. 'He hadn't been to a meeting in a long time, but the fact was that when he was there he was bloody good. He was very direct and he had the wind up most of them as well, which was handy.'[14] The day after the board discussion, the front page of the *Daily Telegraph* carried a story saying that Packer was going to be sacked for non-attendance. Pemberton was appalled: 'That was an absolutely disgraceful breach of security. It was embarrassing for me, embarrassing for Kerry.'[15]

When Packer came to a subsequent meeting he spoke angrily to the members: 'The chairman can't tell you blokes anything. Anything he tells you, he's going to read in the newspapers.' He proposed to Pemberton a simple, brutal remedy: 'If someone leaks, they go. They can't stay on the board.'[16] The president found it simpler not to tell the board anything related to sensitive or confidential dealings.

Packer, who remained on the board for just the first two years, found himself increasingly exasperated during the early arguments arising from the AOC's stranglehold on SOCOG's budget. Coates had sent a strong legal letter to Pemberton reminding him that, since the AOC was due to receive 90 per cent of any surplus from the Games, the board had a fiduciary duty to the AOC to maximise the amount of that surplus in everything they did. Pemberton then took to asking Coates before meetings began if he would release directors from such fiduciary responsibility in respect of any decisions they might be asked to make: 'If you want this meeting to go ahead, Coatesy, you've got to give us a release from any action that might result out of decisions we make during it.'[17] This kind of pantomime kept the tension high, but hardly contributed to effective board deliberations.

'Coates' technical, legal argument was that for the purpose of delivering the Games we, SOCOG, were in effect an agent of the AOC,' Pemberton later recalled.

> We did in a sense have a fiduciary obligation to maximise their profit. Of course what didn't help was that the government was indemnifying the Games on the downside, so arguably I had the same fiduciary relationship with the government to minimise their loss. I'd say to Coatesy, 'Look, I'm the schmuck here taking the public accountability for all these decisions, and I've got to get your consent. And I personally, and the members of this board, are at risk to either you or theoretically to the government if you take a view contrary to the one we've agreed. This just doesn't work…'[18]

Packer, meantime, wanted action: 'Listen, doesn't anyone realise what a big job we've got to do? This is going to be a bigger television broadcast operation than any existing structure in the world. For God's sake, can't we just get on with planning and building venues?' And again: 'Dammit. Let's just get on with the job … of staging a great Games for Sydney and Australia and stop this preoccupation with unnecessary crap!'[19]

Once Pemberton told the board: 'Look, I can't conduct a board meeting, and I'm not prepared to conduct a board meeting, if I'm going to be personally liable when the AOC doesn't like something we do. I would counsel the rest of you as directors to take a similar view.'[20] With AOC members of the board absenting themselves from the vote because of perceived conflict of interest, the board agreed that an unworkable relationship existed. It was soon after this meeting that the government concluded that the only way ahead was to buy out the AOC. This led in turn to the Knight of the Long Prawns in March 1996, the passing into law of the SOCOG Amendment Bill and the establishment of the SOCOG Sports Commission (both in June 1996).

The jousting between Pemberton and Coates never had a personal edge. The two men enjoyed each other's company, had no great love for formalities, and occasionally made their farewells from stuffy overseas ceremonial functions simultaneously, and early, to meet up again at sportsmen's bars, yarning, drinking beers and eating hamburgers. Pemberton said later of their confrontations over fiduciary responsibility: 'None of this was done with any animosity. In fact there was a bit of good humour to it. Everybody except Coatesy and I seemed very distraught about it. I sensed, I don't think he ever told me explicitly, but I certainly had the conviction that this was part of a game that was going to go the way it did ... he used his strongly worded letter [about fiduciary obligation] to precipitate a situation where the government had no option but to buy him out.'[21]

Six years later, Knight expressed a similar viewpoint: 'John had been thinking ahead from the beginning, and he had a whole lot of contractual positions. He knew he had to do a deal. He couldn't sit there with the veto. He forced the issue at a very propitious time. It was a great time to negotiate. He had a new minister learning the ropes. The US TV rights were yielding much more than had been budgeted for. There was a feeling of more money coming in, and euphoria. It was leading into Atlanta, so everyone was enthusiastic about the Australian team and the AOC. It was a time of strength. So he forced the circumstances for a buy-out.'[22]

A bit Machiavellian? Well, probably. Certainly it was an exercise characteristic of the man's style. Coates was later asked about his personal feelings as SOCOG was being rendered impotent by clauses in the endorsement contract he had engineered. Cryptically, and with a benign smile, he responded: 'I knew it was headed in the direction it was. It was okay for us.'[23] In the circumstances, it seems fair to assume that the buy-out solution occurred to him a long time before it did to any politicians.

When Pemberton retired in March 1996, many believed he had found the SOCOG boardroom — and specifically the constraints woven by Coates, mainly through his endorsement contract — simply too difficult to handle. This wasn't the case, he declared later: 'I just didn't want to spend another five or so years doing this, and being in a fishbowl. I'm essentially a private person. I wasn't particularly comfortable with this public life, this exposure. I guess I was sensitive.' He added:

> Certainly I didn't think I could get through to 2000 in this kind of environment. I just didn't want to do it. I also could sense the way things were going. I believed ultimately the government was going to do it [take over] anyway, and inevitably the relationship between Knight and myself would come under pressure. I didn't need that either. There was only going to be room for one dog at the bone, and if I was in the government's position I wouldn't want it to be Pemberton. And it wasn't a comfortable situation, in terms of accountability. The government auditor was checking the number of chocolate biscuits in the premier's office, and I was out there negotiating a billion-dollar deal. No, although there was a natural assumption that I'd had enough of the wrangling over Coatesy and his hold over the budget, the bottom line is that if that issue had never existed, I would still have chosen to go when I did. It wouldn't have mattered if Coatesy didn't have the leverage to get his 100 big ones. If that issue was never there, I would have done exactly what I did. I'd served my four years.[24]

Pemberton had told Knight of his decision to retire in early February 1996, and refused to be dissuaded. Knight then asked Pemberton for a big favour: 'There's a federal election coming up. Let's not have you resign until afterwards. Why don't I find a replacement, and actually announce your resignation and introduce your successor at the same press conference?'[25] Pemberton agreed, and soon after the pair of them flew to Lausanne on a routine reporting visit to Samaranch.

After that session, Knight spoke alone with the IOC president and told him of Pemberton's impending departure as SOCOG president. 'I know,' was the predictable enough response. 'John Coates telephoned last night to tell me.' Then Samaranch said, 'You should take that job.'[26] Knight was taken aback. He argued that such a move would be politically impossible, that it would be seen as unwanted government interference, that since the SOCOG chief was a businessman it was important to replace like with like. Knight later recalled what followed: 'Samaranch argued very strongly in favour of a government person taking the presidency. I was quite surprised, and that was the first time anyone had

Michael Knight (Minister for the Olympics) announces major changes to SOCOG, 6 March 1996. From left: John Iliffe (incoming president of SOCOG), Bob Carr (premier of New South Wales), Knight, Gary Pemberton (outgoing president of SOCOG). (Peter Rae / *Sydney Morning Herald*)

suggested it. I'd never even thought about the possibility. Anyway, I explained to Samaranch the need for secrecy until after the election and after we'd found a replacement.'[27]

The election was lost, and a replacement found. John Howard succeeded Paul Keating, and John Iliffe followed Gary Pemberton. Iliffe, 58, then chairman of Woolworths, GIO Australia and AWA, had a reputation as a trouble-shooter. He was a director of three other companies, but decided after his appointment to SOCOG to relinquish a number of positions. In the late 1980s he had been called in to help rescue Wormald after it had been pillaged by a Malaysian entrepreneur. Next he had taken on a fix-it role with the ailing electronics group AWA, which had lost direction and been subject to a number of takeover bids. He had become chief executive in a subsequent shake-up, and there were claims that he had pulled the group out of a death-spin. An inveterate smoker, he had been involved in sport as a first-grade rugby referee.

While SOCOG had been making headlines, many of them a result of internal discord and board leakages, another authority had arrived without much fanfare on the planning scene: the Olympic Co-Ordination Authority. It was a statutory body that resulted from the merging in 1995 of five government departments, all of which had been undertaking some Olympic work. Its primary missions were to deliver new facilities and venues for use at the Olympics and the follow-ing Paralympics, to coordinate and monitor all government activities in support of the Games, and to develop and manage the 760 hec-tares of land at Homebush Bay. SOCOG and OCA had been designed to complement each other; according to Michael Knight's simplified explanation, OCA would build the theatre and SOCOG would put on the show. That was the early intention, anyway. The roles would change a lot along the way.

The man chosen as director-general of OCA was David Richmond. He had been the state's most senior public servant in health, author in 1983 of the controversial but respected Richmond Report on mental health services. He had endured some major public rows, including the doctors' dispute of 1984–85, and at one stage of his career had received police protection after receiving death threats. He came to the Olympic task with a couple of firm resolves — to get the job done, and to keep out of the newspapers — and achieved both objectives pretty well. He became in fact the quiet achiever of the organising team. When he and OCA began in 1995, they inherited a construction program at Homebush Bay that was two years behind schedule. The only completed venue was the swimming pool, and the rowing and canoeing course was three-quarters built. Under Richmond, after the spending of $3.3 bil-lion, the entire building program envisaged in the original bid proposal was completed in record time, 12 months before the Games.

OCA director-general David Richmond (left), with IOC vice-president Anita DeFrantz and Olympic transport chief Ron Christie. (News Ltd)

That included the Olympic Stadium, the Sydney Showground (home to seven sports and the main press centre), the NSW Tennis Centre, the Super-Dome, the State Hockey Centre, the Sydney International Archery Park, the Dunc Gray Velodrome, the Sydney International Equestrian Centre, the Penrith Whitewater Stadium, the Sydney International Regatta Centre, the Blacktown Olympic Centre, the Sydney International Shooting Centre, the Ryde Aquatic Centre, the Beach Volleyball Stadium, the Rushcutters Bay Marina, the Olympic Park Railway Station, the Olympic Village and two hotels (the Novotel and the Ibis) at Homebush Bay. It was OCA that transformed Homebush Bay from an ugly wasteland — a place that had been the location for abattoirs, brickworks, factories and a rubbish dump — into the Olympic Park complex, one of the world's great sporting and industrial parklands.

For a time there was a distinct rivalry between SOCOG and OCA, with OCA consigned to the role of poor relation. SOCOG had the higher profile, maybe because it was seen to be the key organising body, maybe because its very fractious existence was earning it greater public awareness. To many, SOCOG was something of an elite club — a private organisation not unlike ACOG, the committee which had run Atlanta's privately funded Games — and OCA was a bunch of bureaucrats. At the Atlanta Olympics the SOCOG team, numbering more than a hundred, was led by its new president John Iliffe, board members Rod McGeoch, Nick Greiner, Donald McDonald, Frank Sartor and Anna Booth, and chief executive Mal Hemmerling. Most worked hard in the Atlanta heat, although Kevan Gosper later claimed that Iliffe had been 'almost invisible'.

Richmond and his senior OCA observers, Bob Leece and Mick O'Brien, were allocated accreditations that were inferior even to those of junior members of the SOCOG observation team. They had no access to seating or to lounges, they were billeted in low-quality hotels, and they were given no vehicle facilities other than a railway pass. This turned out to be an advantage. While SOCOG board members were able to enjoy the comforts of luxury hotels and limousine transport, the OCA observers endured first-hand the traffic shambles that existed in Atlanta. They were caught in railway jams, traffic jams, pedestrian jams. From that coalface observation of Atlanta's misfortunes, Richmond was later able to devise and recommend to Knight a scheme of traffic control for the Sydney Games. Until Atlanta, the plan had been that SOCOG would run transport at the Games, but this idea was abandoned as a result of Richmond's report. The new proposal involved coordination, through a single powerful body, of all forms of public and private transport in Sydney. That body was established in April 1997 and given the name Olympic Road and Transport Authority (ORTA). It was responsible for the integration of all transport in Sydney during the Games, involving everyone from athletes to spectators to IOC dignitaries, and it was to succeed spectacularly.

Knight summed up the change: 'In Atlanta the organising committee had responsibility for transport, tried to run it by contracts, and it plainly didn't work. An alternative for Sydney [to SOCOG control] might have been to have the government's department of transport take charge. What David [Richmond] came up with was a hybrid, with government clout, but involving all the private operators. It was responsible to the Minister for the Olympics rather than the Minister for Transport. We thus got government muscle and the Olympic focus.

That was a really critical change that grew from a real-world experience in Atlanta.'[28]

There were other real-world experiences. Richmond said later:

Because of the denial that existed in SOCOG of the government's involvement in the Games, it was very hard for me and my team to get accreditations that would take us officially into places [in Atlanta]. We had very limited access to anywhere. We resorted to all kinds of devices to get into venues. There was a venue inspection they [ACOG] were supposed to organise for visiting observers, but it broke down because they were in such chaos. My creative colleagues soon worked out that one of the best things to have was a tag that said, 'Cleaning Supervisor'. Cleaning supervisors for all those dunnies got into every kind of location. In today's climate of much enhanced security, subterfuge like that probably wouldn't work, but we had to do that sort of thing. We also forged some contacts with people who owned some of the venues, and we started to deal direct with them, rather than go through SOCOG or ACOG. There's no doubt our lowly stature meant that we had to improvise a lot.[29]

Knight avoided much of the cocktail circuit in Atlanta. He spent most of his time there in shorts, joggers, polo shirts and sunhat, looking backstage:

I spent time in the police centre, I crawled over buildings, I climbed on waste trucks, whatever. I wanted to see how things worked, the mechanics of it all. And I saw a lot of sport … it was my first Olympic Games, and I felt that maybe I'd be too busy for that in Sydney, or maybe we'd lose the election. It was in Atlanta that David and I had a vision of what the Games would actually look like if they worked — what it would be like on the trains, what it would be like around the city. We wanted people happy and celebrating in the city in the night. We wanted to minimise the disruption, maximise the fun. Much of what happened later in Sydney — the planning for all the areas between the venues, the six Olympic live sites, all equipped with giant TV screens, at key locations like Circular Quay and Martin Place — grew out of that vision.[30]

It was during the Atlanta Games that the SOCOG president, John Iliffe, who had been in the job a little over four months, decided to retire. He had been absent on a private trip to New Orleans when the bomb exploded in Centennial Park, and was thus unable to join others, including Knight, Hemmerling and McGeoch, in observing how the authorities dealt with the problem. Gosper wrote later that this absence was 'the final straw' for 'those of us who were already beginning to think he was not up to the job'.[31] Iliffe later told Knight that the difficulties facing organisers in Atlanta had convinced him that SOCOG needed stronger government involvement at the top.

'He said he knew he'd given me a commitment that he would stay through to the Games,' Knight later recalled. 'But he said he was prepared to step aside as long as it was part of structural change. He could see how the private sector was struggling to cope in Atlanta. The lack of liaison between them and the government bodies was very strong. And he felt that in a smaller country like ours, if we were going to deliver a quality Games, the government influence needed to be at the highest level. If we changed the SOCOG Act to ensure that the Minister — not necessarily me, because there was an election coming up in March 1999 — became president, he believed we could make a similar change.'[32]

Others were thinking the same way. Coates had told Knight not long after Pemberton decided to go that he should take the job, either immediately or after the Atlanta Games. The experience of those Games reinforced his view, and he let Knight know. Gosper briefly took the view that Coates should become president, and when the response from Coates to that was lukewarm, he floated without success the notion that the pair of them might consider a joint presidency. Knight had meantime given serious thought to Samaranch's arguments that he should become SOCOG president, and warmed to the idea. After a short return visit to Sydney on government business, he tried to arrange a meeting in Atlanta to discuss the matter further. When that proved impossible, he decided to fly home via Lausanne and call on the IOC president.

There he told Samaranch: 'Look, you put this view to me before. Now John Iliffe wants it to happen. John Coates wants it to happen. I want it to happen. This will be difficult, my position will be bipartisan. I am not going to do this unless you are wholeheartedly behind it.'[33]

SOCOG members at a press conference in Atlanta (from left: IOC member Phil Coles, Michael Knight, SOCOG chairman John Iliffe and chief executive Mal Hemmerling). (News Ltd)

Samaranch declared that it would be a sensible move, and stressed that he was prepared to offer public support. Ultimately the NSW premier, Bob Carr, agreed and the SOCOG legislation was changed. Thus, out of Atlanta, Michael Knight, Minister for the Olympics, became president of SOCOG on 27 September 1996.

Eight months later, in May 1997, John Iliffe died of a brain tumour, aged 60. Some newspaper reports had cited ill health as the reason for his resignation. Kevan Gosper took the view that his unassertive performance in Atlanta had probably been caused by his illness.[34] Six years later Knight disagreed emphatically: 'John Iliffe had no idea he was sick until six months after he stopped being president of SOCOG. I went to his 60th birthday party, and in fact his kids did a skit at the party based on a tour of his brain — they were finding all these strange things in his brain and so on. It's not the sort of thing that would have happened if there had been any inkling he was ill, particularly in that way. At the time he thought he was in perfect health. We thought he was in perfect health. As it turned out, he would have died before the Games. But he had no idea, we had no idea. He resigned from SOCOG wholly and solely to make the transition seamless, so that the government and the organising committee could come together. His was a selfless act.'[35]

CHAPTER FIVE

A dangerous culture

The sheer immensity of the task of organising the Sydney Olympic Games impressed key planners in diverse ways. Sandy Hollway could envisage the result in the simplest of terms as 'great sport on great fields of play in great venues in a great city', but he saw the business of achieving it as comparable to the Allied military invasion of Europe in 1944. 'It involved similar management principles,' he said later. 'You needed an early positioning stage, then strategic and tactical planning, plenty of training and rehearsal. There's a command control and communication structure which allows the top leadership to take the really big decisions once the battle is on, but allows each platoon high discretion to fight for its life on the beaches and in the hedgerows.'[1]

Michael Knight, shunning beaches and hedgerows, saw it in starker terms: 'When you actually confront [the task] in the flesh, it becomes a very big animal. Up close.'[2] After attending the Atlanta Games David Richmond likened the Sydney challenge to grabbing hold of the city and shaking it: 'You had to take it, shake it hard, put it on its side for three weeks...that's your city...then afterwards you shake it again and put it back. It will never be quite the same again...It has had this rare, amazing experience.'[3]

Seasoned Games-watchers like Kevan Gosper were convinced the goodwill that embraced the city from that night in September 1993, when the Games were won, would never last. 'There is no project with as many faces as an Olympic Games,' he said later. 'It is so big globally, it involves major architectural opportunities, it involves governments and people feeling good about themselves, it involves bringing the whole focus of the world on a single city, watching sport. It's seven years of planning for 16 days of competition. And seven years is too long a period to sustain a common enthusiasm. There are cycles by which the public interest ebbs and flows. With Olympic planning, organisational fatigue can set in. We've traced the histories, and there's always a disillusionment factor. In the IOC, we call it the 'organising committee curve of confidence'. What it means is that, whatever the host city, you're going to have periods that are downers.'[4]

Major downers came to Sydney after the Atlanta Games in the wake of a couple of resignations from SOCOG, both of which generated much controversy and critical media comment. Mal Hemmerling, the chief executive officer, departed suddenly in March 1997 amid rumours that his resignation had been forced by Michael Knight. Hemmerling, the former organiser of Adelaide's Formula 1 Grand Prix, had joined SOCOG as marketing manager in early 1995. He had performed well in that role and had a harmonious relationship with Gary Pemberton; in September 1995, when Pemberton stepped away from the chief executive role to concentrate on the presidency, Hemmerling had been given the job.

As chief executive Hemmerling worked comfortably in his new role under Pemberton, who later described him as 'a good operator'.[5] This was unsurprising, since part of Hemmerling's brief in the marketing job had been to act as deputy CEO. But after Pemberton's departure and Iliffe's brief, passive term as president, he found himself increasingly at odds with Knight, by then Minister for the Olympics and president of SOCOG. Pemberton later speculated that Hemmerling had been frustrated — as he himself had been — by an inability to retain some independence from government control.[6] Hemmerling had worked with Pemberton on overseas TV agreements, and after Pemberton's departure had negotiated the Japanese TV deal. He had also overseen sponsorship arrangements with Westpac and Ansett. But there were reports that he had been increasingly isolated inside SOCOG, that decisions had been taken out of his hands, that people under his responsibility had been advised to report directly to Knight. His main problem, it seemed, amounted to a difficulty in adapting to the changing identity of SOCOG in its steady progress away from a corporate culture towards the public sector.

In accordance with the terms of a severance settlement negotiated

Sandy Hollway, chief executive of SOCOG. (Andrew Meares / *Sydney Morning Herald*)

at the time of Hemmerling's departure, neither he nor Knight was able to speak to this writer (or any other) about any aspect of their relationship. But some measure of the fractured condition of that relationship might be gleaned from the fact that, when the three-volume Official Report on the XXVII Olympiad — the report produced by contractual obligation with the IOC — was released in 2001, Hemmerling's name was not mentioned once. He had occupied the cockpit of SOCOG for 18 months, but the weighty tomes that constituted the official report did not acknowledge his existence.

Hemmerling's successor was Sandy Hollway, who had no problems with the public sector. Hollway was an accomplished bureaucrat who had headed two Commonwealth government departments — in Employment, Education, Training and Youth Affairs, and in Industry, Science and Technology. He had held senior posts under prime ministers Bob Hawke and Paul Keating, had been Hawke's chief of staff for three years, and had spent 16 years with the Department of Foreign

Affairs, with four postings overseas. He was not intimidated by big budgets or major management tasks: at Employment, Education, Training and Youth Affairs he had managed a budget of $16 billion, a salary bill of $750 million and a staff of 15,000.

Hollway had been recruited through Graham Richardson late in 1996 to become one of two deputies (with Jim Sloman) to Hemmerling, and had been with SOCOG for two months. The day he became CEO he vowed to work 'hand in glove' with the NSW government to produce an integrated organisational plan. 'What we need,' he said, 'is a clear game plan that stretches out over the year ahead and that fully integrates all the organising bodies.' He and David Richmond had been working on a 20-point plan, covering everything from transport to accreditation, accommodation and security, aimed at bringing the government and SOCOG closer together. Coordination had been starting to happen under Hemmerling's leadership, he said, but 'it needs now to be driven through very strongly'.

The second significant exit was that of a leading board member, Rod McGeoch, who had played a heroic role as chief executive of the bid team that had won the Games for Sydney. McGeoch, a man of considerable charm, had been widely touted as a likely president of SOCOG if Labor was tipped out of office at the NSW elections due the following March; but such an appointment wasn't a realistic prospect. Not only did he not have the support of the AOC heavyweights Coates and Coles, not to mention Knight, but Coates had told him even before Sydney won the bid, over a steak and a bottle of red at New York's Waldorf-Astoria Hotel, that he did not think him suitable to become chief executive or president of SOCOG. What this statement underlined was the power the AOC had over all senior appointments. After McGeoch quit and the New York conversation became public, Coates told reporters, 'I don't know if he was disappointed. I can't remember what he showed...as usual, we had a good red wine.' The resignation came in November 1998, after damaging allegations had been made about McGeoch, suggesting that he had attempted to profit as a professional public speaker from his role as a member of the SOCOG board. McGeoch, who had spent almost exactly five years on the board, denied this strenuously.

Announcing his decision to resign, McGeoch accused unnamed

Rod McGeoch, chief executive of the successful Sydney bid team and a director of SOCOG until his resignation in November 1998. (News Ltd / Alan Pryke)

people of conducting a campaign of personal vilification and destabili-sation against him, as well as invasion of privacy and misuse of emails between his staff members and other people. He claimed there were people who were prepared to damage the Games in pursuit of their own agendas, and added: 'SOCOG has a huge job ahead of it. Sydney's Games will be the greatest Games ever. But there is a hell of a lot of work to do…the athletes, staff, sponsors and others do not need the distraction of political and Olympic muck-raking.'[7] Recalling the affair in 2003, McGeoch told this writer: 'The crazy thing is that I was never at any stage interested in becoming president of SOCOG. I had told John Fahey long before we even won the bid that I had no interest in a full-time job with the organisation…that I didn't want to become CEO

The premier of New South Wales, Bob Carr, Majorie Jackson and Michael Knight after the announcement of Jackson's appointment as a director of SOCOG, 14 December 1998. (News Ltd)

or president, that I just wanted to be a director. With the [New South Wales] elections coming, there was some opposition speculation, but nobody ever consulted me. I simply never entertained the idea of being president. In fact, I once told the board that if the coalition was elected, the only person to take over should be John Coates.'[8]

McGeoch's successor on the SOCOG board was Marjorie Jackson, then 67, the former Lithgow Flash and double gold medallist of the 1952 Helsinki Olympic Games. Jackson had been working almost full-time on a campaign to raise funds for leukemia research, which had dominated much of her life since the death of her husband, Olympic cyclist Peter Nelson, in 1977. She brought with her a refreshing sense of integrity, enthusiasm and political innocence. 'At my age, who wants to get involved in politics or anything like that?' she asked. 'I'm not here for any political reason, ego, or anything like that...I'm just here for the athletes.' Told that Aboriginal leader Lowitja O'Donoghue had said it was a disgrace that she had been overlooked for the position, Jackson said: 'She's entitled to her opinion. If they'd appointed another man, they'd be criticised. I've already read that my appointment was a token gesture. I guess whatever they did they couldn't win.' With former union leader Anna Booth, Jackson was one of the two women on the board.

After the McGeoch departure, the *Sydney Morning Herald* published a profile of the SOCOG board, under the banner headline 'OUT OF CONTROL'. The article claimed that McGeoch's resignation had stunned fellow directors, and added that he had 'made no secret...that he blamed Coates, his offsider Phil Coles and board president Michael Knight for the leaks that had brought him down'.[9] During a later briefing session to the IOC in Lausanne, Knight denied that he had sought the resignation. Whatever the case, that headline reflected a mood of disenchantment that existed in the media at that time with SOCOG and Games preparations. The disunity at the highest levels, the bitter boardroom arguments and accusations, were inevitably leaked and publicised, helping to shape a fairly constant pattern of negativity.

What Sydney and the Games needed badly just then, close to the end of 1998, was some good news. What they got instead, within days of McGeoch's divisive departure, was a scandal that engulfed the entire Olympic movement, humiliated the IOC and its president, and threatened Sydney's Olympic Games. It began with a television news report in Salt Lake City, sparked by an anonymous tip-off, that the Salt Lake Organising Committee for the 2002 Winter Games had been paying university fees for a student, the daughter of a Cameroon IOC member. Follow-up stories in the local media in that final week of November 1998 claimed that since 1991 — beginning soon after Salt Lake City had lost the 1998 winter bid to Nagano — individuals had received scholarship assistance worth almost $US 400,000 from the Salt Lake bid committee, or SLOC. Of the 13 recipients of the scholarships, at least six had been close relatives of IOC members.

That first leaked tip-off was like the distant lighting of a grassfire that quickly exploded into a huge, uncontrollable bushfire. In Lausanne on 1 December 1998, Marc Hodler, of Switzerland, a former IOC vice-president and current member of the executive board, shocked his colleagues by alleging that at least 5 to 7 per cent of IOC members had taken or solicited bribes from cities bidding to host the Games. Corruption existed in the bidding system, he said, to a degree that there were agents who would, for fees of up to $US 1 million, undertake to deliver blocs of IOC votes to hopeful bid cities. Hodler, 80, was a highly respected figure: he had run the International Ski Federation for 47 years, had been the IOC member for Switzerland for 35 years, and was one of only four life members of the IOC. He felt the Olympic host city bidding process encouraged corruption; he had long wanted to take the selection of host cities out of the hands of IOC members, and entrust them to the executive board.

Hodler's outburst created front-page headlines around the world and ultimately confronted the IOC with its worst moment ever. IOC members found it hard to believe what was happening. Theirs was an organisation that had been assailed over the decades by issues like terrorism, boycotts and drug abuse, and had taken them in its stride. Now it was absorbing awful punishment — and the damage was being inflicted from the inside, by one of its own most distinguished leaders. 'This has affected me deeply,' said Samaranch. 'After 18 years of watching the organisation grow and prosper, these charges are extremely hard to accept.'

The revelations just kept coming, seeming to feed off each other.

Marc Hodler, a member of the executive board of the IOC, created a furore when he alleged that the host-city bidding process encouraged corruption. (IOC Archives, Lausanne)

Hodler's allegations had been of a general nature, and were largely unsubstantiated. But what emerged over the next three months was a huge body of specific evidence that made it clear that many IOC members had been earning either big bundles of cash or lavish favours by selling their votes to cities bidding to host future Games. The favours came most notably in the form of scholarships and jobs for relatives, expensive gifts and free medical care. Samaranch acted quickly to set up an inquiry into the Salt Lake bidding process; it took the form of an ad hoc commission, headed by Dick Pound, a Canadian Queen's Counsel and senior IOC member. A spate of separate investigations was soon under way — by the Salt Lake organising committee, the US Olympic Committee, the US Justice Department and the US House of Representatives. Even the FBI became involved.

Some of the disclosures demonstrated behaviour that was both blatant and bizarre. In Salt Lake City Jean-Claude Ganga, an IOC member from the Republic of the Congo, who was president of the Association of National Olympic Committees of Africa, became known to insiders as 'the human vacuum cleaner': he was guaranteed to suck up any material object that came his way. He made six visits to Salt Lake City, during which he received treatment for hepatitis, his mother-in-law underwent total knee replacement surgery, and his wife had cosmetic surgery — all of it paid for by the organising committee. An enterprising man, Ganga formed an investment company with the SLOC bid committee president Tom Welch, bought land, sold it quickly, and reaped a profit of $US60,000. Travel expenses for Ganga and his family exceeded $US115,000, and he received an unexplained direct payment from the bid committee of $US70,010. Nobody doubted that Ganga had clout in terms of African votes; it was he who had orchestrated the African boycott of the 1976 Montreal Games.

General Zein El-Abdin Mohamed Ahmed Abdel Gadir, the Sudanese IOC member, managed to persuade the SLOC to send payments of $US1000 a month to his student daughter Zema in London. When it later transpired that he didn't have a daughter, someone worked out that the fictional daughter's name was an acronym for the initials of his first four given names. When he was later expelled from the IOC, Gadir set a record unlikely ever to be equalled. He became the only person in history to have been expelled twice from that august body. He was first thrown out in 1987 for having missed three meetings without providing an excuse beforehand; his absence was understandable really, given that he was in prison throughout that time after a difficult experience in a coup d'état. Following his release from jail, he was reappointed to the IOC, where he remained contentedly until his second expulsion in 1999.

John Kim, the son of the Korean IOC member Kim Un-Yong, was the beneficiary of an unusual employment arrangement. Tom Welch found him a no-work job with a satellite communications company, the Keystone Corporation, on the basis that his salary of $US75,000–100,000 was reimbursed to Keystone by Welch's Salt Lake bid committee. The money was laundered as 'consulting fees' from the committee, and the fake job enabled Kim to obtain a visa allowing him to live in America. The scholarship of Sonia Essomba — the subject of the tip-off that began the entire scandal — involved rent, tuition and expenses worth $US115,000. Ms Essomba was the daughter of Rene Essomba, a surgeon from Cameroon, an IOC member for 20 years. His family enjoyed expensive, extended stays at the Hotel Intercontinental in Paris on their journeys to Salt Lake City. Essomba died in August 1998, so the issue of expulsion didn't arise.

Variations on the corruption theme were diverse. Sergio Santander Fantini, IOC member from Chile, asked the bid committee cheekily for a contribution to an election campaign in which he was a candidate, and received $US20,050. When he was beaten in the poll, he asked for another $US20,050 to help pay debts he'd incurred during the failed campaign — and got it. The sons of Mali's IOC member Lamine Keita and Swaziland's David Sibandze received around $US100,000 apiece for scholarships and living expenses while attending US universities. Nancy Rignault Arroya, daughter of Augustin Arroya, IOC member for Ecuador, liked Salt Lake City so much she stayed there from 1992 to 1995, with living expenses paid by the bidding city.

The pattern of IOC corruption was exposed in Salt Lake City, and its most outrageous documented excesses occurred there, but its roots were elsewhere. There were three main contributing factors: the recent prosperity of the Olympic movement, the fallibility of the host-city bidding system, and the dangerous culture of largesse that existed in the IOC:

> ▶ Until 1984 it was a risky proposition financially to host the Olympic Games. Then, in Los Angeles, Peter Ueberoth designed a corporate version of the Games that yielded a profit of US$215 million. After that, as television and sponsorship revenues created an increasingly wealthy environment, the number of cities keen to

stage the Games multiplied. Competitive bidding between aspiring host cities intensified, to a degree that all kinds of lures were being offered to win votes from those lucky people who would make the choice: the members of the IOC. Lobbying had changed a lot since the days when a nervous delegation from Melbourne sought votes for the 1956 Games by sending food parcels and bottles of wine to London. A new breed of Olympic consultant had emerged — the middle-man whose role it was to make deals between IOC members and bidding committees. In the quest for bigger, better pay-offs, unscrupulous IOC members were not beyond playing one bid committee against another.

▶ In the post–Los Angeles era the process of selection of host cities became unwieldy, expensive and difficult to control. Certainly it was very vulnerable to corruption. By the 1990s, around 150 people — members and partners — were zigzagging around the world to visit candidate cities continuously over a two-year cycle. For the 1992 summer and winter Games there were 13 simultaneous candidates, seven summer and six winter. Many of those who were making trips to evaluate winter Olympic sites came from countries which had no snow or ice; what some were having was a series of junkets, accompanied by extreme hospitality, with kind hosts to greet them and load them with lovely gifts. IOC evaluation committees were visiting candidate cities and reporting on them, but that had no effect on the steady traffic of IOC members. No system of surveillance existed. The IOC became aware of abuses, and of the existence of agents who undertook to deliver votes for bidding cities at a price; it discussed the issue at board level and suggested guidelines, but took no meaningful action. Inevitably it gave the impression that it tolerated a system which it knew was deeply flawed.

▶ To be a member of the IOC has always been to be a member of a select club, a recipient of much indulgence. The fancy hotels, the limousines, the first-class travel, the general mood of largesse are not matters of individual choice. They come with the territory. In the old days there was an accent on titles and personal wealth. As Samaranch told this writer in 1997: 'The composition was dif-

Juan Antonio
Samaranch and
IOC vice-president
Dick Pound, 1999
(News Ltd,
AFP photo)

ferent then. There was so much aristocracy... princes, marquises, barons, counts and so on. Now we are trying to appeal to a new aristocracy, the aristocracy of the athletes. We have 17 members who won medals in Olympics, nine with gold medals.'[10] Despite this laudable thrust, a sense of privilege and patronage still pervaded the IOC, even though its 114 members were unpaid and many of them were not wealthy. Members were never elected, always co-opted; from 1981, their travel and accommodation expenses were paid by the IOC; they had the job until they turned 80. Some of them, a greedy minority, saw the perks that came their way, particularly the fawning attention of host cities, as genuine fringe benefits. They accepted the favours unquestioningly, as if they deserved them.

By the end of March 1999, after the findings of the Pound commission and the Salt Lake City inquiry, four members of the IOC had resigned and another six — including the aforementioned Ganga, Gadir, Arroyo, Fantini and Keita, plus Paul Wallwork of Samoa — had been expelled. Another whose expulsion had been recommended, Charles Mukora of Kenya, had resigned. In the face of world-wide vilification of the IOC, and widespread, taunting calls for him to step down in the wake of the scandal, Samaranch was hurt but defiant. 'I have been elected by members of the IOC, not by outside people,' he told those who questioned his right to remain. He put his leadership on the line at the March session, and made a speech before the vote outlining his many achievements as president. The vote was 86–2 in favour of him remaining in the job. After that the IOC addressed its many problems. It embarked on a process of reform for both host-city bidding and membership of the IOC.

It established an Ethics Commission, whose task was largely self-evident, and an IOC 2000 Commission, which was given the daunting challenge of reforming the entire structure of the Olympic movement. The 2000 Commission's report, which was endorsed in full by the IOC in December 1999, involved 50 recommendations. Prominent among them was an overhaul of membership rules: retirement at 70; fixed eight-year terms; creation of new categories to include 15 active athletes, 15 presidents of international federations, 15 presidents of national Olympic committees and 70 elected members; and a procedure for selecting and electing new members. On host-city bidding, the new regulations involved a ban on IOC members visiting candidate cities.

Australia and the Sydney Games team did not emerge from the corruption crisis unscathed. Hodler made early suggestions, which he later withdrew, that the bid was tarnished. Coates made an admission that he had promised grants worth $52,500 apiece to two African IOC members for their national Olympic committees (of which they were also presidents) on the eve of the 1993 vote in Monte Carlo. Phil Coles was accused of having received favours from the Salt Lake City bid committee, and later given a 'most serious warning' by the IOC; the charges against him began a punishing five-month saga that damaged the Games, wrecked friendships and caused him much personal agony.

More than a year after the scandal erupted, Gosper, a member of the Ethics Commission, faced (and successfully defended) accusations that he had also broken the rules in accepting Salt Lake City hospitality.

When he first made his allegations in Lausanne, Hodler was asked whether Sydney's bidding process had been clean. 'I would be surprised,' he replied. 'I know what happened but I don't want to disclose it. I can't imagine that Sydney is different from the others. Sydney pretends it is completely clean, clean, clean.' Following angry denials in Sydney, and a demand by Coles that he apologise, Hodler backed away from the claims: 'I don't know anything about Sydney. I only know that Sydney very firmly says they never did anything against the existing rules.'

Soon afterwards, Coates admitted publicly that he had made a deal with Charles Mukora, of Kenya, and Major General Francis Nyangweso, of Uganda, in Monte Carlo before Sydney won the vital vote. Certain grants had been contingent on Sydney winning the bid. In Lausanne that night an agitated Gosper, who had been unaware of Coates' disclosure beforehand, told reporters after the news broke that questions were already being raised about whether Sydney should be allowed to proceed with the Games. A flurry of phone calls followed between Gosper, Knight, Coates and Coles. Coates explained that Gosper was unaware of the grants because he had not been on the Sydney bid committee's board, and had been living in London. What did not help matters was the certainty that Mukora was no innocent in the Salt Lake City affair. Because he had been paid $34,650 directly by the bid committee, the Pound commission had recommended his expulsion from the IOC. He resigned before the axe fell.

On 24 January, after consultation with Gosper, Coates faxed some relevant information to Samaranch: An annually audited program of assistance by the AOC for 11 African nations had been widely known. What had not been highlighted before was an amount of $52,500, by way of $7500 a year, that had been promised to the Ugandan Olympic Committee towards costs of the Ugandan national games. The grant to the National Olympic Committee of Kenya of $52,500 was for special projects, one of which had been a visit to Australia by a schoolboy athletic team. Before leaving on their vote-seeking mission to Africa in 1993, Coates and Gough Whitlam had taken advice from former US ambassador Andrew Young on the dispensation of US government aid to African nations during Atlanta's similar quest for votes, and been guided by it. 'The AOC did not breach any IOC bidding guidelines by supporting the NOCs of various developing countries,' Coates told Samaranch. And he linked the conditional nature of the grants to other undertakings. The $US30 million Sydney offered in 1992 to allow athletes and officials to travel to the Games, as well as the 1993 offer of US$7 million for transportation of rowing and canoe craft, and for horses, had both hinged on Sydney winning the Games.

Next morning, fronting a large media conference at a school near his home, Coates was candid about the circumstances of the last-minute offers. 'I thought the vote was slipping away. That's when I went to the two IOC members and said, "If we win we would also make available $52,500 to each of your national committees for other programs."' Had he done wrong? His response reflected his tough, realistic approach: 'We didn't win it [the bid] on the beauty of the city and sporting facilities we had to offer. We could have chosen not to go down this path [of making offers]. We could have chosen to give them the Ken Done scarf or whatever it was, and settled for that. We've spent cumulatively $50 million-plus on the three bids for Brisbane, Melbourne and Sydney. I had some responsibility. I wasn't going to die wondering.'[11]

Even two years after the Games, Coates was uncertain whether Mukora and Nyangweso had voted for Sydney: 'You never quite know. Of the 11 African votes I think we got five or six, which we normally [in previous bids] didn't get.'[12] What mattered was that Sydney had won by two votes.

Although an IOC investigation pronounced the Sydney bid as clean, Knight decided to call an investigation into the conduct of the entire process. He had been influenced by a letter from the chairman of the Independent Commission Against Corruption, Barry O'Keefe, who felt the whole affair threatened the reputation of Sydney and New South Wales. Tom Sheridan, a former attorney-general of South Australia, was appointed Independent Examiner for SOCOG. Coates argued before the inquiry that he had made the African offers on behalf of the AOC, which was not an agent of the bid. On the morning of his cross-examination, he had found a clause in his faithful document of last

Michael Knight
(left) and
Tom Sheridan,
15 March 1999,
releasing the
report on
Sydney's Olympic
bid. (News Ltd /
Paul Burston)

resort — the endorsement contract — spelling out the AOC's independence from the bid company, and thus exemption from IOC guidelines. One of Sheridan's conclusions was that uncertainty existed about how or whether those guidelines applied to NOCs, and he recommended the removal of this uncertainty.

The Sheridan Report, delivered on 12 March 1999, found that Sydney's bid had breached official guidelines but that there had been no corruption. The Sydney bid company had spent $386,000 on gifts for IOC members, exceeding the $320-a-gift limit specified in the guidelines, but there was no misconduct: 'The gifts...were generic and not of a type designed, or likely, to influence the vote of an IOC member.' Sheridan found that a number of actions by the bid company had been in contravention of the spirit of the IOC guidelines, 'if there is such a thing'. These included the presence for four months of a lobby team in Paris, costing $160,000, under the direction of Coles; the African tour by Coates, the Whitlams and Perry Crosswhite; and several side-trips within Australia for visiting IOC members to destinations like the Gold Coast and the Great Barrier Reef.

Sheridan summed up the breaches as often 'technical', falling far short of abuses that occurred in Salt Lake City, and suggested that Sydney might not have won the Games had it not committed them. The IOC guidelines, he pronounced, were ambiguous, riddled with loopholes, often ignored, and not policed.

CHAPTER SIX

The battler from Bondi

The public agony of Phillip Walter Coles, born 20 July 1931, lasted five months, from his drag-on entrance to the IOC corruption stage in February 1999 until his forced departure from the SOCOG board in June the same year. The personal agony lasted much, much longer.

The whole Coles saga turned out to be the saddest, most demeaning personal drama enacted during the organisation of Sydney's Games. As it unfolded, in the eyes of the media and much of the community Coles came to be seen as a serial freeloader, a virtuoso veteran of the IOC junket circuit. Knight and members of the SOCOG board, including his close friend Coates, came to regard their colleague variously as an embarrassment and an unwanted hindrance, particularly after he received a couple of serious censures from the international body. Coles saw himself as a victim, a scapegoat, a kind of martyr — although he did admit to occasional lapses of judgment. His image throughout the whole wounding affair became that of some kind of pop-up duck in a carnival shooting gallery. He kept being hit and knocked over, but each time he would just flip back up again, full of defiance, until the next shot took him down. A Monty Python knight once fought like that, down to his last limb. It shouldn't have happened that way for Phil Coles.

Coles was a Sydney County Council plumber and a knockabout surf club member when he was first selected in the Australian kayak team for the Rome Olympics. As the planning for Sydney advanced, he could have felt considerable satisfaction in the contribution he had made to the Olympic movement since 1960 — as an athlete and an administrator. He had played an influential role, during his four-month posting to Paris in 1993, in securing votes in Europe for the Sydney bid. He was director of international relations for the AOC, a foundation

director and vice-president of SOCOG, and chairman of the torch relay committee. He had a reputation as a decent, easy-going man, justifiably proud of his record. The prospect of hosting fellow IOC members at an Olympics in his home city — an Olympics that he had helped win and plan — loomed enticingly, a splendid culmination to 40 years of positive involvement.

There was some irony in the fact that his first implication in the corruption scandal followed within days of his own outraged call for the whistle-blower Marc Hodler to apologise for his mild slur on

Phil Coles in his
paddling prime.
His first Olympic
selection was in
the Australian
kayak team for
Rome in 1960.

Phil Coles
alongside Prince
Charles on the
sand of Bondi,
1966.

Sydney. On 10 February 1999 the report of the Salt Lake City Organising Committee's board of ethics claimed that Coles and his family had visited the city four times between 1991 and 1995 at the expense of the organising committee. The report stated that they had stayed at expensive hotels, and had been guests at a Super Bowl match in Miami. Coles denied any wrongdoing, claimed he had been defamed, and advised Knight that he would withdraw from SOCOG activities until the matter was settled.

There was little doubt that Coles and his partner, Patricia Rosenbrock, had benefited from considerable hospitality in Salt Lake City and the surrounding ski fields; his major problem was that he hadn't asked too many questions. He later conceded that he had been naive: 'I should have questioned more. I was naive to think that the invitation was based on friendship rather than me being an IOC member ... I considered I was visiting friends.'[1] Two years after the Sydney Games he told this writer:

> The initial inspection visit we made was legal. When we went back later — and I stress that this was after Salt Lake City had won the vote, and had nothing to gain from me — it was legal, too. We paid our own fares. I've got the vouchers and the travel documents to prove it. When we got there we paid our own grocery bill, we fed ourselves in the apartment, paid for our ski tickets. The error of judgment we made was to accept someone's word: 'It [the apartment] is owned by a friend of mine. He's not using it. It's yours.' And we used the place three times. The other time I went the accommodation was provided by Jim Easton, another IOC member. I was made a scapegoat. Everyone knows that now. The IOC knows it.[2]

On 12 March 1999 the IOC's Pound commission made the recommendations that led to the expulsion of six IOC members and the resignation of four others. It also found that Coles 'did not ... exercise his best judgment, and his repeated acceptance of benefits ... should have been avoided'. It decided that 'whilst [he] should have been much more careful, his behaviour does not justify a proposal of expulsion'. He was warned and told that a repeat performance would expose him to expulsion. Nine other IOC members who had been investigated were

Phil Coles, *chef de mission* at the 1980 Moscow Olympics, with some of the Australian team (from left: Rosemary Brown, Georgina Parkes, Lisa Curry, Michelle Ford, Michele Pearson, Coles, Stephen Foley and Lisa Forrest). (AAP picture / R. McPhedran)

given similar warnings. Coles admitted to reporters that night that in hindsight he knew he had been careless and should have been 'more circumspect'. He swiftly resigned his $140,000 job as director of international relations for the AOC, citing stress as the reason, but remained a member of the IOC and the SOCOG board.

Separately, though, new allegations had surfaced a week beforehand that he and his former wife, Georgina Coles, had received valuable jewellery, including a gold necklace worth $10,000, from a Greek businessman associated with the failed Athens bid for the 1996 Games. Again Coles denied it, claiming that all he had received was a pair of silver cufflinks 'worth $20 or $30'. The IOC set up another investigation on 22 March. On 1 April the SOCOG board sacked him from a job he cherished — the chairmanship of the torch relay committee. He was bitterly disappointed, more so when told that his fellow AOC members of the board — Coates, Gosper and secretary-general Craig McLatchey — had abstained from voting on the issue. 'When I took on that job I told Michael Knight it would be very expensive, but sponsorship would cover it,' Coles said in 2002. 'I told him that if it was done properly it would unite the people for the Games like you've never heard before. The only consolation when I look back is to be able to say that 95 per cent of the work was all done when I left.'[3]

By this stage the Coles affair was receiving headline treatment daily. His health was suffering, his relationship with old buddies like Coates was fraying, public support for the Games was reported to be eroding, and SOCOG directors were expressing concern about the impact of the continuing scandal on sponsorships and the impending release of ticketing. Knight and the premier, Bob Carr, were calling for his resignation from the SOCOG board. He had been the subject of vilification before, when he stood his ground as *chef de mission* during the huge controversy over Australia's participation in the 1980 Moscow Olympics, but the pressure had been nothing like this. Once he broke down in tears during a radio interview, after John Laws asked him whether he was running out of money and mates.

'It was a terrible time for him,' Coates recalled. 'He was almost under siege.'[4] Gosper said: 'He was being just trammelled by the press. Let's face it, he did step out of line and he was managing the press very badly, being very badly advised.'[5] Coles' recollection: 'No one should ever be put through what I endured. After all I'd put into it, everything was crashing around me. I had no support anywhere. I didn't have anyone to help me. People were saying I should go and hide. [Broadcaster] Alan Jones took me away from the media to his hideout down the South Coast. Alan looked at all my diaries — I keep impeccable diaries — and measured the charges against what happened. That's why he took up my case.'

Then on 5 May, as the IOC was meeting to consider the charges relating to the $10,000 necklace, there was another shooting gallery hit. ABC radio revealed the existence of 400 pages of secret documents from the Sydney bid, which had turned up mysteriously in the possession of the Salt Lake City Organising Committee. It broadcast sample extracts from the files, which it said were also in the hands of the *New York Times*. Newspaper front pages and TV bulletins around the nation were abundantly fuelled again. The documents had been prepared by Coles and Patricia Rosenbrock, but Coles denied they had been provided to the Salt Lake organisers. They listed the personal likes and dislikes of most IOC members, including even Samaranch, and opinions they had proffered. They consisted of typed reports by Coles, written during his stay in Paris during the Sydney bid, with added handwritten notes below by Rosenbrock. This last material was mainly chatty, trivial and at times almost coy — 'has passed on her beauty secrets to me', about an executive board member — and in most cases included references to likely voting intentions for the 2002 winter Games. Of IOC heavyweight Pound, the assessment was, 'I think Salt Lake would be Dick's second vote.' Of Prince Albert of Monaco, who 'always greets me with a warm embrace', there was, 'Discussed Salt Lake City with him & he said it was a great bid & will win next time.'

The revelation of the existence of these documents provoked a rash of editorials calling for Coles either to remove himself or be removed from SOCOG. The *Australian* said on 6 May 1999: 'He should in all decency do what the *Australian* recommended months ago and resign his Olympic jobs. His reputation is in tatters — it cannot be restored by him staying on and meanwhile Australia's reputation as host nation suffers.' The *Sydney Morning Herald* said on the same day: 'The sooner he goes, the sooner the focus can be turned away from controversies and back on the 2000 Games.' The *Age* accused Coles of 'refusing to put the good of the whole [SOCOG] team ahead of his own interests by gracelessly refusing to go'.

The Coles dossiers prepared for the Sydney bid were not improper. It is normal practice for bidding cities to assemble profiles on IOC members, and to include confidential assessments of voting intentions. Coles had been part of an intelligence team which put together information to aid Sydney's candidature, and only a small number of people had been privy to the reports. These included the six senior members of the bid committee — McGeoch, Coates, Bruce Baird, Graham Lovett, Geoff Wild and Coles. What caused outrage was not the compilation of such profiles, but the passing of them to the planners of another city's bid, which Wild — a former advertising executive who was a vice-president of the Sydney bid company — described as a betrayal. Also worrying was the pattern of references in the handwritten notes to voting attitudes on Salt Lake. Coles was adamant that he was not responsible for the presence of the files in Salt Lake.

Three years later he told this writer: 'They [the dossiers] were made over the course of many, many months for the benefit of our own bidding team, and we never gave them to anyone. I was an agent of that bid. Patricia was an agent too.'[6] For whom were the dossiers intended? 'For no one, for our own use. For anyone within the Sydney bidding process who wanted to look at them.'[7] Could he not have allowed the Salt Lake team access to them as a means of repaying hospitality? 'No. What we did with the Salt Lake people, because I knew them personally, when we met internationally, we'd sit down and compare notes on how we thought bidding was going.'[8] He had nothing further to offer on that issue.

After consultation between Knight, Gosper and Samaranch, the IOC executive board decided to set up a third inquiry into a Coles issue, to be headed by Judge Keba Mbaye, of Senegal. Gosper later explained: 'They felt comments by Phil and Patricia were not the sort of communications you would expect a member and his partner to be making about other members, and the third-party references on Salt Lake City's prospects really worried them.'[9] Meantime the ABC, which had decided to release the entire Coles files to the IOC, handed them over to Gosper through its Olympic journalist Kevin Wilde. When Knight asked Gosper if SOCOG could have copies of the files, Gosper took advice from Mbaye. The judge consented, on the basis that the papers were not secret, had been in the hands of the *New York Times*, the ABC and the Salt Lake committee. Also, he pointed out that they rightfully belonged to SOCOG, as successor to the Sydney bid team.

Gosper gave the files to Knight, who promptly released them to the media. Gosper later wrote, a little ambiguously, 'Several IOC members were critical of the Minister's decision to do so, which I found a bit odd.'[10] Coles said:

> That was the final stroke that finished me off as far as SOCOG was concerned … those notes were personal and private, but they fell into the hands of journalists. Kevan and I met at the AOC office. He declared in front of a witness that he would take those notes direct to the IOC, and nobody else would see them. He went across the road, straight to Knight's office, and between them they made the notes public. They would never have seen the light of day if he'd kept his promise to deliver them to the IOC — very wrong decision. Every trick in the book was tried to make me resign from SOCOG, and ultimately it came down to them releasing those documents to the media.[11]

That night Gosper told Kerry O'Brien on the ABC's '7.30 Report' that Coles had been 'guilty of a continuous pattern of misjudgment in his role as an IOC member'. Rejecting Coles' claims that he was the victim of a conspiracy, Gosper said that Coles had nobody but himself to blame, and added: 'I know of no persons, I know of no information, that suggests there is a conspiracy against Phil Coles. And I told him that.'

Knight defended his decision to release the dossiers:

> Once Kevan told the media he had given me a set I didn't believe I had any choice but to make them available generally to the media. Not surprisingly, several journalists quickly came beating on my door demanding a copy. If they applied under Freedom of Information legislation — legislation which applied to material I as a government minister had in my possession, but which did not apply to either the AOC or the IOC in the same way — I would almost certainly have had to provide them with a copy within 30 days. Remember, two media organisations, the ABC and the *New York Times*, already had copies. Any delay would have just been perceived as being obstructionist on my part. Indeed, some journalists perversely may have accused me of being involved in a cover-up. I recognise that some IOC members were not happy with my action, but, like Kevan, I see the problem as having been

Phil Coles and Kevan Gosper arrive at the crucial IOC meeting in Lausanne, Switzerland, March 1999, which followed the Salt Lake City corruption scandal. (News Ltd / Jayne Russell)

with the creation of the documents, not their release to some additional journalists over and above those who already had them.[12]

A few days later one of the dossiers, containing personal references to Gosper's wife Judith, was published on the front page of the *Sydney Morning Herald*. Among the handwritten comments on the file of the Russian IOC member Vitaly Smirnov was the cryptic sentence, 'They both hate the Gospers (particularly Judy).' Gosper was furious, and wrote later, 'It was at this point that Phil Coles, suddenly and finally, lost me.'[13] Soon afterwards he advised Samaranch that he would refuse to take part in any further IOC discussions on Coles.

Throughout May the pressure on Coles to resign from the

SOCOG board intensified, with political leaders Kim Beazley and Tim Fischer echoing Knight's argument that the whole drama was damaging Sydney's Olympic efforts. Headline writers invented a word to portray his dogged refusal to go — 'philibuster'. He could not be forced out: under the original SOCOG legislation, his role as an IOC member guaranteed his right to sit on the board, worth $50,000 a year. Sandy Hollway telephoned Coles and told him: 'Look, mate, I have to tell you it would be best for you to leave the board of SOCOG. It's causing too much harm.' Much later Hollway said: 'It wasn't an easy message to receive, especially from somebody like myself, a relative Johnny-come-lately. But he took it well and with dignity.'[14] Hollway then told the media: 'I'm the person in charge of bringing off the biggest peacetime event on earth ... I just don't need day after day front-page and other news stories that are crowding what we should be thinking about — which is the sport, the athletes, the Games themselves. The ongoing and protracted controversy is particularly unwelcome. A number of sponsors have made their concerns clear to me.'

Coates said he agreed with Hollway that Coles' refusal to budge was hurting the Games. 'This is very difficult for me,' he said. 'We're talking about one of my oldest and dearest friends. It is someone I've worked with a long time, but I could not dispute what Sandy put to me.' Coles still refused to walk, saying, 'All I'm asking is for Knight to stop the persecution and give me a fair go.'

In mid-June the affair finally ended. Mbaye's IOC investigation commission (consisting of the judge, Anita DeFrantz and Marc Hodler) found Coles had been guilty of 'serious negligence' in failing to ensure that dossiers written by himself and Patricia Rosenbrock about IOC members did not go outside the Sydney bid committee. It found it was reasonable to believe that the person writing them intended them for another bid city, Salt Lake City, but added that 'the facts ... do not prove beyond doubt that Mr Coles directly committed an act constituting a breach of his oath'. In his defence to the commission, Coles had vehemently denied that either he or his companion had provided in any way a copy of the documents to anyone from Salt Lake City. He had claimed that Rosenbrock had written the notes for her own use 'because she wanted to complete her records, and the issue of Salt Lake City came

up as a matter of conversation in her encounters with IOC members'. The IOC decision, based on the recommendation of the Mbaye commission, was to maintain the severe warning given to Coles the previous March, to reprimand him afresh for serious negligence, and to suspend him from all committees for two years. The commission ruled there was insufficient evidence to make a finding on whether he had accepted the jewellery.

Coles resigned from SOCOG after the IOC director-general, Francois Carrard, phoned and offered him the choice of either resigning or being forced off the board. Afterwards he told reporters: 'To be honest, I've been thinking about it for some time — I got to the stage where I thought it's probably going to be best for the Sydney Games.'

He wondered aloud whether he still might have a role to play with the sports commission. But Knight declared: 'Out is out. Mr Coles has resigned from SOCOG. I take that to mean he is off everything…the board, the sports commissions, the Sydney Olympic Broadcasting Organisation and the torch relay committee.' Hollway said he hoped the scandal was over: 'Now we can get on with the task, free from what has been a major distraction and controversy.'

An unfortunate casualty of the whole episode was the friendship that had existed between Coles and Coates since they met at the 1976 Montreal Olympics. They became the CoCo twins, inseparable mates for 23 years, as they moved through the ranks of administration and into two of the most senior jobs in the Australian Olympic movement. Coates had supported Coles through the early days of the scandal — 'he's hardly the gravy train type, he's the battler from Bondi, I can tell you' — but as the drama wore on the bond between the two men became increasingly strained. When Coates advised Coles to resign his post as director of international relations for the AOC — and receive another year's salary — before the first IOC warning was handed down, he believed he was achieving the best result possible for Coles. 'Look, Phil,' he told him by phone, 'If there's an adverse finding you'll get nothing. We'll be forced to terminate your contract because you'll be seen to have brought the Olympic movement into disrepute and thus be in breach of the contract. I can clearly advise that's what will happen. But if you retire now we can pay you a year's salary and allowances, but no car.'[15] Coles accepted the deal reluctantly.

In 2002 Coates said: 'He didn't trust me. To this day he believes he was pushed by me into resigning when he wouldn't have had to.'[16] Coles told the *Weekend Australian* that Coates' advice had come as 'a kick in the guts'. He added: 'I was shocked that John would do anything like that. I came up in the lifesaving movement, where friendship, loyalty and mateship were a huge bonding thing.'[17]

In a cover story in *BRW* magazine in September 1999, Coles conceded that in the case of Salt Lake City he had overstepped the mark, that he had accepted hospitality outside IOC guidelines. The authors of the article said they had seen documents showing that he and his partner had over-indulged themselves, and that 'he now recognises this'.

Much more significantly, the magazine article said that Coles believed Coates had abandoned and betrayed him. He was quoted as saying: 'I put it that if you were in the trenches with John Coates, he wouldn't desert and leave you. He'd hold you up in front of him as a shield.' That was the end for Coates. He said in 2002: 'Coles suggested in that article that I wanted him out so I could become an IOC member. It was so wrong. By that time the reforms were in place, the route for me to the IOC wasn't that way. And if he goes, Australia will have only one member in that category. So that was just a nonsense. Anyway, that was it for me.'[18] In 2002 Coles was asked whether he regretted having made the 'trenches' remark. 'I never made it,' he said, straight-faced. Huh? 'It was a throwaway line by another person … I didn't say it, but when it was said, I know it was said as a throwaway line. It was printed, the thing is it was printed.' Did he never publicly deny it? 'No, I've got to live with it.'[19]

Various mutual friends, including Peter Montgomery, J. J. Brown and Jon Donohue, afterwards tried to make peace between the two men. Coates' response to all of them: 'What would you do if someone did that to you?'[20] The bitter fall-out between the pair had the effect of bringing Gosper and Coates close together as planners, if not as friends. 'In the start it was rather like the way I found I had to work with Michael Knight after we did the buy-out deal,' Coates recalled. 'The thing was too big. Phil and I had to work with Kevan whether we liked him or not. What happened was that Phil fell by the wayside and Kevan and I became close.'[21]

A late, unexpected target in the Salt Lake corruption scandal was Gosper, then an IOC ethics commission member and likely contender for the presidency after Samaranch. When claims were made that he and his family had been the beneficiaries of $50,000 worth of gifts and accommodation from Salt Lake City, he referred them immediately to the ethics commission. The claims focused on a stopover holiday taken by Judith Gosper and their two children in Salt Lake City during the family's return from Gosper's London post to Melbourne. The ethics commission (with Gosper standing aside) found the following May that there had been no evidence of misconduct, but still turned the matter over to a senior New York legal firm — Watchell, Lipton, Rosen

Phil Coles and partner Patricia Rosenbrock at the Sydney Opera House, 31 December 1999. (News Ltd / Mark Williams)

and Katz — for independent inquiry. The senior investigator, Martin Lipton, reported that there was 'no basis to conclude that the Gospers either knowingly or negligently violated IOC rules'. When it was all over, Gosper retained a strong conviction that he had been set up by an IOC colleague.

Phil Coles had certainly made some errors of judgment (some conceded as such by him, some not), but there seemed little justification for the treatment dished out to him in the year 2000 on the issue of the torch relay. Coles received a letter dated 28 October 1999, from SOCOG's torch relay director Di Henry, advising that he would have the honour of carrying the torch 500 metres along Bondi Beach on Day 99 of the relay. It added that the exact location of the run on Bondi Beach would be communicated about six weeks beforehand 'so your family and friends can share in this momentous occasion'. Coles had expressed an early preference to carry the torch there, but now that the arrangement was confirmed he was delighted. It all seemed so appropriate, because that beach had been part of the man's life. He had patrolled it as a lifesaver for ten years without missing a single patrol, and such was his sentimental attachment that he was already planning for his ashes to be scattered in the surf.

Coles had recently celebrated his 50th anniversary as a member of the North Bondi Surf Club, and was one of 19 club members who had represented Australia at the Olympics. He had won five national surf championships while a member of the club, had captained the first Australian surf team to compete in the United States, and had translated his surf-paddling skills to the Olympics with some effect, representing Australia in kayak events at three Olympic Games. He had also been chairman of Sydney's torch relay committee until his sacking in March 1999. The North Bondi club was so chuffed about the decision that he would be carrying the torch that it circulated a letter advising all life members, 50-year members and sponsors.

On 10 July 2000 Coles received a second letter from Di Henry, advising him of a change of plan. He would not be running on the beach, after all. He had been allotted instead a segment of the relay on the same day, but along Curlewis Street, Bondi, from houses No. 45 to No. 271, the latter on O'Sullivan Road.[22] His run on the beach had apparently been awarded instead to Jim Walker, another fine (but less controversial) North Bondi paddler who had competed at the 1996 Olympics. It is hard to avoid the conclusion that this relegation of Coles, from the high-profile run on the nation's most famous beach to 400 metres of a suburban street, was petty and spiteful. Certainly it was personally hurtful to a man who had already taken plenty of punishment for his lapses. The surf club, while still asserting its pride in Walker, protested that the change was perplexing.[23] One radio broadcaster, Mike Carlton, branded the demotion of venue 'an act of bastardry'. Another, Alan Jones, who had previously defended Coles, conducted an audited phone poll among listeners that provoked a jam of 1000 calls every half-hour. The question was: 'Should Phil Coles be allowed to run on Bondi Beach?' The result was 7574 votes for yes, 363 for no.[24]

(Around the same time, Dawn Fraser, who had been openly critical of the IOC, was advised of a similar change of plans. She had received an invitation from Di Henry in October 1999 to carry the torch at another of the nation's iconic sites, the Sydney Opera House, on Day 99. Then, in July 2000, another letter from Henry advised her that her leg of the torch relay would be along George Street, central Sydney, from Bridge Street to Martin Place. That was where she finally carried the torch.)[25]

On 20 July 2000, following sustained criticism early that day by talk-back hosts Jones and John Laws, the directors of SOCOG considered Coles' relay demotion — and in effect whether he should run on sand or asphalt. It was now 15 months since Coles had been removed from the board. Graham Richardson argued strongly that he had been punished enough for his Salt Lake City indiscretions, and was supported by ABC chairman Donald McDonald, investment broker Brian Sherman, Sydney mayor Frank Sartor and NSW opposition frontbencher Chris Hartcher. The *Australian* reported that Craig McLatchey, the AOC secretary-general, was also believed to have supported Coles' right to run on the sand. After a 6–5 vote, the SOCOG board decided to reinstate him at Bondi Beach. Afterwards Michael Knight, who abstained with Kevan Gosper from the vote, said simply, 'Sydney has always been the city of redemption.'[26]

Soon afterwards, Coles received formal notice that he would be back on the beach. A letter from Dani Elliott, Torchbearer Manager, advised him that, 'due to unforeseen circumstances, we have had to make an amendment to your Torchbearer Position'.[27] He was to receive the flame close to Bondi's Olympic volleyball stadium, then carry it north, up the ramp in front of the North Bondi Surf Club, then south along the walkway to the next ramp. Jim Walker was to receive the flame from a surfboat, run the first leg along the beach, then hand it to Coles.

That was how it happened on 14 September, the day before the opening ceremony. While an armada of surfboats, surf-skis and surfboards drifted offshore in calm seas, Walker accepted the flame from Jessie Miley-Dyer, the state's junior lifesaver of the year, who had carried it in a surfboat from Bronte. Fifty thousand people packed the beach as

Walker handed the flame to Coles near the volleyball stadium. Coles, with an escort of surf Nippers around him, jogged slowly with the flame to his old surf club, where he stopped and raised both arms in salute to the club and the surf lifesaving movement. It was an immensely satisfying moment, one that he could really savour after a couple of pretty awful years. The pity was that it had almost been spoiled by an apparent conviction, somewhere deep in SOCOG, that the punishment of an amiable, occasionally fallible battler from Bondi should not be allowed to end.

CHAPTER SEVEN

A difficult year

John Coates remembers it as a time when 'the media didn't stop bashing us'.[1] For Sandy Hollway the whole year was gruelling, but the last five months were the darkest period of all — just hard slog, sleepless nights and constant criticism. And Michael Knight reflects candidly: 'If you had asked me in November 1999 did I think we could deliver a quality Games in September 2000 I would have told you no. I didn't believe we could deliver anything like what we did ultimately.'[2] That was the kind of year 1999 was, an *annus horribilus*, a year of scandals, disappointments and declining optimism. With the corruption affair finally subsiding, the organisers found themselves facing a couple more crises — on the issues of marching bands and ticketing. SOCOG's handling of both was greeted by the media and the public with criticism that was fierce and merited.

Sometime during the year, a notice was unofficially distributed among SOCOG staff members. Its sardonic tone fitted the rather embattled mood of the organisation, and it found its way onto numerous notice-boards and walls. It said:

> ANYONE WHO HAS BEEN ASSOCIATED WITH ANY PROJECT, WHETHER SAVING THE WORLD OR A LAMINGTON DRIVE, KNOWS THAT THERE ARE SIX PHASES. PIN THEM UP ON A WALL AS A REMINDER OF THE EVENTS OF 1993 TO 2000.

> 1. EUPHORIA
> 2. DISENCHANTMENT
> 3. SEARCH FOR THE GUILTY
> 4. PERSECUTION OF THE INNOCENT
> 5. SUCCESSFUL COMPLETION

And, finally

6.   GLORIFICATION OF THE UNINVOLVED

In 1999, SOCOG staff felt, Phase 4 was in rampant mode. The marching bands rumpus — like a concurrent, thankfully unsuccessful campaign to keep the beach volleyball away from Australia's most famous beach, Bondi — stirred many parochial passions. It followed a proposal by Ric Birch to Michael Knight to mark the 2000 Games by having a band of 2000 youngsters from around the world march into the stadium during the Olympic opening ceremony. What he wanted to create, he said, was 'a wall of sound'. Birch, the director of ceremonies, had a triumphant record in helping to produce wondrous ceremonies at the Los Angeles and Barcelona Olympics and the Brisbane 1982 Commonwealth Games. Knight, though, was not a total fan: he later described Birch as 'terrific broad brush, but problems with the detail'.[3]

Knight liked the proposal for an international band and took it to the SOCOG board, which embraced it. 'What we thought we were getting was a band made up from as many countries as possible,' Knight recalled. 'We loved that. What we got contractually — in a contract that was signed by the chief executive, but which the board never saw until long after the event — was a marching band that was predominantly American and jack else.'[4] Birch's plan in fact was to have a band comprising 1300 Americans, 500 Australians and a balance from other nations, including 200 Japanese. He explained the accent on US bands: only American bands had the expertise to march to complex patterns while playing, and few Australian players had been trained in the distinctly American art of marching in steps of 22.5 inches.

What began as a communication problem at SOCOG, with the board quite unaware of the detail of an arrangement it had already endorsed, developed into another unwanted controversy. Although the original arrangement had been made in March 1998, and selected US and Japanese youngsters had been working at odd jobs since then to raise their own fares to the Games, it was not until June 1999 that the bands issue caused a public outcry. Victor Grieve, director of a Sydney brass band called the Golden Kangaroos, began a media campaign to protest against US domination of Birch's proposed marching band.

The marching band segment, subject of so much fuss in 1999, turned out to be a huge success at the Sydney Olympic opening ceremony.

When radio talk-back hosts John Laws and Alan Jones took up the cause, the air waves were suddenly filled with outrage. The reaction ranged from proudly patriotic to unabashedly jingoistic, and the unrelenting message was: 'It's Australia's Games, Australia's opening ceremony. Why import foreigners to perform in what should be a showcase of Australian culture?' Birch did little to hose down the mood when he attempted to justify his action on radio: 'Australians march like soldiers, American marchers *perform*.' After Laws read out Birch's fax number on air, the director of ceremonies received more than 1000 abusive fax messages. In the face of all this anger, the SOCOG board quickly caved in. Knight announced that there had been 'very strong, indeed overwhelming community opposition to foreign musicians', and that SOCOG had decided 'not to proceed with the overseas component of the massed band segment'.

This knee-jerk reaction caused international embarrassment, media assaults on Australia (with one Californian columnist dismissing Australians as 'low-down, back-stabbing rats'), orchestrated protests to Australian diplomatic posts, talk of $10 million compensation, and great disillusionment for 1500 young musicians whose invitations to Australia were cancelled. Birch said he came close to quitting, but was influenced to stay by his responsibility to 24 members of his support team. When American band-leaders came to Sydney to protest, Graham Richardson blasted them on his 2GB radio show. Richardson, a SOCOG board member since 1996 and recently appointed as mayor of the Olympic Village, declared: 'You're not going to be in the opening ceremony. If you don't like it, if you find it unacceptable, go ahead and sue us. We'll give you nothing. [The kids] won't be appearing anywhere.'

Eventually, after more belligerent rhetoric and several attempts at compromise, a settlement was reached — with much guidance from Hollway — at a cost of around $1 million. A 'truly international' band would march, with 900 Australians, slightly fewer Americans, 200 Japanese and another 200 from Africa and Europe. 'We got a better outcome,' Knight summed up. 'Not the outcome we were initially promised, but we got closer to it than what the public was furious about.'[5] (In fact the pattern-marching segment of the opening ceremony turned out to be a huge success.) The double back-down over a fairly trivial issue, driven mainly by shock-jocks, cost SOCOG more credibility and good-will than it could afford.

Selling tickets to the Games was expected to be easy. Certainly the signs looked good to SOCOG's ticketing sub-committee — Graham Richardson (chair), John Valder, John Coates and Donald McDonald — when the first ticket book was released on 30 May 1999, carrying messages of welcome from Mark Taylor, former Australian cricket captain, and Sandy Hollway. Taylor wrote that 'more than 5 million tickets have been reserved specially for us — every Australian has an equal chance'. Hollway, who became the public face of the ticketing drive, stated that there was a choice of '5 million tickets, more than 640 sessions of 28 different sports'.

What unfolded from that point was an unremitting nightmare for SOCOG, a catalogue of failed promises and dented expectations that amounted to a public relations disaster. At one stage the process drew intervention from the Australian Competition and Consumer Commission, whose chairman, Allan Fels, accused SOCOG of having breached the Trade Practices Act with misleading and deceptive advertising. Later Knight, Hollway and Richardson, among other senior SOCOG executives, were called to face a NSW parliamentary inquiry chaired by the Rev. Fred Nile. Finally there was an independent review of the ticketing process, conducted in November 1999 by John Shirbin, solicitor, of Clayton Utz, and Rory O'Connor, auditor, of Deloitte Touche Tohmatsu — both of whom had occupied advisory roles during Tom Sheridan's independent examination of the Sydney bid six months earlier. Their ultimate findings were extremely critical of SOCOG senior and middle management, and of the board itself.

Apart from that, the botched ticketing affair had significant impact on the course of Olympic planning, most notably affecting the roles of Sandy Hollway and David Richmond from November 1999. Hollway remained chief executive of SOCOG, but from that point his responsibilities were downgraded, as Richmond's authority increased in inverse ratio. Richmond went on to become director-general of Sydney 2000, director-general of OCA and SOCOG, responsible for overall command and coordination of the Games. OCA, which had been seen early as a poor relation of SOCOG, progressively became the dominant

David Richmond, director-general of the Olympic Co-Ordination Authority and ultimately director-general of the whole Sydney 2000 organisation. (News Ltd / Michael Amendolia)

partner. 'It was virtually a takeover of SOCOG,' Richmond remembered, 'but we didn't call it that. Sandy, who had never seen himself as the chief operating officer, increasingly moved away from the centre. He was very good at strategic thinking, a very good communicator, wrote very well, but he was not the person to make hard decisions. What I did was form an alliance with Jim Sloman, his deputy, and effectively we changed arrangements so that meetings were jointly chaired. I didn't want to alienate people too much, but equally I wanted to make sure we were getting the right result — because the government was now putting more money into the Games, and we had to make sure that a lot of things were delivered correctly.'[6]

When the Games were over, Knight came to regard the ticketing scandal as an ugly kind of blessing:

> It was the watershed. If the ticketing crisis hadn't happened we might never had got the quality Games we did. Although it was the biggest crisis we faced, and for a period it destroyed public confidence, the truth is that out of it came an imperative to fix problems, and not just in ticketing. It led immediately to Michael Eyers taking over half the SOCOG organisation. It led to Alan Marsh, chief executive of the Darling Harbour Authority, taking over the ticketing. We went from a position of zero credibility on ticketing to the highest percentage sell-through in Olympic history. We went from that moment to make some very dramatic changes, including the integration of SOCOG, OCA and ORTA, which was pivotal to the delivery of the Games.[7]

SOCOG operatives (from left: Michael Knight, Sandy Hollway, David Tierney and Paul Reading) meet for the NSW parliamentary inquiry into Olympic ticketing, November 1999. (News Ltd / Brett Faulkner)

So what had gone wrong with the ticketing process? Mostly it was a case of overblown promises, inefficient delivery, communication problems (an affliction common to SOCOG) and downright deception. The whole system, borrowed uncritically from Atlanta, was revenue-driven rather than customer-driven. The accent was on greed, not service to the customers. When the public ticket ballot was launched, SOCOG promised 3.5 million tickets for purchase by the Australian public in the first draw. The ballot in fact contained around 420,000 fewer tickets. Given the huge demand for the most popular events, many prospective buyers were bound to miss out. In the high-demand sport of diving, for instance, just 16 A-grade tickets were included in the ballot.

The public sense of outrage increased when it was revealed that the SOCOG manager in charge of ticketing, Paul Reading, had secretly set aside a pool of around 360,000 tickets to high-profile events for sale to wealthy individuals, companies, agents and clubs at inflated prices. The objective was to raise $35.5 million. Reading, who described himself as 'the ugly face of capitalism', told a NSW parliamentary inquiry in November 1999, 'My job was to maximise revenue.' Undeniably SOCOG was under enormous budgetary pressure at the time, still $140 million short of its revenue target.

By the end of October, Knight offered a public apology for the mess and SOCOG began paying $5.4 million in refunds to disgruntled ticket-buyers who had either received tickets they didn't want or received no tickets and been charged $15 for an unwanted program. A clearly distressed Hollway admitted that he was never informed about the number of tickets actually available in the contrived public ballot. He said he had been too tied up with the day-to-day running of SOCOG to have concerns about the tickets. 'Ticketing has been an issue of high importance, but only one of them,' he told the *Sunday Telegraph*. 'I didn't ask the question of the numbers of tickets by sport or by session. But as a CEO, I won't duck the problem. I should have asked. I don't think the guys were keeping it from me.'

Some days earlier Hollway was reported to have offered his resignation to Knight. What he had written in fact was a letter offering to resign if the president and board of SOCOG felt that such a course was in the best interest of the Games. This offer, which Knight convinced him to withdraw, was seen by Knight as shifting the onus of the decision to himself and the board. On 22 October, three days before the scheduled release by SOCOG of details of the number of tickets that had actually been in the public ballot, session by session and category by category, Hollway began two weeks' leave. It was unfortunate timing, with SOCOG clearly heading into the worst crisis it had faced, but he needed the break. He had planned to take a holiday earlier, but this had been deferred during the controversy of the marching bands. On 4 November, with Hollway still away, Knight called a meeting at SOCOG to assure staff that, contrary to rumours, Hollway was not about to quit. Not only had he talked Hollway out of resigning, he said, but he had full confidence in him.

Interviewed in 2002, Hollway spoke about 'the darkest period of it all':

> We'd been working massively long hours and on very tough issues, under very considerable stress…It is easy to look back now and say it was a tremendous success, but we didn't know that then. We knew enough about the project to know how much could go wrong…Not just me, but every general manager would be waking up at 3 o'clock in the morning. There'd be a million things in your mind, people would be getting up writing notes to themselves. We'd all worked ourselves very hard, to a point where we needed a break. After discussion with Michael I decided to go ahead. I went to Coolum and I went to Pacific Palms, near Foster. I think the darkest period of it all was the series of months in late '99 when we worked our way through the ticketing controversy.[8]

On 29 October, after apologising publicly for the ticketing fiasco, Knight announced that he was ready for 'some action to take us forward'. That action, apart from an agreement with Fels on marketing practices, was the setting up of the Shirbin–O'Connor independent review, whose progress was monitored by David Richmond and Jim Sloman. The judgment, delivered on 22 November, confirmed that (1) SOCOG had offered fewer tickets in the public ballot than it had promised, (2) unacceptably low numbers of tickets had been allocated for some high-demand sessions, and (3) SOCOG had removed tickets and sold or reserved them at premium prices. There were a number of

During the ticketing crisis. From left: Michael Knight, Kevan Gosper, Paul Reading, John Coates and Graham Richardson. (News Ltd / Brett Faulkner)

damaging findings, most important of which was that the whole affair had been 'caused by management failures on the part of SOCOG's senior and middle management, and oversight failures on the part of the board as a whole'. There was criticism of the ticketing sub-committee, which 'did not meet regularly ... [and] did not have sufficient rigour in its processes to compensate for the lack of checks and balances in the ticketing management structure'.

The report made a recommendation that was distinctly unhelpful to Hollway's cause. It said that he 'put to the Review that it was important to maintain SOCOG's present management model, which involved extensive delegation of responsibility. The Review's findings demonstrate that the model did not work properly in ticketing. It is the

Review's opinion that it was the absence of basic management controls combined with the excessive delegation of responsibility that has led to [the ticketing mess].'

Knight made some harsh assessments soon after, revealed for the first time to this writer in December 2002. He declared:

> When Sandy took leave on the eve of what was clearly going to be the biggest crisis SOCOG had faced, it was obvious to me he would not be able to play a major role in the delivery of the Games. The pressures were only going to increase. The real issue was never the one the media focused on, namely whether or not Sandy Hollway should be sacked. The real issue, which Sandy had effectively determined himself, was whether he could continue to have a central role in the delivery of Sydney 2000. Once the answer to that was 'no', we moved on to arrangements recognising that fact. What this meant was that, while Sandy continued to hold the title of 'chief executive officer of SOCOG' from November 1999 onwards, he was chief executive in name only.[9]

Knight went on: 'As I progressively integrated the operations of SOCOG, OCA and ORTA, David Richmond became the director-general of the whole Sydney 2000 organisation. Within SOCOG, key management decisions were no longer taken by Sandy or referred to him. They were made by SOCOG's existing chief operations officer, Jim Sloman, or by the new deputy chief executive officer, Michael Eyers, appointed in November 1999. Sloman and Eyers reported to Richmond, or, on occasions, directly to me.'[10]

Knight claimed that Hollway had not been sidelined because of findings in the Shirbin–O'Connor report; that that decision had already been made. He added: 'We went out of our way to make sure that Sandy was not publicly humiliated. Neither the public nor the media generally was aware of the extent of the arrangements, but Juan Antonio Samaranch and Jacques Rogge were fully aware … In the last year Sandy did some valuable work in the areas of protocol and international relations. He did those things very well. They were important but were not at the core of the delivery of the Games.'[11]

Unsurprisingly Richmond, the man who took over leadership of the integrated operation, had reservations about aspects of SOCOG

Clearing another hurdle. Michael Knight and Sandy Hollway after announcing that an extra 500,000 tickets would be available to the public. (News Ltd / Grant Turner)

performance under Hollway. 'He had set forward a very good agenda when he came in,' he pronounced. 'But when it came to some of the hard decisions, he didn't take them. He'd agree to a decision, and a week later you'd talk to somebody in SOCOG who'd say they didn't know anything about it. Things didn't seem to percolate down because there was a strong sense of people deciding their own destiny. That was okay, but sometimes the destiny they were deciding was the future of the whole Games. You had to take a decision … now go and do that, not what you like to do but what I'm telling you to do.'[12]

Coates said later: 'If you were judging the split-up of credit for the Games … while others ended up administering the Games, there is no doubt that Sandy carried the motivation side for the staff, and kept them together and focused through all those crises. People were going home and copping it off their families, sometimes from their friends, over the ticketing. He's a lovely bloke, and he saw them through it. Although he wasn't a key player in terms of who called the major shots at the end, I think he was very important.'[13]

Hollway's attitude to his staff was summed up in a letter he circulated to all of them at the end of the Games:

> We all know that the inherent problems of organising something as massive and complex as the Games were greatly compounded by the fact that we hadn't done it before and we only got to do it once … Above all, you were not deflected by hard times and bruising controversy. There are very few organisations — in fact none come to mind — which have shown the strength of character which you showed in gritting your teeth, focusing on the job and just ploughing ahead. We sustained each other with shared confidence that the work we were doing was good, and that we would be vindicated in the end by a great Games.

The obvious collision between Knight and Hollway, like the Coles–Coates and Coles–Gosper conflicts, gave an edge of personal drama to the events of 1999. Knight, whose tall, forbidding presence at times gave him the look of a bossy funeral director, seemed to spend much of that awful year bullying, cajoling and offending people. He was never any sort of candidate for a popularity poll, and he seemed content about that. From the time he took on the SOCOG presidency he had been a driven man, undeterred by a fairly constant pattern of abuse, prepared to elbow out anyone who got in his path, convinced in his own mind that he had to do it his way. If being branded as arrogant and dictatorial and a control freak bothered him, he didn't let it show. He made it known that he had only one objective: a successful Games. If people got hurt along the way, bad luck.

Hollway, unlike Knight, enjoyed being loved by those around him. Also unlike Knight, he related well to people around him and was able to inspire loyalty from those in the workforce below him. He was affable, courteous, urbane, consistently considerate. Throughout his time at SOCOG, even during the punishing troughs of the ticketing affair, he was the organisation's most popular figure, held in genuine affection by staff, the public and the media. Long after major powers had been stripped from him, he continued to be seen as the Games supremo.

When, at the end of the Games, the IOC honoured Knight, Coates and Richmond with the rare gold version of the Olympic Order, there were protests that Hollway should have received a similar award. Knight, identified publicly (and correctly) as the person who stood between Hollway and a gold Order, received a mauling on talk-back radio, with even IOC vice-president Dick Pound condemning him as 'mean of spirit'. In the *Sydney Morning Herald*, David Humphries commented that Knight, who had 'a vindictive spirit', had ensured he would be remembered 'more for his mostly stupid and irrelevant acts of bastardry than for his competence…' Hollway was among seven key organisers who were nominated by Knight to receive the silver Olympic Order. The others were: Jim Sloman, deputy chief executive of SOCOG and chief operating officer during the Games; Michael Eyers, deputy chief executive of SOCOG; Bob Leece, director of construction and deputy director general of OCA, and chief executive of ORTA; Mick O'Brien, deputy director general and director of operations at OCA, with primary responsibility for the athletes' village and media village; Bob Elphinston, general manager of sport, and formerly general manager of the Sydney bid; and Margaret McLennan, the longest-serving female executive in the Sydney bid and organising team.

Knight had not nominated himself for any award, and said later that he had expressly asked that he should not receive one: 'The really unfortunate thing was that the IOC insisted on giving me an Order. People thought it was all to do with "my Order"… Now the simple reality was that I said to the IOC all along, "Don't give me an Order. I'm happy to recommend who else gets Orders." The IOC invariably gives one to the president of the Games, though, whether it's been a good Games or a bad Games. It's a courtesy.'[14] He finalised his recom-

Michael Knight is presented with the Olympic Order by Juan Antonio Samaranch while John Coates looks on. (News Ltd)

mendations to the IOC in August 2000, a month before the Games. The list was known and approved by Samaranch and the vice-president who would later succeed him, Jacques Rogge. On the day of the closing ceremony, Dick Pound and Anita DeFrantz argued at an IOC executive board meeting that Hollway should receive a gold award. Rogge was asked by Samaranch to sound out Knight about such an upgrade. Knight's response was brusque: 'It wouldn't be fair to others. You know where people fit in. If you really want to give him gold, give him the one you want to give me.'[15] This was later leaked inaccurately to the media as an ultimatum: 'If Hollway gets gold, I'll refuse mine.'

When it was put to Knight in September 2002 that many people still saw his attitude on the Hollway award as churlish, he said: 'It would have been easy for me to say, "Sure, go ahead. Give it to him." But how do you then justify elevating someone above people like Leece and Sloman? It was a very simple matter of principle and fairness. And hey, if I have to take some personal abuse and flak for standing up for a principle, it certainly wouldn't be the first time.'[16]

Hollway remained diplomatic and distanced from the issue. 'I didn't see it as a matter of great consequence,' he said in 2002. 'What mattered to me was that, despite problems and some mistakes along the way, in the end the staff had been vindicated. It was good to be able to say to staff people on the closing night, "Have some champagne. It's very rare in your life that you'll be able to walk away from something saying that by geez we nailed that — that it was an unqualified triumph".'[17] He said it mattered more to him when, during the International Year of the Volunteer in 2001, he attended a major Rotary conference in western New South Wales and was awarded the organisation's highest honour: 'That was nice, because that was about being recognised by Australians in the volunteer movement. And anyway, why should I aspire to get anything more than Jim Sloman or Bob Elphinston?'[18]

Hollway considered for a moment or two, then added: 'Summing it up, my feelings were that (a) I was in excellent company, (b) my own country mattered more to me than the IOC, and (c) the Games were such a conspicuous success that all the rest was trivia.'[19] For Hollway *and* Knight, however their relationship travelled, that last sentiment meant everything.

CHAPTER EIGHT

Changing the mood

Ever since it was conceived for the Berlin Olympics in 1936, the torch relay has been seen as a symbol of unity and goodwill. The mission statement of the Sydney relay organisers echoed that theme, stressing that the relay embodied 'a sense of sharing — from the simple connection of two individuals as the torch is passed from one to the next, to the sharing of the spirit … with all Australians and the entire world'.

A sharing of the spirit? One problem in May 2000, in the early stages of the flame's 61,000-kilometre journey from Olympia, Greece, towards the main stadium at Homebush Bay, was that the Olympic spirit didn't look to be in great shape in Australia. What was being shared among many ordinary citizens, after the IOC scandals and the almost unrelenting controversy that had attached itself to SOCOG, was a mood of disappointment, disgust and even apprehension. This communal unease was not helped in the earliest stages of the relay, when it was perceived that Kevan Gosper had taken advantage of his position as an IOC vice-president to gain preferential treatment for his daughter Sophie as a runner in the relay.

In terms of geographic sweep and individual involvement, the Sydney 2000 torch relay was certainly the most ambitious in history. Its most significant accomplishment, though, was that it somehow managed to transform that overwhelmingly negative national sentiment into something that fairly glowed with goodwill. In its earliest days the cynicism in the air was almost palpable, as the Games continued to be identified with bungling, bribery, privilege and organisational insensitivity. It was not helped by sections of the media which seemed at times to be besotted with the notion of belting SOCOG at all costs.

But during the 27,000-kilometre passage of the torch between those two defining landmarks of Australia, the ancient rock of Uluru and Joern Utzon's audacious Sydney Opera House, something wonderful happened. Not only did that cynicism evaporate. What took its place, gently at first, was a blend of pride, enjoyment, wonder and bonding — a reinforced sense of national identity — and that blissful mood continued to saturate Sydney and the entire country throughout the Olympic Games. The torch relay, impeccably and creatively organised under a team led by Di Henry, ushered in a period of sheer, enduring happiness, even rapture, possibly unmatched in Australian history. For most of us it was, quite simply, the time of our lives.

The relay did not begin well, though. First the Olympic flame failed to ignite during the traditional ceremony at the Temple of Hera, set among the ruins outside the ancient town of Olympia. When clouds rolled across the site and blocked the sun's rays, a flame kindled during a rehearsal the previous day had to be substituted to light the torch for the first runner, the high jumper Lambros Papacostas. That small hiccup did little to detract from an elegantly choreographed passage of the flame, in the care of 25 lissome young actors and dancers masquerading as priestesses, from the temple to the starting point on the track where heroes of the ancient Games used to perform.

Even as the long, four-month journey began, Kevan Gosper was embroiled in a controversy that would wound him deeply, torpedo his hopes of succeeding Samaranch in the IOC presidency, and make SOCOG again the subject of public derision. His acceptance of an invitation for his 11-year-old daughter, Sophie, to carry the torch meant that she became the first Australian to do so, taking over for the last 300 metres of the kilometre allocated to Lambros Papacostas. This distinction was to have gone to another schoolgirl, Yianna Souleles, 16, of the beach suburb of Maroubra, who had travelled with classmates from Sydney's St Spyridon College for the torch-lighting ceremony. She had been allocated seventh spot in the relay, through the centre of Olympia, following an approach by her school to the town's municipal council.

Gosper's invitation had been offered in Lausanne a month before by the Greek IOC member Lambris Nikolaou, who was also president of the Hellenic Olympic Committee. It was later suggested that Nikolaou had his own agenda — that the invitation had been part of a pitch to

Yianna Souleles at Athens Airport after her participation in the torch relay. (News Ltd / Angelo Soulas)

woo Gosper into supporting his bid to become a member of the IOC's executive board. 'I made a serious mistake then,' Gosper reflected later. 'I didn't ask him what he had in mind, where she might run, what day it would happen. I will never regret that I let her run, but I do regret that I didn't see anything sinister about the offer. I should have asked more about it. I think I might have found a solution, or I'd have sensed that this wasn't quite right, that this is a bit dangerous, that I won't even ask

Sophie.'[1] He did none of those things. After discussion with his wife Judith, he accepted happily. He was motivated largely by family associations: his brother Peter had run with the Olympic torch on its way to Melbourne in 1956; his father had been the official organiser for the 1956 relay for northern New South Wales; his son Richard had run in the Atlanta relay four years earlier. He was also aware that Sophie, at 11, was too young to run in Australia during the torch relay.

The news that the daughter of an Australian vice-president of the IOC had been given priority in the torch-bearer order caused outrage in Australia. Gosper was blasted by politicians, athletes, the media, talk-back listeners and letter-writers — accused of nepotism, queue-jumping and failure to abide by the Olympic spirit. Dawn Fraser said his behaviour was outrageous, Ron Clarke felt he had blundered, Bob Carr railed at the Gosper ego, and in Canberra the Senate passed a solemn motion expressing its 'very deep regret' at the treatment accorded Yianna Souleles. The *Australian* caught the mood well in an editorial:

> Kevan Gosper, how could you? Just when the current of public opinion was beginning to flow in favour of the Sydney Olympics, you have ruined it with a piece of nepotism. The start of the Olympic torch relay should have been the turning point in public perceptions of the Games. Four years of squabbling and scandal over the preparation could finally be put aside. In its place would be the inspiring sight of an Australian schoolgirl carrying the Olympic torch on its journey here for the world's greatest sporting event. Instead of this unifying image, you have treated us to the spectacle of the girl who was promised the honour of being the first Australian torchbearer being replaced by your daughter. It is hard to imagine how anyone could get it so wrong.[2]

On the morning the relay began, as the extent of the rage in Australia became known to SOCOG powerbrokers in Olympia, Knight, Coates and Hollway all tried to defuse what was shaping up as yet another crisis. Separately, each of the three suggested that he reconsider his acceptance. At first Gosper refused to budge, taking the view that the Hellenic Olympic Committee had given the invitation as 'a simple and generous gesture', and that it would be ungracious to refuse. He told the media: 'I haven't interfered in this from the start. I've had no play

Marie-Jose Perec (France) wins her 400 metres title in Atlanta, with Cathy Freeman (left) a gallant second. The win made Perec the first athlete of either sex to win the 400 metres twice.

Carl Lewis leaps high and hard in Atlanta to take his fourth long-jump gold medal.

The Oarsome Foursome (from left: Mike McKay, Nick Green, Jamie Tomkins and Drew Ginn) after their back-to-back win in the coxless fours at the Atlanta Games.

In Atlanta Michael Johnson became the first man in history to win the 200 metres–400 metres double.

Kieren Perkins, triumphant after his mighty win in the 1500 metres freestyle in Atlanta.

Susie O'Neill powering along on her way to gold in the Atlanta 200 metres butterfly.

Gillian Rolton about to take a fall (and suffer some broken bones) with Peppermint Grove during the cross-country phase of the Atlanta three-day equestrian event.

After the gold. Australia's winning equestrian team at the Atlanta Games (from left: Andrew Hoy, Wendy Schaeffer, Phillip Dutton, Gillian Rolton).

The celebrating Hockeyroos display the passionate sense of togetherness that took them to gold in Atlanta.

Canada's Donovan Bailey after his world-record run in the Atlanta 100 metres.

Heartbreak time. Shane Kelly walks away from his bike after his foot slipped from the pedal in the 1000 metres time trial in Atlanta. (News Ltd / Nick Wilson)

Nova Peris-Kneebone setting out on the first leg of the Sydney torch relay. Behind her are some of the traditional custodians of Uluru. At right is Olympics minister Michael Knight. (News Ltd / Marco Del Grande)

Evonne Goolagong was surrounded by excited children during her leg of the torch relay. (News Ltd)

Wendy Craig Duncan carried the Olympic flame underwater at Agincourt Reef on Queensland's Great Barrier Reef. (News Ltd)

Stockhorses thunder into the arena for the Sydney Games opening ceremony.

Aboriginal women dancers at the Sydney opening ceremony.

Wildflowers bloom as the opening ceremony takes on the look of a vibrant garden.

Ned Kellys roam at the opening ceremony.

The Australian team marches in to the stadium.

Cathy Freeman stands proud and still in the circle of fire that later became the cauldron.

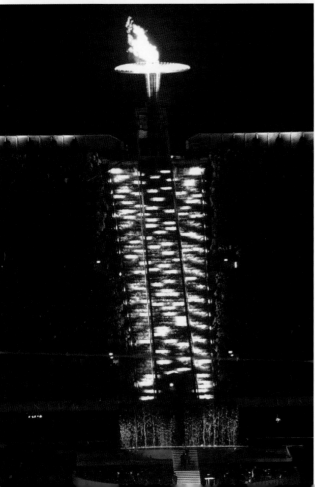

Fire and water in the Olympic Stadium . . . a majestic voyage for the cauldron.

The women sporting legends who brought the Olympic torch into the stadium gather round Cathy Freeman after the flame had been lit.

The first night of the Games: Ian Thorpe wins gold — twice.

The triumphant men's 4 x 100 metres freestyle relay team (from left: Ashley Callus, Chris Fydler, Michael Klim, Ian Thorpe).

Susie O'Neill won gold in the race she didn't expect to — the 200 metres freestyle.

Dutchman Pieter van den Hoogenband (left) outswam Ian Thorpe in the 200 metres freestyle to take home the gold.

Grant Hackett celebrates after his magnificent victory over Kieren Perkins in the 1500 metres freestyle.

Grant Hackett (left) and Kieren Perkins after the 1500 metres.

Australia's silver-medal-winning 4 x 200 metres freestyle relay team. From left: Susie O'Neill, Kirsten Thomson, Giaan Rooney, Petria Thomas.

in it. It's a matter for the Greeks.' Three hours before the relay was due to begin, at the suggestion of Hollway, he approached Nikolaou with a view to juggling the relay order so that the two young girls could swap positions. Until this stage Nikolaou had neglected to tell him one very important fact: that his own (and the HOC's) authority over the selection of torch runners was limited to the first runner in Olympia and the last into Athens. Local authorities along the torch route had sole responsibility for the choice of all other runners.

Gosper told Nikolaou: 'Look, this thing has caused a huge storm in Australia. It can't be that big a deal to let them change places. Maybe you can let the other girl run, and then hand over to Sophie.'

Nikolaou said he would try, but returned soon after to report: 'I can't make such a change. Either Sophie runs or she doesn't, but I can't make changes. The decision is yours.'

Gosper: 'Sophie has crossed the world in expectation that she will carry the torch, and I'm not going to take that away from her. She'll run.'[3]

As the furore mounted at home, Sydney's *Daily Telegraph* published a front page that hurt him deeply. Across the page it spelled the name GOSPER — Greedy, Obstinate, Selfish, Pompous, Egotistic,

Kevan Gosper, IOC vice-president and SOCOG director.

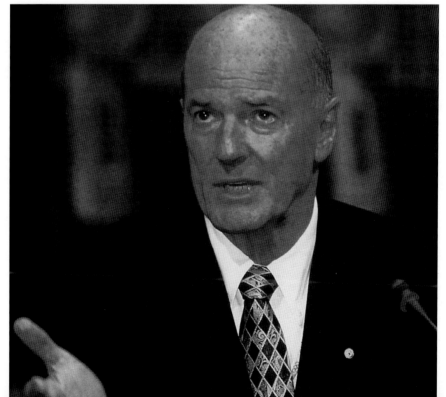

Reptile. He brandished a faxed copy at reporters: 'I'm appalled,' he said. 'What crime have I committed? How do you think I feel? They didn't even talk about the enemy during the war like that.' Later, though, after flying from Athens to London, he issued a public apology: 'My fatherly pride simply clouded my judgment,' he said. 'In retrospect, I now know my acceptance on behalf of my daughter was a mistake. It has led to a perception of undue influence by me as vice-president of the IOC, and has upset many Australians ... I apologise to all who have been upset by my lapse in judgment, especially Yianna Souleles. I also regret that my decision led to unfair criticism of the IOC, and has diverted attention from the torch relay.' As penance, he relinquished his planned leg of the torch relay at the Melbourne Cricket Ground, which was later taken over by Australian cricket captain Mark Taylor.

Gosper, a patrician figure who took himself and his many Olympic roles very seriously, had been behind the play from the time he arrived in Athens from China on his way to Olympia. At an embassy reception the night before the Australian party left for the flame-lighting rehearsal, he told friends proudly that Sophie would be running in the relay. He had no idea when. 'You'll be told when you get to Olympia,' he was advised by Greek officials. When he and his family reached the rehearsal site, an excited Nikolaou greeted him and the media simultaneously with the news that Sophie would be second runner. Asked whether another Australian girl was running, Nikolaou said: 'I know nothing about that.' Gosper still saw no danger signals. Dealing with the Australian media that early morning, he misread the public mood at home, becoming defiant at a time when he should have been placatory. He seemed unable to understand what the fuss was all about.

Essentially he had made a wrong judgment, accepting a favour without asking questions or considering the implications — rather like Phil Coles in Salt Lake. When it came to a final crunch — withdraw Sophie or invite more trouble — he acted more like a doting father than a seasoned IOC diplomat. It was not a huge sin, and hardly seemed to equate with the extreme vilification that came his way. Perhaps the explanation was that for a few days, in the eyes of most Australians, he became a symbol: the haughty face of all that was seen to be wrong with the IOC.

A few days later in Lausanne the IOC ethics commission chairman, Judge Keba Mbaye, and chief investigator Martin Lipton announced the findings that cleared Gosper of any impropriety relating to his family's stay in Salt Lake City in 1993. Mbaya's commission also examined the Sophie Gosper episode in Olympia, and decided that no action should be taken. The IOC chief of protocol, Pal Schmitt, discussed the affair with Samaranch, who agreed that it was a domestic Australian affair. Even so, events in Olympia cost Gosper dearly. When Gosper's biography, *An Olympic Life*, had been released earlier in the year, it had been seen by many as the starting point in his campaign for the IOC presidency. Even as it was being printed, the Salt Lake City investigation was launched. The findings of that inquiry did him no harm, but the torch relay furore effectively ended his dream of succeeding Samaranch. He did not announce his decision not to stand until after the Olympics, but he later told this writer: 'After Olympia I knew my prospects [for running for the presidency] were gone.'[4] And the book? It died in the bookstores, a victim of dreadful timing.

For ten days the flame snaked its way through towns and villages of Greece, to fishing ports and islands in the Aegean Sea, and often along the route flowers were tossed in the path of the torch-bearers. The torch, on display for the first time, owed its colours and slender, graceful design to the Sydney Opera House, the blue waters of the Pacific and the curve of the boomerang. From Athens the flame moved by chartered plane through the Oceania region, stopping at Guam, Micronesia, Nauru, the Solomons, Papua New Guinea, Vanuatu, Samoa, American Samoa, the Cook Islands, Tonga and New Zealand before its arrival at Uluru. A military coup, also unfortunately timed, caused Fiji to miss out.

A barefoot Nova Peris-Kneebone, one of 11 Aboriginal members of the 2000 Australian Olympic team and a hockey gold medallist from the Atlanta Games, was the first of 11,000 Australians who carried the torch over 100 days. She was joined in jog by her nine-year-old daughter, Jessica, and was followed soon after by the double Wimbledon champion Evonne Goolagong Cawley. Cawley became the first of many to share her brief tenure of the flame with others. The route had been devised so that it passed within an hour's drive of 85 per cent of

Samantha Riley
runs into the
QE II Stadium,
Brisbane, during
the torch relay.

the population, and the flame was carried by an improbable range of conveyances. A prawn trawler, a camel, a surf boat, a bicycle, a Royal Flying Doctor aircraft, a pearl lugger, the Indian Pacific train, the *Spirit of Tasmania*, a chair-lift, the *Puffing Billy* steam train, a Murray River paddle steamer, snow skis, a Holden V8 racing car, a sculling shell and a Sydney Harbour ferry-boat all had a share in its progress.

For 2 minutes 40 seconds it was dunked below the waters of the Great Barrier Reef as its carrier, Wendy Craig Duncan, scooted among coral and fish during a historic diving expedition. At Townville, where young swimmers had set world records in 1956, the same swimmers, much older and sometimes plumper, swam relay races against each other and local school-kids. In Port Lincoln, home of the 1984 weightlifting gold medallist Dean Lukin, a fleet of tuna boats assembled themselves on the bay in the formation of the five Olympic circles. In Grafton, a town fabled for its magnificent jacaranda trees, the trees were not yet in flower — so citizens compensated by decorating buildings, fences and trees along the route with purple crepe paper, and many sported purple wigs. At the Melbourne Cricket Ground, Ron Clarke and John Landy carried the flame and re-enacted roles they had taken during the 1956 Melbourne Olympics: Clarke had lit the cauldron at the opening ceremony, and Landy had recited the athletes' oath. Everywhere, every day, local heroes and local history were acknowledged and celebrated.

When the planning team for this remarkable, romantic and sometimes quirky exercise began its task, it articulated a series of prime objectives — which amounted to a desire to share the experience with most Australians, deliver the precious flame safely and on time, generate enthusiasm for the 2000 Olympics and 'showcase Australia and Australian innovation to the rest of the world'. It did all that and a good deal more. From the time the relay began, as it snaked its way through the red sandhills around Uluru and headed off in a roundabout way towards Sydney, it was as if it was telling the story of Australia. As if it was defining the country, exploring its very identity as well as its geography.

The journey cut across desert and jungle, through wilderness both exotic and harsh. It probed paths traversed by tribal blacks and white explorers, some of the latter of whom had been both intrepid and

Camel rider Jamali Bintalib carries the torch at Cable Beach in Western Australia. (News Ltd)

a bit mad. It touched lonely outback settlements, mining and farming towns that had known better times, grand and gloomy sweeps of suburbia, sky-scraping colonies along the coast. It visited Broome, the most polyglot community in Australia, and Darwin, the resilient city that had been devastated four times — three times by cyclones, once by Japanese bombers. It went to Kalgoorlie, where an Irishman called Paddy Hannan once discovered gold, and another, Charles O'Connor, conceived the ridiculously bold scheme of pumping water vast distances. It spent a night in Cowra, scene of the bloodiest prison break in world history — a town which houses an extraordinary Japanese garden and Australia's World Peace Bell, and has quietly become a place for pilgrimage, a centre of reconciliation. The relay made its salutes to Ballarat's Eureka Stockade, Bowral's Don Bradman, Lithgow's Marjorie Jackson,

Bendigo's Chinese joss houses, Glenrowan's Kelly Gang, Rockhampton's Rod Laver, Broken Hill's flying doctor service.

In those hundred days the torch relay didn't miss a thing. It celebrated every aspect of the nation: its environment, its sporting, political and cultural heritage, its history, its industries, its tragedies and triumphs and shame. It did not just share the spirit. It changed it. John Coates, a man who by his own admission had never understood the potential of the torch relay, could hardly believe the transformation:

> I wasn't big on the relay. I hadn't paid much attention to it in other Games cities. I'm not big on symbolism, I guess. I felt some newspapers were very anti-us, anti-SOCOG, and I kept feeling they were not helping people to enjoy the approach of the Games. I didn't much want to be in the spotlight then. I wanted to keep my head down. I decided around then I wouldn't run with the torch ... I gave my spot to [broadcaster] Norman May. I wanted as low a profile as I could get. I didn't go to Uluru to meet the flame. I sent [AOC vice-president] John Devitt. But from that point it was all different. The image of Evonne Goolagong with those kids on the front page of the *Australian* was enduring. [Governor-General] Bill Deane was outstanding. I think the Gosper thing was then over, forgotten. I continue to be amazed at how the torch relay brought our Australian community to a crescendo. It was a huge impact, and it played right through to the opening ceremony.[5]

What helped the mood play through was the fact that the athletes were beginning, rightfully, to occupy centre stage. Teams were being chosen, Olympians were being identified, communities were able to associate themselves not just with past champions but with members of the Australian team that was in the process of selection. Gold medals were being forecast.

Coates set the bar high by suggesting that Australia was on target to finish in the top five on the Sydney medal tally, with a record 60 medals — 19 more than it had won in Atlanta. Basing the predictions on an AOC analysis of results in all 28 Olympic sports over the previous two years, he nominated a total of 19 gold medals, nine of them in swimming. Australia's head swim coach, Don Talbot, was unsurprisingly peeved about this, claiming that the optimistic forecast would put extra pressure on his swimmers and provide motivation for other nations. 'They [the AOC] are saying we are going to win. Our opponents will be saying, "Like hell you will".'

Cathy Freeman had turned 27 in February of that Olympic year. She was a stronger runner now than she had been when she won silver in Atlanta, pushing the 400-metres champion Marie-Rose Perec so very hard. She was tougher mentally, more experienced as a runner and an individual, and since Atlanta she had won back-to-back world championships over the distance in Athens (1997) and Seville (1999). She

The torch approaches Parliament House in the nation's capital. (News Ltd)

had also been married, in a small ceremony in California in 1999, to Alexander 'Sandy' Bodecker, an executive of the Nike sportswear corporation. Freeman was Australia's only realistic gold-medal hope in athletics, hopefully on track to join the luminous company of Marjorie Jackson, Shirley Strickland, Betty Cuthbert, Debbie Flintoff-King, Maureen Caird and Glynis Nunn.

In swimming a new generation led by Ian Thorpe and Grant Hackett had moved in, making it clear that they were ready to take over. As Kieren Perkins, now the elder statesman of Australian swimming, watched in admiration and just a little apprehension, those two fought like hungry barracudas to snap at his most revered records, set over 400 metres and 1500 metres. Thorpe, who would not turn 18 until soon after the Olympics, had first grabbed world attention in the 1998 world championships in Perth when he stormed past Hackett in the last few metres of the 400 metres freestyle — to become, at 15, the youngest world champion in history. From then on he made winning look easy.

Despite an early allergy to chlorine, which he thankfully grew out of, the portents for greatness had been there for quite a while: at 12, in a state short-course meet, Thorpe competed in 13 events and set under-age NSW records in all of them. 'I knew then,' his father Ken said later, 'that we had a very special boy on our hands.' Thorpe had grown up in the southern Sydney suburb of Milperra, and his sister Christina had been a promising swimmer who swam the 400 metres freestyle in the 1995 Pan Pacific titles but failed to reach the 1996 Olympic team. A bright student who was dux of his year at East Hills Boys Technical School, he quit school at 14 to concentrate on swimming — but continued to study at home. Even then he was a young man of rare poise and commonsense, and his intention was to go to university later, maybe to qualify in medicine or psychology.

Thorpe had been large-framed since his earliest teens, and at 17 stood 195 cm tall, weighed 100 kg, with an arm-span of 190 cm and size 17 feet which propelled him like pumping flippers. Aided by coach Doug Frost, he had developed a long, almost languid, gliding stroke and a lethal, outboard-motor kick that enabled him to run down opponents as he powered through the last lap. As his first Olympic Games approached, he had broken ten world records, one less than the career total of dual Olympic champion Perkins. His serial bursts of world-record-smashing had included four in four days at the 1999 Pan Pacific championships, and three in three days at the Olympic trials. One of his conquests at the PacPacs had been Perkins' cherished 400 metres free-style record, which had stood for five years. Thorpe then emphasised his point by breaking it again at the Olympic trials. Young Australian of the Year in 1999, he had endeared himself to the public at the PanPacs by donating to children's cancer research the $25,000 he won as first swim-mer to break a world record in the Sydney Aquatic Centre. Expectations for Thorpe were ambitious; when he swam, the fans wanted not just victories but more world records. His own expectations were also invariably high.

Traditionally, Australia's strongest single event in the Olympics has been the 1500 metres freestyle. The line began with Frank Beaurepaire and Boy Charlton, and has included such world-beating swimmers as Murray Rose, John Konrads, Bob Windle, Steve Holland and Kieren Perkins. In the interval between Atlanta and Sydney, a period when Perkins had some illness but largely took a holiday, Hackett had ruled the distance — winning the world, Commonwealth, Pan Pacific and Australian championships. He had also duelled with Thorpe over 200 metres and 400 metres for a long spell; he often came off second-best, but had some notable triumphs. At the 1999 national titles he toppled Thorpe over 200 metres, set a world record the next night for the same distance, then downed Thorpe a month later over 400 metres at the world short-course titles in Hong Kong, setting a world record in the process. Hackett had grown up on the beaches of Queensland's Gold Coast with his older brother Craig, surfing for fun and competition. Both trained under the coach Denis Cotterill, but Craig finally opted to concentrate on the surf, going on to become one of Australia's leading Iron Men. Grant was disenchanted with the vagaries of surf swimming, where some results are influenced more by the luck of a timely wave than by speed through the water.

When Hackett won the 1500 metres selection trial in May 2000, his former idol Perkins was runner-up, and still ominously optimistic that he would make it three in a row. No Australian had done that since Dawn Fraser, no 1500 metres swimmer had ever done it, and adoring fans at the Olympic trials made it clear that they dearly wanted it to happen for Perkins. So strong was the mood that Perkins made a plea to his fans not to play favourites when the two met in their Olympic showdown. He was responding to a media report that said Hackett might as well be American for all the support he would receive when taking on Perkins. 'That's a bit rough,' he told reporters. 'We're both Australians; whichever one of us touches the wall first and gets the gold medal, fantastic. Let's just hope that the other bloke picks up the silver and it's a quinella for the country.' Perkins was 27 now, and Hackett 20. Hackett was not only younger but also stronger and fitter. He had not yet threatened Perkins' world record of 14 minutes 41.66 seconds, but was the only other swimmer in the world who had bettered 14 minutes 50 seconds for the distance.

Susie O'Neill, now 26, had dominated butterfly swimming over 200 metres for five years, but had never been able to slice the world record that had belonged to the great American Mary T. Meagher since 1981. She had inherited Meagher's sobriquet, Madame Butterfly, but not the record, the oldest in the books. She had been chipping away at it in vain since her gold medal in Atlanta. At the Australian championships in May 2000 she finally rectified that state of affairs with a swim of 2 minutes 5.81 seconds, and celebrated as soon as she climbed out of the water with a goofy, arm-swinging, cross-legged shuffle. It was a cross between the Charleston and a chicken dance, and she gave it a plain, uncompromising name: 'my world record dance'. Normally a most undemonstrative woman, she had invented the routine at a night club the previous year, and had promised her husband, Cliff Fairlie, that if and when she broke that record she would perform it. 'I felt like an idiot,' she said later, 'but it meant a huge amount to me.'[6] Sadly, the same meet ended the career of her training partner Samantha Riley, formerly the dominant breaststroker in the world; Riley failed to qualify for either the Olympic 100 metres or the 200 metres.

Meantime, other significant things were happening. After March 2000, by which time all the refunds and other legacies of the ticketing disaster had been dealt with, ticket sales surged, aided considerably by a sales promotion undertaken by the News Ltd publishing group. The compression of SOCOG, OCA and ORTA into a single framework —

an exercise that had been triggered by the ticketing shemozzle and subsequent budget problems — continued apace, with the leaders of those bodies joined by police commissioner Peter Ryan and Paul McKinnon, of the security unit, and later by Manolo Romero and Gary Fenton, of the Sydney Olympic Broadcasting Organisation. The Olympic Village, home for 16,780 athletes and team officials, opened on 2 September, becoming the first such complex in the history of the Games to house every athlete. A huge army of volunteers, 46,967 of them, was assembling to begin an ambitious operation that would do much to ensure the success of the Games. Transport was being orchestrated to ensure seamless journeys between homes and venues — wherever they were.

The final composition of the SOCOG board, which was effectively submerged early in 2000, was: Michael Knight (president), John Coates (senior vice-president), Frank Sartor, Kevan Gosper (vice-presidents), Chris Hartcher, Craig McLatchey, Anna Booth, Nick Greiner, Graham Richardson, Brian Sherman, Marjorie Jackson-Nelson, Donald McDonald, John Valder (directors) and Sandy Hollway (chief executive). McLatchey had replaced Perry Crosswhite in September 1995, after taking over as AOC secretary-general. Hartcher, as shadow minister for the Olympics, had had the briefest tenure — since April 1999. Only Coates, Sartor, Gosper and Greiner had lasted the whole voyage since November 1993.

The key single outfit into which all the major planning organisations integrated was called the Games Coordination Group (GCOG), and it had clout. 'That's where the real decisions were made from the beginning of 2000,' Knight recalled. 'It had no formal power. The IOC didn't create it or approve it. Cabinet hadn't approved it. The premier didn't know it existed at the start. No, it had no formal power, but it still exercised it ruthlessly. That's where all the integrated decisions happened under the pressure of presenting.'[7] He went on:

> One of the ways the group worked was this. We'd say: 'Okay, we want to know how the city is going to function the night the torch relay comes in, and we want the SOCOG torch relay people, the OCA city operations people, the ORTA streets and transport people and the cops to all go and get their act together. You'll be presenting collectively to

us how it is going to function at next Monday's GCOG meeting.' The GCOG was an important part of driving that integration we needed, because if they came to us separately and started playing little territorial rivalry games they were going to get it wrong. They had to get their collective, integrating act together in order to make those presentations. And that was a very important discipline GCOG created.[8]

The continuing integration of all the various planning bodies, begun in December 1999, was an exercise in cooperation and the slimming-down of individual authority. The coordination group, headed by Knight, Coates and Richmond (who chaired meetings whenever Knight was absent), met fortnightly from February 2000, then weekly, then daily during the Games. With the sidelining of SOCOG's board, Knight and Coates took charge of all decision-making in the lead-up to the Games and during them. This arrangement, between those two men who had been feuding very publicly in early 1996, inevitably caused newspapers to dub them the Gang of Two.

Athletes' villages have been part of the Olympic scene since 1924, but until Sydney's opened at Newington, Homebush Bay, they had always involved some form of division. Various teams or disciplines had found themselves housed separately from the rest, either because of politics (as in the Cold War) or plain geography (as when some sports, like rowing or sailing, had been conducted at distant venues). This time there were no such problems: international politics did not intrude on the Games, and the village was immediately adjacent to Sydney Olympic Park, where 17 of the 28 sports were conducted. The venues for sailing (Sydney Harbour), rowing (the Penrith Lakes) and equestrian events (80 hectares inside Sydney West Regional Park) were unaccustomedly close, with the farthest competition venue no more than 40 minutes away by bus.

The man who presided over the village was Graham Richardson, 'Richo', who had been installed as mayor by Coates in November 1997, without the bother of consulting other SOCOG board members. When some of them, most notably Nick Greiner, expressed outrage at the appointment and the manner of it, branding it a case of jobs for the boys, Coates' response was tersely defiant. 'So what?' Coates told 'Four

Corners', at a time when he was feeling distinctly embattled. His right to make the appointment, through the sports commission, didn't really bear questioning. Characteristically, he had a clause in a document to prove it; it was part of the charter he had negotiated with a compliant SOCOG after the Knight of the Long Prawns.

A typically cheerful group of Olympic volunteers. There were nearly 47,000 like them.

Richardson, who turned 51 in the September of the Games, had been known as Mr Fixit during his 11 years in federal politics. He had had a few others labels — as a wheeler-dealer, a head-kicker, a king-maker. Bob Hawke once testified to the man's influence: 'I am indeed the only person in the world who had Richo's kind services to help me become prime minister and to help me not be prime minister.'[9] The title of Richardson's autobiography, *Whatever It Takes*, said much about his style, but those who worked with him claimed he always plotted from the front. One colleague said of him admiringly, 'There's one thing you can be sure of with Graham — if you get knifed by him, it's going to be in the guts, not in the back.'

Richardson had been on the SOCOG board since 1996, was a member of the sports commission, and chairman of the board's troubled ticketing sub-committee. He had two deputy mayors: Sallyanne Atkinson, former lord mayor of Brisbane and leader of Brisbane's unsuccessful bid to host the 1992 Games, and Julius 'Judy' Patching, former secretary-general of the (pre-AOC) AOF and Australia's *chef de mission* at the 1968 and 1972 Olympics. Atkinson, a former senior trade commissioner in Paris, was director of protocol; importantly, that involved responsibility for the welcome ceremonies that were accorded every team, and the greeting of visiting VIPs, who included Nelson Mandela and J. A. Samaranch. Patching's task, as director of *chef de mission* support and relations, was largely to be Judy Patching; because of his knowledge, his easy manner and his strong Olympic involvement since 1956 (when he was chief starter), he was a hugely respected figure around the village. When there were gripes, he was sought out; he had long possessed a special capacity for listening, then solving — usually behind the scenes.

Richardson's appointment, which the then NSW opposition leader Peter Collins branded in 1997 as 'political patronage gone mad', in fact worked out very well. What the man took to the village most significantly was his legendary capacity to get things done. He also took as his main assistant Simon Balderstone, who had worked closely with him in politics. At the meetings each morning with team bosses from all nations, his usual response to problems was to announce, 'I'll see what I can do.' Invariably, with his own brand of affably tough persuasion, he was able to sort things out. His approach was distinctly hands-on. Once, after complaints from village volunteers that they had to wait up to 40 minutes for their late-night shuttle bus to Lidcombe railway station, and official reassurances that this couldn't be happening, he stationed himself on a street on the edge of the village. At 1 am the control post received a phone call from him: 'I'm at the bus stop now. The people are waiting, and the shuttle's not happening.'[10]

The Olympic Village was one of the many responsibilities of the sports commission, whose challenging task it was to transform the label

'Athletes' Games' from an enticing phrase into a reality. Coates had pledged seven years before, when Sydney was awarded the Games, that this would happen, with 'every athlete offered the best opportunity ever to excel'. Under the chairmanship of Coates and the management of Bob Elphinston, the commission oversaw innovations that promised to set benchmarks for future Olympics.

It followed through on promises made during the bid process to provide free travel for all athletes to and from the Games, as well as free freight passage for all canoes, kayaks, rowing shells, sailing boats and horses. Forty test-event programs were conducted, embracing every Olympic sport except beach volleyball. Doping controls took place on an unprecedented scale: out-of-competition tests, including for the first time blood and urine checks for EPO (erythropoietin), began the day the village opened. (The fact that a number of selected athletes decided

Torch-bearers Dawn Fraser and Murray Rose, both winners of four Olympic gold medals.

at a late stage not to make the trip to the Games, after all, was probably not unconnected to the new out-of-competition and EPO testing.) Two new sports, taekwondo and the triathlon, were added to the 26 already on the Games program. Thirty-three first-time events, 23 of them for women — including water polo, weightlifting, hammer throw and pole vault — were also introduced.

'Urban Domain' is not a phrase to induce excitement, but that was the name of the program that enabled Sydney to convert itself into a virtual disco-by-the-Harbour, bopping and bouncing throughout the Games. The scheme had its beginnings in Atlanta, as Knight and Richmond wandered through crowded, often unattractive streets and talked about 2000. 'We had a vision, David and I, of what the Games would look like if they worked,' Knight remembered.

> I don't mean a grand vision of wonderful and happy. We had a vision of what it would be like on the ground, if the Games were working, what it would be like on the trains, what it would be like around the city. We had specific ideas. We wanted people happy and celebrating in the city in the night. So we thought ... how do we minimise the disruption, how do we maximise the fun? How do we still get deliveries through to businesses? We had very concrete visions. What happened in Sydney grew out of the good and bad things we saw Atlanta.[11]

What they did to encourage the mood was place six live Olympic sites around the city, at Circular Quay, Martin Place, the Domain, Belmore Park (next to Central Station), Darling Harbour and Pyrmont Bay Park (next to the Star City Casino). Each was equipped with a 30-square-metre video screen showing the Olympic action, on-stage entertainment, food-and-beverage stalls and information booths, and 1.5 million people gathered at them during the Games. There was street theatre at every site, and jugglers, clowns, comics and jazz musicians worked the crowds, as well as the queues at transport hubs. Concerts in the Domain, with Neil Finn and Paul Kelly as performers, attracted crowds of 100,000. Buildings were washed with colour in an illumination project called the Sydney Skyline Spectacular, and the sails of the Opera House glowed in a range of hues throughout. In and around the city, the Games were just one long party.

ORTA's integrated transport system, born out of David Richmond's observations amid the traffic chaos of Atlanta, and led by Ron Christie, functioned 24 hours a day throughout the Games. Between the first and last days, it carried 4.45 million people — 76 per cent by rail and 24 per cent via a mixed bag of public and private bus routes. Its big test came on Super Friday (22 September), the last day of the swimming and the first of the track-and-field program, when some sort of stampede was feared at Central Station and Homebush Bay. Trains packed with 1800 passengers arrived at Homebush Bay station every two or three minutes, and through the day 400,000 moved to and from Olympic Park without significant delays. The premier, Bob Carr, was moved to say: 'This is monumental. We are moving more people than have ever been moved in wartime or in peacetime on this continent. This is bigger than D-Day.'

No matter how efficiently the paid organisers and administrators did their jobs, no matter how superbly the athletes performed, it was the volunteers who made the whole show come together. Certainly, more than any other group, it was this collection of gaudily clad individuals who helped make Sydney the happiest place in the world for 17 days. Not only were they unfailingly friendly and helpful: they were also knowledgeable and efficient — a consequence of an intensive program which saw one million hours of training delivered in the three months before the Games. They were ordinary citizens who did an extraordinary job. Six thousand had specialist roles, but most simply wanted to be there, manning gates or desks, patrolling aisles in the stands, standing on corners giving street directions — anything that would help. The training had begun as early as 1997 for a core group of 500, who became known as the Pioneer Volunteers, but the major recruiting did not begin until the end of 1997.

Of the 46,967 volunteers at the Games, 53 per cent were female. Thirteen per cent were aged between 50 and 59, 20 per cent between 40 and 49, 24 per cent between 18 and 24, 18 per cent between 25 and 34. Altogether 75,000 people volunteered to work at the Olympics and the following Paralympics, with 78 per cent from New South Wales. All who did the job were unpaid, and they worked difficult hours without complaint: each was allotted a minimum of ten eight-hour shifts during

Pat Rafter and Olivia Newton-John with the flame at Sydney's Opera House.

the Games; some worked more than 20. Without much doubt, the marked difference between the impact the volunteers made in Sydney and the one they made in Atlanta had less to do with attitude than with communication and training. In Atlanta they were wonderfully courteous, made visitors welcome, and really wanted to help, but they didn't have too many answers. The Sydney volunteers had been thoroughly drilled, starting with interview sessions conducted by senior university students, then in 52 orientation sessions conducted around Australia, finally with intensive training, specific to their jobs. They worked hard, their own evident enjoyment was contagious, and they were unfazed by the trickiest questions.

Dorothy Williams, a pioneer volunteer with her husband Norm, recalled the mood of an early session: 'We were training to be team leaders from 4 pm to 10 pm each night. One night people from the university came in to ask us questions. One of the questions to my group was: "What would you do if you were a team leader for the Olympics, and you walked in on one of the people in your team making passionate love to another volunteer?" I answered, "Well, if it wasn't my husband, I'd say, 'Go for your life'." I'm not sure if I lost points for that.'[12]

Afterwards Samaranch, who talked to scores of volunteers, wrote of them: 'In Sydney, one of the truly great performances was turned in by the volunteers. Their work and dedication helped make the 2000 Olympic Games the best Games in Olympic history. Everywhere I went, I saw smiling, helpful volunteers ensuring everyone's needs were well taken care of. They were the best hosts the Olympic movement could have hoped for.'[13] The volunteers' street parade through Sydney after the Games was the longest that Sydney had seen. They deserved all their plaudits. Their performance was a reminder that throughout the nation's history — in wartime, on the beaches, in bushfires and other natural disasters — volunteers have invoked the spirit of Australia.

CHAPTER NINE

The big secret

The Olympic Games are almost as redolent with ritual as the Vatican, and one of the most important rituals concerns the lighting of the cauldron as the torch relay ends at the main stadium. It signals the end of the opening ceremony, the beginning of the actual Games — and over the years it has produced some glistening moments. Paavo Nurmi, one of the Olympic movement's most enduring idols, did the job in his home town of Helsinki in 1952, and to be there that day was to be in the company of history. Nurmi had once been excluded from the Olympics, and his triumphant return said much about the spirit of reconciliation. A Japanese youngster who had been born in Hiroshima the day the atom bomb dropped on that city had the role in Tokyo in 1960, and that moment offered more to contemplate than just a wondrous spectacle. In Mexico City, after the flame had tracked the ocean voyage of Christopher Columbus in 1492, the stadium fire was lit for the first time ever by a woman. In the gender context of 1968, when female participation at the Games was 13 per cent and female representation on the IOC was nil, that was a breakthrough to remember.

With the most recent Games of 1992 and 1996, the ceremony had taken on different, quite breathtaking elements of theatre. Barcelona added a dimension of incredulity when Antonio Rebello, a Paralympic archer, sent a burning arrow across the stadium and into the flame dish. And the most sublime moment of Atlanta's centennial opening ceremony was the unexpected, unsteady lighting of the cauldron by the most outstanding sports personality of the 20th century, Muhammad Ali. As this proud man whose physical capacities had been diminished by Parkinson's disease stood in the spotlight, his hands clasping the torch — those hands that had once stung like a bee to the dance of a butterfly — were trembling very visibly. The moment represented a triumph of the spirit over physical adversity, a message of hope in a racially troubled city. It was an impossible act to follow, a challenging one even to attempt to echo. But now, with the Sydney Games coming up, it was time to think about a new spectacle, new symbolism, and a new person centre-stage.

Unsurprisingly, for nearly four years an abiding subject of debate and conjecture around Australia was the identity of the person who would fill that final role at 9.45 pm on 15 September 2000. On a slow news day editors could always rely on it to provide a readable range of opinion, sometimes passion, and to seed an argument that wouldn't be settled until the big night. Radio talkback callers couldn't get enough of the theme, and newspapers published all kinds of public opinion polls, not always rigorously researched. Although the usual suspects who figured in the polls were mostly distinguished gold medallists, there was a public awareness that nothing in the Olympic charter demanded that the cauldron should be lit by an Olympian. After all, in Melbourne in 1956 the honour had gone to a junior runner, a lad called Ron Clarke.

One whose name cropped up a lot was Sir Donald Bradman. In a nation that thrived on hero worship, this man was the ultimate hero, and durable too. At times when Australia had needed something to feel good about, during the Depression and immediately after the most horrifying war in history, he had provided comfort, a sense of pride, a little zest. In the first half of the 20th century, during the sometimes lurching progress towards national identity, Bradman had been a beacon. He was not only the greatest batsman of them all; the prime minister, John Howard, pronounced him to be the greatest living Australian. He had been for decades Australia's counterpoint to Babe Ruth, and he was the closest approach to a Muhammad Ali that the country could offer. Almost certainly, Bradman would have declined any proposal to light the flame. He was 92 in 2000, but he still continued to score well in the polls. On the eve of the Games he sent a message to the Australian team, stressing that it was competing that mattered, not winning or losing. He died in February 2001.

Just as prominent amid all the speculation was the name of Dawn Fraser, a formidable figure who had somewhere transcended the boundaries of sport and embedded herself in folklore. The trappings of legend had been there from the start: her playground as a kid had been a disused coal-mine, she had been afflicted early by all kinds of respiratory troubles, also by a disqualification at the age of 14 for alleged professionalism. She was a larrikin who could swim better than any other woman in the world. She was the first in her sport of either sex to win the same event at three consecutive Olympics. She held 39 world records, 27 of them individual. Such was her dominance of the 100 metres that she had custody of the world record for 16 years, until the arrival of Shane Gould. Her non-conformist nature had brought her into conflict often with administrators, and caused her career to end prematurely, but it was an attribute that endeared her to most Australians. Her credentials were impressive, some almost felt too much so: she had been honoured at the Atlanta Games among the greatest living Olympians, and named at the Vienna World Sport Awards in 1999 as the Female Swimmer of the Century. She dearly wanted that date with the cauldron, but her uneasy history with authority gave her some doubts. Also in 1999, in the wake of all the scandal, she had declared memorably, 'The IOC has forgotten what the Olympics is all about.'

Later she wrote:

> Of course I would be lying if I said … I didn't want to light the cauldron. It would be the biggest honour I could imagine. Just thinking about it gave me goose bumps. I felt I had a fair chance because I had the greatest number of Olympic achievements in Australia, and also because almost every part of the media had called for me to light the cauldron after I was named World Female Swimmer of the Century. Yes, I definitely wanted to light it, and a little part of me deep inside kept that hope alive right up until the night before the opening ceremony. Another little part of me, however, whispered that they would never choose me in a million years.[1]

Mike McKay, chairman of the AOC's Athletes' Commission and double gold medallist from the Oarsome Foursome, was one who took the view, wrapped in great respect, that Fraser might not be an ideal choice. 'I know she's won those four gold medals, but I think it should be someone a bit more contemporary,' he told reporters. 'The Olympics

Shane Gould's enjoyment is obvious as she skips with the flame to the waiting Debbie Flintoff-King during the final lap of the torch relay at the opening ceremony.

has the potential to lose a little bit of relevance sometimes when you just keep bringing out older, long-retired athletes rather than younger people who have achieved just as well.' He suggested Kieren Perkins or Susie O'Neill as more appropriate candidates.

Other favourites, still close to the age bracket of Fraser, included Betty Cuthbert, Shirley Strickland, Marjorie Jackson, Herb Elliott and Murray Rose. Cuthbert, the Golden Girl of the 1956 Melbourne Games and winner of four gold medals, was confined to a wheelchair now, a victim of multiple sclerosis. Strickland's total of seven medals on the track (three of them gold) had never been bettered. Jackson, the Lithgow Flash and winner of two track gold medals in Helsinki, had a large sentimental following as a result of her enduring quest to defeat leukemia. Elliott had been the world's greatest middle-distance runner, winner of a most emphatic 1500 metres in Rome in 1960 — in a time that would have won a gold medal in Seoul (1988), Barcelona (1992) or Atlanta (1996). Rose, in company with Fraser and Cuthbert, owned four gold medals. Some observers felt that Shane Gould, triple gold-medallist in Munich in 1972, might get the nod because of her comparative youth. Other candidates included Perkins, O'Neill, McKay, James Tomkins, Andrew Hoy, Matt Ryan and Andrew Gaze.

Nelson Mandela, former president of South Africa and one of the most admired world leaders, was favoured by some commentators, and the knowledge that he would be in Australia for the Games gave the theory some credence. The respected commentator Roy Masters wrote in the *Sydney Morning Herald* of that prospect: 'It would be a great signal to the world of Australia's commitment to peace and racial accord.'

The two people who would make this important choice were John Coates, as president of the AOC, and Michael Knight, as president of SOCOG. Coates, a man who knew how to duel by document, had decided a long time before that this was how it would be. Later, in a recollection that offered rare insight into the sheer craftiness of the Coates negotiating style, he had this to say: 'You want the history? After we won the Games and we had the host-city contract, I trawled through just about everything just to see what else we ought to get into an agreement early, while other people weren't thinking about it. We came up with a document which is down there [indicating a desk drawer], called the joint marketing agreement. Included in that is a stipulation that the president of the national Olympic committee would decide on the athlete and official to take the oaths in the opening ceremony. It continued that the chief executive of SOCOG and the secretary-general of the AOC would jointly decide who was to light the flame, but in the event of any disagreement between them it would be sorted out by the two presidents. So that was it. Effectively it was down to the presidents.'[2]

If Sandy Hollway, as chief executive of SOCOG, or Craig McLatchey, secretary-general of the AOC, harboured any illusions that they, as the officials nominated, might have had a say, these were quickly dispelled. Coates' accomplice in this arrangement, Michael Knight, remembered with the cheerful candour of a successful conspirator: 'John and I said from the word go that there's going to be a dispute here. Just leave the choice to John and me. That's all we wanted. Otherwise we would have contrived a dispute anyway.'[3]

Coates and Knight first discussed the matter informally in September 1999, about a year out from the Games. No short lists were offered. Mainly they talked about principles rather than identities. Coates felt adamantly that the chosen person should be an Olympian and an Australian, and Knight quickly agreed. 'This eliminated the Bradmans, the Nobel Prize winners, and all that sort of stuff, the politicians,' Coates recalled.[4] It also took Mandela out of contention — although even on the night of the opening ceremony rumours still spread through newsrooms that he would light the flame. Coates and Knight made a pact after that first talk not to discuss the matter again, even privately, for some months. 'We wanted to be able to say truthfully whenever the media asked us — and that was often — that we hadn't met to discuss the flame,' said Coates.[5]

In March 2000 Knight called Coates and told him he thought it was time they met to talk about the issue. They settled on 31 March, and both men came to the meeting with prepared notes. This time Knight threw in an idea he had been nursing — that since the Games were celebrating a century of women's participation since the first mixed Games of 1900, the final runners inside the stadium should all be women. 'Let's have our female legends handle the last lap,' he proposed. 'You and I can select those people — that won't be hard. Perhaps symbolically we can have Herb Elliott, as the last runner outside the stadium, hand over to the first of the women.'[6] It was Knight's idea, his alone — and Coates loved it.

They talked for a while about the notion of a young girl lighting the cauldron as a symbol of the future, as the youthful Clarke had in Melbourne in 1956. 'Quite frankly I didn't want the Old and Bold,' Coates remembered. 'I thought, and still think, the Ron Clarke thing had the right youth element for Melbourne. I argued that, as in Melbourne, it should be someone young...to show we were looking to the future. For the Melbourne Games, though, you have to remember that they didn't have someone already in the team who loomed as a symbol.'[7]

Both men, it transpired, had Cathy Freeman in mind, but for different roles. As their arguments converged, they effectively peeled away layers of nominated candidates. Coates' attitude about 'the Old and Bold' effectively meant a thumbs-down for great names from the past — like Fraser, Cuthbert, Strickland, Jackson, Rose and Elliott. He wanted them honoured, but not during the lighting of the flame. He favoured someone from the 2000 team, and Knight's women-only emphasis had the effect of eliminating another layer: males like Perkins, Hoy, Ryan, Gaze, Mike McKay and his Oarsome pals. Fragments of dialogue, remembered separately by each man, show how the choice took shape.

Coates: 'I went to that meeting with three names in mind, three high-profile women in that team: Susie O'Neill, Rechelle Hawkes and Cathy Freeman. I had taken along some extra notes about why it might well be Cathy, so at one point I started to read from them. I said that athletics was the best-known Olympic sport, and she was the best-known athlete we had in the team, largely because of her Aboriginality. She was a current world champion, an Olympic silver medallist in the event she was going to contest. I thought it was most important that she was indigenous, and I said so. This was before the "sorry" thing became a big issue, but I knew she could offer an important message. I had also observed my own children — my daughter had read her book, and they loved her. I'd gone to the Australian track and field championships at Stadium Australia, and I saw the adulation that was exhibited to her as she came off the track, by all kids. So I had all these arguments. And they added up to the fact that she was an important role model for her own people and for all children.'[8]

Knight: 'I outlined my plan for the torch-bearers inside the stadium, still with the last one being a young girl, probably chosen in some way by the Games Co-Ordination Group, which was the key driver of the Games during that final period. I took John through the ages of the legends in that lap, and when we got to the end I quite nervously suggested to John that we might use Cathy as the second last runner to hand it to the young girl. I thought I would have difficulty with John, because John has always been careful not to single people out from the team, and he's always been wary about putting pressure on athletes. I thought it was a big ask of me to see how he'd feel about Cathy being second last. Then John said to me, "Well, why can't Cathy be the last? Why can't she light the torch?" He had all these arguments to support such a choice.'[9]

Coates: 'I said I thought it should be Cathy Freeman. He was a bit tentative. He didn't embrace it straightaway. He was asking, "Are you sure it won't potentially affect her performance?" I said, "Yeah, that's a problem we have to talk through." Then Michael said that maybe I ought to talk to her, explain to her what's involved. He said, "She might be scared of fire, and she needs to know that the rehearsal's going to be late at night." He seemed to be putting obstacles in the way, but it was certainly important for us to find out how she felt about the whole thing.'[10]

Knight: 'We agreed that John would talk to Cathy, ask her if she wanted to be considered for a role in the stadium, tell her that we weren't going to make a final selection until later, but that we needed to know her feelings.'[11]

When that meeting ended after around 90 minutes, the young-girl idea had been discarded — along with the names of most of the fancied candidates. The two arbiters had arrived, after some circuits and bumps, at their joint first preference. They had also settled on a list of legends to carry the torch inside the stadium. Very soon afterwards Coates' personal assistant, Pamela Harris, was checking diaries and airline timetables.

On the evening of Sunday, 21 May 2000, Coates took Cathy Freeman and her husband Sandy Bodecker to dinner at an Italian restaurant, *Il Piccolino*, in Los Angeles. Coates had arranged to pass through that city, where Freeman was training and living, on his way to a meeting of the Association of National Olympic Committees in Rio de Janiero. He had explained by phone that he wanted to talk about something very important and very confidential. Naturally enough, when they all sat down, the couple told him they had been intrigued.

Coates explained that the theme of the final torch relay would be to celebrate 100 years of female participation, and that all the relay spots inside the stadium were for women. He named people who would be taking part — Fraser, Strickland, Cuthbert, Raelene Boyle, Shane Gould, Debbie Flintoff-King — and then said, 'We'd like to see if you would light the flame for us.'[12]

Freeman was dumbfounded — 'blown away', as she put it later. 'Why me?' she asked. 'There are so many more important people, people like the ones you've just mentioned.'[13]

Coates offered the kind of arguments he had used with Knight, stressing her significance as an Aboriginal, her appeal to young people, her role as a symbol for reconciliation. Bodecker was supportive, agreeing that these were all the right reasons, telling her finally, 'You should do this.' Coates stressed to them both: 'I want to make sure you don't prejudice the most important thing. That's winning gold. I have to tell you there's going to be a lot of pressure.'[14]

Freeman grinned at him. 'John, I like pressure. That's when I perform at my best.'[15]

Coates told her more, about the need for strict confidentiality, about the fact that even the late-night rehearsals would be secret. He told her too that Knight was keen to talk to her soon in England, where the couple intended to base themselves. As Coates put it later, he knew when that meal was finished that Cathy Freeman was 'hot to trot'.[16]

As the three of them left the restaurant, she sidled up to him and whispered shyly, 'John, I'll understand if you change your mind.'[17]

Towards the end of July Knight caught up with Freeman and Bodecker during a stopover in London on his way to Athens. They met at her home in Windsor, close to the castle, and this time Knight had a number of diagrams with him, including an artist's representation of the cauldron. He told her: 'Cathy, I know John's raised the prospect of you lighting the cauldron. I want to tell you now, in extreme confidence, that we both want you to do that. We'd love you to do it. It'd be terrific. But I'm going to give you all the reasons why you shouldn't.'[18]

Knight talked mainly about the extra pressure the ceremony would put on her, about the possibility of it interfering with her focus on the 400 metres. She turned to her husband and asked him, 'What do

Betty Cuthbert (in wheelchair) and Raelene Boyle enter the stadium during the final torch-relay lap at the opening ceremony.

you think?' He answered, 'Just do whatever you like, hon.' She said then, 'Yes, I'm going to do this.'[19]

She and Knight did not meet again until a week before the Games, when he attended a prime minister's fundraising dinner in Melbourne and took a video of the test lighting of the cauldron out to her home. Freeman was overwhelmed by the scope of it, but very enthusiastic.

The guesswork about the lighting intensified as the Games drew very close. On the day before the opening ceremony, John Coates told Dawn Fraser of the illness of Juan Antonio Samaranch's wife (who in fact died during the Games). He said that Samaranch wanted her to be his partner at the opening ceremony, as First Lady of the Games. Her reaction to this invitation, which she accepted, was a little brusque. 'So I guess that counts me out of lighting the cauldron?' she responded.[20] Not necessarily so, he said. Afterwards she wrote that when she learned that she was going to miss out, she felt 'let down, hurt, sad and disappointed'.[21] She became further upset when she learned that Coates had visited Freeman in Los Angeles four months before the Games to sound her out. It was uncharacteristic of Fraser to let her personal emotions show, much less any sense of vulnerability. But she really did want that assignment with the cauldron, and missing it was immensely difficult to accept.

Such was the emphasis on confidentiality that preparations for the rehearsals for the final lap assumed an almost theatrically conspiratorial air. The six chosen to join Freeman's distinguished little gang had all been contacted personally by either Coates or Knight. A big problem was that all of them might have been seen as potential candidates for the lighting of the cauldron, and any knowledge of their identities could have provoked some educated arithmetic, simply by elimination. The task of briefing them, bringing them together from different parts of the country, rehearsing them after darkness, keeping them as unaware as possible of the identities of each other, called for a talent for subterfuge. Coates and Knight, both acclaimed as successful plotters in their fields, were up to it.

Flintoff-King, who had won gold in the 400 metres hurdles in Seoul in 1988, received her phone call from Coates in mid-August. He asked her if she would like to be involved in the final phase of the torch relay, and she said yes. At the end of a conversation in which he gave her no clues about what or who else might be involved — just the advice that there would be a rehearsal, that she must not tell a soul, and that she would be contacted again — she was weeping with joy. Then came a long wait, so long she thought there had been a change in plans, until four days before the opening ceremony. Knight called this time, telling her that she would be flying into Sydney on the eve of the ceremony for a late-night rehearsal. The airline ticket would be in her husband's name, she should fax her measurements to Knight's office so that a uniform would be ready, and she should come incognito. When her late-afternoon flight arrived that Thursday, she was met by a driver holding a sign saying 'King' and driven to the Novotel Hotel close to the stadium. He gave her a room key so there would be no risk of her being recognised during the checking-in process. The driver relayed an instruction: she was to stay inside, but be ready for a pick-up at 10.30 pm, wearing black clothes and a hat. Agents dropped behind enemy lines used to behave like that.

When she emerged from the hotel, she was escorted to a car containing Freeman and Bodecker. The couple had been booked into another hotel in Sydney, the Observatory, by Knight's chief of staff, Michael Deegan, and registered as Mr and Mrs Deegan. Together with Deegan, the three of them were driven to the stadium, where they waited in a lounge until the arena below was clear. Still nothing was said about the cauldron. It was only when their rehearsal of the final change-over began that Flintoff-King became aware of the role Freeman would play. Soon after midnight (and now the day of the opening ceremony) Flintoff-King passed the flaming torch for the first time to Freeman, who was wearing a fireproof body suit. Then, ankle deep in water, Freeman leaned forward and plunged her torch into the cauldron. The final duet was enacted many times, until two o'clock in the morning. Then Flintoff-King returned to her hotel, and Freeman continued to practise alone until almost 5 am.

Raelene Boyle, who had been contacted by Knight on 18 July before she underwent major abdominal surgery to remove a cancer, had no contact with any of the others before or during her rehearsal. She remembered: 'I received a phone call on the Thursday and was told to be at my hotel in the Rocks at 7 pm. I was picked up in an Olympic car, and the driver wouldn't tell me anything about what was happening. He kept saying he knew nothing. We went to the stadium. I was met, then told that I'd be pushing Betty Cuthbert in her wheelchair from the end of the entrance tunnel, where Herb Elliott would be handing me the torch. Betty wasn't there for the rehearsal. I was briefed on the distance, and did the walk. I had a uniform fitting near the tunnel. I didn't have a wheelchair, just pretended I did. I was a bit worried that the cabling under the tracks might cause problems for Betty's wheelchair. I didn't see Dawn, didn't know I'd be handing over to her. I got to the stadium without a clue about who would be lighting the cauldron, and still didn't have one when I left.'[22]

Michael Knight recalled:

We wanted this secret to be very tight. I told David Atkins, the artistic director, because I trusted him implicitly. I'm not saying other people can't keep secrets, but I knew David could — and I wasn't taking any risks. Full-dress rehearsals of the opening ceremony were held on the Monday and Wednesday evenings, but they did not of course involve any of the torch women. Dawn, Shirley [Strickland] and Shane [Gould] rehearsed together on the Thursday, unseen by any of the others. They were called simply runners two, three and four. They now knew about each other, but didn't know who came before or after. Not one of them knew about Cathy's role. It's fair to say the toughest job anyone had that night at the rehearsal belonged to the guy who had to take Dawn out the back on the track and brief her. A close friend of my chief of staff did that. Then we had the last two, Cathy and Debbie. All of these rehearsals, and the transport involved, were coordinated by Michael Deegan. The secrecy was kept. It was perfect. On the night we marched Cathy with the team, and everyone thought, 'Well, that rules her out if she's with the team.' John Coates [who led the march as *chef de mission*] had the job of getting her off the ground. We had Dawn sitting in the box with Samaranch, so people assumed she wasn't involved. It all worked perfectly. We kept the secret until the very last moment.[23]

In the days before the Games Coates had 11 other selection tasks which were his alone. He chose Rechelle Hawkes to take the oath on behalf of the assembled athletes, water polo referee Peter Kerr to take the officials' oath, Andrew Gaze to become team captain and carry the Australian flag ahead of the team in the march of nations, and the party of eight whose job it was to carry the Olympic flag around the track. Hawkes, competing in her fourth Olympics, had been a member of the gold-medal teams of 1988 and 1996, and had recently celebrated 250 international matches for Australia. The only other Australian athlete ever to have taken the oath had been John Landy in 1956. Gaze was captain of the basketball side and a five-time Olympian, ranking second overall in Olympic scoring to Brazil's Oscar Schmidt. His father, Lindsay, had been a member of the 1960, 1964 and 1968 Australian basketball teams, and had coached the 1972, 1976 and 1980 sides — giving the pair of them an unbroken 40-year link with Australian Olympic basketball.

Of the flag-carrying party, Coates said later: 'I wanted a balance of men and women. But I couldn't advise them too early, nor could I tell any of them who any of the others were. By elimination, people might have been able to work out things.'[24] The eight selected were Bill Roycroft, Murray Rose, Leane Tooth, Gillian Rolton, Marjorie Jackson, Lorraine Crapp, Michael Wenden and Nick Green, who spanned Olympics from 1952 to 1996, and between them had won 17 gold medals.

Rechelle Hawkes takes the oath on behalf of the assembled athletes.

A solemn moment as eight Olympians, representing 17 gold medals, carry the Olympic flag.

The rehearsal for the carriage of the flag did not go well. Jackson had been discharged from hospital after major back surgery only two days previously, and was in considerable pain. Roycroft, then aged 85, was limping heavily with an arthritic knee, one that had been kicked by a horse a long time ago. The intention was for them to carry the flag a full lap, but at rehearsal this task took the group an unworkable eight minutes. After a quick conference between David Atkins and John Coates, it was agreed to shorten the journey to 200 metres. On the big night Jackson took a morphine tablet an hour before the flag procession, and was ferried to the starting point in a wheelchair. She was still in pain, but full of spirit. 'I'm not going to miss this,' she told Coates. 'I'm doing it for my grandchildren.'

The opening ceremony was exuberant, funny, quirky, stunningly choreographed — and successful beyond most anticipation in celebrating the character, history, culture and environment of Australia. From the moment it exploded into life with the thunderous arrival of whip-cracking cavalry in the form of 120 stockhorses and their riders, until it ended with the flaming cauldron rising above and around Cathy Freeman, the whole spectacle crackled with energy, passion and wit. The creative team, led by Ric Birch as director of ceremonies and David Atkins as artistic director, took on the challenge of presenting what had to be a risky balancing act. On one level the show amounted at times to a mischievous collage, a gentle exercise in self-mockery — from Ned Kellys on stilts to explorers on bicycles and wandering windmills. On another it explored one of the most profound challenges confronting

Stockhorses gallop as the opening ceremony of the Sydney Olympic Games begins.

Australia, the issue of reconciliation between indigenous Australians and the overwhelmingly white population whose first representatives arrived as settlers more than 200 years ago. That the many diverse themes blended so comfortably, evoking overwhelming sentiments of pride, wonder and plain enjoyment, was a tribute to the imagination of the segment directors — Ignatius Jones, Meryl Tankard, Stephen Page, Rhoda Roberts, Atkins, Peter Wilson, Nigel Jamieson, Lex Marinos, Nigel Triffitt and Lloyd Bond. Birch led a team of 12,700 cast members and 5000 backstage workers.

Dancers tapped their way through the building of a bridge during the opening ceremony.

'Hero Girl' Nikki Webster soars high above giant jellyfish during the opening ceremony.

Moments to savour were abundant. The robust opening gallops of the stockhorses awoke memories of Light Horse charges, that man from Snowy River, the gallantry of Olympic riders like Bill Roycroft in Rome and Wendy Schaeffer in Atlanta, a procession of first Tuesdays in November, sun-squinting drovers, the rollicking verse of the bush balladeers. Nikki Webster, a remarkably talented and intrepid 13-year-old, soared 30 metres above the arena on a tracking wire, swimming, diving, drifting and somersaulting among exotic seahorses and giant jellyfish in a surreal ocean. This girl dominated the show, linking the seven creative segments in her role as Hero Girl, in company with her guide Djakapurra Munyarryun, the renowned tribal dancer who took the part of Songman.

A slow-moving, hunch-shuffling, chanting congregation of 350 Central Desert women spread across the arena, singing to the Dance of the Seven Emu Sisters as drums beat; Arnhem Land clans gathered, eucalyptus leaves were burnt, smoke gathered. A bolt of lightning engulfed the arena, and after the resultant fire the process of regeneration of the charred earth began. Fresh green shoots appeared, flower-buds swelled and bloomed, and the bush and rivers came alive to the strident laugh of the kookaburra and the screeching of parrots. The stadium took on the look of a vibrant, living garden.

Explorers pedalled their bikes with their telescopes and sketchbooks, Ned Kellys stalked high in Sid Nolan helmets, sheep were shorn,

Farm machinery and water tanks were powered by pulleys, bicycle chains and human muscle during the 'Tin Symphony' segment of the opening ceremony.

lawnmowers danced a quadrille, waves of immigrants arrived, construction workers tap-danced their way through the building of a bridge. And finally homage was paid to a reformed alcoholic called Arthur Stace, whose penchant it was to chalk the word 'Eternity' over the pavements of Sydney. The pace was fast, the mood affectionately irreverent, and the snapshot that emerged from it all was of a place that had a rich history but didn't take itself too seriously.

And the 2000-strong marching band, the subject of so much talkback ire 15 months earlier, vindicated Birch's vision by providing just the kind of rousing 'wall of sound' he had first predicted. It represented 20 countries, was the biggest marching band ever assembled, and it welcomed parading athletes with some distinctive melodies — 'Born in the USA' for the Americans, 'Guantanamera' for Cuba, 'Pomp and Circumstance March' for Britain, 'The Land Down Under' and 'The Road to Gundagai' for Australia.

If evidence that the true Olympic spirit was alive and well, it was provided in the parade most poignantly by the delegation from the two Koreas. Although competing separately, the teams from both sides of an uneasy border marched together, with one from each nation leading the contingent and those behind locking hands. John Farnham, Olivia Newton-John, Vanessa Amorosi, Tina Arena and the Children's Choir of the Greek Archdiocese of Australia all sang, and Samaranch showed off his mastery of the local accent: 'G'day, Syd-er-ney, G'day, Australia.'

The final lap with the torch offered not only the opportunity for the 110,000 crowd to salute a magnificent medley of six Australian women who had between them won 15 gold medals. Inevitably it also involved a kind of crossing-off process in solving the identity of the person at the core of the big secret. So it wasn't Betty? Not Dawn either? Not Shirley, eh? After Gould skipped her way to Flintoff-King, who then passed the torch to Freeman, the picture was suddenly clear, and somehow just right. Homage had been paid to the past, with a treasured group of female champions marking a centenary of women's participation in the Games. A wonderful relay that had begun with one young indigenous woman, Nova Peris-Kneebone, had ended with another. The Freeman culmination, at the end of a ceremony that had emphasised Aboriginal heritage and addressed the issue of reconciliation, amounted to a quietly eloquent statement about the kind of nation Australia aspired to be. It underlined itself boldly as a significant moment in the nation's history.

Freeman ascended four flights of stairs carrying the torch, then walked across a shallow circular pond to an island in the centre, where she dipped the torch low, then swept it around her to ignite a ring of fire. The pond concealed a submerged cauldron, and the circle of fire consisted of 150 nozzles around the rim of its gas-burner. The whole

To a wave of applause, the two Korean teams march into the stadium as one.

Andrew Gaze leads the Australian team into the opening ceremony. *Chef de mission* John Coates is on the left.

Cathy Freeman carries the torch on the final leg of its journey.

concept, this tableau that represented a memorable marriage of fire and water, was the brainchild of Ric Birch; he had nursed it since he first took it to engineers and project managers in 1995, and had somehow kept it secret. Freeman stood motionless as the now-flaming cauldron rose around her, like a cascading umbrella, then walked from the pond and stood, a solitary figure, torch aloft. She stayed like that for a long time, because a freak signal had caused a glitch in the computer that drove the cauldron on rails to its place above the stadium. For what seemed an eternity it didn't move, and Freeman remained there, space-suited, still as a sculpture, and very wet. Then two attendant engineers, Peter Tait and Rob Ironside, re-programmed the computer, made the winch system work, and the cauldron made its slow, majestic voyage upwards, against a waterfall background.

Afterwards Samaranch described the opening ceremony as the most beautiful of his presidency. Since opening ceremonies did not become extravaganzas until he took over in 1980, that was no empty praise. More significant, though, was the fact that this ceremony had ushered in a Games the Olympic movement really needed. Symbolically, it put an end to two painful years.

The cauldron rises to begin its passage to the top of the stadium.

190

CHAPTER TEN

'The best minute, the best hour ...'

When Juan Antonio Samaranch offered his judgment — 'You have presented to the world the best Olympic Games ever' — it surprised nobody. We knew it, mainly from our warm inner glow. Sure, there had been some apprehension beforehand about all kinds of potential problems: latent scandal, train derailments, sharks in the harbour, drunks in the city, terrorist outrages, Aboriginal demonstrations, cold and/or rainy weather, wind in the stadium, unsold tickets, disgruntled sponsors, etcetera. Perhaps the considerable shortcomings of Atlanta four years earlier had conditioned some people to believe that something would have to go wrong. David Williamson, the playwright, had a view: 'Six months before the Games, we were certain we were headed for disaster. We were gripped in a lacerating orgy of self-doubt ... Coming up to the Games, our fear that we would stuff up the whole thing became intense.'[1]

Perhaps. But from the moment the first stockhorse and rider galloped in to the centre of the opening-ceremony stage, any such feelings dissolved, and the public sentiment became one of overwhelming confidence. The weather remained friendly, and considerate too: when the rain tumbled down, it was on track and field's only rest day. The venues, the crowd control and the public transport system were perfect, the volunteers a delight. We just *knew* that nothing would mar these Games, that they really were the best ever. For 17 days, from opening to closing, the whole experience had an almost other-worldly quality to it. To be in the streets was to be surrounded by a smile. To be at a venue, any venue — but perhaps more relentlessly than anywhere else, at the volleyball on Bondi Beach — was to be in the presence of a throbbing, pumping beat. Smiles begat smiles, and the beat made for good, easy vibes. The mood of mutual enjoyment was infectious and at times a little dream-like. It was as if everyone in the streets of Sydney and inside its Olympic venues was on happy pills. Late in the second week people would confide to each other that they didn't want this state of bliss to end. But it was just too much to expect that such a condition of suspension from the real world, from politics and share markets and a diving dollar, could ever be permanent.

Steve Redgrave made it five gold in a row when he took Britain's team to victory in the men's coxless fours.

Like all Olympic Games, Sydney 2000 showcased heroes and heroines and yielded lifetime memories that encapsulated proud and often improbable spectacles, as well as performances that prickled our deepest emotions. The arithmetic was simple and not really conducive to individual optimism: 10,561 athletes from 200 countries competed for 300 gold medals. As if those odds were not miserly enough, some athletes refused to settle for just one lump of gold. Six of them won three apiece: Ian Thorpe (Australia, swimming), Marion Jones (US, athletics), Inge de Bruijn (Netherlands, swimming), Leontien Zijlaard-ven Moorsel (Netherlands, cycling), Jenny Thompson (US, swimming) and Lenny Krayzelburg (US, swimming).

Steve Redgrave took his tally of gold medals to five, over five consecutive Olympics, as he led Britain's crew to victory in the men's coxless fours. The Americans Marion Jones and Maurice Greene proved themselves the fastest sprinters on earth, and Haile Gebrselassie, of Ethiopia, won again over 10,000 metres. Greene, a man with a fine talent for swagger, celebrated his 100 metres win by hurling one of his golden-soled shoes high into the grandstand, making the catcher, a young apprentice jeweller from Wagga Wagga, potentially richer by a cool $US100,000. Ms Jones would have liked to emulate Jesse Owens (1936) and Carl Lewis (1984) by adding a long jump to her successes in the 100 and 200 metres, but her technique over the jump pit didn't quite match her ambition. She had a couple of rare consolations. One was the knowledge that her winning margin over the shorter sprint was the widest ever recorded at an Olympic Games. The other was that her tally of five medals (gold in both sprints and the 4 × 400 metres relay, and bronze in the long jump and 4 × 100 metres relay) was unmatched by any other woman. Her conqueror in the long jump was a woman of extraordinary athletic longevity: Heike Drechsler, 36, of Germany, had won her first world title seventeen years previously, and a previous Olympic gold medal in 1992.

Michael Johnson, upright as an exclamation mark amid a field of surging italics, continued to compete in a zone of his own, becoming the first man in history to defend a 400 metres title at successive Olympics. The main interest in his final was not whether he would win — he *owned* the distance — but whether he would break his own world record. He didn't, but he was in great company: for the first time since 1948 not a single world record fell during the entire track and field program. This itself constituted something of a record.

For Australia, these were Games to bask in. Its team of 632, aided by support staff of 374 (including 137 coaches and 90 medical personnel), was the largest the nation had ever fielded. Some had considered

'See these,' Maurice Greene seems to be saying, 'they've just carried me to gold in the 100 metres.'

Marion Jones had much to celebrate at the Sydney Olympics, winning three gold medals (100 metres, 200 metres and 4 × 400 metres relay) and two bronze medals (long jump and 4 × 100 metres relay).

John Coates (*chef de mission* for the fourth consecutive time) more than a little foolhardy when he predicted a top-five finish, with a record total of 60 medals. In fact, Australia finished fourth among nations (behind the powerhouses of the United States, Russia and China) with 58 medals — 17 more than ever before — culled from 20 different sports, which set another record. This result represented justification not only for the absolute dedication of so many fine athletes but also for the $60 million

the AOC had spent on their preparation. The team won 16 gold medals (eclipsing the record total of 13 gathered in Melbourne 44 years earlier), along with 25 silver and 17 bronze. And the sheer range of them! Whereas the tally of 35 medals in Melbourne had been restricted to just seven disciplines, the Australians of 2000 ventured successfully into a whole raft of comparatively infant Olympics sports — such as women's water polo, beach volleyball, taekwondo, women's triathlon, women's pole vault, men's trampoline and men's and women's synchronised diving.

Michael Johnson leads the way as he powers towards the finish line in the 400 metres.

Undoubtedly, the finest individual performances came from Cathy Freeman and Ian Thorpe. From the moment Freeman took the torch from Debbie Flintoff-King in the opening ceremony, these were indelibly her Games. It was as if her part had been scripted, just a bit outrageously. How very appropriate it was that her victory in the 400 metres final (which occurred in the second week and will be dealt with at more length in the next chapter) should have represented the 100th gold medal in Australia's Olympic history! For that we can hold that improbable script responsible, just as we can for the cauldron lighting, for the companionship of the Australian and Aboriginal flags during her victory lap, for the chorus of what seemed to be 100,000 voices greeting her victory with the national anthem. There was often about this woman an aura of shy nobility. At times, one of them immediately after her win, she seemed to retreat somewhere deep within herself. But when her face split into her natural wide and toothy grin, as it did on the rostrum when she came to terms with her triumph, her glowing happiness amplified on giant television screens, it became the face of the Sydney Olympics — then and forever.

Ian Thorpe's introduction to the Olympic Games occupied one crowded hour on the first night of swimming competition, and yielded two gold medals plus a couple of world records. Thorpe has never been a boisterous person, but after the second event he was unaccustomedly exuberant. 'This is the best minute, the best hour, the best day of my life,' he said of his stunning arrival. 'To be able to dream and fulfil it is the best thing an individual can do.' Rather like Michael Johnson, he had assumed the personal proprietorship of a distance. The distance (like Johnson's) was 400 metres, the discipline freestyle swimming. Since he had taken Perkins' mantle, Thorpe had overcome distractions — a broken ankle, ridiculous drug insinuations from Germany (some even related to the size of his feet), the rumpus that preceded the intro- duction of bodysuits at the Games — to reach this moment of truth, equipped with a philosophy to match his talent.

As world champion and world record-holder over the distance, and the creator of six recent world records, he was well aware that he was carrying an enormous weight of expectations. But, at 17, he pos- sessed an astonishing degree of cool maturity. His theory was that if

Ian Thorpe acknowledges the crowd after his gold-medal-winning swim in the 400 metres freestyle.

he could turn those expectations into something positive, they would amount to sheer support; if they were allowed to become a negative, they would translate to unwanted pressure. He did not concern himself much with the opposition. His attitude was taut: 'I have a lane and I swim. I can't affect the performance of my competitors...If I focus all my energy and attention on what I'm trying to do, I'm going to be able to get my best performance. It's as simple as that.' Around the pool deck he was known as Big Foot. Nobody could ever think of him as Big Head.

As he padded towards the starting blocks at the Sydney Aquatic Centre Thorpe looked as unflustered and relaxed as if this was just another meet. Above and around him, the bulk of the 17,500 crowd

Daniel Kowalski responds to the deafening reception the Australian team received during the opening ceremony.

were stomping and chanting: 'Thor-pee! Thor-pee!' While he continued to appear unaffected by the din, he later confessed that he felt like a gladiator walking into the Coliseum. He hit the surface hard at the start, and after the first half-lap was ahead by nearly a body length. Scything through the water with his long, languid-looking stroke and explosive kick, he led by a full second at the first turn. From then the only question was whether he would break a world record. This he dutifully did, completing eight withering laps in 3 minutes 40.59 seconds, shaving 0.74 seconds from the mark he had set 12 months previously. As he touched the wall he looked at the scoreboard, then acknowledged the crowd with raised fists, but stayed calm and controlled. He whispered an omnibus 'thank you' — to God, to the crowd, to his family, to his country, to everything that had brought him to this place — before leaving the water. 'I think he was born to swim,' said the Italian Massi Rosolini, who finished an unthreatening second in 3 minutes 43.40 seconds, the fourth fastest time in history. Thorpe owned the other three. The American Klete Keller collected bronze with 3 minutes 47 seconds, and Australia's other finalist, Grant Hackett, weakened in the late stages to come in seventh in 3 minutes 48.22 seconds. After the race Thorpe told reporters: 'I just felt this surge of sheer energy inside of me when I touched the wall and realised I had the world record.'

It was a night when sheer energy would come in handy. After a few anxious moments between races when Thorpe's jet-black swimsuit split at the seams — it took him ten minutes to be squeezed into his spare suit — he joined his team-mates Michael Klim, Chris Fydler and Ashley Callus for his next big test, the 4 × 100 metres relay. This was an event the United States had never once been beaten in since its introduction to the Games program in 1964. The stranglehold had almost been prised loose just once, in Atlanta in 1996, when its anchor man, Gary Hall Jr, had been forced to swim the fastest relay leg in history to bring the team home. This time the same Gary Hall had unintentionally provided the Australians with a motivational tool by declaring in print that the US team would 'smash Australia like guitars' in the swimming events. He would later explain that he had meant no disrespect — that the remark had been less a taunt than a joke that didn't work too well. No matter — it became a handy spur.

Members of the winning men's 4 × 100 metres relay team strum mock guitars in response to a jibe from the American Gary Hall Jr. From left: Ashley Callus, Michael Klim, Ian Thorpe.

Klim fairly flew from the blocks and thrashed his way to a handy opening lead, covering the first 100 metres in 48.18 seconds to shave three-tenths of a second from the world record held by the great Russian Alex Popov — who happened to be Klim's training partner at the Australian Institute of Sport in Canberra. Fydler and Callus both held their opponents well on the second and third legs, and as the anchor men hit the water for the final two laps, Thorpe had a narrow margin over Hall. Hall, a much more seasoned sprinter, reeled Thorpe in, and when he took a lead of half a body length into the final turn the Americans' unbeaten record looked intact. With his powerful, so-very-relaxed stroke and furious size-17 kick, Thorpe kept on gaining ground until he caught Hall in the final metres and touched the wall just in front. The winning relay time was another world record — 3 minutes 13.67 seconds. That anchor leg had been a magnificent effort from a youngster who until then had not taken himself too seriously as a sprinter. (Unfamiliar with the limits of the distance, he had not been sure at first whether Klim had even broken the world record: 'I really had to think about it, because I'm not really a 100 metres swimmer.') After he did check, he was able to advise Klim before he took off on his final leg that, yes, he was 'pretty sure' it had been a record. His own magnificent effort in upsetting the most highly regarded relay swimmer in the world had owed less to muscle and power than to passion, courage and self-belief.

Afterwards Hall had to endure the painful sight of the Australian quartet strumming away at non-existent guitars in a not-too-subtle jibe at the prediction that bounced. The winners, even including the normally reserved Thorpe, were ecstatic — hugging, punching high in the air, roaring their joy. They knew they hadn't just won an important race and set a world mark; they had annexed a tradition of American swimming. Twenty minutes after the race, Hall was still close to disbelief. The Americans had broken their own world record by almost one-and-a-half seconds, yet had lost the men's 100 metres relay for the first time in history. Dawn Fraser, the matriarch of world swimming, called it 'probably the greatest race I've ever seen'. Thorpe, asked to choose between those two debut gold medals, said afterwards that the relay meant more to him. 'Being able to share that experience with three other swimmers was incredible,' he enthused. It was no wonder that for him it would always be the best minute. When he returned to the Village from the pool, Thorpe was asked by a security guard to empty his pockets of metal objects. Obligingly, he plonked down two gold medals on a plastic tray.

If after that first night Thorpe had taken on an aura of invincibility — and he had — it was soon to be cracked. Another cool-headed young man five years his senior, the Dutchman Pieter van den Hoogenband, made that very clear when he set a world record mark

Dutch swimmer Pieter van den Hoogenband was victorious in both the 100 metres and 200 metres freestyle.

of 1 minute 45.35 seconds in his 200 metres freestyle semi-final. Soon after, in the second semi-final, Thorpe cut through the four lengths to finish in 1 minute 45.37 seconds, just two-hundredths of a second outside the new record. The prospect of that final the next night was one to salivate about, and the *Australian* greeted it, in a banner headline across the top of the front page, as the race that would stop the nation. That was fairly true. All Australia did seem to be watching and listening as van den Hoogenband and Thorpe battled to decide who was the fastest swimmer in the world over 200 metres. The winner was the Dutchman, who equalled his own world record and earned for his country its first male Olympic gold medal in history. Afterwards his father, Cees-Rijn, looking at a crowd that was generous in its ovation but still in an obvious state of shock, summed up the magnitude of the feat: 'We came into the lion's den, and we did it.'

Mainly, it was a victory for tactics. Van den Hoogenband and his coach, Jacco Verhaeren, had devised a plan five months earlier to attack hard early and try to burn off the Australian, whose usual preference was to swim faster in the late stages. The Dutchman did just that, exploding from the blocks and stealing a lead he would not relinquish in the final 50 metres, even to the man who had swum down Gary Hall. Thorpe spent much of his energy counter-attacking in the third lap, and they shared the lead at the final turn. Unbelievably, even as Thorpe was changing gears and engaging the most powerful six-beat kick in the world, van den Hoogenband was inching ahead. Thorpe could not quite catch him, finishing second in 1 minute 45.83 seconds, with Italy's Rosolini third. The Australian, who complained of flatness before the race, was as gracious in defeat as in victory: 'I'm happy I gave it my best shot,' he said. 'I'm a little disappointed at the time [his fourth best over the distance] but not in the result — I don't think it would've mattered how I swam that race because in the last part I couldn't have given anything else. I gave my all to that race. I hurt a lot at the end.' The Dutchman just kept saying, 'I can't believe I won.' Even on the victory dais, with the gold-medal evidence looped around his neck and the national anthem of the Netherlands being played, he was still shaking his head. Later this very modest young man would defeat both Alex Popov and Gary Hall in the 100 metres to make it a sprint double.

The entrenchment of Ian Thorpe in Australian Olympic history took just four days. It was on the fourth that he combined with Klim, Bill Kirby and Todd Pearson to smash all opposition and the world record in the 4 × 200 metres freestyle relay final. Australia had always been rated a strong chance in this event — a consequence of its sheer depth in the 200-metre zone, where six Australians were among the ten fastest in the world. The win made Thorpe the first Australian triple gold medallist at a single Games in 28 years, sharing that distinction

The victorious 4 x 200 men's relay team (from left: Todd Pearson, Bill Kirby, Michael Klim and Ian Thorpe).

with Betty Cuthbert (1956), Murray Rose (1956) and Shane Gould (1972). His overall tally was three gold and one silver, which gave him the most significant Olympic debut since another teenage marvel, Gould, in Munich. It was the first time Australia had won the men's 200 metres relay in 44 years (since Melbourne, 1956), and curiously the only other such win had been 44 years before that (in Stockholm, 1912).

The relay team's strategy was a simple one: to demoralise any potential challengers. Instead of anchoring the squad, as he did in the shorter relay, Thorpe led off, and he set the race up perfectly. Klim dived in second and increased the lead. Pearson swam his leg well, and by the time Kirby entered the water for the race home, American and Dutch swimmers on the deck were already congratulating the Australians. Kirby still had the world record to swim for, and he made sure of that with a spirited finish that stopped the clock at 7 minutes 7.05 seconds — 1.74 seconds inside the old mark. Four Australians had battled in the morning heat for the honour of joining Thorpe and Klim in the final. The two who missed out were Daniel Kowalski and Grant Hackett, both of whom were still rewarded with gold medals.

For Susan O'Neill, 27, these last Olympics of a glorious career ended paradoxically: she won the race she didn't expect to, and lost the one that everyone expected her to win. Although as the year began she had been ranked No. 1 in the world in both the 200 metres butterfly and the 200 metres freestyle, the latter stroke was not one in which she fancied her chances. Butterfly was the discipline she loved and identified with: she was the conqueror of them all, the undisputed Madame Butterfly, and the night she broke Mary T. Meagher's 19-year-old world record in May 2000 would always be, for her, the highlight of her career. Freestyle was just something else she did, not always with great enthusiasm, and during the previous year she had become disenchanted enough with the stroke to consider giving it away. She had made an agreement with her coach, Scott Volkers, that if she broke the Commonwealth record at the national championships she would never have to swim freestyle again; so impressively did she smash that mark that Volkers refused to keep his side of the bargain and insisted she keep going.

As the Games approached, O'Neill continued to wonder whether she ought really to be contesting the 200 metres freestyle. 'It was always in the back of my mind that I wouldn't swim that race,' she told this writer in 2002. 'Apart from other considerations, the final of the free-style was just before the semi-final of the 200 butterfly on the Olympic program, and I was worried about that. But I'd backed myself into a bit of a corner, especially after I was ranked No. 1 in the world. Also, the 4 × 200 metres freestyle relay was something of an incentive to keep going with the stroke. I really thought we could win that relay.'[2]

Even though she was the fastest qualifier of the semi-finalists in the 200 metres freestyle, O'Neill was still doubtful about her own prospects and sincerely talking up those of others. 'I still think the ones to

At her last Olympic Games as a competitor, Susie O'Neill took gold in the women's 200 metres freestyle.

beat are Martina Moravcova and Claudia Poll,' she told reporters after the semi. She recalled how she felt on the day of the final, the following day:

> I was a lot more nervous that day than for the 200 'fly. I knew that I could do the time to win [the freestyle] ... I'd seen the heat times, and it was nothing special. But I wasn't sure I was going to pull it out. I started having doubts, and they magnified. I rang Cliff. He was on the beach at Bronte, and I was crying. I was a bit sleep deprived, and quite emotional. I said, 'I'm not going out to the pool ... I'm over it.' He talked some sense into me, saying it was only a swimming race and trying to put things into perspective. I still said, 'I don't want to do this.'[3]

As the finalists were led across to the starting area, the fans in the bleachers at the handsome shed that was the aquatic centre were stomping, and the decibel levels were explosive. Surveying the raucous crowd and the tension-charged pool deck, Volkers was moved to remark: 'People are trembling tonight, people who have never trembled before.' O'Neill remained undistracted and swam the race exactly as she and Volkers had planned — leading through the first 100 metres, and taking command after a strong third lap. The challengers came at her in the final stretch, first Moravcova (Slovakia), then Poll (Costa Rica), but she defied each assault to win in 1 minute 58.24 seconds. Her freestyle victory made her the first Australian woman since Dawn Fraser to win gold medals in successive Olympics, and the first since Shane Gould to win gold in separate disciplines. With the crowd all around her roaring and chanting 'Susie, Susie', she confessed that it had been a very painful swim. 'Thank goodness that's over,' she said of the race that had been almost as much an ordeal as it was a triumph.

O'Neill's defeat in the 200 metres butterfly final represented one of the most stunning upsets of the Sydney Games. She had been unbeaten for six years, and it seemed there was nobody in the final field with a hope of challenging her. Then Misty Dawn Hyman emerged, seemingly from nowhere, but in fact from Mesa, Arizona. A former high school prom queen, she had received her unlikely Christian names because she was born very early on a slightly rainy morning. Hyman, 21, had raced against O'Neill unsuccessfully in the Pan Pacific titles — trying to steal races by leading out hard early, but always weakening in the final stages. In the lead-up to Sydney she had been thinking about quitting swimming. In this final she didn't perform her normal fade: she led for 150 metres, then held off the Australian duo, O'Neill and Petria Thomas, in the final lap. O'Neill, who had been uncharacteristically tense throughout the week, had these memories of the race:

> To be perfectly honest, I thought I was going to win. I certainly didn't think Misty Hyman was a threat. If anyone, I thought Petria [Thomas] probably was. If I swam it again, I would not think so much — just try and keep my key words ('long' and 'strong') in mind, and not worry. I remember even in the last lap hearing a loud roar and seeing Misty Hyman, and thinking, 'Oh, my God!' And you are really trying to speed up, and then it doesn't work. So if I did it again I'd just close those

In one of the most stunning upsets of the Games, Misty Dawn Hyman won gold in the 200 metres butterfly.

curtains and swim my own race. Even so, I was less than a second outside my best time. Hers was an amazing swim…she did a Jon Sieben or a Duncan Armstrong, really. She's a nice girl. She was almost embarrassed to see me afterwards.[4]

On that same night O'Neill and Thomas were members of an Australian 4 × 200 metres relay squad that broke the world record but still finished second behind a US team anchored by Jenny Thompson. By the end of the week Susie O'Neill had surpassed (by one) Shirley Strickland's tally and equalled Dawn Fraser's record of eight Olympic medals. O'Neill's total was: 2 gold (Atlanta 200 metres butterfly, Sydney 200 metres freestyle); 4 silver (Atlanta 4 × 100 metres medley relay, Sydney 200 metres butterfly; Sydney 4 × 200 metres freestyle relay, Sydney 4 × 100 metres medley relay); 2 bronze (Barcelona 200 metres butterfly, Atlanta 4 × 200 metres freestyle relay). When the carnival was over, she announced her impending retirement from swimming in typical fashion — quietly and without any fanfare. 'I've had a great career,' she said. 'I'm at a point in my life where I want to do other things, spend more time with my husband.' Fittingly, when athletes of the world voted during the Games for eight of their number to become members of the IOC Athletes' Commission, Susan O'Neill was one of those elected.[5] Rarely, if ever, has Australia produced an athlete with more grace, courage and character.

It was a copious season for superlatives and for races anticipated to 'stop the nation'. One such duel was that between Kieren Perkins and Grant Hackett in the 1500 metres freestyle final on the final swimming day. It possessed elements of classic drama: the young gun versus the last-time veteran, the unawed challenger from the beach facing off the sentimental favourite who specialised in winning against the odds, plus an interesting mix of form slumps and mind games. Hackett, 20, had won world, Pan Pac and Commonwealth gold medals, and had not once been beaten over the distance — but he was unaccountably off form in the early stages of competition. Even though he had been a world 200 metres record-holder, he missed selection in Australia's final 4 × 200 metres relay team. Nobody, including Hackett, seemed to know what was wrong that week, much less how to correct it.

Perkins, 27, had won in Barcelona in 1992, and almost miraculously overcome all kinds of adversity to do it again in Atlanta in 1996. To win for a third time in Sydney would not only establish him as the finest distance swimmer in history: it would rank him alongside Dawn Fraser as a three-time winner in the same event. He had not won a race in four years — but suddenly, in that first week of competition, he was on song. In his heat of the 1500, he broke 15 minutes for the first time since Atlanta, with a time seven seconds faster than that of his closest rival, who wasn't Hackett. More than that, he radiated confidence, punching a fist high after the qualifier, talking up his chances. Perkins moved to favouritism, and there was even talk that the American Erik Vendt, the second fastest qualifier, would deny the Australians a quinella.

Before the start of his last event ever, Perkins took time to savour the moment. 'For the first time,' he said later, 'I just stood behind the blocks to sort of have a look up into the crowd and absorb the noise and feel what it was like.'[6] The Australian pair made clear in the early laps that it would be *their* race, nobody else's. Right from the start Hackett attacked, and after 100 metres he looked comfortable and controlled. He swam as Perkins had in Atlanta, assuming mastery early, defying others to tackle him. After two laps he was telling himself, 'You can really win this, Grant.' Perkins challenged hard but could not stay with him. He summed up the race: 'I knew if I wasn't in front by a substantial margin with 100 to go I wouldn't be able to beat Grant, because he had more speed … but every time I'd pick up the pace, he'd pick up the pace too. He had me covered on all angles. I gave it my best shot and it wasn't enough.' And later: 'I didn't allow myself to consider the fact before the race, but the reality was that Grant was bigger, stronger, faster. It was his time.'[7]

Hackett covered the distance in 14 minutes 48.33 seconds to become the Olympic champion, the sixth Australian ever to win that event. After an agonising week, he yelled, punched into the water, embraced Perkins and waved towards his parents, Nev and Margaret. Perkins finished eight strokes behind, recording his fastest time in six years, and for the first time in history four swimmers finished in under 15 minutes. Such was Perkins' popularity that one writer observed that if he suffered a humiliating defeat Hackett would go down in history

as the man who shot Skippy. That's not the way it happened. Perkins
emerged from that race as the most successful 1500 metres swimmer
yet. Only America's Michael Burton (1968 and 1972) and the Soviet
Union's Vladimir Salnikov (1980 and 1988) had ever won double gold
in the event, and neither had managed silver as well. Perkins had been
Hackett's early inspiration, and it was appropriate that immediately
after the race Perkins reached across and anointed Hackett with the
quiet words, 'You deserve this, mate.'

In taking the silver medal behind Grant Hackett, Kieren Perkins still became the most successful 1500 metres swimmer the Games had seen.

Afterwards Hackett was frank about the sense of desolation that had accompanied his worrying lack of form in the shorter distances early in the week. 'I bawled my eyes out after the 4 × 200 relay final,' he confessed as he sat in the media conference room alongside Perkins. 'That was a very hard win to take. I was the world record-holder in that event just a year ago. I still get a gold medal out of it, but it would have been great to swim in the final. I have had a lot of pressure coming into this race — I blocked out what everyone else was saying. I had a job to do and I knew I could do it. I had a lot of anger within from what people were saying. People were even asking my parents what was wrong. I had unbelievable support from the likes of Murray Rose and Steve Holland calling me, and Peter Brock came to visit me in my room.'

The youngest member of the Australian swimming team, Liesel Jones (15), on her way to winning silver in the 100 metres breaststroke.

Australia emerged from the swim program as second top nation (behind the United States) with five gold medals, nine silver and four bronze for a total of 30 medals — its best performance in almost 30 years. Members of the team set a remarkable range of records: 4 world, 6 Olympic, 12 Commonwealth and 17 Australian. Twenty-six personal-best times were recorded, and 26 of the 44 team members won medals. The youngest of them, Liesel Jones, who turned 15 just before the Games began, won silver behind Megan Quann (US) in the 100 metres breaststroke. The US team remained supreme with 14 gold, 8 silver and 11 bronze. Lenny Krayzelburg, who had immigrated to America from the former Soviet Union with his parents as a teenager, won both back-stroke gold medals and another in the medley relay. Jenny Thompson brought her amazing total of relay gold medals to eight (Barcelona 2, Atlanta 3, Sydney 3). The Dutchwoman Inge de Bruijn was quite as dev-astating as her compatriot van den Hoogenband; she won two freestyle

Inge de Bruijn from the Netherlands was devastating in the pool, winning two freestyle sprints and the 100 metres butterfly.

sprints and the 100 metres butterfly, while he won the 100 metres and 200 metres freestyle. And Eric 'the Eel' Moussambani, from Equatorial Guinea, did well to reach the end of his 100 metres freestyle heat without sinking. The magnificent ovation he received underlined the sentimental significance of Pierre de Coubertin's assertion that the important thing is just to compete.

When a bunch of boys from the bush galloped through a couple of laps of honour after winning the three-day equestrian event at Horsley Park, the omni-present Dawn Fraser was of course on the spot, urging them on. 'Go on, boys,' she shouted. 'Go around again.' This they did, for an unprecedented third victory lap, to the strains of the theme from 'The Man from Snowy River'. That was as it should have been, not just because these men had demonstrated the kind of gritty perfection that warranted a Banjo Paterson ballad. One of them had just joined Ms Fraser in history. Andrew Hoy, 41, who grew up on a farm near Culcairn in New South Wales, became the first Australian other than her to have won three consecutive gold medals. Hoy's team-mates were Phillip Dutton, 37, Matt Ryan, 36, and Stuart Tinney, 35, but it was understandable that the crowd was drawn irresistibly to the chant, 'Aussie, Aussie, Aussie — Hoy, Hoy, Hoy.' Ryan, winner of individual and team gold in Barcelona in 1992, also collected his third gold medal.

For Australia, long considered a specialist only in the cross-country stage of the event, the equestrians gave a superb all-round performance. The team rode brilliantly through the dressage phase to begin the cross-country in first place — a most unusual luxury. The pivotal Australian ride came from first-time Olympian Tinney, a former cattle

Andrew Hoy on the mighty grey Darien Powers during the three-day equestrian event.

First-time Olympian Stuart Tinney ... a pivotal ride in the three-day equestrian event.

musterer from Maralyla in northern New South Wales, on Jeepster, a horse that one New Zealand rider derided as 'a showjumping donkey'. Tinney rode third, following rounds by Ryan and Dutton, and negotiated all the difficult jumps before dislodging a single rail. This ice-cool ride made it almost impossible for the second-placed team, Britain, to overhaul the Australians. It gave Hoy and his mount, the mighty grey Darien Powers, a barrier of 30 penalty points, which meant that they would have to knock down six rails for Australia to lose gold. Three rails fell, but the medal was safe, leaving Britain with silver and the United States bronze.

Afterwards the Australians, despite their fancy red riding gear, all confirmed that their skills harked back to their bush beginnings. 'I really think one thing that's contributed to my riding — was that

I grew up on a farm and was chasing cattle and sheep around a paddock,' said Hoy, to general nods from his team-mates. The victory gave a dimension of symmetry to the Sydney Olympics, whose opening ceremony had begun with a great massed ride that acknowledged the fundamental place of the horse in Australian history. After Australia's unprecedented third successive victory in this event, nobody would dispute that it now had a similar role in the nation's Olympic history. Hoy later made the Games even more memorable personally when he won silver in the individual three-day event, finishing second on his mount Swizzle In to the American rider David O'Connor.

When Michael Diamond won the Olympic men's trap gold medal in Atlanta in 1996, he became the first Australian to win a shooting event at the Games since Donald Mackintosh in 1900. In Sydney he made history again, and consolidated his place within the pantheon of great marksmen, by winning back-to-back gold. Only one trap shooter had ever done that before — Italy's Luciano Giovenetti, who won the event in Moscow (1980) and Los Angeles (1984). The trap is an event that has endured since the 1900 Olympics. It requires constant concentration, with the shooter having about three-tenths of a second to react to the projection of targets (representing birds) from below and in front. If the first shot misses, a shot from the second barrel might still score.

Diamond, 28, entered the Games as world trap and double trap champion. In the final, over three rounds, he hit every one of the 75 targets — small orange discs of clay, flying at speeds of around 100 kilometres an hour from unpredictable angles — to win by five targets from Britain's Ian Peel. He started the last day two targets ahead of his nearest rivals, then shot two perfect qualifying rounds of 25 to enter the final four shots clear. His shooting during the final was again flawless, giving him a total of 147 out of 150 shots. He rarely needed to resort to the second barrel of his Perazzi MX8 shotgun, his first shot almost invariably reducing the orange disc to fine powder. When he smashed his final target, the cheering at Cecil Park was deafening: he estimated that half his home town of Goulburn had bought tickets to the event.

Afterwards the unflinching self-control that Diamond had shown throughout the competition melted away, as he hugged his mother and dedicated the gold medal to his father, Constantine, who had died the previous May. It was Con who had introduced him to shooting at the age of six, and had been his coach, mentor and psychological support for more than 20 years. He had never before competed in a major tournament without Con by his side. 'I've heard his words all through the Olympics,' he said afterwards. 'They were the same words I heard prior to the Atlanta final. He said to me then, "Don't move the gun before you see the target. When you see the target, shoot it with a controlled amount of aggression. Don't back off. You're in the final now — go and finish it off." And, bugger it, he didn't teach me for 20 years for me to just walk out there and fail. I just stuck to my guns and did what he told me. It may sound like a very few words, but it was a million dollars worth of advice.'

Australia's only cycling gold medal came in an event that was new to the Olympic program, the madison — a two-man race demanding teamwork, endurance, sprinting ability and strategy. It is conducted over 60 kilometres (240 laps), with sprints every five kilometres and team-mates propelling each other into the action by means of 'hand-slings'. The winners, Brett Aitken, 29, and Scott McGrory, 30, both overcame intense personal stress just to be there. McGrory's infant son Alexander had died earlier in the year, as a result of a heart deficiency. Aitken's daughter Ashli, aged two, had been diagnosed months earlier with Rhett's Syndrome, a disability affecting movement and communication. The motivation of both riders had been affected deeply for a time, but both had managed to convert their private agony into a deep desire to win.

The Australian duo worked together smoothly and methodically from the start, finishing second and first in the first two sprints. By the halfway mark they were 11 points clear. Such was their precision and stamina that they were placed in nine of the twelve sprints. During the final dash, after Aitken catapulted his mate into the final sprint, an ugly fall threatened the charge for victory. Three riders around McGrory went down, but he came through the hurtling mass of bikes and bodies to sprint to the line for gold. The cycling team finished with one gold, two silver and three bronze medals. The veteran Gary Niewand, 34, won silver in the keirin event (also new to the Games) and bronze in the team sprint, adding to his bronze from 1988 and his silver from Barcelona.

On the day Simon Fairweather, of Strathalbyn in the Adelaide Hills, won the world archery championship in Poland in 1991, his future in the sport looked very bright — so bright that a sponsor signed him for a two-year contract. He was 22 and already an Olympian. What followed in fact were nine years of frustration and comparative obscurity, in which the archer struggled to regain the technique and mind-set that had taken him to that first great win. He failed to win anything much and was quickly dropped by his sponsor. His participation in the Seoul, Barcelona and Atlanta Olympics yielded no trace of his early promise; his finishing places in individual events at those three Games were 16th, 25th and 52nd respectively. After Atlanta, he seriously considered giving the sport away. That's when he met the coach who turned his career around, the Korean master coach Ki Sik Lee. Lee was the former South Korean national coach, whose teams won a total of eight gold, five silver and three bronze medals at four Olympics. The Australian Sports Commission poached him in 1997 to coach at the Australian Institute of Sport, and he quickly became Australia's secret archery weapon. The Korean, convinced of Fairweather's huge potential, persuaded him to give the sport another try — then went to work on his technique and mental approach.

In Sydney, nine years after his early brush with fame in Poland, Fairweather finally delivered, reeling off bullseye after bullseye from 70 metres in the gusty winds of Homebush Bay. He stamped his authority on the competition in the opening round, when he equalled the Olympic record for an 18-arrow match. In the final series of knock-out matches he defeated in succession a Cuban, a Russian, and then the Dutch bronze medallist Wietse van Alten. In the gold-medal shoot-out against America's Vic Wunderle, he shot nervelessly to hit two bullseyes and a nine with his opening arrows, setting up an unassailable lead. He drove a fist high in the air after he shot the final arrow to clinch a 113–106 victory. Afterwards Fairweather embraced the Korean coach, whose simple instruction before the last shot was: 'Just shoot for the gold [inner target] and the averages will carry you through.' He did. And they did.

CHAPTER ELEVEN

A creature of destiny

It is possible that some other Australian athlete — some other *athlete* — has carried as burdensome a cargo of expectations into an event as Catherine Freeman did when she lined up for her final at Stadium Australia on 25 September 2000, but no name comes readily to mind. Not Cuthbert, or Fraser, or Strickland or the schoolgirl Shane Gould in Munich. Not Elliott, or Rose, or Perkins, or even the unfortunate young Steve Holland in Montreal. Lleyton Hewitt and Greg Norman didn't come close. Bradman maybe? Not really. He was said to be misty-eyed that last time at the crease, the time he made a duck, but he didn't walk out there carrying the weight of a nation on his shoulders.

It is also possible that at some time, somewhere, there has been an explosive fusion of pride, exultation, goodwill and nationalistic fervour to compare with the one that greeted Freeman's victory on the red rubber track that night. Again, none comes to mind. Ian Thorpe's victory from behind in the final relay leg a few days earlier had been courageous, even inspirational, but it assumed no degree of deep national significance. What made Freeman's captivation of the nation such a rare and precious moment in our history was that it seemed to be ordained. As events had unfolded, and not just in the preceding week, she had assumed without intent the role of a creature of destiny. She had also become a symbol of identification with Australia's past and of reconciliation. As well as the hopes of nineteen million people, she seemed that night to be carrying the extra load of two hundred years of history. And when the night was over, she had not just won the race of her life: she had delivered one of the most powerful gestures of reconciliation in the nation's history.

All this seems an awesomely heavy agenda for an unassuming

young woman from Mackay, Queensland, whose nonchalance and charming skittishness seemed early in her career to outweigh any sense of dedication. She was always a natural who loved to run harder and jump higher than anyone else, but her biographer Adrian McGregor records that even as her prodigious talent was asserting itself at national age championship level, she was prone to eat a Mars bar just before a final, or fiddle with an errant singlet while heading flat-chat into the straight.[1] She won her first Queensland state high-jump title after throwing down her marker and declaring casually, 'I think I'll jump from here', without even measuring her mark-up. She was remarkably good at winning, less so at training. Her sports coordinator at St Joseph's Primary School, Mackay, Bessie Bauldry, remembered that an eight-year-old Freeman could easily outrun kids three years older, but at training time she was invariably hard to find. She had to be dug out of hiding places, sometimes in the library or the toilets.

In any charting of Freeman's passage towards her Olympic gold medal, several pertinent markers beckon. There was the time she was asked as a small schoolgirl why she liked athletics. 'I have a sister, Anne-Marie, who has cerebral palsy, and my mother told me that I had two good arms and two good legs, so use them,' she replied. And one day a vocational officer asked Freeman, then aged 14, what she wanted to do when she left school. 'I want to win gold medals at the Olympic Games,' she said. What about after the medals and the Olympic Games? came the question. 'Oh, I don't care,' came the reply. She set about the task of using those good legs with some resolve, surprising everyone by making Australia's 4 × 100 metres relay team that won gold at the Commonwealth Games in Auckland in 1990. She was then just 16.

But perhaps the real story had begun earlier, when Cathy's grandmother, Alice Sibley, was taken from her parents to Palm Island, a government mission 60 kilometres north of Townsville. Alice was light-skinned, the daughter of a Syrian immigrant, Willie Assad, and Dora Brook, of the Kuku-Yalanji tribe, near Tully in north Queensland. She became part of the stolen generations, one of an estimated 100,000 Aboriginal children taken from their mothers by government direction from 1930 to 1960. Alice was eight, and able to speak her tribal language fluently, when she was taken away — assigned first to foster parents and later to a mission dormitory. Years later Alice's mother, Dora, was also sent to Palm Island, but by then Alice had lost the dialect and their natural bond was lost. It was Alice Sibley, known always to Cathy as 'Nanna' Sibley, who kept the small Cathy in touch with her Aboriginality, telling her stories from the Dreamtime. Cecilia Barber, Alice's daughter and Cathy's mother, was born in the mission on Palm Island.

It was on Palm Island that Alice's second husband, Sonny Sibley, helped lead a strike against the mission superintendent in 1957, a year after the 1956 Melbourne Olympic Games — 'the Friendly Games'. He and six other ringleaders were shipped off the island in handcuffs, some of them in leg-irons, to another mission, Woorabinda, 600 kilometres south, where their families were later sent to join them. Cathy became aware from an early age of the injustices suffered by her grandmother and the Sibleys, and it seems reasonable to suggest that this knowledge contributed over a long period to what eventually became a remarkable toughness of mind and spirit.

Freeman told McGregor about the sense of shame she experienced in growing up black in the white-dominated community of Mackay, where she was born on 16 February 1973, christened Catherine Astrid Salome Freeman. 'The black people I grew up with, my family, friends and relatives, were very shy,' she said. 'They had low self-esteem. Because they were like that, I was like that too. I thought it was normal... When we walked into new places we were just totally intimidated because we felt that, being black, we had no right to be there. In a group we felt better, but individually we lacked confidence... We were too ashamed to go mixing with people in the white world. That was our mentality. I think it was a carryover from our ancestors, being institutionalised, like my nanna. That's why a lot of people stay on missions and don't venture into the mainstream.'[2]

The childhood hurts, the background of enforced family dislocation, all served to emphasise in Freeman during her teenage years a distinctive sense of identity — one that was compounded largely of pride, resilience and disciplined defiance. Freeman asserted publicly for the first time her sense of Aboriginality when she won gold in the Commonwealth Games in Victoria, Canada, in 1994. She trotted 50 metres of her victory lap after the race carrying the Aboriginal flag draped like a cape around her shoulders, then borrowed a national Australian flag from someone in the crowd to complete the run. In a sense it was a coming out, a celebration of both her Aboriginal roots and her love of her country. Afterwards she was admonished by the team's *chef de mission*, the venerable Arthur Tunstall, who was offended by the very notion of one athlete with two flags, but she also received a congratulatory message from the prime minister, Paul Keating.

Freeman's business and athletic career was guided by her partner, Nick Bideau, from 1991 until after her magnificent race against the defending champion Marie-Jose Perec at the Atlanta Olympics. Bideau, a former sportswriter and a master tactician of the track, had spotted Freeman as a raw teenager with no mental horizons, and during their seven years together he was the most significant influence in her life. It was during this period that she matured and toughened as an athlete, learned about preparation and strategy, and earned a lot of money. She and Bideau split as a couple after Atlanta, but he continued to manage her affairs — albeit a little uncomfortably — for another year, during which she won the world 400 metres championship in Athens.

By the time the Sydney Games were close, Freeman was a confident, assured young woman of 27. She had successfully defended that world title in Seville, had married the new man in her life, Alexander Bodecker, and had sacked Bideau as her manager, declaring that she was ready to handle her own affairs. This last action provoked a legal wrangle over disputed contractual arrangements, and the mood of mutual acrimony was not helped much when he asserted in an interview in the *Australian* that Aboriginal athletes had a tendency to 'self-destruct'. The timing of the whole affair, coming as it did at a critical stage in Freeman's pre-Olympic preparation, was plainly awful.

In mid-July, from her base in London, Freeman surprised many people by projecting herself into the reconciliation debate, speaking out with passion about the stolen generations and the Australian government's refusal to apologise for past treatment of Aborigines. Until then she had stayed well clear of the reach of such arguments, and if she had remained with Bideau it is most unlikely that this situation would have changed. She was her own woman now, though, and in an interview with the London *Sunday Telegraph*, she gave expression to a quiet anger she had nursed for a long time. She said it was important for black and white Australians to start accepting 'each other's history', a history she wanted a British audience to understand. She went on:

> My grandmother was taken away from her mother because she had fair skin. She didn't know her birthday, so we didn't even know how old she was when she died. You have to understand that when you have a government that is so insensitive to the issues that are close to people's hearts, that have affected so many lives for the worse, people are going to be really angry and emotional — I was so angry because they were denying that they had done anything wrong, denying that a whole generation was stolen. The fact is, parts of people's lives were taken away. They were stolen. I'll never know who my grandfather was, I didn't know who my great grandmother was. All that pain, it's very strong, and generations have felt it. There's a sense of sadness and anger, and people underestimated that — and it's why things are being said.

Her comments elicited considerable reaction, most of it sympathetic. Neither this diversion, nor the prospect of a protracted legal case with Bideau, appeared to affect the momentum of her progress towards Sydney. Through her season in Europe she was running more easily, more authoritatively. She was virtually unchallenged over the 400 metres, winning with times half a second faster than those of her nearest rivals. The spectre of Marie-Jose Perec was always close, but the double Olympic champion pulled out of every race she was supposed to run against Freeman. With Bideau gone, her coach Peter Fortune imposed more rigorous training disciplines, and she reacted positively. A valid query before the 2000 campaign began might have related to the question of who, in the absence of Bideau, would supply the steel to reinforce the planning; the answer was that it was Freeman herself. She returned to Australia in late autumn to complete her preparation for the race of her life — or what the *Sydney Morning Herald* nominated, all the way across its front page, as 'the race of our lives'.

Freeman's lighting of the cauldron was the best-kept secret of the long build-up to the Games. John Coates and Michael Knight had chosen to take the risk of adding to the pressure that inevitably accompanied favouritism and national idolatry, and their judgment was greet-

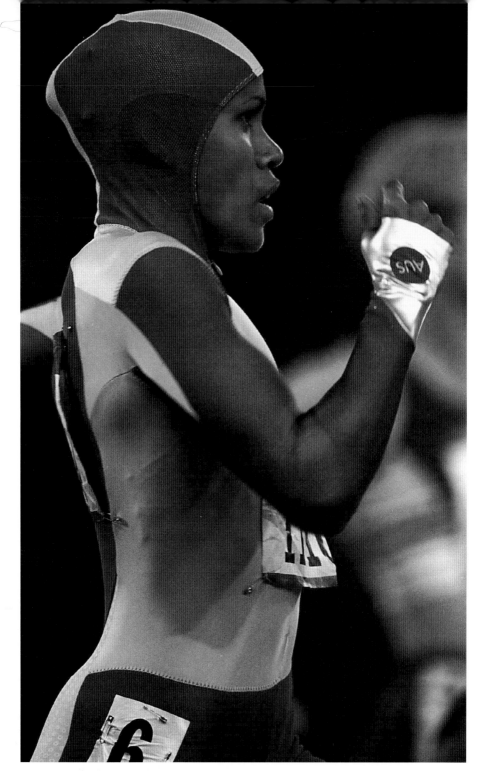

In winning the 400 metres final, Cathy Freeman established herself as the Athlete of the 2000 Games.

ed with huge public approval. The symbolism was drenching. Freeman was one of eleven Aboriginals in Australia's team, and her choice meant that the first and last athletes to handle the torch in Australia were both Aboriginals. The Games represented the 100th anniversary of women's participation in the Olympics, and a significant part of the opening ceremony was largely based on a theme of Aboriginal and non-Aboriginal reconciliation. Freeman handled the pressure of her role in the ceremony comfortably, with poise and rather more precision than the cauldron itself, which had provided cause for some tension during its interrupted ascent above the stadium.

This ability to deliver, at a time when others might be stressed, is an intriguing aspect of the Freeman make-up. She is an exquisite contradiction: delicate, anxious to please, and shy at times to the point of apparent vulnerability, but with iron in her soul. She can give the impression of being almost fragile, yet her self-confidence is boundless, and when she is striding out hard on the track she seems to be running with an arrogance that separates her from the rest. She giggles a lot and is devoid of guile; her manner is self-deprecating and at times almost excessively casual. But for all that, never very far away is a built-in discipline, a sense of resolution that reflects the remark she made to John Coates the night he wondered in Los Angeles whether the cauldron task might be too much to handle just days before her race: 'John, I like pressure. That's when I perform at my best.'

After the ceremony she confessed at a media conference that she had been embarrassed as she waited to accept the torch from Debbie Flintoff-King. *Embarrassed*? 'I really was,' she said. 'More than anything my main focus was being concerned about what other people would think about Cathy Freeman lighting the cauldron. But all that went out of my head when I got the flame. I felt the energy and emotion of all the people in the stadium.' When someone asked about her role as a link between white and Aboriginal Australia, there was diplomacy as well and good sense in her simple response: 'I like to typify any Aboriginal person in Australia who is taking advantage of the opportunities available in Australia to anybody. That is what I am about.'

While all this was happening, Marie-Jose Perec was being deeply mysterious. She had not faced Freeman in either of her world championship races, and had raced over 400 metres only once during the year. At their only meeting since Atlanta, Freeman had beaten her in Brussels. Mostly, she had become a specialist in the no-show: she had withdrawn late from no fewer than six races during the European summer. There were Garbo touches when she arrived in Sydney wearing a wig and dressed entirely in black, and immediately retreated into seclusion in a Darling Harbour hotel.

Despite a personal plea from the head of the national sports federation, Perec declined to march with the French contingent in the opening ceremony, or to join the national team in the athletes' village. She refused another request to join the track team at its training base in Narrabeen, preferring to hire a small oval in Sydney for a private work-out. On her personal website she complained of persecution, and betrayed real fears about the impending 400 metres showdown with the message: 'I'm freaking out.' Freeman told questioning reporters: 'I don't know what's been happening with her. I saw her on the TV when she arrived at the airport and ran away, and that's her prerogative if she wants privacy. I hope you have been treating her nicely and with respect. I would like her to be happy, healthy and comfortable in my country.' Perec, a proud woman and a diva of the track, clearly never intended to expose herself to the risk of defeat in Sydney. Her final action in leaving town suddenly for Paris on the eve of the heats, without ever joining the French team, confirmed what most insiders were well aware of: that the 400 metres crown had long passed from her to Cathy.

Eleven nights after she lit the cauldron, Freeman fulfilled the mission that had absorbed her throughout her running life. She won the 400 metres Olympic final, and in doing so she established herself unquestionably as the Athlete of the 2000 Games. She also made all kinds of dents in history. Not since Ralph Doubell equalled the world record over 800 metres in Mexico City in 1968 had an Australian won an Olympic race on the flat. Not since Betty Cuthbert in 1964 had a woman done so — and there was symmetry in the knowledge that Cuthbert, an enduring heroine of Olympic folklore, had also won over 400 metres. Cathy Freeman's victory that night made her the first Aboriginal ever to win individual gold at the Games, and the hundredth gold medallist in the nation's Olympic history. This blessed coincidence of arithmetic, as well as the almost surreal quality of two evenings — that of the victory, and that of the opening ceremony — provoked this writer to remark in the *Australian* the following morning: 'It is as if Cathy Freeman was born for these Olympic Games.' There surely had to have been a master script somewhere.

Clad in a full-length hooded lycra bodysuit of silver, green and gold — there was a touch of the Phantom about it, or maybe Spiderwoman — Freeman lined up in lane six for the big race, as the commentator Bruce McAvaney conveyed the seriousness of the occasion: 'We're all on the edge of our seats ... it's fate of a nation time.' She was fourth out of the blocks, with the South African beside her, Heide Seyerling, opening more explosively. Sometime after the 100-metre mark McAvaney was cautious, seeming to prepare the stadium crowd, as well as millions of TV viewers, for the unthinkable: 'She's got a lot of work to do.' She did the work, and looked utterly relaxed as she settled into her flowing, ground-devouring stride (2.33 metres a time) along the back straight. On the bend Lorraine Graham (Jamaica) looked poised to pounce on Freeman, with Katherine Merry (Britain) not far behind. She held her nerve, though; it still wasn't time to attack hard — she needed all her reserves for the final straight. Off the bend she began to catapult herself clear of her rivals. She grimaced, she dug deep, and with each huge stride over the last 50 metres she moved further ahead. Halfway down the straight the noise from the 112,524 people in the stadium was deafening; it grew to another level, avalanche level, as she crossed the line in 49.11 seconds to win from Graham and Merry.

The important indicator of Freeman's dominance was not just the remarkable winning margin of three metres — a full half-second. It was the knowledge that the silver and bronze medallists, as well as the fourth runner, Donna Fraser from Britain, had all run personal-best times, with the first five recording less than 50 seconds. Freeman was outside the time she ran in Atlanta, but nobody cared. What was clear was that if anybody in the field had been able to run faster, she would have done so too.

When it was over, when she was home, free of that awful ballast of a nation's hopes, there were no emotions to show. No hugs, no kisses, no waves — not yet. Her face remained sombre, almost mask-like, as she peeled off her hood, shook her head free, then continued to sit slumped on the track, her mind somewhere else, for what seemed an age. The impression was of a lone, stone sculpture. She looked quite drained. Sitting there in a kind of daze, blinking after a time, she could have been a survivor from a train wreck rather than the fresh heroine of a nation. It had been a punishing ordeal, that race and the journey towards it, and this was recovery time. This was time to comprehend, to allow sheer relief gently to invade her mind and body. Her state of stillness, her process of transformation, in fact occupied all of three minutes. Then suddenly, with the din intensifying all around her, she

As Cathy Freeman sat, head bowed, on the running track after the race, the impression was of a lone, stone sculpture.

Cathy Freeman, adorned in the Australian and Aboriginal flags, acknowledges the crowd as she heads around the arena in a victory lap.

was back with us — her face split wide by that great grin, her signature grin. She was ready to wave to friends, to her mother and family, to applaud the masses that had turned out to watch. She was ready for a joyous victory lap.

That victory lap was her powerful declaration on reconciliation. One writer, Michael Gordon, described it as 'a defining moment in the forging of a national identity that celebrates the unique heritage, culture and contribution of the nation's first people'.[3] Not since the Americans

Tommy Smith and John Carlos gave their gloved 'black power' salute in Mexico City in 1968 had such a strong statement been made on race at the Olympics. Theirs had been a gesture of defiance. Cathy Freeman's was one of inclusiveness, of mutuality, an embrace of old and new Australia. She kicked off her red, black and yellow shoes and headed around the arena, her body adorned with knotted Australian and Aboriginal flags. She walked, jogged, even danced a barefoot jig. When she had carried the two flags six years before, she had been reprimanded. Now there was just a joyous, loving reception. From the time her race ended, she had been accorded what might well have qualified as the longest standing ovation in sports history.

Later, after Kevan Gosper had presented her with her gold medal, she talked about her feelings after the race. 'When you have dreamt something for so long and it finally happens, it really spins you out,' she said. 'It turns your world around and upside down. I could feel the crowd totally over me, all around me. I felt everyone's emotions being absorbed into every pore of my body. I just had to sit down and try to make myself feel normal and comfortable. I have dreamt of this since I was a little girl — I'm still a little girl, and I suppose I will have to grow up sometime.' A British reporter asked if she thought the symbolism of the two flags and what she had achieved could have an effect on reconciliation. She did not have to ponder: 'I'm sure what's happened tonight and what I symbolise will make a difference to a lot of people's attitudes... All I know is I've made a lot of people happy from all kinds of backgrounds who call Australia home. And I'm happy.'

Even as Cathy Freeman was making people happy that night, provoking warm feelings about the union of old and new Australia, a representative of the new was distinguishing herself on the same arena. Tatiana Grigorieva, 24, blonde and pony-tailed, had been born in St Petersburg, Russia, had immigrated to Australia in 1996, and suddenly that night there she was — not just giving the performance of her life but imparting a dimension of theatre to the brand-new women's pole-vault competition. Before her great lunges into the air, she flirted with an already euphoric, now suddenly infatuated crowd — first putting her fingers to her lips to demand silence from all those throats as she contemplated her approach, then later signalling that she wanted all the noise they could give her. Shamelessly and charmingly, she milked the gallery's emotions, fed off them — and the chemistry of the mutual rapport yielded superb results. She soared 4.55 metres, higher than she ever had before, to win the silver medal behind the US world champion and record-holder Tracy Dragila. At one stage Grigorieva asked gamely

Tatiana Grigorieva lunges for the bar in the pole vault.

Soaring 4.55 metres, Tatiana Grigorieva took the silver medal in the pole vault, behind Tracey Dragila of the United States.

for the bar to be lifted to world-record level. She failed, but only Dragila (4.60 metres) managed to catapult herself higher than she did.

Grigorieva, 178 centimetres tall and weighing 65 kilograms, had switched from hurdling to the pole vault three years earlier, and after an unimpressive year she didn't look to be a serious Olympic contender. At the world championships in 1999 she had managed 4.45 metres to come within 15 centimetres of the world record, but she had struggled all through the 2000 season, failing to better 4.30 metres. Her commitment was extreme, but when she wasn't vaulting she was in some demand as a photographic model. Like a number of other members of the team, she had posed nude for a publication called *The Sydney Dream*, which went on sale just before the Games. Her husband, Viktor Tchistiakov, did well to finish equal fifth (with team-mate Dmitri Markov) in the men's pole vault. Two sad, early eliminations from that competition were Sergei Bubka, 36, the world record-holder and outstanding competitor of his generation, and Emma George, the Australian pioneer and former world record-holder, who had cleared 4.60 metres.

Australia's other silver medal in athletics came from the self-confessed party animal of the team, Jai Taurima, who let it be widely known that he smoked a pack of cigarettes a day, loved a drink and never went to bed before midnight. Taurima, who sported a Superman tattoo on his left arm, behaved in the long jump as if he really was invincible, hurling himself 8.49 metres to break the Australian record and look for a time to be the likely gold medallist. He also enjoyed himself mightily. He played to the crowd as Grigorieva had done, gesticulating often with both arms high to rev up the roars that accompanied each charge along the runway. The Cuban world champion Ivan Pedroso finally spoiled his party, reaching 8.55 metres and confronting him with the challenge of beating that mark with his last leap. Taurima could manage only 8.28 metres, but had the huge satisfaction of knowing that he had become only the third Australian in history to win a long-jump medal. (The others were Theo Bruce, London 1948, silver; Gary Honey, Los Angeles 1984, silver.)

As always, there was heartbreak for some. Jane Saville was leading the 20 kilometres walk and about to enter the Olympic Stadium, with the finish line only 150 metres away, when she was disqualified. The Italian judge Lamberto Bacchi stepped into her path and held up a card that signified she had just committed a third breach of the rules on 'lifting' — and thus was out. It was a cruel moment, reminiscent of the cyclist Shane Kelly's pedal mishap in Atlanta. Saville, who had seemed set to become Australia's first walk gold medallist of either sex ever, was at first disbelieving, then distraught, then so embarrassed that she ran from the stadium. But afterwards she was remarkably controlled and gracious. 'It's a subjective sport,' she said, 'and anyway I'm in good

In the new Olympic sport of triathlon, Michellie Jones won silver.

company' — a reference to the fact that the Chinese world champion, Liu Hongyu, had also been disqualified. There was anguish too when the women's 4 × 100 metres relay team spilled a baton in a botched change between Elly Hutton and Lauren Hewitt in the first round. Overall, though, the three medals won represented Australia's best athletic performance at a non-boycott Olympics since 1968.

In acknowledgment of the centenary being celebrated, and the participation of 4069 women (38.2 per cent of the total, against 34 per cent in Atlanta), some commentators dubbed these the Games of the Dames. Certainly Australian women turned in some magnificent performances. Away from the swimming pool (where four out of five championships went to the men), female competitors won six of the remaining eleven gold medals. Apart from the individual wins by Freeman and the taekwondo exponent Lauren Burns, Australian women's teams had victories in the water polo, beach volleyball, hockey and 470 sailing. The basketball team, the Opals, didn't drop a match on their way to the final match against the overwhelming favourites, United States. Their silver medal made them the most successful Australian basketball team, male or female, in Games history, and the performance of their standout player, Lauren Jackson, 19, caused experts to nominate her as the best young basketballer in the world. The softball women won six of seven games, defeating the United States and China, to reach the semi-final round, and finished with their second bronze medal in two Olympics. Triathlon, like taekwondo, was introduced to the Olympic program at these Games, and Michellie Jones took silver behind Switzerland's Brigitte McMahon. Kate Slatter, a gold medallist from Atlanta, teamed with Rachael Taylor to win silver in the coxless pairs rowing, and the tiny Maria Peklik collected Australia's first medal in judo since 1964 when she won bronze in the 52–57-kilogram division.

Water polo for men has been an Olympic sport since 1900. It took another century for the women's game to be admitted to the Olympic program, and that initiative owed much to the determined campaigning of Australian and American women players. The struggle to persuade the sport's governing body, the *Federation Internationale de Natation* (FINA), and the IOC to admit the sport to the Games began in the 1980s, but both bodies were steadfastly, emphatically, against it. This wasn't due to rampant misogyny, although there was undoubtedly some of that about in the higher reaches of international sport. Water polo can be a tough, very physical sport, and a prevailing view among senior administrators seemed to be that matches between women had the potential to be a little too unladylike for the Olympic Games.

After lobbying campaigns for the admission of the sport for the 1984, 1988, 1992 and 1996 Games had all successively failed, the Australian team captain, Debbie Watson, retired in despair. Then in

1997, when it was learned that a group of high-ranking FINA delegates were due to arrive at Sydney airport, the Australian players tried a radical approach to campaigning. The FINA people disembarked to be confronted by the sight of about thirty lissome young women — all dressed only in swimsuits, all of them brandishing placards and demanding that the barriers to the Olympics be taken down. They had been rounded up at short notice by the team's goalkeeper, Liz Weekes, who explained much later: 'At times it was like bashing our heads against a brick wall. But we had a dream, and we weren't going to let anyone stand in our way.' This

Rowers Rachel Taylor (left) and Kate Slatter won silver in the coxless pairs.

Taryn Woods looks for a team-mate to pass the ball to in one of the heats in the water polo competition.

unconventional protest received widespread media coverage and was reinforced by support and diplomacy from John Coates. An unexpected ally turned out to be IOC president Juan Antonio Samaranch, who happened to be pursuing his own campaign to change the male, sexist culture of the Olympic movement. Later the same year it was announced that women's water polo would be added to the program for the Sydney Games. Debbie Watson's first reaction to this news was that she couldn't believe it; her second was to come out of retirement.

It was clear from the opening matches that women's water polo was not a dainty sport. In Australia's first-round clash with Kazakhstan, which the home side won 9–2, swimsuits were routinely ripped apart and players were kicked, belted in the face and dunked underwater for long periods. One Australian, Taryn Woods, 25, was held below the surface for so long that she pushed her hand in the air like a submarine

periscope, undoubtedly to remind the referee that she was still down there. Appropriately enough, it was the campaigning nations Australia and the United States that lined up against each other for the final in front of 15,000 people at the Aquatic Centre. The Australians, who had beaten Russia in the semi-final, came from behind twice against the Americans after some freakish saves by Liz Weekes, 29, to be level at the three-quarter break. Later, with 1.2 seconds left to play, Yvette Higgins, 22, unleashed an incredible left-handed shot from long range — one that tore through the hands of US defenders, past the grasping goalie, into the back of the net. Confusion followed, then a short-lived protest by the Americans, who claimed that the match had finished before the shot was taken. Then it was official: Australia had beaten the powerful US team 4–3. 'This is a fairytale ending for me,' said Watson, the team veteran at 34. 'It's as if my mum wrote the script.'

The victorious Australian water polo team during time out.

Among all the venues at Sydney's Olympics, among all the 104 years of Olympic history, nothing compared with the beach volleyball stadium at Bondi. It was sport dressed up as a party, Club Med with gold medals. The sport had been introduced to the Olympics, on 16,000 tonnes of artificial sand a long way from any ocean, at the Atlanta Games four years earlier — and its impact at the time was muted. This time, alongside the Pacific on the sands of the most famous beach in the nation, it evoked the boisterous spirit of these happiest Games ever. The action itself, in a sport that demands extreme fitness, courage and skill, was riveting — lithe, tanned bodies leaping, lunging, diving, smashing, and sometimes finally collapsing — and it was watched throughout in

The power play of Natalie Cook and Kerri Pottharst in the beach volleyball kept spectators enthralled at Bondi.

disciplined hush. But between plays, the gallery of 10,000 in the tempo-rary stadium bopped, stomped, executed slow-motion Mexican waves to the unlikely strains of 'Swan Lake', danced the 'Macarena', and bounced along with 'Zorba the Greek'. The music was thunderous — Queen, Village People, Men at Work, and Tchaikovsky for the odd change of pace — and the reception raucous. A comic MC who called himself Dave the Lifesaver seemed to be in charge, but he had competition from a squad of swimwear models and an enormous Brazilian cheerleader in a white wig. Nowhere was the fun of the Games more undiluted than at the beach volleyball. It was hard afterwards to reconcile that success with the recollection that, during Sydney's season of discontent 18 months earlier, some Bondi protesters had been prepared to lie down in front of bulldozers to prevent an 'outrageous act of desecration'.

At Atlanta four years before, Natalie Cook and Kerri Pottharst had won bronze. It was a happy enough result, but they wanted gold. They split up, tried themselves with other partners, then re-formed a year before the Games. They employed a full-time coach, hired a physi-cal trainer, then took on an American 'success' coach, Kurek Ashley. As part of Ashley's doctrine of self-belief, they once even walked over burning coals. Before the Games they adopted another of his philoso-phies, 'thinking gold', and surrounded themselves in their team living quarters with gold objects — even down to toothbrushes. They needed some self-belief in the final: their opponents, Brazil's Adriana Behar and Shelda Bede, were ranked number one in the world, and had won more tournaments, including world championships, than any other pair ever. In a dozen matches against them, Cook, 25, and Pottharst, 35, had won only twice. This time, though, they produced a stunning exhibition of power volleyball to overcome the Brazilians in straight sets.

The Australian pair, aided by a 'no guts, no glory' philosophy that added up to a commitment to take risks, clawed back from a deficit in each set. They were down 6–10 in the first, saving two set points to even the score at 11-all before Cook sent across a crushing, angled ace. It hit the net, wobbled, landed on the right side of the net, settled the set and dented the confidence of the Brazilians. Pottharst unleashed some screaming serves in both sets, the fourth of them, at 85 kilometres an hour, the fastest in the short history of Olympic beach volleyball.

Australia's gold-medal beach volleyball players Cook and Pottharst embrace after their thrilling final against the Brazilians.

The Brazilians collected themselves enough to hold a 10–8 lead in the second set, but the Australian pair, powering all the way on a wave of emotion from the crowd, came back to win the next three points. At match point, 11–10, Pottharst served, Bede dug the ball up, and Behar gambled by slamming for the line. It landed just wide and the match was over. Pottharst remained prostrate with her head buried in her arms in the sand, apparently in emotional overload. 'I just lost it,' she explained afterwards. 'I couldn't believe our dream for so long had come true.' The Brazilians, idolised in their country, were shattered, choking on tears. 'We are warriors who lost the war,' said Behar simply. And on the beach at Bondi the party raged on, and on.

In the twenty years since women's hockey was introduced to the Olympic program, Australia is the only nation to have won the gold medal more than once. At Homebush Bay the Hockeyroos won back-to-back Olympic gold, and scored Australia's third victory in four Games. In doing so they confirmed their status as the finest women's hockey team ever, and in fact as one of the greatest teams ever to have represented Australia in any sport. Their 3–1 victory against Argentina in the final represented a fitting farewell for two of the most significant Australians in the sport: Rechelle Hawkes and Ric Charlesworth. Hawkes, a member of the winning 1988 and 1996 Olympic teams and the only survivor from the Seoul gold-medal side, joined Dawn Fraser and Andrew Hoy as a member of the exclusive band of people who have won gold at three separate Olympics. Like Cathy Freeman, during these Games she had become a symbol as well as a champion: two weeks earlier she had sworn an oath of behalf of all competitors to uphold the values of sport. Charlesworth, himself a four-time Olympian, had coached the side to nine major international trophies during his eight-year term. Under him, the Hockeyroos had developed into the world's fittest team. Their flair and skill had always been there, but it was Charlesworth who instilled the work ethic, discipline and determination that separated them from all the rest.

Such was the quality of those Hockeyroos that they came to be compared with some of the most famous Australian teams in history — such as Don Bradman's 1948 Invincibles, John Bertrand's 1983 America's Cup crew, the 1984 Wallabies, winners of rugby's coveted grand slam, and rowing's Oarsome Foursome.[4] Their record was certainly daunting. Over 12 years, culminating in their gold-medal series in Sydney, the women had won three out of four Olympic tournaments, had clinched two World Cups, five Champions Trophies and won the first Commonwealth Games title. And they had been unbeaten in 18 consecutive Olympic Games matches. The team had had some changes along the way, but nine members of the 2000 team were already gold medallists from Atlanta: Alyson Annan, 27, Lisa Carruthers, 30, Renita Garard, 28, Juliet Haslam, 31, Rechelle Hawkes, 33, Clover Maitland, 28, Jenny Morris, 28, Katrina Powell, 28, and Kate Starre, 29.

The 16 Hockeyroos played fast, selfless, attacking hockey

throughout the tournament, defeating Great Britain 2–1, drawing 1–1 with Spain, downing Korea 3–0 and Argentina 3–1 in the preliminary rounds, then outscoring New Zealand, the Netherlands and China by a total of 13–1. In the tenth minute of play in the final, Annan, the finest player in the finest team, chipped a pass over the Argentinian goalkeeper's head into the net. A clever decoy run from the half-back Haslam resulted in another first-half goal, and Morris virtually assured Australia of the gold medal soon after the interval when she nailed a goal from a penalty corner to make it 3–0. Argentina scored with twenty minutes to go, but it was academic. They had vowed before the match to 'fight like lions' but hadn't been allowed even to growl. Afterwards Hawkes

In winning gold in Sydney, the Hockeyroos confirmed their status as the best women's hockey team ever.

Alyson Annan, 'the finest player in the finest team'.

tossed her stick into the crowd, Maurice Greene style, and announced her retirement, explaining: 'It's time to go. I just don't want to train any more.' Charlesworth, also retiring, said his goodbyes privately to the team. 'He was close to tears,' said Annan afterwards. 'That was enough to have us in tears.'

Lauren Burns, 26, of Melbourne, who won a gold medal in the kicking, punching sport of taekwondo, was never a natural. The child of showbiz parents, 1960s rock star Ronnie Burns and dancer Maggie Stewart, she played little sport early and had minimum urge or encouragement to do so. Hers was an alternative childhood. At the age of 14 she tagged along with her brother Michael to a taekwondo class, was not overly impressed, but returned the next week, and the next — much to the surprise of her family. 'We expected her to get hit in the face and come home crying,' Ronnie Burns explained after his daughter's win in the under-49 kilogram class. 'We thought she wouldn't stick at it, but she proved us all wrong.' Burns stuck at it — 'through determination, inner resolve, never natural talent,' she still insists — so emphatically that she decided to become the best woman of her weight in the sport. To achieve that end she elected to train in Korea — where the sport originated twenty centuries ago as a form of martial arts — under the leading coach Jin Jae Jeong. Burns, a student of natural medicine, deferred her studies for a year to concentrate on preparation for the introduction of the ancient discipline to the Olympic Games.

Along the way, Burns acquired an inner strength and confidence. Her mantra, even against intimidating opponents who were stronger and more skilled, became: 'I don't care whether you're better than me technically, I can beat you. We both have two arms and two legs…the only difference is in the head. I can beat you there.' At the Olympics, where she shed six kilograms to make the weight, she defeated opponents from Chinese Taipei and Denmark to reach the final against Cuba's Urbia Melendez Rodriguez — which she won 4–2. Suddenly she was Australia's newest heroine, in arguably the Games' oldest sport. Her team-mate Daniel Trenton did well, scoring three wins and a loss to take silver in his division.

When Australian crews won both the women's and men's 470 class sailing gold medals on Sydney Harbour, some interesting history was clocked up. Only once before had Australian sailors won two gold medals on the same day — at the 1972 Games events at Kiel, on the Baltic coast. The women — Jenny Armstrong, 29, and Belinda Stowell, 30 — were the first to win in Sydney, and when their craft crossed the finish line, its spinnaker emblazoned with the Australian flag, they became the first Australians of their gender ever to win a sailing medal at the Olympic Games. Theirs was in fact the first sailing gold medal Australia had won in 28 years, since those same 1972 Olympics. The victory also took Australia's gold-medal tally for the 2000 Games to fourteen, breaking the record that had been set in Melbourne in 1956.

In front of a huge flotilla of spectator craft and thousands of people lining the foreshores, Armstrong and Stowell finished 37 seconds ahead of Denmark. Two passing Manly ferries honked their sirens, and the entire following fleet erupted into a cacophony of horns and hooters. The ferry *Queenscliff* stopped as its passengers lined the decks to cheer the winners. Olympic events are usually sailed so far offshore that they possess no sense of intimacy, but this was different: passing Bradley's Head, Stowell had been able to identify a cluster of family members after she heard one of them roar, 'Go, you good thing.' When the final began, the two women had already won three races and needed only a top ten finish in the strong winds to secure gold. Throughout the series they had been very fast downwind, and the final was no exception. After their first spinnaker run they were second behind China, and one leg later had hit the front, where they stayed. It was a multicultural triumph. Stowell, a former swimmer, was born in Zimbabwe. Armstrong came from New Zealand and sailed for that country in the 1992 Olympics. She and their coach, Victor Kovalenko, both became Australian citizens in the lead-up to the Games.

A little over an hour after Armstrong and Stowell sailed into history, their 470-class male counterparts, Tom King and Mark Turnbull, won more gold. King, 27, and Turnbull, 26, who went into the Olympics as reigning world champions, knew that in the final of the eleven-race series they needed only to finish within five places of the American craft, crewed by Paul Foerster and Bob Merrick, to guarantee a win. The two boats circled each other warily and the United States got away better. At the first mark the Americans led, with the Australians buried deep in the fleet. On the next, downwind, the Australians showed their customary speed under spinnaker, and moved up to fifth behind the United States. At the top mark, when the Australians were third, behind the US and Ukraine, their tactic was simply to stay out of trouble. On the last windward leg the Australians crossed once in front of the Americans but didn't fight to stay there. They wound up slicing across the line in second place to the United States — with the gold secure. Afterwards, amid the tooting of a congestion of spectator craft, they hoisted an Australian flag. A hero of the 470s' day of triumph was the Ukrainian coach Victor Kovalenko, who had trained both the men's and the women's crews intensively, meticulously, for three years. King summed up the feelings of all: 'We are where we are because of him.'

After its strong showing in Atlanta (six medals, two of them gold), the rowing team expected to perform at least as well at home, but had to be content with three silver medals (men's eights, lightweight coxless fours and women's coxless pairs) and two bronze (coxless pairs and coxless fours). Oarsome Foursome survivors Mike McKay and James Tomkins took home silver and bronze respectively from the coxed eight and coxless pairs, and the team extracted some satisfaction from the knowledge that ten out of twelve crews had reached finals. Also at the Penrith regatta centre, Australia won medals in the kayak events — Andrew Trim and Daniel Collins silver in the men's K2 500 metres, and Katrin Borchert bronze in the women's K1 500 metres.

After a medal drought of 76 years — since the high diver Dick Eve won gold in 1924 — Australia won two diving medals within an hour at the Sydney Aquatic Centre, both in the new synchronised events. First Loudy Tourky, 21, and Rebecca Gilmore, 21, teamed to take bronze in the women's synchronised 10-metre platform event, then the 3-metre

At the Penrith regatta centre Daniel Collins (left) and Andrew Trim won silver in the K2 500 metres.

springboard pair, Dean Pullar, 27, and Robert Newbery, 21, combined to finish third behind the diving giants United States and Mexico. On the same program the Chinese girl Fu Mingxia, 23, joined the ranks of diving's immortals by winning her fourth gold medal. Only the Americans Greg Louganis and Pat McCormick had performed that feat.

Six athletes were stripped of medals after recording positive drug tests, and for five of them nobody felt much sympathy. The exception was the tiny Romanian gymnast Andreea Raducan, 16, the victim of a foolish team doctor and drug prosecution policy that quite properly doesn't tolerate the notion of mitigating circumstances. Raducan, all 37 kilograms and 147 centimetres of her, won the gold medal in the all-round individual event, then tested positive to the banned stimulant

Katrin Borchert brought home the bronze in the women's K1 500 metres.

Loudy Tourky (left) and Rebecca Gilmore took bronze in the women's synchronised 10-metre platform event.

Robert Newbery (left) and Dean Pullar finished third behind the United States and Mexico in the 3-metre springboard event.

Romanian gymnast Andreea Raducan was the victim of a foolish team doctor and a tough drug prosecution policy. She had won gold in the all-round individual event, but was stripped of it because she had been given pills for a cold.

pseudoephedrine — a substance contained in a couple of cold tablets fed to her by a doctor who was consequently expelled from the Sydney Games and Athens 2004. She explained later: 'I took a pill for a cold. It didn't help me. On the contrary it made me dizzy.' The Court of Arbitration for Sport rejected an appeal against the IOC's automatic disqualification. Unmoved by such factors as her age, weight, reliance on the team doctor and the knowledge that the drug had not enhanced her performance, it ruled that 'the Anti-Doping Code must be enforced without compromise'. Even the IOC's drug chief, Prince Alexandre de Merode, was embarrassed by the affair, declaring that the doctor had been responsible, not the athlete. Raducan was allowed to keep medals she won in two events for which she did not test positive: a team gold and an individual silver in the women's vault.

While it was easy to feel sorry for Raducan, the confiscation of other medals after positive drug tests evoked feelings of disgust and relief that the culprits had been caught. To nobody's great surprise, they included three Bulgarian weightlifters — Izabela Dragneva, Ivan Ivanov and Sevdalin Minchev, who were stripped of gold, silver and bronze respectively after they all tested positive to diuretic furosemide. A couple of other Bulgarian lifters had already been snared by pre-Games tests in the athletes' village. One wrestler, the German Alexander Leipold, who cheated with nandrolene, had his gold medal taken away after an IOC Medical Commission hearing in Lausanne two weeks after the Games. The highest-profile drug offender at the Games was C. J. Hunter, world shot-put champion and husband of the greatest woman athlete in the world, Marion Jones. Hunter, who tested positive four times during the year for the banned steroid nandrolene, withdrew as a competitor on the eve of the Games, citing a bad knee, but remained accredited as a coach. When he sought to attribute his excessive doses of nandrolene — in one case a thousand times the legal limit — to nutritional iron supplements, IOC heavyweight Dick Pound remarked dryly: 'He'd have to be pretty rusty.' To her everlasting credit, Jones rose above the scandal.

Overall the drug testing program at the Games, which saw the introduction of combined blood and urine tests for EPO (erythropoietin), worked effectively. The combination of out-of-competition and EPO testing from 2 September deterred a number of chosen athletes, including a reported 27 from China, from attending the Games. More than 400 athletes were tested before the Games and 2788 during them, and 11 were disqualified after testing positive.

At the end of Sydney's Games, the Happy Games, George Vecsey, the *New York Times* columnist, offered this judgment: 'The Games were great, but the Australians were greater, and they bought a whole lot of time for the survival of the Olympic Games.' Certainly between them the athletes, the crowds, the volunteers and the mood contributed much to the healing of an Olympic movement that was suffering badly from self-inflicted wounds. What they also managed to do, with unmatched exuberance, was turn on the greatest marathon of revelry the nation had ever seen.

Appropriately enough, after 17 days it all ended with a closing ceremony that was really an excuse for a garish, unapologetic, raucously unabashed party. After the entry of the 199 flag-bearers (including Ian Thorpe for Australia, Steven Redgrave for Britain, Inge de Bruijn for The Netherlands) and the storming of the arena by 3500 athletes, the formal part did not last long. Even Samaranch showed a touch of self-deprecating humour. 'Seven years ago, I said: 'And the winner is — Syd-er-ney.'' Well, what can I say now? Maybe, with my Spanish accent, Aussie, Aussie, Aussie!' He paused, and from around the entire stadium came the so-familiar response: 'Oi! Oi! Oi!' He resumed: 'These are my last Games as IOC president. They could not have been better. Therefore I am proud and happy to proclaim that you presented to the world the best Olympic Games ever.' It was an accolade that had been notably absent in Atlanta. Michael Knight told the athletes: 'You have given us the time of our lives and left us with memories to last a lifetime.' Samaranch presented the Olympic Orders in Gold that had caused some controversy — to Knight 'for a perfect organisation' and to John Coates 'for fulfilling the promise of these being the Athletes' Games' — and announced that the IOC's Olympic Cup would go to the people of Sydney. The ceremonial Olympic flag was handed over to the mayor of Athens, 'Hero Girl' Nikki Webster sang 'We'll be One' high on a platform beneath the cauldron, and, as she finished, the flame that had been burning throughout the Games dimmed and died. At that exact time, an RAAF F-111 thundered overhead, just 160 metres above the cauldron, a plume of flame from its afterburner lighting up the night sky. It was as if the Olympic flame had been snatched and carried away. There was a huge, communal sigh, maybe just of awe, maybe of sadness provoked by the knowledge that the spell that had been cast over Sydney was on its way out.

Then came the real party, a David Atkins indulgence that amounted largely to a kaleidoscope of kitsch, as well as a thumping, over-the-top send-up. Clichés were rampant. Kylie Minogue sat astride

Paul Hogan aboard the huge Crocodile Dundee hat that served as a float during the closing ceremony.

an enormous thong, hauled by a hundred lifesavers, Elle Macpherson emerged from a large camera, Greg Norman teed off from atop a shark covered in Gladwrap, Paul Hogan shaved with *that* knife aboard a huge Crocodile Dundee hat. Jimmy Barnes sang from the grill of a giant barbecue, and was buzzed by a huge blowfly as he growled his way through 'Working Class Man'. There were prawns on bikes, lizards on unicycles, water buffaloes on scooters, kewpie dolls, drag queens aboard the bus from *Priscilla: Queen of the Desert*, Bananas in Pyjamas, stilt-walkers with Hills Hoists on their backs. In glitzy homage to the film *Strictly Ballroom*, 960 couples in fluorescent costumes whirled through laps of samba, tango and sheer jive to the beat of John Paul Young singing 'Love Is in the Air'. When Slim Dusty sang 'Waltzing Matilda', the whole

255

stadium joined in. And, despite the irreverence and extravagance, the thematic undertone of reconciliation that had permeated the opening ceremony was never too far away. It was there in the Aboriginal flags and 'sorry' statements adorning the clothing of some of the entertainers. But it was asserted most in the hard-edged lyrics of message songs from the groups Yothu Yindi and Midnight Oil.

Finally, to the strains of Wagner and Mahler, came an enormous fireworks display that began at the stadium and moved 14 kilometres down the Parramatta River to Sydney Harbour. The audience in the stadium watched its progress on the giant screens, then began to drift away. The cauldron was dark. The show was over. There was nothing left now but the memories.

Bondi lifesavers were part of the exuberant, over-the-top kaleidoscope of kitsch that was the closing ceremony.

After the Games were over

In Moscow in July 2001 Juan Antonio Samaranch relinquished the presidency of the International Olympic Committee, which he had led for exactly twenty years. He was one day away from his 81st birthday, and may have stayed a four-year term too long in the job, but his achievements were considerable. He had inherited the leadership of the Olympic movement from the benign Irishman Lord Killanin at a difficult time. The three most recent Games until then — Munich (1972), Montreal (1976) and Moscow (1980) — had done little to enhance the image of the Olympics. Boycotts abounded. Cold War politics dominated sport, the threat of terrorism had spooked the movement since Munich, drug-taking was largely unchecked (particularly in Eastern Europe). South Africa was an outcast. Aggressive amateurism reigned, to the degree that it was distorting the spirit of Olympism. The cost of staging an Olympics was daunting enough to frighten off most potential host cities. The bad news didn't end there. Through its 85 years of existence, through six presidents (including the revered creator of the modern Olympic Games, Pierre de Coubertin), women had been virtually ignored — both as athletes and administrators. The IOC, while not broke, didn't have the money it needed to assert authority. It had been run in the kitchen-table style that had characterised amateur sport for many years.

What the Olympic movement had needed was a revolution, and Samaranch had supplied one: quietly, diplomatically. These are some of the things that happened under his regime. Amateurism died, and with it, a great deal of hypocrisy. Women's participation in the Olympics increased to 38.2 per cent. The boycotts ceased (after one tit-for-tat exercise in Los Angeles in 1984). The movement prospered, with world-

In July 2001 Juan Antonio Samaranch relinquished the presidency of the IOC, a position he had held for 20 years.

wide sponsorships and huge television audiences. The IOC was run like the giant corporation it became. Far from being financially fearful of holding the Games, prospective host cities jostled to bid for the privilege. Athletes were given a role in running the movement through the Athletes' Commission and the IOC itself. The IOC led the way in tackling the problem of drugs in sport.

If Samaranch had stepped down in 1997, he would probably have been remembered as a great reformer. But vanity intervened. He wanted to be in charge of the movement during the change of centuries, just as Coubertin had been. Future historians will have to weigh the many achievements of Samaranch against the fact that under his watch the IOC was stained by the 1999 Salt Lake City corruption scandal, an affair that resulted in the forced departure of ten members. In any final assessment, though, he ought to win some credit for the vigorous manner in which he tackled the consequential process of reform for both host-city bidding and IOC membership.

The man who took over as president was Jacques Rogge, 59, an orthopaedic surgeon and former Olympic sailor (1968, 1972, 1976) and rugby player from Belgium. He became the eighth leader in the IOC's 107-year-old history, and the second Belgian. (The first, Count Henri Baillet-Latour, had been in charge from 1925 to 1942.) Rogge was one of five candidates. The others were: Dick Pound, 59, a Canadian lawyer and Olympic swimmer; Anita DeFrantz, 48, an American former Olympic bronze-medal rower; Pal Schmidt, 59, a Hungarian diplomat and twice Olympic gold-medal fencer; and Kim Un-Yong, 70, a South Korean businessman and government adviser whose son had been provided with a mock job with the help of the Salt Lake City bid committee. Kevan Gosper, who had withdrawn from the presidential race, was reprimanded by the IOC's ethics commission for having endorsed the candidature of Pound. Rogge made it clear from the start that his would be a different style, insisting that he would not stay at a Salt Lake City hotel during the 2002 Olympic Games. He lived inside the athletes' village.

The new IOC president Jacques Rogge, a former Olympic sailor from Belgium. (News Ltd)

At the same meeting of the IOC in Moscow, John Coates became a member under the new rules that allowed the admission of up to 15 presidents of national Olympic committees. Two months earlier, in May 2001, he had been elected president of the AOC for another four years. His IOC nomination had been proposed to the executive board by Kevan Gosper, and seconded by Jacques Rogge. He became the fourth Australian IOC member, behind Gosper, Phil Coles and the double gold-medallist Susan O'Neill, who had been elected on the vote of international athletes in Sydney's athletes' village. Coates became a member of the IOC's juridical commission and a newly formed study commission, which was given the brief of exploring the means by which the costs and complexity of organising the Games could be reduced. In the week of his election to the IOC he was named as chef de mission of the Australian team for Athens in 2004 — his fifth consecutive such appointment. Another IOC member who had achieved that distinction was Jacques Rogge, who had led the Belgian team to five Olympics.

For Coates, a vice-president of the International Council for Arbitration of Sport and a council member of the International Rowing Federation (FISA), the pace of life hardly slowed after the Games ended and SOCOG was wound up. He remained a partner in a law firm (now Kemp Strang) and a director of David Jones, and became chairman of a public relations company and a member of the advisory board of a merchant bank. Much of whatever spare time he's had since the Games has been spent close to his favourite sport of rowing — mainly at the Sydney Rowing Club, where all six of his children have rowed.

Three days after Sydney's closing ceremony, Michael Knight surprised everyone, including his premier and his parliament, by announcing that he was quitting politics after 19 years. Fittingly enough, the decision came at a time when he was at the centre of a fierce controversy, caused by his refusal to countenance the award of a gold Olympic Order to Sandy Hollway. Knight says that he chose the timing of his announcement to fit between the day of the street parade of the Australian team and the day of the Olympic volunteers' parade 'so as not to take any of the media's focus away from either of those important events'. By the end of the year SOCOG no longer existed and much of the structure that was Sydney 2000 had been disassembled. Knight left parliament in

January 2001 and set up as a private consultant — 'to a variety of businesses, with the accent on problem solving'. In a voluntary capacity, he continued some Olympic work, as a member of the IOC Coordination Commission for the Athens 2004 Games and an occasional adviser to the organisers of Beijing 2008.

He remembered: 'It was a great privilege for me to lead the team which delivered something special for both the Olympic movement and for Australia. The most common thing people said to me during the Games, or have said since them, is how proud they felt to be Australian. Australians are normally very reticent about openly expressing their patriotism (except during wartime or when supporting Australian teams or athletes competing against other countries)... Hundreds of thousands of Australians contributed to delivering what is widely regarded internationally as "the best Games ever". That adds enormously to our nation's reputation in the rest of the world and justifiably enables all Australians to feel pretty good about themselves, our country, and what we are capable of.'

The IOC's two-year suspension of Phil Coles from all committees ended in June 2001, and not long afterwards he was appointed to the organisation's program commission and radio and television commission. He became a consultant to the Olympic TV rights holder, the Seven Network, and the radio rights holder, station 2GB. The IOC troubles had not affected one of his major roles in Sydney, as chairman of the NSW Institute of Sport, and he continued in that job after the Games. His appointment late in 2002 to the NSW premier's Major Events Board gave a clear enough signal that, at least as far as the highest levels of state government were concerned, all had been forgiven.

In his new major-events role Coles found himself attending meetings alongside a man he had worked with for Sydney's Games, David Richmond, as well as old friends and sporting heavyweights Sir Nick Shehadie, Jon Donohue and Alan Whelpton. Coles continued to have an occasional paddle in the surf, and to visit both the North Bondi surf club (where he received his 50-year gold medal in August 1999) and the Bronte surf club. He remained steady in his conviction that he was a scapegoat of the IOC scandals, and claimed that ordinary Australians shared the same view. 'I go out to dinner, I go to public places, I go to football, I go to cricket, and all the time I'm stopped by people who say, "Phil Coles, you're a good man…Can I shake your hand, have your autograph." Someone stopped me the other day, gave me his card, and said, "If you ever need anything please let me know."'

Susan O'Neill's projection towards the upper levels of Olympic administration began while she was training for the Sydney Olympics. Herb Elliott persuaded her to nominate for a poll being conducted by the Australian Athletes' Commission, aimed at selecting an Australian candidate for the election to be held in the athletes' village during Sydney 2000. She won that vote, thus becoming one of 44 athletes to contest the eight positions available in the IOC Athletes' Commission. The four who polled most heavily would win eight-year terms with the IOC, the second four four-year terms. She finished third, and has been on a major learning curve ever since: 'I had to get used to the meetings, the sessions, the men-in-suits type of thing.' At her first IOC session in July 2001, she found herself voting on such significant matters as the site of the 2008 Olympics (Beijing) and the selection of a new president (Rogge). Soon after, following a brief spell with the IOC's Women in Sport working group, she became a member of both the World Anti-Doping Agency and the 2008 Beijing Coordination Commission.

O'Neill became a hard liner on drug penalties — she'd like offenders banned for life, with their gold medals confiscated and world records erased — but her experience at major anti-drug conferences in Copenhagen and Montreal convinced her that the whole subject was fraught with legal, logistical and human-rights problems. 'The great need is for uniformity,' she said. 'We need to get governments on board as well as sports federations.' When Claudia Poll, 1996 Olympic 200 metres freestyle gold medallist, tested positive for a steroid drug in February 2002, O'Neill was far from surprised. While not bitter, she saw a certain irony in the fact that Poll and the Irish triple gold medallist Michelle Smith, both of whom she swam against in Atlanta, had since proved to be drug cheats. Her role on the Beijing commission excited her: 'It will be intriguing to watch, over the next five years, the whole process of putting a Games together.' She had no nostalgia for her glory days: 'I'm not missing the early-morning training, I'm not missing being nervous before a race.'

David Richmond, who oversaw during 2000 all operations of the Sydney Olympic Games and the Paralympic Games, was rewarded with the IOC's highest honour, the Olympic Order in gold, and, on Australia Day 2002, Australia's AO (Officer in the Order of Australia) award. After the Games he became a consultant, providing strategic advice to government and business, as well as to major event organisers. He gave advice to the organisers of the Athens 2004 Olympic Games, and was appointed chairman of the board of the Sydney Olympic Park Authority. With a small group of former Sydney 2000 executives — Sandy Hollway, David Churches and Bob Adby — he provided assistance to the Beijing 2008 organising committee and to the Beijing city government as part of a program designed to help Australian companies seeking Olympic contracts in China.

A consummate bureaucrat, Richmond continued to tread surely through the avenues of state government machinery. He served as an adviser to the NSW government, and during 2002–2003 was chairman of the board of the State Rail Authority responsible for Sydney's passenger train services. With former Olympic colleague Bob Leece, he carried out a review in 2001–2002 of management strategy for key government-owned industrial and port sites around the industrial city of Newcastle. Through 2003 he was chairman of a task force reviewing NSW government strategy for capital works such as schools, roads and hospitals. He was a member of the NSW Major Events Board, on which Phil Coles also sat.

From the end of 2000, Sandy Hollway followed through on two of the main legacies of Sydney's Games: the boost to volunteering, and the competitive edge of Australian companies that demonstrated their capabilities in helping deliver the Best Games Ever. He led the activities in New South Wales of the International Year of the Volunteer in 2001, and became actively involved in efforts to win business for Australia with other major events, notably the 2006 Asian Games and the 2008 Beijing Olympics. He was an adviser to the Beijing bidding committee ahead of the Moscow meeting at which the Chinese won the right to stage the Games. He handled a range of business consultancies and chaired the Economic Development Organisation of the Central Coast of New South Wales. Following the devastating bushfires that struck the nation's capital in January 2003, he accepted the ACT government's invitation to become chairman of the Canberra Bushfire Recovery Task Force.

Sandy Hollway said his enduring memory of the Games was the joy, pride and enthusiasm of the community. He stressed often after Sydney 2000 that 'while the organisers provided the muscle, bone and sinew to make this huge event work, it was the Australian people who provided the heart, soul and spirit'. And he added: 'What the Olympics demonstrated was that Australia has no need for self-doubt...that we can accomplish anything if we put our minds to it.'

Marjorie Jackson, who replaced Rod McGeoch on the SOCOG board, was appointed Governor of South Australia in November 2001 (following a laudable trend set when another member of the 1952 Olympic team, John Landy, took up a similar post in Victoria earlier that year). McGeoch, who had been president of New South Wales' Law Society and managing partner of a law firm, moved into business as a director and consultant, travelling widely overseas. He summed up his Olympic journey: 'The great golfer Bobby Jones once said of his experiences at St Andrews, "If I took all of the experiences out of my life except those at St Andrews, I would still die a happy man." I feel the same way about my Olympic experiences.'

Kevan Gosper continued as a vice-president of the IOC until July 2003, and remained during the Rogge regime with his job as chairman of the IOC Press Commission. Jacques Rogge appointed him to two new roles, as deputy chairman of the Solidarity Commission, and deputy chairman of the Beijing Coordination Commission (on which two other Australians, O'Neill and Simon Balderstone, also sat). Apart from his AOC involvements, he served as a trustee of the Melbourne and Olympic Parks Trust, and was a director of three companies — the Crown casino group, the Visy packaging group and the brewers Lion Nathan. In 2003 his children Richard (19) and Sophie (14) were Victorian state swimming champions.

Although the IOC had imposed an age limit of 70 on members elected after December 1999, a grandfather clause allowed earlier members to stay until they turned 80 — if approved. At the time of the 2004 Athens Games Gosper would be 70 and Coles 73, and it was Gosper's great hope that sometime during the decade Coates would take over from one or both of them as an elected IOC member rather than one from the category of NOC presidents. 'He's one of the most outstanding individuals in the Olympic movement,' Gosper declared. 'I have no doubt he'll become one of the key players.'

In November 2001 Craig McLatchey, who had been a member of the SOCOG board, resigned his post as secretary-general of the AOC to become chief executive officer of Olympic Games Knowledge Services in Lausanne. This was a joint venture of the IOC and Monash University, whose task it was to formalise the transfer of accumulated knowledge from one Games organiser to the next. In this role McLatchey worked under the chairmanship of Kevan Gosper. McLatchey was succeeded as secretary-general of the AOC by Bob Elphinston, who had been SOCOG's general manager of sport until he joined the AOC after the Games as director of sport. When Elphinston moved up, that post was taken by Craig Phillips.

'Have Ideas, Will Travel' was a recurring theme in the life of the restlessly talented Ric Birch, director of ceremonies at the Sydney Olympics. After the Games he returned to his base in Los Angeles, where he had set up his Spectak production company in 1985 'to create special events on an international scale'. He renewed an old association in Los Angeles with News Corporation, but much of his post-Games working life was spent outside the United States. In Paris he worked on a theme park development with a French partner. In Milan he became involved with an Italian company that was bidding to stage the ceremonies for the Turin 2006 winter Olympics. He bought a house in Istanbul and joined in a land development project in southern Turkey, where he hoped to create an entertainment precinct.

Birch looked back on the Sydney Olympics with mixed emotions: 'The ceremonies were a great success because a brilliant creative team of Australian directors, designers and choreographers came together for a common purpose. The volunteer performers dedicated hundreds and thousands of hours, and a professional production staff gave years of their lives to show the world their Australia. I hoped that the ceremonies would be a force for social change and not just an isolated highlight in Australia's history — but I can't see that happening yet.'

In late November 2000 in Monte Carlo, the International Athletic Foundation confirmed what most Australians already knew: that Cathy Freeman's win in the 400 metres was the emotional high point of the Sydney Olympics. The foundation, an agency of the governing body of track and field, the International Amateur Athletic Federation, awarded her its Inspirational Award for 2000, labelling the gold medal run the most dramatic performance of the year.

Freeman, who handled pressure so well at the Sydney Olympics, faced some personal crises after them. In mid-2002 she and her husband, Sandy Bodecker, learned that he had cancer — a tumour at the back of his mouth. She took a long break from running to care for him during his course of chemotherapy, but at his urging joined the Commonwealth Games team for the 4 × 400 metres relay in Manchester, helping it to win gold. By the end of the year doctors pronounced that Bodecker was cured. Then, in February 2003, Freeman announced that the marriage was over. She said: 'As a couple, we have had our shares of highs and lows, and through that both of our lives have changed … our respective careers have put extreme pressure on the relationship, and this has led to my decision to separate.' She said it was time to get on with the rest of her life, and that she was optimistically looking forward to the future.

By mid-2003, after she had failed to reproduce anything like her best form, Freeman became increasingly uncertain about the direction of that future. She had plainly lost some of the motivation that had driven her since early childhood, as well as a certain edge … 'I've lost a little bit of that steeliness,' she conceded. On July 15 she announced her retirement, explaining that she no longer possessed her old passion, or the hunger she could see in the eyes of other athletes. There were simply no more goals to reach, she said. It was a judgment that did not bear querying. Cathy Freeman owed nobody anything. She had carried more than enough expectation, and there was nothing left to prove. The mountain had been climbed. The destiny had been fulfilled.

Marion Jones, triple gold medallist, charging for gold in the 100 metres.

On the winner's podium after the 200 metres (from left: Pauline Davis-Thompson (Bahamas), Marion Jones, Susanthika Jayasinghe (Sri Lanka).

Michael Johnson after his win in the 400 metres. He became the first man in history to win that race twice in a row.

Maurice Greene (centre) wins the 100 metres final from Ato Boldon (Trinidad) and Obadele Thompson (Barbados).

After the 400 metres . . . The strain shows on Cathy Freeman's face.

Cathy Freeman on the winner's dais
after her 400 metres victory.

Jai Taurima winning silver
in the long jump.

Haile Gebrselassie (left) wins the 10,000 metres.

Cyclists Brett Aitken and Scott McGrory were victorious in the madison — an event that demands teamwork, endurance, sprinting ability and strategy.

The Hockeyroos win gold again.

Andrew Hoy, whose victory in the three-day team equestrian event gave him three consecutive gold medals. He also won silver in the three-day individual event.

Tatiana Grigorieva, a study in concentration before taking silver in the pole vault.

Simon Fairweather shoots for gold.

Michael Diamond after being presented with
the gold medal for his victory in the men's
trap shooting.

Jenny Armstrong and Belinda Stowell won gold in the 470 sailing class.

Lauren Burns, victorious in the ancient discipline of taekwondo.

Tom King and Mark Turnbull emulate the women's success in the 470s.

Members of the women's water polo team celebrate their victory.

'I couldn't believe our dream for so long had come true.' Kerri Pottharst and Natalie Cook won gold in the beach volleyball.

The beach volleyball court at Bondi Beach, the site of one long party during the Games.

A cruel moment to come. Jane Saville before her disqualification in the 20-kilometre walk. Afterwards she was remarkably controlled and gracious.

Michellie Jones savours the moment, after winning silver in the triathlon.

The closing ceremony fireworks light up the Harbour Bridge and Opera House.

Steven Bradbury during a heat on his way to gold in the 1000 metres short-track speed skating at the Salt Lake City Winter Games.

Steven Bradbury on the winners' podium at Salt Lake City.

Alisa Camplin performing the triple somersault that won her gold in Salt Lake City.

Alisa Camplin exultant after her victory.

PART THREE

CHAPTER TWELVE

Gold in the cold

For many years, until comparatively recently, the winter sports used to be regarded as the poor relation of the Australian Olympic movement. Administrators at first ignored the ice and snow athletes, then later accepted them grudgingly as part of the wider Olympic family — but still tended to resent and ridicule them. The Queenslander Tom Blue, whose task as chairman of the Australian Olympic Federation's justification committee from the 1960s to the 1980s was to scrutinise the credentials of all nominated athletes, reflected the general attitude well. Once, when winter officials were pleading their case for the admission of six cross-country skiers to the Australian team, Blue declared: 'What you're really asking for is seven places.' Puzzled, they asked what he meant. 'You'd need to keep one spot for a St Bernard dog to find them after they got lost,' he explained, to the chortling amusement of most of his colleagues.

Not all the heavyweights of the AOF (which became the AOC in 1991) were so keen to humiliate the winter people. But a pervasive view existed that the skiers and skaters were token athletes, no-hopers really, from privileged backgrounds. The fact that when they did travel to winter Olympics they were forever unplaced had the effect of reinforcing this stance. Hugh Weir, an Australian member of the IOC, expressed the general sense of disdain once when he boasted matter-of-factly to an audience at an Olympic conference: 'I'm a summer man, myself.' Contributing to the uninterested attitude was a common belief that Australia was devoid of tradition or history in skiing or skating.

Most of these assumptions were of course wrong — particularly about the history. Skis were used in Tasmania as early as the 1830s by fur hunters, and Norwegian gold-miners took their skis with them as they joined the gold rushes of the 1850s to Kiandra, New South Wales, and Harrietville, Victoria. One of the oldest ski clubs in the world was formed at Kiandra in 1870, and by the 1880s downhill races were being organised there, billed as championships of Australia. A ski club was formed at Mt Kosciusko, the highest mountain in Australia, in 1909, and in the years immediately afterwards Kosciusko became a tourist destination, catering for skiers, tobogganists and skaters.

Australia's first artificial indoor ice rink was opened in 1889, and by 1903 Melbourne, Sydney and Adelaide all possessed rinks that attracted speed and figure skaters, as well as ice-hockey players. Ice hockey was being played in Australia in 1904, before organised competition began in the United States, and in 1908 a match took place in Melbourne between sailors from the USS *Baltimore*, part of the visiting

Speed skater Kenneth Kennedy, the first person to represent Australia at a winter Olympics.

Great White Fleet, and a Victorian representative side. One of the finest early exponents of all three branches of ice sports was Ted Molony, national speed-skating champion, a figure skater and ice dancer of renown, and captain of Victoria's ice-hockey team from 1925 to 1936.

Far from being pampered losers, most of the skaters and skiers who represented Australia at winter Olympics for more than half a century were dedicated athletes, almost invariably competing against the odds, often prepared to make huge sacrifices for their sport. The pioneer was Ken Kennedy, who paid his own way from Britain to skate as a one-man Australian team in three speed events at the 1936 Olympics. He played ice hockey with the Birmingham Maple Leaf team from 1935 to 1937, and for two of those years was Britain's indoor skating champion over a half-mile and mile. (Another Australian who competed at the Berlin Games — but wasn't in the national team and didn't make too many sacrifices — was a playboy called Freddie McEvoy, a close friend of the dashing film actor Errol Flynn. McEvoy, nicknamed 'Suicide Freddie', captained the British four-man bobsled team that won bronze, and carried Great Britain's flag in the opening ceremony. McEvoy, whose exploits were dealt with in more detail in *Australia and the Olympic Games*, was a likeable rogue who lived by his wits and his looks. He was sometimes called a cad, often a gigolo. He drowned after his ketch, loaded with Scotch whisky, was wrecked in a storm off the north African coast in 1951.)

Ted Molony's daughter, Gweneth, was a figure skater with the first real Australian team at the winter Olympics — in Oslo in 1952. The team consisted of five skiers and four skaters. She later married Geoff Henke, once a teenage rink rat at the St Moritz in Melbourne, later an ice-hockey player who captained Victoria, still later an AOC vice-president and *chef de mission* of six Australian winter Olympic teams. Henke was himself once the victim of the Cinderella syndrome, which translated really as an administrative contempt for the winter sports. Henke and other leading ice-hockey players expected to go to Cortina in 1956 for the winter Games; the Australian Ice Hockey Association raised the money to fund their trip, and officials of the association claimed they had been told that the AOF would endorse the sending of the team. That was all they needed: formal approval. They waited and waited, until the last ship that could transport them to Europe had sailed, and no word came. The players and their association claimed with some justification that they had been let down by an Olympic committee that just wasn't interested. When Henke later moved into the upper levels of Olympic administration he resolved to change the culture.

From 1952 to 1992 Australia sent teams to eleven winter Olympics, mostly with discouraging results. They were hampered by distance, shortage of funds and a consequential lack of competition between Games, and for a long time by an abiding sense of official indifference. Among the athletes were some marvellous battlers, maybe best characterised by the speed skater Colin Hickey, who became hooked on the sport at the age of 15, after his father took him for an outing to the Melbourne Glaciarium. He sold newspapers to earn the money to buy his first pair of skates, at Myer's on lay-by, and took to skating seven

Speed skater Colin Hickey (right) competing in the 500 metres event at Oslo, 1952 (Colin Hickey)

nights a week and all day on Saturdays. Small and lightly framed (162 centimetres and 56 kilograms), he took a ship to Europe at the age of 18 to try his luck in the speed-skating hub of Norway. He found work as a lumberjack, learned to speak Norwegian, and applied himself totally. 'We just slept, trained, skated and travelled,' he said later. 'We did it hard, lived maybe two weeks at a time on muesli — What was good was that they [the Australian authorities] had no control over me. All they'd do was tell me what times I had to do for selection and it would be up to me.' He found the conversion from the indoor skating of Australia to the outdoor, natural rinks of Europe dramatic: 'It was like going from ping-pong to lawn tennis, from dirt track to Grand Prix.'[1]

Hickey represented Australia in three Olympics, from 1952 to 1960, with his best results two seventh placings in the 500 and 1500 metres in 1956. His times in both those events would have won gold medals at the previous Olympics. He finished third over 500 metres at the 1960 world championship in Davos, Switzerland. He was an inexpensive investment for his national Olympic committee, as was demonstrated in this interview with the writer:

> We didn't get a uniform. I never had an Australian blazer once in three Olympics. In 1952, because King George had died, they issued us with a black armband and tie for the opening ceremony. Nothing else. You wore it with whatever you had. I had a green sweater and ski slacks. In 1956 I was issued with no gear at all, even though I was the best-performed member of the team by about a hundred per cent. I couldn't march without any kind of uniform, so I stayed in the hotel. In 1960 they gave us a duffle coat and a sweater, and that covered everything you had. That's the way it was. You had to look after yourself.[2]

Another colourful and highly competent speed skater was Colin Coates, one of the only six people ever to have competed at six Olympic Games. Coates was an extraordinary athlete: three times Australian speed-skating champion, triple Australian and ten times Victorian champion in 14-foot sailing dinghies, a competent ice-hockey player and cyclist. Originally from Elwood, Melbourne, he was in the same journeyman-skater mould as Hickey, and he made similar sacrifices. To be close to the skating action of Europe, he spent fifteen winters in

Holland, working at his trade as a plumber. Once, while skiing, he fell 25 metres on to an ice ledge, breaking both arms, his jaw, his left shoulder and his nose. He had ten metal pins inserted in his body, but was back skating and racing on ice within three weeks. His performance in finishing sixth in the 10,000 metres at Innsbruck in 1976 was the finest recorded by an Australian at a winter Olympics until 1994. For his last Games, in Calgary in 1988, he was listed not as a contestant but as a coach–manager, but still contrived to have a place on the entry list for

Colin Coates, who finished sixth in the 10,000 metres speed skating at Innsbruck in 1976.

the 10,000 metres — and skated against the express orders of the team's *chef de mission*, Geoff Henke. He finished 26th, in the best time he had ever recorded. Henke abused him afterwards, but after the congratulations began to flow in on Coates' historic six-Olympics feat — with one from the prime minister, Bob Hawke, telling him he had made all Australians proud — the team boss relented. 'I stopped going crook,' Henke said later. 'The man was a public hero — his was an incredible performance.'

Geoff Henke reprimands Colin Coates after he disobeyed orders and competed in the 10,000 metres race in Calgary in 1988. (Geoff Henke)

Malcolm Milne,
one of Australia's
finest skiers.

Among the skiers in the dog days of Australian Olympic winter competition were the Milne brothers, Ross and Malcolm. Ross, who captained the ski team at the age of 19, died in a crash during a training run at the 1964 Olympics in Innsbruck. Afterwards Hugh Weir reported that the IOC was concerned that Australia might have been sending 'inexperienced people to compete in ... snow sports which contain an element of danger'. One effect of the tragedy was to give extra motivation to Milne's younger brother Malcolm, who was 15 and a junior national champion at the time of the accident. He heard of suggestions from Europe that skiers from minor (winter sport) countries like Australia and New Zealand should not be allowed to race on difficult downhill courses ... that such accidents might not happen if less experienced skiers were barred from competition. 'I was only young at the time,' he said later, 'but I knew very well that was a cover-up kind of story. It made me want to prove that we *were* capable of racing downhill.'[3] He went on to become easily the finest Australian skier of his era.

Malcolm Milne raced well in the 1968 Olympic downhill to finish 24th of 86 starters, with a time only 5.51 seconds behind that of the great French champion Jean-Claude Killy. Afterwards the team manager, Bruce Dyson, reported: 'This was by far the best Australian skiing result in any Games.' Milne finished 12th in the overall alpine placings. In the winter of 1971–72 he won a World Cup race at Val D'Isere, France, then won a US title at Bear Valley, California, and finished third in a world championship. He turned professional after the 1972 Sapporo Olympics and joined a troupe formed by Killy. He later made an observation that reflected the sense of inferiority ingrained into many Australian skiers of the time: 'Someone once said to me that for us to beat the Europeans at winter sports was like Austria tackling us at Test cricket. I reckon it's an accurate judgment.'[4]

When attitudes in the AOF began to change, it was mainly due to Geoff Henke, the ice-hockey player who had been left high and dry by an administration that didn't care. Julius Patching, the revered secretary-general of the AOF, later declared: 'The old guard simply never accepted the winter Games and never got behind them. Until Henke came along and changed the culture, the attitude was, "We'll fix 'em up".'[5] Henke began by inviting the AOF's executive board to Trackers Lodge at Falls Creek for a weekend retreat to learn something about the winter experience. Patching recalled:

> He was patient and shrewd and broke down the barriers, because the winter sports were pretty much a token. Hugh Weir, Harold Alderson and Edgar Tanner were never really behind them, never really tried to understand them, and the legacy from them remained negative. Geoff explained that there were well over 500,000 active skiers in Australia. Tom Blue was sceptical at first, but the whole executive finally accepted Geoff's invitation to see the sport at close range. We travelled cross-country and all tried ourselves on skis, with spectacular results. Kevan Gosper could ski well, but most ended up in some dreadful tangles. John Rodda was taken up in a ski lift and came down like an avalanche. We all came away with a better appreciation of what the winter people

were up against. It was a subtle exercise, because Henke was infiltrating old attitudes. But it worked.[6]

A quiet but very influential businessman, Henke progressed steadily as a sports administrator, becoming in turn president of the Australian Ski Federation, a vice-president of the AOC and the first Australian member of the Federation Internationale de Ski, the controlling body of world skiing. He was also *chef de mission* of the six Australian teams that attended winter Olympics from 1976 to 1994. Largely through his efforts, by the time the AOF had transformed itself into the AOC in 1991, it was finally taking the cold sports seriously. He was instrumental in the establishment in 1993 of Sonnpark, a training and base camp at Axams, near Innsbruck, in the Tyrol region of Austria. Zali Steggall, alpine slalom world champion in 1999 and Olympic bronze medallist in 1998, was one of a large number of Australian skiers who used Sonnpark as their European base until its sale in 2002. Major initiatives that followed were the setting up in 1995 of the Australian Ski Institute (in which enterprise Henke had significant help from the construction tycoon Rino Grollo, owner of the Mt Buller ski lift), and its succession after the 1988 Nagano Olympics by the AOC's Australian Institute of Winter Sport, which became the Olympic Winter Institute on 1 July 2001. Fittingly, Henke was its chairman.

Australia's first taste of success at a winter Games came in Lillehammer in 1994 when the short-track skating relay quartet of Richard Nizielski, Steven Bradbury, Andrew Murtha and Kieran Hansen won bronze. These four had gone to the preceding Albertville (1992) Games with John Kah as reigning world champions, but had been eliminated in a semi-final after two of them fell. With that nightmare fresh in their memory, they resolved before the 45-lap Lillehammer final that whatever happened they would stay on their feet. A member of the world champion Canadian team crashed, but the Australians stayed safe and upright to finish third, behind Italy and the United States. At the same Games Australia's Kirstie Marshall finished sixth in the final of the newly introduced aerial freestyle skiing competition — matching Colin Coates' speed-skating sixth in 1976, until 1994 the finest Australian winter performance ever.

In winning bronze at Lillehammer in 1994, the short-track relay team was the recipient of Australia's first winter Olympics medal (from left: Andrew Murtha, Kieran Hansen, Steven Bradbury, Richard Nizielski and John Kah (reserve). (APL)

By the time the 1998 Nagano Olympics arrived, Australians had made huge headway in the fledgling sport of aerial skiing — with Kirstie Marshall, 28, winner of the 1997 world championship, and team-mate Jacqui Cooper, 25, ranked No. 2 in the world. Marshall, a former gymnast whose 1997 victory had made her the first Australian individual world champion in any winter sport, was rated the outstanding contender among the 27-strong Australian team. Another highly performed skier was Zali Steggall, 23, already a double Olympian, who had become the first Australian woman ever to win an alpine skiing World Cup event when she won the slalom at Park City, Utah, three months earlier. Steggall had followed her win with a fifth, sixth and tenth to become (at No. 6) the highest ranked Australian skier in alpine history. All three attributed much of their success to the infant Australian Ski Institute, where they had come under the influence of two high-calibre coaches — the American aerial specialist Frank Bare and the Austrian alpine mentor Helmut Spiegl.

In what turned out to be a day of torment for the Australians, it took less than an hour for Marshall, Cooper and their male colleague Jono Sweet (ranked No. 8 in the world) to be eliminated during their Olympic qualifying rounds in Nagano. They all had their worst day in the snow for years. Marshall was unable to land the first of her two jumps. She did better with her second, the triple-twisting double somersault she had pioneered, but finished in 14th position, with the top 12 progressing to the final. Cooper slammed her face into the landing

hill with her second jump, finishing the competition with concussion and the desolation that came with the knowledge that she had finished 23rd. Sweet, 24, was badly rattled by the pressure and failed to complete the triple twisting triple somersault jump he had nominated before the competition. He later explained that he had been off-balance on take-off and had to abandon the jump to avoid serious injury.

Kirsty Marshall (left) and Jacqui Cooper at Nagano.

It was left to Steggall, a girl from Manly (Sydney) who had learned to ski at the age of four, to redeem a sense of prestige for Australia by winning bronze in the women's slalom. She became the first Australian woman to take a medal at the winter Games, and the first Australian skier to do so, when she finished behind Germany's Hilde Gerg and dual gold medallist Deborah Compagnoni, of Italy. Steggall, whose family went to Morzine in the French Alps when she was a toddler, and stayed ten years, was on the French national junior team at the age of 14. Her grandfather John had played ten Tests for Australia as a member of the rugby union Wallabies team. Ron Reed, of the Melbourne *Herald Sun*, commented that Steggall's performance had kept Australia's winter-sport dream alive, 'albeit weighed down by the usual slew of uncompetitive performances and results'. He added truthfully: 'This was not necessarily the athletes' fault. Most of them were under-funded, under-equipped and under-trained.' Acknowledging this state of affairs, John Coates told officials: 'If we're going to participate in the winter Olympics, then let's get serious. We need to be fair dinkum.'

It was in an effort to get serious that the AOC upgraded and expanded the Australian Ski Institute, renamed it the Australian Institute of Winter Sports, and ploughed funding into it. Two years later it was renamed the Olympic Winter Institute (OWI) of Australia, as a partnership program with the Australian Institute of Sport, with support from the Australian Sports Commission. It had a budget of $1.65 million, of which the AOC provided half. Its major objective was to develop and prepare elite Australian athletes for participation in winter Olympic Games, world championships and World Cup events. It employed seven coaches and provided opportunities for up to 37 athletes across six winter disciplines: alpine, mogul and aerial skiing, snowboard, short-track speed skating and figure skating.

The results were swift and positive. In 1989/1999, the OWI's first year of operation, two of its athletes — Jacqui Cooper (freestyle aerial) and Zali Steggall (slalom) — were among the 13 skiers who won world championships in various disciplines. Zali's brother Zeke (snowboard) won a world championship bronze medal, and Cooper won an overall World Cup title as well as three individual World Cup gold medals. In the second year, 1999/2000, Cooper won another three World Cup events and the overall World Cup for the second year in a row, Zeke Steggall had two snowboard World Cup wins, and individual World Cup minor

Zali Steggall and *chef de mission* Ian Chesterman celebrate her medal-winning performance in Nagano.

medals went to Cooper, Zeke Steggall, snowboarder John Fletcher and a new aerial skier, Alisa Camplin. In 2000/2001, Cooper made it a hat-trick of World Cup titles, Maria Despas won silver to give Australia its first-ever medal in a mogul skiing world championship, and the aerial team took out seven World Cup medals (Cooper 6, Camplin 1).

By the time the 27-member Australian team arrived in Salt Lake City for the 2002 Games, a certain modest confidence existed — alongside the harsh awareness that the nation's record at winter Olympics had long been unimpressive. The *chef de mission* Ian Chesterman, who had been second-in-command to Henke in Lillehammer and was in charge in Nagano, referred to both when he addressed the team on the eve of the Games. 'Historically our winter teams have been the child racked by self-doubt, shy in nature as we saw our big brother, our summer Games team, take on and conquer the world,' he said. 'But over time we have

developed a belief in ourselves ... It has been a gradual process, but in recent years has gathered momentum.' He referred to this writer and his history, *Australia and the Olympic Games*, and challenged the team to provide the next chapter. 'It may not take as long to read [as the chapters on Sydney],' he declared, 'but there will be great stories of triumph and disappointment, for such is the nature of every Olympic Games.'

Ian Chesterman could hardly have realised then the truly prophetic nature of his words. What unfolded in the days that followed was not just the story of Australian success and redemption after 66 years, an Olympic lifetime, in the winter wilderness. With it came two of the most remarkable gold-medal adventures ever, as well as the tragedy of an awful crash that ended the hopes of an athlete acknowledged as the most accomplished female skiing acrobat in the young history of the sport.

Jacqui Cooper had won three World Cups and a world championship since Nagano, and was considered by many good judges to be a certainty for an aerial gold medal. She was on her very last training jump — a routine (for her) double twisting triple somersault — when she landed awkwardly and in a moment wrecked the campaign that had absorbed her for four years. The precise moment was captured on camera by coaches videotaping the session, and Cooper's instant scream of pain and horror was shrill and chilling. It continued — or was it

Ian Chesterman,
Australia's *chef
de mission* at the
Salt Lake City
winter Games.

the echoes? — as she slid through the snow down the Deer Valley hill. She said afterwards that she had felt something go in her left knee 'like a little explosion'. What had happened, it emerged after an afternoon of x-rays and scans, was that she had ruptured the anterior cruciate ligament, fractured a tibia bone and suffered severe bone bruising. Her Olympics were over; an early knee reconstruction was necessary. She wept as she told reporters: 'I knew straightaway that my Olympic dream was over … My knee is broken, my heart is broken, but my spirit is not. I have worked so hard to get myself into a position to win. This is a nightmare for sure. It's an enormously emotional time for me.' Her less experienced team-mates Alisa Camplin and Lydia Ierodiaconou had been in the vicinity when she crashed, although Camplin said later that she didn't see the crash or hear the scream. Both received counselling from team officials.

Within days two extraordinary events had occurred. The understudy Camplin, a city girl had been a comparative stranger to snow before she bought her first pair of skis at the age of 21, and Steven Bradbury, a skater who managed to stay on his feet when all around him were falling down, had given Australia the most unexpected gold medals of the 2002 Olympics. Officials, even the athletes themselves, found it hard to believe: twice within 48 hours 'Advance Australia Fair', which had never once had an airing at a winter Games, was echoing around the podiums of Salt Lake City. Postage stamps bearing the images of Camplin and Bradbury were being sold in Australia. Pictures of them adorned the front pages of newspapers in London and New York, and both were having multiple interviews with US television networks such as NBC (whose 'Today Show', somebody quipped after about the sixth such appearance, should be renamed the 'G'Day Show'). Both had been fairly broke when they came to Salt Lake City — she had to sell her car to get there, and he had to borrow $1000 from his parents to fix his to get to training — and suddenly, as advertisers and marketers courted them, their separate earning potentials were spearing north. This was due not only to the nature of their victories but also to the refreshing, even appealing, manner in which they had reacted to them.

Bradbury, whose spiky, luminously bleached hairdo and pierced left eyebrow were somehow in harmony with the bizarre nature of his

Steven Bradbury during the short-track speed-skating competition in Salt Lake City.

win, was the first to take gold. His victory in the 1000 metres short-track speed skating final, after three rounds of racing in which his competitors stumbled, fell and were disqualified around him, caused him to be dubbed the 'Accidental Hero'. Certainly his pathway to that moment when he crossed the line, arms outstretched and a look on his face that somehow managed simultaneously to convey joy, amazement and disbelief, had been paved by default. He had won his heat convincingly, but then been drawn to skate against the two hottest prospects in the field — American favourite Apolo Anton Ohno and the Canadian multiple world champion Mark Gagnon — in the quarter-finals. With only two men qualifying for the semi-final, it looked as though Bradbury's

Olympics were over, but Gagnon was disqualified for impeding another skater, giving the third-placed Bradbury a free bunk into the semi-finals. For the semis, after consultation with his coach Ann Zhang, he decided on a specific tactic: to skate deliberately behind the pack, stay out of trouble and wait for opportunities and accidents, which are essential elements in the nature of the sport. When defending Olympic champion Kim Dong-Sung (South Korea), Li Jianjun (China) and Matthieu Turcotte all went down in two separate crashes, Bradbury sneaked through in second place to qualify for the final. These were his feelings:

> Leading into the semi-finals, I had already achieved all I wanted from those Olympics, because I'd skated as well as I could at the age of 28 (I was the second oldest in the field of 32), because I was one of the fastest nine guys in the world, which I was really happy with. I looked at all the other names and thought, 'I've got to be realistic about this ... I can't beat any of these guys. They're all skating better than me.' I went out there very relaxed because I knew that whatever the result I'd be happy with it, so it didn't matter. I had a little bit in the legs left at the end, but I stayed out of the way and didn't waste any energy. I was right there and able to capitalise when there was a mistake. By the time the final came I was very tired. Each round is half an hour apart, and after three goes at it that night ... I wasn't good at that backing-up thing.[7]

For the five-man final, Bradbury decided to use the same wait-at-the-back tactics. This time he was influenced by a very real consideration: he was too leg-weary to do anything else. But, he said later, he also realised that 'there was a massive chance I was going to pick up a medal because there was a big chance of some sort of accident, collision or whatever.' Why such confidence?

> If you have a look at the rest of the field there in the final, probably in every case they were a little bit over-trying. The American guy [Ohno] was pumped up by the media to win four gold medals, it was his first event up, and he had heaps of pressure on him. The expectation on him was very unrealistic. But he was a big chance to win and he had all that pressure of the home stadium and all the media on his back. He was only interested in coming first. Then you had the Chinese guy Li.

I think he's got four or five silver medals in his kitbag, and I'm sure he wasn't shooting for another one of those [silvers]. And the Canadian guy Turcotte, he was skating in only that one event, the 1000, because it's a very competitive team to make, the Canadian, there's such a depth of skating there. That was his only skate in the Olympics and he was all driven on getting a gold. And the Korean guy who had hardly been in international competition before…he was just skating awesomely, and being from South Korea he has to do whatever the coach tells him, and the coach obviously only tells him he's got to win, and that's it. So I was really the only guy out there in the final with some kind of different plan. I knew my chances were pretty well zero of winning the race, but that was never the plan. The plan was to have some kind of accident occur and sneak in for a bronze. That was a realistic plan with a high chance of success, but things obviously worked out a little better than that.[8]

Bradbury had read the field, and the aspirations of all his rivals for a medal that was gold, no other colour, very well indeed. As the four of them jockeyed for position on the final bend, the Chinese Li was the first to fall, then Ohno. Turcotte and the Korean Ahn Hyun-Soo collided, tumbled and slid across the ice, leaving Bradbury alone to skate past the finish line. He had been more than 15 metres behind the others when the mayhem occurred. Ohno and Turcotte scrambled to the line afterwards to secure the minor placings. It was easy to write off this gold medal as a piece of outrageous fortune, and some did. *USA Today* columnist Mike Lopresti, who called Bradbury 'the luckiest guy at the Olympics', went on: 'The first winter gold medal in the history of Australia fell out of the sky like a bagged goose. He looked like the tortoise behind four hares.' Bob Ryan, of the *Boston Globe*, called the win 'a reminder that we live in an imperfect world', and added: 'Oh, I forgot. It's short track, and those of us who don't follow this goofy little enterprise are supposed to understand that multiple crashes that allow the wrong person to win are part of the deal.'

Bradbury himself struggled with conflicting emotions about his gold medal. As the judges talked after the race, he circled around the middle of the rink slowly. 'The other guys had gotten off the ice, and everyone was looking at the judges, wanting to know whether there would be a re-race. Then the official announcement came and it clicked with me that I had actually won. There was a lot of disbelief, a lot of emotion, a lot of tears and that sort of stuff, and the rest of the guys from the team were there quickly. It didn't sit quite comfortably with me, being the guy that won because everybody else fell down. It just didn't feel right.'[9] It was another member of the Australian team, Andrew McNee, who suggested the exact perspective he needed to feel at ease with the win. 'Don't think about it as a reward for the minute and a half of that race,' he said, 'but for the last 12 years.' As he headed for the media conference where he knew he would be asked whether he deserved to win, Bradbury reflected on that advice, and was grateful for it. He said later: 'I didn't have any answers for myself, and it was good that Andrew helped me with that. From that time, I thought, "I'll take it." I was asked the question a lot that night, and have been ever since, and I have no problems now justifying the fact that I'm a deserving winner. It was pretty difficult then, though.'[10]

Those last 12 years had been interesting for Bradbury, as a journeyman of the speed-skating world through four Olympics and a couple of horrific injuries. His moments of glory came when he was a member of the four-man relay team that won gold at the 1991 world championships and bronze — Australia's first winter Olympic medal ever — in Lillehammer in 1994. At those same Olympics, in an individual race for which he was among the favourites, he had been knocked down by another skater and eliminated. A year later, in another crash during a World Cup competition in Montreal, Canada, the blade of a rival's skates sliced into one side of his right thigh and out the other. He recalls: 'It cut through all four of my quad muscles, sliced the femoral vein, the ileo-tibial, basically anything else that got in the way. I lost four of my six litres of blood and could feel my body starting to shut down. It was right at the end of a 1500, so my heart rate would have been going close to 200 and blood was pumping very fast. There was no way I was going to close my eyes because I thought I would be dead. I thought, if I lose consciousness here I'm never waking up again.'[11] Three weeks and 111 stitches later, he was back on the ice — although it took about 18 months for the leg to regain full strength.

Steven Bradbury and Alisa Camplin show off their gold medals in Salt Lake City.

Bradbury was again a serious medal contender in Nagano in 1998 but was the victim of another knockdown. Then in September 2000, the day before the summer Games began in Sydney, he crashed head-first into a barrier during training in Brisbane and broke his neck. He had been trying to hurdle another skater who fell in front of him, had caught his toe on the way across, and had fractured the C4 and C5 vertebrae. He had a halo fitted for five weeks, with four pins into his skull and screws bolted onto plates on his chest and back. Doctors told him he wouldn't skate again, but the whole episode provided him with the motivation for one more crack at the Olympics. 'Me not skating was never going to happen,' he said later. 'Now I just wanted to skate my best at the Games. Through 1994 and 1998 I knew that I had the ability to win a medal, but I hadn't been allowed [through crashes] to skate as well as I could. Now my goals were changed. I knew I wasn't the serious contender I had been, but I also wanted to give it everything, skate the best I could.'[12]

Twelve years of dedication to a low-profile sport had done little to enhance the Bradbury bank account. He ran a backyard skate-boot business in Brisbane — the Revolutionary Boot Company — with former Australian speed champion Clint Jensen, and supplemented the modest income from that with a $20,000-a-year grant from the Winter Olympic Institute. Before the Salt Lake City Games he e-mailed Apolo Ohno, to whom the company supplies free boots, asking him to give the company a plug if he won the 1000 metres gold medal, as he was expected to do. 'I guess I can do that myself now,' said Bradbury with a grin afterwards. His mother, Rhonda, who worked in the tuckshop of one of three rinks managed by his father, John, told the media: 'He needs some publicity, because he's flat broke. He had to borrow $1000 out of our Salt Lake food kitty to fix his car before he came over. He wants to be a fireman when he gets a real job.'

When Alisa Camplin soared through two perfect triple twisting double somersaults to win the freestyle aerial gold medal at Deer Valley, she ended one of the more unlikely journeys in the history of Australian sport. She was 27 years old, and for 22 of them her ambition — sometimes obsession — had been to compete in an Olympic Games. For most of that time she had thought that it would be the summer Games, in track and field. She had been such a late starter in the winter version that, while she could twirl and flip, almost trace flower patterns in the air, she was far from an expert skier on the ground. The jumping had always come first, and in the lead-up to the Olympics she was still receiving skiing lessons from Helmut Spiegl, Zali Steggall's coach. Even as she skied away from the gold medal presentation, she took a small tumble. Watching her charm interviewers after her victory, appreciating her pleasant looks — she is petite (158 centimetres and 48 kilograms), with blue eyes and an easy, bubbling personality — it would be easy to misread Camplin: she is as disciplined and tough-minded as any elite athlete in any sport, and her talent is bolstered by an appetite for hard work and huge reservoirs of self-belief.

Camplin can remember distinctly the two occasions on which she saw snow before she was an adult. Once, when she was quite small, her parents, Geoff and Jenny, took her and her two younger sisters to the Dandenong Ranges, outside Melbourne, to let them take a look at the white stuff. Then, when she was in seventh grade at Methodist Ladies' College, there was a class outing for a day at the Mt Buller resort. She had been a successful runner, jumper and hurdler in Little Athletics, training two mornings and five afternoons a week at the age of nine, but suffered what she later called 'an emotional blow' when she failed to make the state under-12 team. At MLC she turned to gymnastics, reached Level 8 after three years, but suffered stress fractures in her lower back and failed to make the Victorian team in 1990. 'That was a real shame, my second big setback,' she said later. 'I guess when you're younger you're always looking to get your state team tracksuit. I was a really good runner and a good gymnast.'[13] She played hockey for a time, then trained in athletics again at Doncaster under the coach Tom Kelly, who felt she could be a prospect for the marathon at the Sydney Olympics. Through all of these sporting preoccupations, she talked constantly of going to the Games:

> People think it's all huff and puff, but I swear to goodness that every time I cut a cake, blew out a candle, made a wish, blew an eyelash off my finger or saw a ladybird, I wished to go to the Olympics Games and win a medal. It was just a dream. From the time I was five years old I wanted to be great at some form of sport … to go to the Olympics. Even missing out on the track and field nationals, missing out on the gymnastic nationals, I didn't lose the desire. I really had to prove something to myself. I think there had been this internal gnawing, that I'd not achieved anything. I have hundreds of trophies and medals, but I still couldn't tell myself that I'd done enough. Some of my training partners got to the Atlanta Games, but I was still there, wishing. I needed a direction.[14]

The direction came quite accidentally in 1994, after she had begun a tertiary course — for a Bachelor of Information Technology at the Swinburne Institute of Technology. In May that year, when she was 19, a friend from Swinburne persuaded her to go with him to a Ski Expo at the old Exhibition Building. He intended to go on a family trip to Canada, and for her ' it was just something to fill the day … I had nothing else to do.' Team Buller, the ski group based at the mountain, had rigged up a trampoline for demonstration shows, with Jacqui

Cooper doing exhibitions. Supervising the show was Geoff Lipshut, later chief of the Olympic Winter Institute, who was seeking to identify potential talent for the new sport of aerial freestyle skiing. Rather than taking ordinary skiers and turning them into aerialists, he was keen to find gymnasts who could be taught to ski. It was a variation, in a winter sense, of the notion of finding good young paddlers in the surf and turning them into kayakers. At $5 a time, visitors to the Expo could be strapped into a harness with bungy ropes and throw themselves around the trampoline. Camplin was keen:

> I hadn't done any flipping and twisting since 1990, when I'd finished gymnastics. So I got in and had a go, and people kept asking me if I could do this and that. I could do everything. Because you're suspended like that, you can get more height than you can normally on a trampoline. When I got off the trampoline, Jacqui was all excited, and Geoff Lipshut was saying: 'That was great. You should do aerials. You're exactly what we've been looking for.' I spoke to them for a while. We established that I couldn't ski, but I guess it was a convenient time in my life … The biggest risk for me was financial — that and the big unknown. I made an agreement with Geoff that I would ski with the Mt Buller junior ski team for one year, one Australian winter, and then he would give me one Australian summer of practice, doing backflips, back somersaults, on the Australian Water Jump site just outside Lilydale. To be honest, the only reason I started was that aerials were an Olympic sport. I told him right from the start that I was only having a go because I wanted to go to the Olympics. I thought it was my last chance. It was either that or marathon running.[15]

The cost of tackling a new sport was a problem. Camplin worked twenty hours a week at the ANZ Bank, delivered pizzas on Tuesday nights and worked as a cleaner on Thursdays — all to raise enough money to ski. She took out a loan to pay for a season's pass, and borrowed clothes and ski equipment for her sessions in the snow. The only item of ski clothing she owned was a pair of boots. (It was not until three years later that she could afford to buy her own set of skis.) She tried the rudiments of skiing: 'I'm a tenacious person. I took thousands of falls, took out trees, concussed myself, was laughed at and ridiculed by seven-year-olds.'[16] The grandly named Australian Water Jump where she and other aerial skiers learned their basic flips is unlike the fancy clear-water facilities that exist for such purposes in Canada and the United States: it is a muddy, unaerated dam, infested with leeches, without stairs or ladders out of the water — just a mud embankment to clamber up. She didn't complain: 'It was the only thing I'd ever known. There was a jump and water, and that's all I thought I needed.'

Camplin's passage to the Olympics amounted overall to a seven-year procession of somersaults, always increasing in complexity, improving in finesse — and it was littered with accidents. She broke her collarbone and a hand, separated her shoulder, dislocated her sternum twice, ripped her hip flexor out of her groin, tore an Achilles tendon, broke both ankles, tore her right knee, suffered nine serious concussions and cracked twelve ribs. Mostly it was bad landings that were to blame. Once she caught a tailwind in Switzerland, overshot the landing area and came down hard on her head on a patch of ice; she was airlifted to hospital. The worst experience was of a kind that air pilots fear: she became lost and disorientated in mid-air during a double twisting double somersault — looking for the ground, seeing only sky, and travelling at about 57 kilometres an hour. 'I was mentally and physically exhausted, wasn't focused when I came off the jump, started twisting too early. I landed square on my face. I didn't break any bones, but it was truly scary.'[17]

By the time Salt Lake City approached, Camplin knew she had progressed from being a participant to being a competitor, then from a competitor to a potential medallist. She calculated that she had done 800 more jumps than any of her rivals in the past year. She sold her car and spent $150,000 on the final campaign, hiring two Americans — Todd Ossian as her coach and Barbara Meyers as her sports psychologist. A year after the Games, she was still repaying the outlay. It was when she found that her relationship with team-mate Jacqui Cooper was inhibiting her — they had lived and trained closely when she was a developing athlete, but now there were tensions, mainly because they each needed space — that she had made the new coaching arrangement with the blessing of Geoff Lipshut, the team's technical director. It left the Australian coach Peter Judge free to concentrate on Cooper.

Her entire energy was devoted now to just one thing: going to the Deer Valley site on the big day, landing two good jumps and winning that gold medal. It loomed as the culmination of all those years, the bulk of her life in fact, and everything else was simply shut out. She moved (at further cost that she couldn't afford) into separate quarters, away from Cooper and other team-mates. She visited the Olympic site while the temporary bleachers were being built, took photographs, familiarised herself with the surroundings, visualised her jumps and conjured in her mind the noise of the MCG on grand final day. Ossian had taken video footage the previous year of the same site on exactly the day of the finals competition, and they studied the movement of the sun, even the shadows of the trees. 'I was prepared for that site, that atmosphere, well before the Games,' she said later. 'It was all a deliberate plan to be comfortable with the environment. It was Todd's and Margaret's idea.'[18]

She banned her family from attending the Games, because she didn't want distractions. She resolved not to attend the opening ceremony: 'I was one of about five people in the place who didn't go. I'd decided that with Barbara two months before. My whole life I had wanted to go to the Olympics, and I didn't want to go to that ceremony and have it slap me in the face, overwhelm me. I was determined not to be an Olympic tourist.' To that end she did not do what most athletes do: 'I didn't take any photos, didn't swap any pins, didn't run around buying things, didn't go to the international zone in the village. I stayed at another site.' She and Ossian decided that he would grind all the colour off her fluorescent green boots for the Games and spray-paint them black: 'If I had my feet slightly apart with those green boots on, it would be more obvious to the judges, and we didn't want to lose one point from any judge.'[19] When she suffered a bad foot injury a month out from the Games, she handled it characteristically:

> On the second day of training at Apex I was too slow coming into a jump, mainly due to a severe headwind. I didn't make the landing hill and finished on the hard ice. I was in severe pain. I couldn't walk, couldn't put my feet down … it was severe impact bruising. I was in complete agony. I iced my feet in an icing machine eight hours a day. My feet were completely numb all day, every day. The only way I could get around

Seven years of hard work and injuries are forgotten as Alisa Camplin celebrates her success at Salt Lake City.

was on my knees. It was all tiled and wood flooring, and I finished up with massive bruising on my knees from the constant crawling. I missed four competitions before the Games, all the competitions in January, but I didn't fall apart. I knew I'd be right. I decided that I needed to prove to myself that I still deserved to win. In the last weekend before the Games, the last pre-Olympic competition, I was vomiting with pain from the ankles, which were all purple. I still couldn't walk with the pain. But I did three jumps, the first time in six weeks, and landed okay. I wasn't polished but it meant that eight days out from the Olympics there was hope. So I took two days off to let my ankles de-swell a bit. On the day of the opening ceremony our team's medical director, Peter Braun, sent me to the polar clinic, where they took CAT scans of my ankles. We were going to use injections to block the nerves. It turned out that the bleeding in my ankles, the bruising, had invaded my bones badly. It's like honeycomb, little cavities, and the walls between all the cavities were broken down.[20]

The rest, to recycle the old cliché, is Olympic history, or a lovely piece of it. After seven years of hard labour, Camplin won her gold medal, stretching and spinning high on her second jump, making the best landing of her life to finish ahead of Canadians Veronica Brenner and Deidra Dionne. The Olympics were the first world-class event she had ever won, and members of her family were there to see it. Her mother, Jenny, and sister Georgina had secretly booked their flights and hidden behind an Australian flag during the semis and finals. Afterwards Camplin made another wish: that she would win at the 2003 world championships. (She did that, and for good measure also set a world record and won the World Cup.)

The Salt Lake City Olympics were notable for the feats of the Norwegian biathlete Ole Einar Bjoerndalen — who won four gold medals — as well as a rash of scandals. Three of the best cross-country skiers tested positive to drugs; a corrupt French judge caused the Canadian figure skaters Jamie Sale and David Pelleter to be robbed of a deserved victory (although the IOC later intervened, not to take the gold medals away from the wrongful Russian winners but to present duplicate gold to the Canadians); the Russian team threatened to take their skates, skis and hockey sticks home after what they called serial victimisation; South Korea called in lawyers after short-track skater Kim Dong-Sung was disqualified from the 1500 metres and the gold medal handed to Apolo Anton Ohno, who was later placed under protective police guard.

But for Coates, Henke, Chesterman and stalwarts of the Olympic Winter Institute, Salt Lake City's Olympics were significant for one reason alone: they would always be the Games where Australia proved that it finally *was* fair dinkum about the sports of winter.

Notes

1 Stumbling towards Atlanta

1. *The IOC Official Olympic Companion*, compiled by Caroline Searle and Bryn Vaile, Brassey's Sports, Random House, London, Washington, 1996.
2. K. Perkins, interview with author, 17 April 2002.
3. Ibid.
4. J. Carew, interview with author, 26 June 2002.
5. Ibid.
6. K. Perkins, interview with author, 17 April 2002.
7. Ibid.
8. J. Carew, interview with author, 26 June 2002.
9. Richard Yallop, *Oarsome*, Ironbark Press, Sydney, 1988, p. 13.
10. Ibid.
11. M. McKay, interview with author, 17 August 2002.
12. N. Green, interview with author, 31 July 2002.
13. M. McKay, interview with author, 17 August 2002.
14. W. Schaeffer, interview with author, 31 July 2002.
15. S. O'Neill, interview with author, 5 April 2002.

2 Still the same water

1. K. Perkins, interview with author, 17 April 2002.
2. Ibid.
3. Ibid.
4. Ibid
5. Ibid.
6. D. Kowalski, interview with author, 8 February 2003.
7. S. O'Neill, interview with author, 5 April 2002.
8. M. McKay, interview with author, 17 August 2002.
9. Ibid.
10. Ibid.
11. Ibid.

And so to Sydney...

1. Five-page letter, Luxton to Kent Hughes, 18 February 1952.
2. Brundage press conference, 11 April 1955.
3. IOC executive committee, 9 June 1955.
4. Ibid.
5. H. Gordon, *Australia and the Olympic Games*, University of Queensland Press, St Lucia, 1994.
6. P. Coles, interview with author, 18 March 1994.

7. Ibid.
8. J. Coates, interview with author, 4 November 1994.
9. Ibid.
10. R. McGeoch, *The Bid: How Australia Won the 2000 Games*, William Heinemann, Sydney, 1994.

3   The Knight of the Long Prawns

1. G. Pemberton, interview with author, 1 October 2002.
2. J. Coates, interview with author, 18 March 2002.
3. Ibid.
4. M. Knight, interview with author, 29 October 2002.
5. J. Coates, interview with author, 18 March 2002.
6. M. Knight, interview with author, 29 October 2002.
7. K. Gosper, interview with author, 18 September 2002.
8. *Sydney Morning Herald*, 13 September 2000.
9. *UNSW Law Journal* (Vol. 22), 1999.
10. J. Coates, interview with author, 18 March 2002.
11. Ibid.
12. K. Gosper, interview with author, 18 September 2002.
13. J. Coates, interview with author, 18 March 2002.

4   'What have I got here?'

1. G. Pemberton, interview with author, 1 October 2002.
2. Ibid.
3. K. Gosper, interview with author, 18 September 2002. Following dialogue confirmed by G. Pemberton.
4. K. Gosper, interview with author, 18 September 2002.
5. G. Pemberton, interview with author, 1 October 2002.
6. K. Gosper, interview with author, 18 September 2002.
7. G. Pemberton, interview with author, 1 October 2002.
8. Ibid.
9. Ibid.
10. Ibid.
11. Ibid.
12. J. Coates, interview with author, 18 March 2002.
13. G. Pemberton, interview with author, 1 October 2002.
14. Ibid.
15. Ibid.
16. Ibid.
17. Ibid. Confirmed by J. Coates.
18. Ibid.
19. K. Gosper, interview with author, 18 September 2002.
20. G. Pemberton, interview with author, 1 October 2002.
21. Ibid.
22. M. Knight, interview with author, 29 October 2002.

23. J. Coates, interview with author, 18 March 2002.
24. G. Pemberton, interview with author, 1 October 2002.
25. M. Knight, interview with author, 29 October 2002.
26. Ibid.
27. Ibid.
28. Ibid.
29. D. Richmond, interview with author, 29 October 2002.
30. M. Knight, interview with author, 29 October 2002.
31. Kevan Gosper with Glenda Korporaal, An Olympic Life, Allen & Unwin, Sydney, 2000.
32. M. Knight, interview with author, 29 October 2002.
33. Ibid.
34. K. Gosper with G. Korporaal, op. cit.
35. M. Knight, interview with author, 29 October 2002.

5   A dangerous culture

1. S. Hollway, interview with author, 22 October 2002.
2. M. Knight, interview with author, 29 October 2002.
3. D. Richmond, interview with author, 29 October 2002.
4. K. Gosper, interview with author, 18 September 2002.
5. G. Pemberton, interview with author, 1 October 2002.
6. Ibid.
7. R. McGeoch, speech, 24 November 1998.
8. R. McGeoch, interview with author, 12 March 2003.
9. *SMH News Review*, 28 November 1998.
10. J. A. Samaranch, interview with author, 7 September 1997.
11. J. Coates, interview with author, 18 March 2002.
12. Ibid.

6   The battler from Bondi

1. *BRW*, 3 September 1999.
2. P. Coles, interview with author, 31 October 2002.
3. Ibid.
4. J. Coates, interview with author, 18 March 2002.
5. K. Gosper, interview with author, 16 September 2002.
6. P. Coles, interview with author, 31 October 2002.
7. Ibid.
8. Ibid.
9. K. Gosper with G. Korporaal, *An Olympic Life*, Allen & Unwin, Sydney, 2000.
10. Ibid.
11. P. Coles, interview with author, 31 October 2002.
12. M. Knight, interview with author, 29 October 2002.
13. K. Gosper with G. Korporaal, op. cit.
14. S. Hollway, interview with author, 22 October 2002.
15. J. Coates, interview with author, 19 March 2002.

16. Ibid.
17. *Weekend Australian*, 26 February 2000.
18. J. Coates, interview with author, 19 March 2002.
19. P. Coles, interview with author, 31 October 2002.
20. J. Coates, interview with author, 19 March 2002.
21. Ibid.
22. Letter, D. Henry to P. Coles, 9 July 2000.
23. Letter, Warwick Morieson, president North Bondi Surf Life Saving Club Inc., To Whom It May Concern, 20 July 2000.
24. Broadcast, A. Jones, 22 July 2000.
25. Dawn Fraser, *Dawn: One Hell of a Life*, Hodder, Sydney, 2001.
26. *Australian*, 21 July 2000.
27. Letter, D. Elliott to P. Moses, 15 August 2000.

7   A difficult year

1. J. Coates, interview with author, 18 March 2002.
2. M. Knight, interview with author, 29 October 2002.
3. Ibid.
4. Ibid
5. Ibid.
6. D. Richmond, interview with author, 29 October 2002.
7. M. Knight, interview with author, 29 October 2002.
8. S. Hollway, interview with author, 22 October 2002.
9. M. Knight, interview with author, 29 October 2002.
10. Ibid.
11. Ibid.
12. D. Richmond, interview with author, 29 October 2002.
13. J. Coates, interview with author, 18 March 2002.
14. M. Knight, interview with author, 29 October 2002.
15. Ibid.
16. Ibid.
17. S. Hollway, interview with author, 22 October 2002.
18. Ibid.
19. Ibid.

8   Changing the mood

1. K. Gosper, interview with author, 18 September 2002.
2. *Australian*, 11 May 2000.
3. K. Gosper, interview with author, 18 September 2002.
4. Ibid.
5. J. Coates, interview with author, 18 March 2002.
6. S. O'Neill, interview with author, 5 April 2002.
7. M. Knight, interview with author, 29 October 2002.
8. Ibid.
9. Quoted by Marian Wilkinson in *The Fixer*, W. Heinemann Australia, Port Melbourne, 1996.

10. S. Balderstone, interview with author, 15 February 2003.
11. M. Knight, interview with author, 29 October 2002.
12. D. Williams, anecdote in *The Volunteers*, by Max Walker and Gerry Gleeson, Allen & Unwin, Sydney, 2001.
13. Message from IOC president Juan Antonio Samaranch, November 2000.

9 The big secret

1. Dawn Fraser, *Dawn: One Hell of a Life*, Hodder, Sydney, 2001.
2. J. Coates, interview with author, 18 March 2002.
3. M. Knight, interview with author, 29 October 2002.
4. J. Coates, interview with author, 18 March 2002.
5. Ibid.
6. M. Knight, interview with author, 29 October 2002.
7. J. Coates, interview with author, 18 March 2002.
8. Ibid.
9. M. Knight, interview with author, 29 October 2002.
10. J. Coates, interview with author, 18 March 2002.
11. M. Knight, interview with author, 29 October 2002.
12. J. Coates, interview with author, 18 March 2002.
13. Ibid.
14. Ibid.
15. Ibid.
16. Ibid.
17. Ibid.
18. M. Knight, interview with author, 29 October 2002.
19. Ibid.
20. Dawn Fraser, op. cit.
21. Ibid.
22. R. Boyle, interview with author, 8 February 2003.
23. M. Knight, interview with author, 29 October 2002.
24. J. Coates, interview with author, 18 March 2002.

10 'The best minute, the best hour...'

1. David Williamson, 'Patriot Games', *Australian* Magazine, 7–8 October 2000.
2. S. O'Neill, interview with author, 5 April 2002.
3. Ibid.
4. Ibid.
5. The athletes elected were: Pole vaulter Sergei Bubka (Ukraine, 1506 votes); swimmer Alex Popov (Russian Federation, 1471 votes); O'Neill (1208 votes); volleyball player Robert Ctvrtlik (United States, 798 votes); javelin thrower Jan Zelezny (Czech, 786 votes); runner Charmaine Crooks (Canada, 733 votes); rower Roland Barr (Germany, 638 votes); water polo player Manuel Estiarte (Spain, 611 votes). The top four were elected for eight years, the others for four years.
6. K. Perkins, interview with author, 17 April 2002.
7. Ibid.

11   A creature of destiny

1. Adrian McGregor, *Cathy Freeman: A Journey Just Begun*, Random House, Sydney, 1998.
2. Ibid.
3. Michael Gordon, *Reconciliation: A Journey*, University of NSW Press, Sydney, 2001.
4. At the end of 2002 the Sport Australia Hall of Fame selected fourteen teams in its inaugural nomination of the finest combinations in the history of Australian sport. They were: The 1868 Aboriginal cricket team that toured England; the 1948 'Invincibles' cricket team; the 1952 Olympic tandem cycling team; the 1960 Olympic three-day equestrian team; the 1959 Canada Cup (now World Cup) gold team; the 2000 Olympic (Hockeyroos) hockey team; the 1992 (Oarsome Foursome) coxless fours rowing team; the 1963 rugby league Kangaroos; the 1984 rugby union Wallabies; the 2000 Olympic men's 4 x 100 metres freestyle relay team; the 1973 Davis Cup tennis team; the 1983 America's Cup crew of *Australia II*.

12   Gold in the cold

1. Colin Hickey, interview with author, 8 April 1992.
2. Ibid.
3. Malcolm Milne, interview with author, 19 December 1993.
4. Ibid.
5. Julius Patching, interview with author, 8 April 1992.
6. Ibid.
7. Steven Bradbury, interview with author, 26 February 2002.
8. Ibid.
9. Ibid.
10. Ibid.
11. Ibid.
12. Ibid.
13. Alisa Camplin, interview with author, 6 May 2002.
14. Ibid.
15. Ibid.
16. Ibid.
17. Ibid.
18. Ibid.
19. Ibid.
20. Ibid.

Bibliography

Boyle, Raelene and Linnell, Garry. *Raelene: Sometimes Beaten, Never Conquered.* Sydney: Harper Collins, 2003.

Cahill, Janet. *Running Towards Sydney 2000.* Sydney: Walla Walla, 1999.

Fraser, Dawn. *Dawn: One Hell of a Life.* Sydney: Hodder, 2001.

Gordon, Harry. *Australia and the Olympics Games.* Brisbane, University of Queensland Press, 1994.

Gordon, Harry. *Golden Heroes.* Melbourne: Australia Post, 2000.

Gosper, Kevin, with Korporaal, Glenda. *An Olympic Life.* Sydney, Allen & Unwin, 2000.

Kelly, Rob (ed.). *Atlanta '96, Official Commemorative Book.* San Francisco: Woodford Press, 2001.

Lyberg, Wolf. *The Athletes of the Games of the XXVII Olympiad, Sydney 2000.* Stockholm: IOC, 2001.

McGeoch, Rod, with Glenda Korporaal. *The Bid: How Australia Won the 2000 Games.* Melbourne: William Heinemann, 1994.

O'Neill, Susie. *Susie O'Neill.* Sydney: Macmillan, 2001.

Richardson, Graham, *Whatever It Takes.* Sydney: Bantam Books, 1994.

Rolton, Gillian. *Free Rein.* Sydney: HarperSports, 2001.

Toohey, Kristine (senior ed.). *Official Report of the XXVII Olympiad.* Sydney: SOCOG. 2001.

Walker, Max and Gleeson, Gerry. *The Volunteers.* Sydney: Allen & Unwin, 2001.

Wallechinsky, David. *The Complete Book of the Summer Olympics.* Woodstock, NY: Overlook Press, 2000.

Wallechinsky, David. *The Complete Book of the Winter Olympics.* Woodstock. NY: Overlook Press, 2002.

Wilkinson, Marian. *The Fixer.* Port Melbourne: W. Heinemann Australia. 1996.

Yallop, Richard. *Oarsome.* Sydney: Ironbark Press, 1998.

Australian Olympic statistics

Key to country codes

Africa

ANG	Angola
CMR	Cameroon
EGY	Egypt
KEN	Kenya
MAR	Morocco
MRI	Mauritius
NAM	Namibia
NGR	Nigeria
RSA	South Africa
SEN	Senegal
TUN	Tunisia
ZAI	Zaire
ZIM	Zimbabwe

Europe

ARM	Armenia
AUT	Austria
AZE	Azerbaijan
BEL	Belgium
BLR	Belarus
BUL	Bulgaria
CRO	Croatia
CZE	Czech Republic
DEN	Denmark
ESP	Spain
FRA	France
GBR	Great Britain
GEO	Georgia
GER	Germany
GRE	Greece
HUN	Hungary
ITA	Italy
LTU	Lithunia
LUX	Luxembourg
MDA	Moldova
MKD	Macedonia
NED	Netherlands
NOR	Norway
POL	Poland
POR	Portugal
ROM	Romania
RUS	Russian Federation
SLO	Slovenia
SUI	Switzerland
SVK	Slovakia
SWE	Sweden

TUR	Turkey
UKR	Ukraine
YUG	Yugoslavia

Asia

CAM	Cambodia
CHN	China
HKG	Hong Kong
INA	Indonesia
IND	India
IRI	Islamic Republic of Iran
JOR	Jordan
JPN	Japan
KAZ	Kazakhstan
KGZ	Kyrgyzstan
KOR	South Korea
KSA	Saudi Arabia
MAS	Malaysia
MGL	Mongolia
PAK	Pakistan
PRK	North Korea
THA	Thailand
TKM	Turkmenistan
TPE	Chinese Taipei
UZB	Uzbekistan

Oceania

AUS	Australia
NZL	New Zealand

North and South America

ARG	Argentina
ARU	Aruba
BOL	Bolivia
BRA	Brazil
CAN	Canada
COL	Colombia
CUB	Cuba
DOM	Dominican Republic
HON	Honduras
MEX	Mexico
NCA	Nicaragua
PAR	Paraguay
PER	Peru
PUR	Puerto Rico
USA	United States of America
VEN	Venezuela

Australian Olympic teams 1996–2002

1996 Atlanta, USA

Chef de Mission: John Coates **Assistant Chefs de Mission:** John Devitt, Peter Montgomery, Keith Murton
Attaché: Alf Nucifora **Administration:** Craig McLatchey (Director), Brad Kenworthy (Finance/Administration Manager), Belinda Lovett and Anne Mousseux (Administration Assistants), Cheryl Ritchie (Assistant to Chef de Mission) **Operations:** Robert Thornton (Director), Craig Phillips (Assistant Director), Tracey Johnstone (Operations Assistant) **Athlete Services:** Michael Wenden (Director), Lynne Bates (Administrator), Debbie Flintoff-King, Herb Elliott and Laurie Lawrence (Athlete Liaison Officers), Megan Sissian (Athlete Services Assistant) **Media Services:** Jim Webster (Director), Ian Heads, Kevin Berry, Michelle Brown, Greg Campbell, Dave Culbert, John Gatfield, Ian Hanson, Robin Poke and Jacqui Williamson (Media Liaison Officers), Rosemary Towner (Media Assistant) **Medical Services:** Dr Brian Sando (Director), Dr Peter Fricker (Deputy Medical Director), Ross Smith (Physiotherapy Director), Graham Winter (Psychology Director), Robert Granter (Massage Director) **Doctors:** Dr Grace Bryant, Dr Warren McDonald **Masseurs:** Bernd Aldoph, Wayde Clews, Narelle Davis, Gerhardt Hechenberger, Bradley Hiskins, Ari Takkinen, Howard Arbuthnot **Physiotherapists:** Elizabeth Austin, Peter Eckhardt **Nutritionist:** Louise Burke **Psychologists:** Jeffrey Bond, Vicki De Prazer, Catherine Martin

Archery
Section Manager and Coach: Stephen Jennison

MEN

Fairweather, Simon	Men's individual	52/64	660 pts (52nd)
	Men's team	4/15	478 pts (4th)
Fear, Jackson	Men's individual	35/64	671 pts (35th)
	Men's team	4/15	478 pts (4th)
Gray, Matthew	Men's individual	26/64	663 pts (26th)
	Men's team	4/15	478 pts (4th)

WOMEN

Bridger, Deonne	Women's individual	57/64	615 pts (57th)
Matthews, Myfanwy	Women's individual	48/64	616 pts (49th)

Athletics
Section Manager: Margaret Mahoney **Head Coach:** Phil King **Coaches:** Robert Bidder, Keith Connor, Peter Fortune, Craig Hilliard, Peter Lawler, Clifford Mallett, Richard Telford, Christopher Wardlaw, John Zanfirache **Doctor:** Dr Peter Brukner **Masseurs:** Barry Cooper, Garry Miritus **Physiotherapists:** Jennifer Davies, Dean Kenneally, Peter Stanton **Psychologist:** Jeffrey Simons

MEN

Abou Hamed, Zid	400 metres hurdles	DNC	Ineligible	
A'Hern, Nicholas	20 kilometres walk	4/61	Final: 1:20.31 (4th)	
Anderson, Chris	High jump	27/38	Qualifying: 2.15 metres	Final: DNQ
Arkell, Simon	Pole vault	31/38	Qualifying: NH	Final: DNQ
Baker, Simon	50 kilometres walk	47/52	Disqualified	
Brimacombe, Stephen	200 metres	9/81	Heat 1: 20.45 (4th)	Quarter-final 3: 20.53 (3rd)
				Semifinal 2: 20.38 (5th)
	4 x 100 metres relay	16/39	Heat 5: 38.93 (1st)	Semifinal 2: Disqualified
Byrne, Paul	800 metres	16/57	Heat 7: 1:47.05 (3rd)	Semifinal 1: 1:47.58 (6th)
Capobianco, Dean	200 metres	81/81	Disqualified	
			(Performance: Heat 8: 20.76 (4th)	
			Quarter-final 2: 21.03 (7th)	
			35th overall)	

307

	4 x 100 metres relay	DNC		
	4 x 400 metres relay	DNC		
Carlin, Sean	Hammer-throw	25/37	Qualifying: 73.32 metres	Final: DNQ
Cleary, Paul	1500 metres	51/57	Heat 5: 3:52.85 (11th)	
Cousins, Duane	50 kilometres walk	37/52	DNF	
Creighton, Shaun	5000 metres	20/41	Heat 1: 14:04.08 (5th)	Semifinal 1: 13:55.23 (14th)
	10 000 metres	25/48	Heat 2: 28:44.29 (13th)	
Currey, Andrew	Javelin	21/34	Qualifying: 77.28 metres	Final: DNQ
De Highden, Roderic	Marathon	23/124	2:17:42.0 (23rd)	
Ferrier, Scott	Decathlon	40/40	DNF	
Forsyth, Timothy	High jump	7/38	Qualifying: 77.28 metres	Final: DNQ
Greene, Paul	400 metres	29/64	Heat 3: 46.12 (3rd)	Quarter-final 3: 46.22 (8th)
	4 x 400 metres relay	12/35	Heat 1: 3:03.73 (4th)	Semifinal 1: 3:04.55 (7th)
Henderson, Paul	100 metres	56/108	Heat 8: 10.52 (5th)	
	4 x 100 metres relay	16/39	Heat 5: 38.93 (1st)	Semifinal 2: Disqualified
Hollingsworth, Simon	400 metres hurdles	51/55	Heat 4: 52.16 (8th)	
Jackson, Tim	4 x 100 metres relay	16/39	Heat 5: 38.93 (1st)	Semifinal 2: Disqualified
Joubert, Michael	400 metres	35/64	Heat 1: 46.30 (5th)	
	4 x 400 metres relay	12/35	Heat 1: 3:03.73 (4th)	Semifinal 1: 3:04.55 (7th)
Ladbrook, Mark	400 metres	34/64	Heat 8: 46.28 (5th)	
	4 x 400 metres relay	12/35	Heat 1: 3:03.73 (4th)	Semifinal 1: 3:04.55 (7th)
Mackenzie, Cameron	4 x 400 metres relay	12/35	Heat 1: 3:03.73 (4th)	Semifinal 1: 3:04.55 (7th)
Mapstone, Rodney	100 metres	62/108	Heat 6: 10.56 (6th)	
	4 x 100 metres relay	16/39	Heat 5: 38.93 (1st)	Semifinal 2: Disqualified
Miller, James	Pole vault	16/38	Qualifying: 5.60 metres	Final: DNQ
Moneghetti, Stephen	10 000 metres	DNC		
	Marathon	7/124	2:14:35.0 (7th)	
Murphy, Andrew	Triple jump	34/44	Qualifying: 16.00 metres	Final: DNQ
Paynter, Julian	5000 metres	26/41	Heat 2: 14:00.25 (11th)	Semifinal 2: 14:23.60 (12th)
	10 000 metres		Heat 1: Did not start	
Quilty, Sean	Marathon	34/124	2:19:35.0 (34th)	
Robinson, Rohan	400 metres hurdles	5/55	Heat 3: 48.89 (2nd)	Semifinal 2: 48.28 (4th)
				Final: 48.30 (5th)
Russell, Dion	20 kilometres walk	47/61	1:30:04.0 (47th)	
Unthank, Christopher	3000 metres steeplechase	13/35	Heat 3: 8:31.86 (8th)	Semifinal 2: 8:25.59 (8th)
Vander-Kuyp, Kyle	110 metres hurdles	7/64	Heat 7: 13.32 (1st)	Quarter-final 4: 13.49 (3rd)
				Semifinal 1: 13.38
				Final: 13.40 (7th)
Wiggins, Paul	1500 metres wheelchair	7/8	3:16.86 (7th)	
Winter, Peter	Decathlon	40/40	DNF	

WOMEN

Anderson, Kate	5000 metres	42/48	Heat 1: 16:17.83 (14th)	
Boegman, Nicole	Long jump	7/50	Qualifying: 6.67 metres	Final: 6.73 metres (7th)
Costian, Daniela	Discus	14/39	Qualifying: 61.66 metres	Final: DNQ
Cripps, Sharon	4 x 100 metres relay	7/22	Heat 1: 43.75 (3rd)	Final: 43.70 (7th)
Crowley, Margaret	1500 metres	5/32	Heat 3: 4:07.51 (4th)	Semifinal 2: 4:06.21 (3rd)
				Final: 4:03.79 (5th)
Freeman, Cathy	200 metres	11/48	Heat 3: 23.25 (3rd)	Quarter-final 3: 22.74 (4th)
				Semifinal 1: 22.78 (6th)
	400 metres	2/49	Heat 7: 51.99 (2nd)	Quarter-final 1: 50.43 (1st)
				Semifinal 1: 50.32 (1st)
				Final: (2nd)
	4 x 100 metres relay	DNC		
	4 x 400 metres relay	DNC		
Gainsford, Melinda	100 metres	DNC		
	200 metres	10/48	Heat 2: 22.70 (2nd)	Quarter-final 1: 22.91 (3rd)
				Semifinal 2: 22.76 (5th)
	4 x 100 metres relay	DNC		
	4 x 400 metres relay	11/15	Heat 2: 3:33.78 (7th)	

Hanigan, Kylie	4 x 100 metres relay	7/22	Heat 1: 43.75 (3rd)	Final: 43.70 (7th)
	4 x 400 metres relay	11/15	Heat 2: 3:33.78 (7th)	
Harvey, Natalie	5000 metres	41/48	Heat 2: 16:06.45 (15th)	
Hewitt, Lauren	4 x 100 metres relay	7/22	Heat 1: 43.75 (3rd)	Final: 43.70 (7th)
Hobson, Susan	10 000 metres	17/35	Heat 2: 32:25.13 (12th)	Final: 32:47.71 (17th)
Inverarity, Alison	High jump	33/33	Qualifying: NH	Final: DNQ
Jamieson, Jane	Heptathlon	20/29	5897 pts (20th)	
Lambert, Jodie	4 x 100 metres relay	7/22	Heat 1: 43.75 (3rd)	Final: 43.70 (7th)
Lightfoot, Lisa	800 metres	25/37	Heat 4: 2:02.88 (6th)	
McCann, Kerryn	Marathon	28/86	2:36:41.0 (28th)	
McPaul, Louise	Javelin	2/33	Qualifying: 62.32 metres	Final: 65.54 metres (2nd)
Malaxos, Suzanne	Marathon	57/86	2:50:46.0 (57th)	
Manning, Anne	10 kilometres walk	19/44	45:27.0 (19th)	
Naylor, Lee	400 metres	32/49	Heat 3: 52.53 (4th)	Quarter-final 4: 53.75 (8th)
	4 x 400 metres relay	11/15	Heat 2: 3:33.78 (7th)	
Ondieki, Lisa	Marathon	DNC		
Poetschka, Renee	400 metres	15/49	Heat 1: 51.55 (4th)	Quarter-final 3: 51.33 (4th)
				Semifinal 2: 51.49 (7th)
	4 x 400 metres relay	11/15	Heat 2: 3:33.78 (7th)	
Risk, Kylie	10 000 metres	35/35	Heat 1: DNF	
Sauvage, Louise	800 metres wheelchair	1/8	1:54.90 (1st)	
Saville, Jane	10 kilometres walk	26/44	45:56.0 (26th)	
Saxby-Junna, Kerry	10 kilometres walk	12/44	43:59.0 (12th)	
Schuwalow, Carolyn	5000 metres	DNC	Heat 3: Did not compete	
Stone, Joanna	Javelin	16/33	Qualifying: 58.54 metres	Final: DNQ
Vizaniari, Lisa-Marie	Discus	8/39	Qualifying: 63.00 metres	Final: 62.48 metres (8th)

Badminton

Section Manager: Peter Roberts   **Head Coach:** Ning On Sze

MEN

Blackburn, Peter	Doubles	9/25	1st round: Defeated Mauritius 15–3,15–8
			2nd round: Defeated by China 15–7,15–9
	Mixed doubles	11/32	1st round: Defeated Belarus 18–14,15–19
			2nd round: Defeated by China 15–12,15–3
Hocking, Murray	Singles	32/49	1st round preliminary: Defeated by Iain Sydie (Canada) 15–9,15–9
	Mixed doubles	29/32	1st round: Defeated by China 15–5,15–4
Staight, Paul	Doubles	9/25	1st round: Defeated Mauritius 15–3,15–8
			2nd round: Defeated by China 15–7,15–9
Stevenson, Paul	Mixed doubles	24/32	1st round: Defeated by Canada 15–9,15–3

WOMEN

Campbell, Lisa	Singles	27/48	1st round preliminary: Defeated by Yasuko Mizui (JPN) 11–0,8–11,11–7
	Mixed doubles	29/32	1st round: Defeated by China 15–5,15–4
Cator, Rhonda	Doubles	21/27	1st round: Defeated by Indonesia 15–9,15–4
	Mixed doubles	11/32	1st round: Defeated Belarus 18–14,15–19
			2nd round: Defeated by China 15–12,15–3
Hardy, Amanda	Doubles	21/27	1st round: Defeated by Indonesia 15–9,15–4
	Mixed doubles	24/32	1st round: Defeated by Canada 15–9,15–3
Yang, Song	Singles	37/48	1st round preliminary: Defeated by Kelly Morgan (GBR) 11–1,11–5

Baseball

Section Manager: Donald Knapp   **Head Coach:** Peter Derksen   **Coaches:** Ron Johnson,
Adrian Meagher   **Assistant Coach:** Dusty Rhodes   **Physiotherapist:** Ian MacIndoe

MEN			
Dawes, Scott	Nakamura, Michael	7/8	Preliminary round:
Doubleday, Mark	Scott, Andrew		Defeated by Cuba 19–8
Hewitt, Jason	Sheldon-Collins, Matthew		Defeated by Netherlands 16–6
Hinton, Steven	Sheldon-Collins, Simon		Defeated Japan 9–6
Howell, Stuart	Thompson, Stuart		Defeated by Italy 12–8
Hynes, David	Tonkin, Shane		Defeated by USA 5–15
Lindberg, Fredrick	Tunkin, Scott		Defeated by Nicaragua 10–0
McDonald, Grant	Vagg, Richard		Defeated Korea 11–8
McNally, Andrew	Vogler, Peter		
Moore, John	Williams, Jeffrey		

Basketball (Men)

Section Manager: Tom York   **Head Coach:** Barry Barnes   **Assistant Coaches:** Alan Black, Brett Brown
Doctor: Dr Peter Harcourt   **Physiotherapist:** Craig Purdham

Borner, Ray	Reidy, Patrick	4/12	Preliminaries:
Bradtke, Mark	Ronaldson, Anthony		Defeated Korea 111–88
Dorge, John	Vlahov, Andrew		Defeated by Yugoslavia 91–68
Fisher, Scott			Defeated Brazil 109–101
Gaze, Andrew			Defeated Puerto Rico 101–96
Heal, Shane			Defeated Greece 103–62
Jensen, Tonny			Quarter-final: Defeated Croatia 73–71
Mackinnon, Samuel			Semifinal: Defeated by USA 101–73
Maher, Brett			Bronze final: Defeated by Lithuania 80–74

Basketball (Women)

Section Manager: Marian Stewart-Hudson   **Head Coach:** Thomas Maher
Assistant Coaches: Jennifer Cheesman, Carrie Graf   **Physiotherapist:** Jillianne Cook

Boyd, Carla	Sporn, Rachael	3/12	Preliminaries:
Brogan, Michelle	Timms, Michele		Defeated Korea 76–61
Brondello, Sandra	Whittle, Jennifer		Defeated Zaire 91–45
Chandler, Michelle			Defeated Cuba 75–63
Cook, Allison			Defeated by USA 96–79
Fallon, Trisha			Defeated by Ukraine 54–48
Maher, Robyn			Quarter-final: Defeated Russia 74–70
Robinson, Fiona			(overtime)
Sandie, Shelley			Semifinal: Defeated by USA 93–71
			Bronze final: Defeated Ukraine 66–56

Boxing

Section Manager: Peter Rogers   **Head Coach:** Albert Beau Gerring   **Coach:** Dennis Welbeloved

Crawford, Justann	Middleweight	9/32	1st round: Defeated Sackey Shivute (NAM)
			2nd round: Defeated by Alexander Lebziak (RUS)
Hosking, Lynden	Welterweight	17/32	1st round: Defeated by Nurzhan Smanov (KAZ)
Hussein, Hussein	Flyweight	9/32	1st round: Defeated Carmine Molaro (ITA)
			2nd round: Defeated by Kelly Damaen (BUL)
Peden, Robert	Featherweight	9/32	1st round: Defeated Mohamed Achik (MAR)
			2nd round: Defeated by Serafim Todorov (BUL)
Rowles, Richard	Light middleweight	17/32	1st round: Defeated by Gyorgy Mizsei (HUN)
Swan, James	Bantamweight	17/32	1st round: Defeated by Kalai Riadh (TUN)
Timperi, Rick	Light heavyweight	17/32	1st round: Defeated by Thomas Ulrich (GER)
Trautsch, Lee	Light Welterweight	17/32	1st round: Defeated by Fathi Missaoui (TUN)

Canoeing (Slalom)

Section Manager: Roy Farrance   **Head Coach:** Robyn Galloway

MEN

C1	Boocock, Justin	16/30	Heat: 237.89 (25th)	Final: 166.96 (16th)
C2	Felton, John	14/15	Heat: 309.82 (15th)	Final: 199.06 (14th)
K1	Macquire, Richard	24/44	Heat: 163.89 (19th)	Final: 153.97 (24th)
K1	Pallister, Matthew	38/44	Heat: 163.89 (19th)	Final: 179.19 (38th)
C2	Wilson, Andrew	14/15	Heat: 309.82 (15th)	Final: 199.06 (14th)

WOMEN

K1	Farrance, Mia	14/30	Heat: 243.77 (15th)	Final: 180.30 (14th)
K1	Woodward, Danielle	12/30	Heat: 178.67 (5th)	Final: 177.60 pts (12th)

Canoeing (Sprint)

Section Manager: Christine Duff   **Head Coach:** Brian Trouville   **Coaches:** Terence Hutchings, Barry Kelly, John Sumegi, James Walker   **Masseur:** Maxwell Metzker   **Physiotherapist:** Mark Winder

MEN

K4 1000 metres	Andersson, Ramon	9/16	Heat 1: 3:11.752 (3rd)	Semifinal 2: 3:01.806 (1st) Final: 2:57.560 (9th)
K2 500 metres	Collins, Daniel	3/23	Heat 2: 1:31.433 (2nd)	Semifinal 2: 3:01.806 (1st) Final: 1:29.409 (3rd)
K2 1000 metres	Leury, Grant	7/24	Heat 3: 3:40.114 (1st)	Semifinal 1: 3:19.056 (5th) Final: 3:13.054 (7th)
K4 1000 metres	Lynch, Paul	9/16	Heat 1: 3:11.752 (3rd)	Semifinal 2: 3:01.806 (1st) Final: 2:57.560 (9th)
K4 1000 metres	Morton, Brian	9/16	Heat 1: 3:11.752 (3rd)	Semifinal 2: 3:01.806 (1st) Final: 2:57.560 (9th)
K1 500 metres	McFadzean, Cameron	9/26	Heat 2: 1:42.160 (2nd)	Semifinal 2: 1:41.083 (4th) Final: 1:41.023 (9th)
K1 1000 metres	Robinson, Clint	3/23	Heat 3: 3:44.768 (2nd)	Semifinal 2: 3:43.657 (1st) Final: 3:29.713 (3rd)
K2 1000 metres	Scott, Peter	7/24	Heat 3: 3:40.114 (1st)	Semifinal 1: 3:19.056 (5th) Final: 3:13.054 (7th)
K2 500 metres	Trim, Andrew	3/23	Heat 2: 1:31.433 (2nd)	Semifinal 1: 1:29.937 (2nd) Final: 1:29.409 (3rd)
K4 1000 metres	Walker, Jimmy	9/16	Heat 1: 3:11.752 (3rd)	Semifinal 2: 3:01.806 (1st) Final: 2:57.560 (9th)

WOMEN

K1 500 metres	Borchert, Katrin	8/23	Heat 3: 1:53.767 (1st)	Semifinal 1: 1:51.142 (5th) Final: 1:50.811 (7th)
K2 500 metres		3/20	Heat 3: 1:43.633 (2nd)	Semifinal 2: 1:43.729 (2nd) Final: 1:40.641 (3rd)
K4 500 metres	Hunter, Natalie	8/16	Heat 1: 1:41.185 (3rd)	Semifinal 2: 1:37.905 (3rd) Final: 1:34.673 (8th)
K4 500 metres	Lehmann, Lynda	8/16	Heat 1: 1:41.185 (3rd)	Semifinal 2: 1:37.905 (3rd) Final: 1:34.673 (8th)
K4 500 metres	Nossiter, Yanda	8/16	Heat 1: 1:41.185 (3rd)	Semifinal 2: 1:37.905 (3rd) Final: 1:34.673 (8th)
K4 500 metres	Oates, Shelley	8/16	Heat 1: 1:41.185 (3rd)	Semifinal 2: 1:37.905 (3rd) Final: 1:34.673 (8th)
K2 500 metres	Wood, Anna	3/20	Heat 3: 1:43.633 (2nd)	Semifinal 2: 1:43.729 (2nd) Final: 1:40.641 (3rd)

Cycling

Section Manager: Michael Turtur **Head Coaches:** Heiko Salzwedel, Charlie Walsh **Coaches:** Shayne Bannan, Damien Grundy, Andrew Logan, Gary West **Mechanics:** James Bullen, Darrell McCulloch **Physiologist:** Neil Craig **Doctor:** Dr Peter Barnes **Masseurs:** Malcolm Morris, Anthony Bond **Physiotherapist:** Victor Popov

MEN

Aitken, Brett	4000 metres team pursuit (track)	3/17	Qualifying: 4:09.750 (3rd) Quarter-final: Defeated USA 4:09.650 Semifinal: Defeated by Russia 4:07.570
Evans, Cadel	Cross-country (mountain bike)	9/44	Final: 2:26:15 (9th)
Hill, Darryn	Individual sprint (track)	5/24	Qualifying: 10.329 (6th) 1st round: Defeated Kamiyama (JPN) 11.192 2nd round: Defeated Clay (USA) 10.811 Eighth final: Defeated Buran (CZE) 11.008 Quarter-final: Defeated by Nothstein (USA) Final for 5–8 place: 11.072 (5th)
Hodge, Stephen	Individual road race	98/194	Final: 4:56:53 (98th)
	Individual time trial (road)	23/40	Final: 1:09:59 (23rd)
Jonker, Patrick	Individual road race	102/194	Final: 4:56:53 (102nd)
	Individual time trial (road)	8/40	Final: 1:06:54 (8th)
Kelly, Shane	1 kilometre time trial (track)		DNF
McDonald, Damian	Individual road race	65/194	Final: 4:56:47 (65th)
McEwen, Robert	Individual road race	23/194	Final: 4:56:44 (23rd)
McGee, Bradley	4000 metres individual pursuit (track)	3/18	Qualifying: 4:27.954 (5th) Quarter-final: Defeated Martinez (ESP) 4:24.943 Semifinal: Defeated by Collinelli (ITA) 4:26.121
	4000 metres team pursuit (track)	3/17	Qualifying: 4:09.750 (3rd) Quarter-final: Defeated USA 4:09.650 Semifinal: Defeated by Russia 4:07.570
Neiwand, Gary	Individual sprint (track)	4/24	Qualifying: 10.129 (1st) 1st round: Defeated Martinez Arroyo (BOL) 14.373 2nd round: Defeated Vassilopoulos (GRE) 11.249 1/8 Final: Defeated Magne (FRA) 11.625 Quarter-final: Defeated Pokorny (GER) 10.794 Semifinal: Defeated by Fiedler (GER)
O'Grady, Stuart	4000 metres team pursuit (track)	3/17	Qualifying: 4:09.750 (3rd) Quarter-final: Defeated USA 4:09.650 Semifinal: Defeated by Russia 4:07.570
	Individual points race (track)	3/28	Final: 27 pts (3rd)
O'Shannessey, Timothy	4000 metres team pursuit (track)	3/17	Qualifying: 4:09.750 (3rd) Quarter-final: Defeated USA 4:09.650 Semifinal: Defeated by Russia 4:07.570
Stephens, Neil	Individual road race	19/194	Final: 4:56:34 (19th)
Woods, Dean	4000 metres team pursuit	3/17	Qualifying: 4:09.750 (3rd) Quarter-final: Defeated USA 4:09.650 Semifinal: Defeated by Russia 4:07.570
Woods, Robert	Cross-country (mountain bike)	16/44	Final: 2:33:14 (16th)

WOMEN

Ferris, Michelle	Individual sprint (track)	2/14	Qualifying: 64.21 (1st) 1/8 finals: Defeated Wynd (NZL) 11.923 Quarter-final: Defeated Wang (CHN) 11.825, 11.932 Semifinal: Defeated Haringa (NED) 12.080, 12.078 Final: Defeated by Ballanger (FRA) (2nd)
Grigson, Mary	Cross-country (mountain bike)	15/29	Final: 2:02:38 (15th)
Tyler-Sharman, Lucy	Individual points race (track)	3/23	Final: 17 pts (3rd)
Watson, Tracey	Individual road race	39/58	Final: 2:42:35 (39th)
Watt, Kathryn	3000 metres individual pursuit (track)	8/12	Qualifying: 3:43.658 (8th) Quarter-final: Defeated by Bellutti (ITA)
	Individual road race	9/58	Final: 2:37:06 (9th)
	Individual time trial (road)	4/25	Final: 37:53 (4th)

| Wilson, Anna | Individual road race | 17/58 | Final: 2:37:06 (17th) |
| | Individual time trial (road) | 10/25 | Final: 38:50 (10th) |

Diving

Section Manager: Michael Corbitt   **Head Coach:** Salvador Sobrino   **Coach:** Tong Xiang Wang

MEN

Butler, Russell	Springboard	28/39	Preliminary: 305.79 pts (28th) (DNQ)
Lawson, Tony	Platform	28/37	Preliminary: 294.75 pts (28th) (DNQ)
Murphy, Michael	Springboard	6/39	Preliminary: 419.12 pts (3rd)
			Semifinal: 639.21 pts (3rd)
			Final: 640.95 pts (6th)

WOMEN

Arlow, Vyninka	Platform	19/33	Preliminary: 243.57 pts (19th) (DNQ)
Baker, Vanessa	Platform	25/33	Preliminary: 225.84 pts (25th) (DNQ)
Rogers, Jodie	Springboard	15/30	Preliminary: 242.19 pts (15th)
			Semifinal: 446.37 pts (15th) (DNQ)
Tourky, Loudy	Springboard	19/30	Preliminary: 229.11 pts (19th) (DNQ)

Equestrian

Section Manager: Russell Withers   **Head Coach (Eventing):** Wayne Roycroft
Assistant Coach (Eventing): Heath Ryan   **Coach (Show jumping):** Rodney Brown
Coach (Dressage): Clemens Dierks   **Chef d'Equipe:** James Dunn   **Veterinarian:** Denis Goulding

MEN

Cooper, David	(riding Red Sails)	Mixed individual jumping	63/82	Qualifying 1: 24 penalties (77th)
				Final: DNQ
Dutton, Phillip	(riding True Blue Girdwood)	Mixed three-day event, teams	1/16	Final: 203.85 faults (1st)
Green, David	(riding Chatsby)	Mixed three-day event, individual	27/36	Final: DNF
Hoy, Andrew	(riding Darien Powers)	Mixed three-day event, teams	1/16	Final: 203.85 faults (1st)
	(riding Gershwin)	Mixed three-day event, individual	11/36	Final: 112.60 faults (11th)
Johnstone, Russell	(riding Southern Contrast)	Mixed team jumping	19/19	Final: 129 faults (19th)
		Mixed individual jumping	59/82	Qualifying 1: 12 penalties (59th)
		Mixed team jumping	19/19	Final: 129 faults (19th)
				Final: DNQ
Ryan, Matthew	(riding Hinnegar)	Mixed three-day event, teams	1/16	Withdrew

WOMEN

Bishop, Nicola	(riding Wishful Thinking)	Mixed three-day event, individual	21/36	Eliminated in endurance test
Hanna, Mary	(riding Mosaic)	Mixed individual dressage	24/25	1383 pts (25th) (DNQ)
Parlevliet, Jennifer	(riding Another Flood)	Mixed team jumping	19/19	Final: 129 faults (19th)
		Mixed individual jumping	77/82	Qualifying 1: 5.75 penalties (40th)
				Final: DNQ
Rolton, Gillian	(riding Peppermint Grove)	Mixed three-day event, teams	1/16	Final: 203.85 faults (1st)
Roycroft, Vicki	(riding Coalminer)	Mixed team jumping	19/19	Final: 129 faults (19th)
		Mixed individual jumping	57/82	Qualifying 1: 8 penalties (41st)
				Final: DNQ
Schaeffer, Wendy	(riding Sunburst)	Mixed three-day event, teams	1/16	Final: 203.85 faults (1st)

Fencing

Section Manager and Coach: Vladimir Sher

WOMEN

Osvarth, Sarah	Epee individual	38/47	Round A, Bout 8: Defeated by Niki Sidiropoulou (GRE) 15–8

Football

Section Manager: Peter Gray   **Head Coach:** Edward Thomson   **Coaches:** Leslie Scheinflug, Raul Blanco
Doctor: Dr Siri Kannagara   **Physiotherapist:** Pedro Ruz

MEN Agostino, Paul   Foxe, Hayden   Petkovic, Michael   13/16   1st round:
Aloisi, Ross   Horvat, Steven   Spiteri, Joseph   Defeated by France 2–0
Babic, Mark   Juric, Frank   Tiatto, Daniel   Defeated Saudi Arabia 2–1
Casserly, Luke   Lozanovski, Goran   Tsekenis, Peter   Defeated by Spain 3–2
Corica, Stephen   Moric, Ante   Vidmar, Aurelio
Enes, Robert   Muscat, Kevin   Viduka, Mark

Gymnastics

Section Manager: Jacquelyn Wood   **Head Coach (Men):** Warwick Forbes
Head Coach (Women): Ju Ping Tian   **Coaches:** Qu Derui, Melijun Techabaev, Valdimir Zakharov

MEN

Dowrick, Brennon	Artistic individual all-round	35/112	Competition I: Floor: 9.200 pts Pommel horse: 9.350 pts Rings: 9.300 pts Vault: 9.350 pts Parallel bars: 9.325 pts Horizontal bar: 9.350 pts Total: 55.875 pts	Competition II: Floor: 9.200 pts Pommel borse: 9.600 pts Rings: 9.400 pts Vault: 0.000 pts Parallel bars: 9.250 pts Horizontal bar: 9.450 Total: 46.900 pts (35th)
Hudson, Bret	Artistic individual all-round	51/112	Competition I: Floor: 8.900 pts Pommel horse: 9.175 pts Rings: 9.075 pts Vault: 9.525 pts	Parallel bars: 9.225 pts Horizontal bar: 8.900 Total: 54.800 pts Competition II: DNQ (51st)

WOMEN

Brown, Kirsty-Leigh	Artistic team	10/12	Vault: 46.574 pts Uneven bars: 47.099 pts Beam: 46.086 pts	Floor: 47.086 pts Final: 186.845 pts (10th)
Hughes, Joanna	Artistic team	10/12	Vault: 46.574 pts Uneven bars: 47.099 pts Beam: 46.086 pts	Floor: 47.086 pts Final: 186.845 pts (10th)
	Artistic individual all-round	34/36	Vault: 9.456 pts Uneven bars: 8.350 pts Beam: 9.162 pts	Floor: 9.600 pts Total: 36.568 (34th)
Kantek, Nicole	Artistic team	10/12	Vault: 46.574 pts Uneven bars: 47.099 pts Beam: 46.086 pts	Floor: 47.086 pts Final: 186.845 pts (10th)
Moniz, Ruth	Artistic team	10/12	Vault: 46.574 pts Uneven bars: 47.099 pts Beam: 46.086 pts	Floor: 47.086 pts Final: 186.845 pts (10th)
	Artistic individual all-round	35/36	Vault: 9.256 pts Uneven bars: 9.525 pts Beam: 8.937 pts	Floor: 8.700 pts Total: 36.418 pts (35th)
Moro, Lisa	Artistic team	10/12	Vault: 46.574 pts Uneven bars: 47.099 pts Beam: 46.086 pts	Floor: 47.086 pts Final: 186.845 pts (10th)

Skinner, Lisa	Artistic team	10/12	Vault: 46.574 pts	Floor: 47.086 pts
			Uneven bars: 47.099 pts	
			Beam: 46.086 pts	Final: 186.845 pts (10th)
	Artistic individual all-round	36/36	Vault: 9.375 pts	Floor: 8.937 pts
			Uneven bars: 9.412 pts	
			Beam: 8.475 pts	Total: 36.199 pts (36th)
Smith, Jennyfer	Artistic team	10/12	Vault: 46.574 pts	Floor: 47.086 pts
			Unovon barc: 47.099 ptc	
			Beam: 46.086 pts	Final: 186.845 pts (10th)
Takahashi, Kasumi	Rhythmic	DNC	Injured	

Hockey (Men)

Section Manager: Kenneth Read   **Head Coach:** Frank Murray   **Coaches:** David Bell, Larry McIntosh
Doctor: Dr Tony Galvin   **Physiotherapist:** Barry Flemming   **Psychologist:** Neil McLean

Carruthers, Stuart	Garard, Brendan	Sproule, Daniel	3/12	Preliminary:
Choppy, Baeden	Gaudoin, Paul	Stacy, Jason		Drew with South Africa 1–1
Davies, Stephen	Hager, Mark (captain)	Wark, Kenneth		Defeated Korea 3–2
Diletti, Damon	Lewis, Paul	York, Michael		Defeated by Netherlands 3–2
Dreher, Lachlan	Smith, Grant			Defeated Malaysia 5–1
Elmer, Lachlan	Smith, Matthew			Defeated Great Britain 2–0
				Semifinal:
				Defeated by Spain 2–1
				Defeated Germany 3–2

Hockey (Women)

Section Manager: Wendy Pritchard   **Head Coach:** Ric Charlesworth   **Coaches:** Kathleen Partridge, Chris Spice
Physiotherapist: Margaret McIntyre   **Psychologist:** Corinne Reid

Andrews, Michelle	Maitland, Clover	Powell, Lisa	1/8	Preliminary:
Annan, Alyson	Marsden, Karen	Roche, Danielle		Defeated Spain 4–0
Dobson, Louise	Morris, Jennifer	Starre, Kate		Defeated Argentina 7–1
Farrell, Renita	Pereira, Jacqueline	Tooth, Liane		Defeated Germany 1–0
Haslam, Juliet	Peris, Nova			Drew with Korea 3–3
Hawkes, Rechelle	Powell, Katrina			Defeated Great Britain 1–0
				Defeated USA 4–0
				Defeated Netherlands 4–0
				Final:
				Defeated Korea 3–1

Judo

Section Manager: Luis Val   **Head Coach:** Trevor Kschammer   **Coach:** Suzanne Williams

MEN

Fagan, Darren	Half lightweight (65 kg)	23/35	1st round, Pool A: Bye
			2nd round, Pool A: Defeated by Israel Hernandez Plana (CUB)
Power, Brian	Extra lightweight (60 kg)	32/34	1st round, Pool B: Bye
			2nd round, Pool B: Defeated by Ricardo Acuna (MEX)
Szabo, Gabor	Half middleweight (78 kg)	33/34	1st round, Pool A: Bye
			2nd round, Pool A: Defeated by Bronislaw Wolkowicz (POL)
Szabo, Miklos	Heavyweight (+95 kg)	33/34	1st round, Pool A: Bye
			2nd round, Pool A: Defeated by Harris Papaioannou (GRE)
Wilkinson, David	Middleweight (86 kg)	19/34	1st round, Pool A: Bye
			2nd round, Pool A: Defeated Sergej Klischin (AUT)
			3rd round, Pool A: Defeated by Darcel Yandzi (FRA)

WOMEN

Brain, Cathy	Half lightweight (52 kg)	13/21	1st round, Pool A: Bye
			2nd round, Pool A: Defeated by Marie-Claire Restoux (FRA)
			Repechage, Pool A: Defeated by Marisa Pedulla (USA)
Burnett, Heidi	Heavyweight (+72 kg)	9/20	1st round, Pool B: Defeated Colleen Rosensteel (USA)
			2nd round, Pool B: Defeated by Heba Hefny (EGY)

Dixon, Carly	Middleweight (66 kg)	16/20	1st round, Pool B: Defeated by Odalis Reve (CUB)
Galea, Natalie	Half heavyweight (72 kg)	15/21	1st round, Pool B: Bye
			2nd round, Pool B: Defeated by Francis Gomez (VEN)
Hill, Narelle	Lightweight (56 kg)	16/22	1st round, Pool A: Defeated by Isabel Fernandez (ESP)
			Repechage, Pool A: Defeated by Zulfiya Guseynova (AZE)
Kirkman, Tina	Extra lightweight (48 kg)	15/21	1st round, Pool A: Defeated by Shu-Chen Yu (TPE)
Sullivan, Lara	Half middleweight (61 kg)	22/24	1st round, Pool B: Defeated by Diane Bell (GBR)

Modern Pentathlon
Section Manager: Kitty Chiller

MEN

Johnson, Alex	Individual	32/32	Shooting: 1144 pts (3rd)
			Fencing: 640 pts (29th)
			Swimming: 1300 pts (6th)
			Riding: 613 pts (31st)
			Riding: DNS
			Total: 3697 pts (32nd)

Rowing
Section Manager: Andrew Guerin　**Assistant Section Manager:** Matthew Draper
Head Coach: Reinhold Batschi　**Boatman:** Paul Fitzgerald　**Coaches:** Brian Dalton, Noel Donaldson, Stephen Evans, Harald Jahrling, Anthony Lovrich, Lyall McCarthy, Timothy McLaren, Ellen Randell, Paul Thompson
Doctor: Dr Bill Webb　**Masseur:** Luke Atwell　**Physiotherapist:** Henry Wajswelner

MEN

Event	Athletes		Heat	Later rounds
Single sculls	Cameron, David	13/21	Heat 2: 7:53.55 (3rd)	Repechage 1: 7:49.24 (3rd)
				Semifinal 3: 7:25.38 (1st)
				Final C: 7:30.55 (1st)
Double sculls	Antonie, Peter	8/19	Heat 1: 6:50.15 (3rd)	Repechage 4: 6:51.98 (2nd)
	Day, Jason			Semifinal 2: 6:39.49 (4th)
				Final B: 6:19.25 (2nd)
Lightweight double sculls	Edwards, Anthony	3/19	Heat 4: 6:49.95 (1st)	Semifinal 2: 6:29.27 (2nd)
	Hick, Bruce			Final A: 6:26.69 (3rd)
Coxless pair	Scott, Robert	2/18	Heat 3: 6:46.12 (1st)	Semifinal 1: 6:46.43 (1st)
	Weightman, David			Final A: 6:21.02 (2nd)
Quad sculls	Free, Duncan	3/14	Heat 1: 6:05.60 (1st)	Semifinal 1: 5:58.41 (2nd)
	Hanson, Boden			Final A: 6:01.65 (3rd)
	Hooker, Janusz			
	Snook, Ronald			
Coxless four	Ginn, Drew	1/14	Heat 3: 6:15.05 (1st)	Semifinal 1: 6:09.95 (3rd)
	Green, Nicholas			Final A: 6:06.37 (1st)
	McKay, Michael			
	Tomkins, James			
Lightweight coxless four	Karrasch, Haimish	6/17	Heat 1: 6:25.87 (3rd)	Repechage 1: 6:02.04 (2nd)
	Belcher, David			Semifinal 1: 6:15.47 (2nd)
	Lynagh, Gary			Final A: 6:18.16 (6th)
	Burgess, Simon			
Coxed eight	Dodwell, Benjamin	6/10	Heat 1: 5:46.83 (3rd)	Repechage 2: 5:31.33 (2nd)
	Fernandez, Jamie			Final A: 5:58.82 (6th)
	Hayman, Brett (cox)			
	Jahrling, Robert			
	Porzig, Nicholas			
	Stewart, Geoff			
	Stewart, James			
	Walker, Robert			
	Wearne, Richard			

WOMEN

Coxless pair	Slatter, Kate	1/13	Heat 1: 7:26.92 (1st)	Semifinal 1: 7:32.47 (2nd)
	Still, Megan			Final A: 7:01.39 (1st)

Double sculls	Hatzakis, Marina Roye, Bronwyn	4/14	Heat 2: 7:20.10 (1st)	Semifinal 1: 7:15.58 (3rd) Final A: 7:01.26 (4th)
Lightweight double sculls	Joyce, Rebecca Lee, Virginia	3/16	Heat 2: 7:33.16 (1st)	Semifinal 2: 7:17.67 (1st) Final A: 7:16.56 (3rd)
Quad sculls	Matzakis, Marina Newmarch, Sally Robinson, Jane Roye, Bronwyn	9/10	Heat 1: 6:48.58 (4th)	Repechage 1: 6:16.85 (3rd) Final B: 6:25.79 (3rd)
Coxed eight	Davies, Alison Douglas, Georgina Hick, Kaylynn Klomp, Carmen Luff, Jennifer Ozolins, Anna Safe, Amy Thompson, Bronwyn Wieland, Karina	5/8	Heat 1: 6:35.69 (4th)	Repechage 1: 6:08.92 (4th) Final A: 6:30.10 (5th)

Shooting

Section Manager: Ray Andrews   **Head Coach:** William Murray
Coaches: Murray Alexander, Claudia Kulla, Paul McCormack

MEN

Adams, Phillip	50 metres free pistol	30/45	552 pts (30th)
	10 metres air pistol	29/50	574 pts (29th)
Cunningham, David	Skeet	20/54	119 pts (20th)
Diamond, Michael	Trap	1/57	149 pts (1st)
Haberman, Stephen	Double trap	17/35	131 pts (17th)
Mark, Russell	Double trap	1/35	189 pts (1st)
	Trap	13/57	120 pts (13th)
Maxwell, John	Trap	4/57	146 pts (4th)
Mueleman, Craig	Skeet	20/54	119 pts (20th)
Murray, Patrick	25 metres rapid-fire pistol	21/23	575 pts (21st)
Sandstrom, Bengt	50 metres free pistol	35/45	549 pts (35th)
	10 metres air pistol	29/50	574 pts (29th)
Wilson, Bryan	10 metres running target	18/20	560 pts (18th)

WOMEN

Banks, Suzanne	10 metres air rifle	31/49	387 pts (31st)
Forder, Annemarie	10 metres air pistol	23/41	376 pts (23rd)
Huddleston, Deserie	Double trap	3/21	139 pts (3rd)
Roberts, Annmaree	Double trap	7/21	103 pts (7th)
Tomcala, Carol	25 metres sport pistol	37/37	558 pts (37th)
	Air pistol	34/41	370 pts (34th)
Woodward, Annette	25 metres sport pistol	23/37	573 pts (23rd)

Softball

Section Manager: Gail Wykes   **Head Coach:** Robert Crudgington   **Coaches:** Carole Peel, Ken Arthur
Physiotherapist: Wendy Braybon

WOMEN	Brown, Joanne Cooper, Kim Crudgington, Carolyn Dienelt, Kerry Edebone, Peta Harding, Tanya Holliday, Jennifer Lester, Joyce	McDermid, Sally McRae, Francine Petrie, Haylea Richardson, Nicole Roche, Melanie Ward, Natalie Wilkins, Brooke	3/8	Preliminary: Defeated by China 6–0 Defeated Taipei 4–0 Defeated by Puerto Rico 2–0 Defeated Netherlands 1–0 Defeated Japan 10–0 Defeated USA 2–1 Defeated Canada 5–2	Semifinal: Defeated Japan 3–0 Bronze final: Defeated by China 4–2

Swimming

Section Manager: Terry Buck   **Assistant Section Manager:** Julie Dyring   **Head Coach:** Don Talbot
Coaches: Glenn Beringen, John Carew, James Fowlie, Paul Hardman, William Nelson, Mark Regan, Brian Sutton, Brian Wilkinson   **Physiologist:** Robert Treffene   **Psychologist:** Clark Perry
Physiotherapists: Roger Fitzgerald, Peter Blanch   **Masseurs:** Patricia Manson, Nick Massaro

MEN

Allen, Malcolm	400 metres freestyle	13/35	Heat 5: 3:54.34 (5th)	Final B: 3:55.48 (5th)
	4x200 metres freestyle relay	4/17	Heat 2: 7:23.24 (2nd)	Final: 7:18.47 (4th)
Coombes, Simon	200 metres individual medley	28/39	Heat 4: 2:07.31 (6th)	Final: DNQ
Dewick, Steven	100 metres backstroke	15/52	Heat 6: 56.35 (6th)	Final B: 56.82 (7th)
	200 metres backstroke	23/44	Heat 6: 2:04.46 (5th)	Final: DNQ
	4 x 100 metres medley relay	3/27		Final: 3:39.56 (3rd)
Dunn, Matthew	200 metres individual medley	5/39	Heat 3: 2:01.44 (2nd)	Final A: 2:01.57 (5th)
	400 metres individual medley	4/27	Heat 3: 4:19.51 (1st)	Final A: 4:16.66 (4th)
	4 x 100 metres freestyle relay	6/20		Final: 3:20.13 (6th)
	4 x 200 metres freestyle relay	4/17		Final: 7:18.47 (4th)
Fydler, Christopher	50 metres freestyle	18/65	Heat 9: 22.98 (6th)	Final: DNQ
	100 metres freestyle	13/61	Heat 7: 50.27 (3rd)	Final B: 50.31 (5th)
	4 x 100 metres freestyle relay	6/20	Heat 2: 3:20.88 (3rd)	Final: 3:20.13 (6th)
Goodman, Scott	200 metres butterfly	3/43	Heat 5: 1:57.77 (1st)	Final A: 1:57.48 (3rd)
Haenen, Toby	4 x 100 metres medley relay	3/27	Heat 2: 3:41.30 (1st)	
Housman, Glen	4 x 200 metres freestyle relay	4/17	Heat 2: 7:23.24 (2nd)	
Klim, Michael	200 metres freestyle	10/43	Heat 6: 1:49.17 (3rd)	Final B: 1:49.50 (2nd)
	100 metres butterfly	6/61	Heat 7: 53.42 (3rd)	Final A: 53.30 (6th)
	4 x 100 metres freestyle relay	6/20	Heat 2: 3:20.88 (3rd)	Final: 3:20.13 (6th)
	4 x 200 metres freestyle relay	4/17		Final: 7:18.47 (4th)
	4 x 100 metres medley relay	3/27	Heat 2: 3:41.30 (1st)	Final: 3:39.56 (3rd)
Kowalski, Daniel	200 metres freestyle	3/43	Heat 6: 1:48.92 (2nd)	Final A: 1:48.25 (3rd)
	400 metres freestyle	3/35	Heat 3: 3:51.67 (1st)	Final A: 3:49.39 (3rd)
	1500 metres freestyle	2/34	Heat 4: 15:12.55 (1st)	Final: 15:02.43 (2nd)
	4 x 200 metres freestyle relay	4/17		Final: 7:18.47 (4th)
Logan, Scott	4 x 100 metres freestyle relay	6/20	Heat 2: 3:20.88 (3rd)	Final: 3:20.13 (6th)
Miller, Scott	100 metres butterfly	2/61	Heat 7: 52.89 (1st)	Final A: 52.53 (2nd)
	200 metres butterfly	5/43	Heat 5: 1:58.97 (2nd)	Final A: 1:58.28 (5th)
	4 x 100 metres medley relay	3/27	Heat 2: 3:41.30 (1st)	Final: 3:39.56 (3rd)
Mitchell, Ryan	200 metres breaststroke	11/36	Heat 3: 2:15.31 (3rd)	Final B: 2:15.63 (3rd)
Perkins, Kieren	1500 metres freestyle	1/34	Heat 5: 15:21.42 (4th)	Final: 14:56.40 (1st)
	4 x 200 metres freestyle relay	4/17	Heat 2: 7:23.24 (2nd)	
Rogers, Philip	100 metres breaststroke	5/45	Heat 5: 1:01.80 (2nd)	Final A: 1:01.64 (5th)
	200 metres breaststroke	5/36	Heat 4: 2:14.97 (2nd)	Final A: 2:14.79 (5th)
	4 x 100 metres medley relay	3/27	Heat 2: 3:41.30 (1st)	Final: 3:39.56 (3rd)
Steed, Trent	400 metres individual medley	15/27	Heat 3: 4:24.39 (3rd)	Final B: 4:29.35 (7th)
Vander Wal, Ian	4 x 100 metres freestyle relay	6/20	Heat 2: 3:20.88 (3rd)	
	4 x 200 metres freestyle relay	4/17	Heat 2: 7:23.24 (2nd)	

WOMEN

Denman, Helen	100 metres breaststroke	11/46	Heat 4: 1:10.64 (5th)	Final B: 1:10.26 (3rd)
	4 x 100 metres medley relay	2/24	Heat 3: 4:08.87 (1st)	
Gartrell, Stacey	800 metres freestyle	11/29	Heat 4: 8:42.39 (3rd)	Final: DNQ
Greville, Julia	200 metres freestyle	7/42	Heat 5: 2:00.44 (4th)	Final A: 2:01.46 (7th)
	4 x 100 metres freestyle relay	6/19	Heat 1: 3:47.94 (2nd)	Final: 3:45.31 (6th)
	4 x 200 metres freestyle relay	3/21	Heat 3: 8:09.33 (2nd)	Final: 8:05.47 (3rd)
Johnson, Emma	400 metres freestyle	12/40	Heat 3: 4:14.13 (3rd)	Final B: 4:15.79 (4th)
	200 metres individual medley	DNF	Withdrew after heats	
	400 metres individual medley	5/31	Heat 4: 4:43.45 (2nd)	Final A: 4:44.02 (5th)
	4 x 200 metres freestyle relay	3/21	Heat 3: 8:09.33 (2nd)	Final: 8:05.47 (3rd)
Kennedy, Angela	100 metres butterfly	18/44	Heat 5: 1:01.89 (7th)	Final: DNQ
	4 x 100 metres medley relay	2/24	Heat 3: 4:08.87 (1st)	
Lewis, Hayley	400 metres freestyle	15/40	Heat 3: 4:17.02 (5th)	Final B: 4:16.92 (7th)
	800 metres freestyle	13/29	Heat 4: 8:45.79 (5th)	Final: DNQ
Mackie, Lisa	4 x 100 metres freestyle relay	6/19	Heat 1: 3:47.94 (2nd)	Final: 3:45.31 (6th)
	4 x 200 metres freestyle relay	3/21	Heat 3: 8:09.33 (2nd)	
Neumann, Nadine	200 metres breaststroke	6/42	Heat 5: 2:29.91 (3rd)	Final A: 2:28.34 (6th)

O'Neill, Susan	200 metres freestyle	5/42	Heat 4: 2:00.89 (1st)	Final A: 1:59.87 (5th)
	100 metres butterfly	5/44	Heat 5: 1:00.55 (2nd)	Final: 1:00.17 (5th)
	200 metres butterfly	1/35	Heat 5: 2:09.46 (1st)	Final A: 2:07.76 (1st)
	4 x 100 metres freestyle relay	6/19		Final: 3:45.31 (6th)
	4 x 200 metres freestyle relay	3/21	Heat 3: 8:09.33 (2nd)	Final: 8:05.47 (3rd)
	4 x 100 metres medley relay	2/24		Final: 4.05.00 (2nd)
Overton, Elli	100 metres backstroke	14/36	Heat 5: 1:03.88 (6th)	Final B: 1:03.69 (6th)
	200 metres individual medley	5/43	Heat 6: 2:15.81 (1st)	Final A: 2:16.04 (5th)
	400 metres individual medley	14/31	Heat 2: 4:49.82 (4th)	Final B: 4:50.73 (6th)
Riley, Samantha	100 metres breaststroke	3/46	Heat 5: 1:09.37 (2nd)	Final A: 1:09.18 (3rd)
	200 metres breaststroke	4/42	Heat 6: 2:28.30 (1st)	Final A: 2:27.91 (4th)
	4 x 100 metres medley relay	2/24		Final: 4:05.08 (2nd)
Ryan, Sarah	50 metres freestyle	20/56	Heat 5: 26.34 (6th)	Final: DNQ
	100 metres freestyle	6/56	Heat 5: 56:07 (3rd)	Final A: 55.85 (6th)
	4 x 100 metres freestyle relay	6/19	Heat 1: 3:47.94 (2nd)	Final: 3:45.31 (6th)
	4 x 100 metres medley relay	2/24	Heat 3: 4:08.87 (1st)	Final: 4:05.08 (2nd)
Stevenson, Nicole	100 metres backstroke	7/36	Heat 3: 1:02.50 (1st)	Final A: 1:02.70 (7th)
	200 metres backstroke	18/33	Heat 4: 2:16.71 (7th)	Final: DNQ
	4 x 200 metres freestyle relay	3/21		Final: 8:05.47 (3rd)
	4 x 100 metres medley relay	2/24	Heat 3: 4:08.87 (1st)	Final: 4:05.08 (2nd)
Thomas, Petria	200 metres butterfly	2/35	Heat 3: 2:10.64 (1st)	Final A: 2:09.82 (2nd)
Van Wirdum, Karin	50 metres freestyle	15/56	Heat 5: 25.88 (4th)	Final B: 26.17 (7th)
Windsor, Anna	4 x 100 metres freestyle relay	6/19	Heat 1: 3:47.94 (2nd)	

Table Tennis

Section Manager: Neil Harwood   **Head Coach:** Lan Sun Zhou

MEN

Langley, Paul	Singles	52/64	Preliminaries: Defeated by China 0–2 Defeated by Belgium 0–2 Defeated by Yugoslavia 0–2	Final: DNQ
	Doubles	30/31	Preliminaries: Defeated by China 2–0 Defeated by Croatia 2–1 Defeated by Austria 2–0	Final: DNQ
Lavale, Russell	Doubles	30/31	Preliminaries: Defeated by China 2–0 Defeated by Croatia 2–1 Defeated by Austria 2–0	Final: DNQ
Smythe, Mark	Singles	57/64	Preliminaries: Defeated by China 2–0 Defeated by Belgium 2–0 Defeated by Yugoslavia 2–1	Final: DNQ

WOMEN

Zhou, Shirley	Singles	34/63	Preliminaries: Defeated by Hungary 2–0 Defeated by Italy 2–0 Defeated Indonesia 2–0	Final: DNQ
	Doubles	26/31	Preliminaries: Defeated by Hungary 2–0 Defeated by Taipei 2–1 Defeated by People's Rep. of Korea 2–1	Final: DNQ
Zhou, Xi Tao	Doubles	26/31	Preliminaries: Defeated by Hungary 2–0 Defeated by Taipei 2–1 Defeated by People's Rep. of Korea 2–1	Final: DNQ

Tennis

Section Manager: Mike Daws   **Coach (Men):** Tony Roche   **Coach (Women):** Lesley Bowrey
Physiotherapist: Geoffrey Mackay

MEN

Philippoussis, Mark	Singles	9/64	1st round: Defeated Paul Haarhuis (NED) 7–6(–4), 7–6(–2)
			2nd round: Defeated Wayne Black (ZIM)j 6–4, 6–2
			3rd round: Defeated by Fernando Meligeni (BRA) 7–6(–7),4–6,8–6
Stoltenberg, Jason	Singles	17/64	1st round: Defeated Sule Ladipo (NGR) 7–6(–4),6–3
			2nd round: Defeated by Kenneth Carlsen (DEN) 6–2,3–6,6–3
Woodbridge, Todd	Singles	9/64	1st round: Defeated Jan Siemerink (NED) 6–2,6–4
			2nd round: Defeated Tim Henman (GBR) 7–6(–6),7–6(–5)
			3rd round: Defeated by Wayne Ferreira (RSA) 7–6(–3),7–6(–5)
	Doubles	1/16	1st round: Defeated France 6–2,3–6,6–3
			2nd round: Defeated India 4–6,6–2,6–2
			Quarter-final : Defeated Spain 6–4,6–1
			Semifinal : Defeated Netherlands 6–2,5–7,18–16
			Final: Defeated Great Britain 6–4,6–4,6–2
Woodforde, Mark	Doubles	1/16	1st round: Defeated France 6–2,3–6,6–3
			2nd round: Defeated Indonesia 4–6,6–2,6–2
			Quarter-final : Defeated Spain 6–4,6–1
			Semifinal : Defeated Netherlands 6–2,5–7,18–16
			Final: Defeated Great Britain 6–4,6–4,6–2

WOMEN

Bradtke, Nicole	Singles	33/64	1st round: Defeated by Iva Majoli (CRO) 3–6,6–3,6–4
	Doubles	28/31	1st round: Defeated by China (Walkover)
McQuillan, Rachel	Singles	33/64	1st round: Defeated by Amanda Coetzer (RSA) 6–4,7–6(–5)
Stubbs, Renae	Singles	33/64	1st round: Defeated by Magdalena Maleeva (BUL) 6–2,6–1
	Doubles	28/31	1st round: Defeated by China (Walkover)

Volleyball, Beach

Section Manager: Steve Tutton   **Coaches:** Stephen Anderson, Paul Smith

MEN

Prosser, Julien	Pairs	9/24	1st round: Defeated Canada 15–6
			2nd round: Defeated by USA 15–10
			Final for 17th place: Defeated New Zealand 15–8
			Final for 13th place: Defeated France 15–13
			Final for 9th place: Defeated by Cuba 15–6
Zahner, Lee	Pairs	9/24	1st round: Defeated Canada 15–6
			2nd round: Defeated by USA 15–10
			Final for 17th place: Defeated New Zealand 15–8
			Final for 13th place: Defeated France 15–13
			Final for 9th place: Defeated by Cuba 15–6

WOMEN

Cook, Natalie	Pairs	3/17	2nd round: Defeated Great Britain 15–4
			3rd round: Defeated USA 15–7
			4th round: Defeated USA 15–13
			Semifinal: Defeated by Brazil 15–3
			Final for 3rd/4th place: Defeated USA 12–11, 12–7
Pottharst, Kerri	Pairs	3/17	2nd round: Defeated Great Britain 15–4
			3rd round: Defeated USA 15–7
			4th round: Defeated USA 15–13
			Semifinal: Defeated by Brazil 15–3
			Final for 3rd/4th place: Defeated USA 12–11, 12–7
Fenwick, Liane	Pairs	7/17	2nd round: Defeated Japan 15–10
			3rd round: Defeated by Brazil 15–13
			Final for 9th place: Defeated Great Britain 15–12
			Final for 7th place: Defeated by USA 15–6
Spring, Anita	Pairs	7/17	2nd round: Defeated Japan 15–10
			3rd round: Defeated by Brazil 15–13
			Final for 9th place: Defeated Great Britain 15–12
			Final for 7th place: Defeated by USA 15–6

Weightlifting

Section Manager: Julian Jones   **Coaches:** Luke Borreggine, Martin Leach

MEN

Botev, Stefan	Over 108 kilograms	3/19	Final: 450.0 pts (3rd)
Brown, Damian	Up to 76 kilograms	17/24	Final: 315.0 pts (17th)
Goodman, Harvey	Up to 91 kilograms	16/25	Final: 357.5 pts (16th)
Kettner, Steven	Over 108 kilograms	15/19	Final: 375.0 pts (15th)
Kounev, Kiril	Up to 83 kilograms	4/20	Final: 370.0 pts (4th)
Nguyen, Johnny	Up to 54 kilograms	17/22	Final: 232.5 pts (17th)
Sarkisian, Yourik	Up to 59 kilograms	7/20	Final: 280 pts (7th)

Wrestling

Section Manager/Coach: Samuel Parker   **Coach:** Anatoli Beloglazov

FREESTYLE

Fitzgerald, Gregory	Up to 52 kilograms	18/19	1st round: Defeated by D. Legrand (FRA)
			2nd round: Defeated by G. Woodcroft (CAN)
O'Brien, Cory	Up to 57 kilograms	19/21	1st round: Defeated by S. Barzakov (BUL)
			2nd round: Defeated by A. Puerto (CUB)
Zaslavsky, Leonid	Up to 62 kilograms	15/21	1st round: Defeated by G. Schillaci (ITA)
			2nd round: Defeated C. Vath (CAM)
			3rd round: Defeated by R. Islamov (UZB)
Weiss, Richard	Up to 68 kilograms	16/19	1st round: Defeated by C. Roberts (CAN)
			2nd round: Bye
			3rd round: Defeated by A. Fallah (IRI)
Ozoline, Reinold	Up to 74 kilograms	17/22	1st round: Defeated by V. Verhusin (MKD)
			2nd round: Defeated by D. Hohl (CAN)
Brown, Cris	Up to 82 kilograms	19/21	1st round: Defeated L. Jabrailov (MDA)
			2nd round: Defeated by P. Penev (BUL)
Renney, Robert	Up to 90 kilograms	18/21	1st round: Defeated by H. Balz (GER)
			2nd round: Defeated by B. Muhammad (PAK)
Vincent, Benjamin	Up to 100 kilograms	18/19	1st round: Defeated by M. Garmulewicz (POL)
			2nd round: Bye
			3rd round: Defeated by S. Kovalevskiy (BLR)
Pikos, Mick	Up to 130 kilograms	16/18	1st round: Defeated by Z. Turmanidze (GEO)
			2nd round: Defeated by P. Bourdoulis (GRE)

Yachting

Section Manager: John Harrison   **Head Coach:** Michael Fletcher   **Coaches:** Nicky Bethwaite, William Hooper, Gregory Johns   **Masseur:** Damienne Cahalan   **Physiotherapist:** Susan Crafer

MEN

470 Class	King, Thomas	23/36	After 2 races: 31 pts (16th)
	McMahon, Owen		After 4 races: 77 pts (23rd)
			After 6 races: 120 pts (24th)
			After 8 races: 164 pts (23rd)
			After 10 races: 206 pts (24th)
			Final race: 213 pts (23rd)
Finn Class	McKenzie, Paul	6/31	After 2 races: 23 pts (12th)
			After 4 races: 71 pts (20th)
			After 6 races: 89 pts (14th)
			After 8 races: 105 pts (12th)
			After 10 races: 115 pts (6th)
Mistral Class	Todd, Brendan	8/46	After 2 races: 13 pts (6th)
			After 4 races: 28 pts (6th)
			After 6 races: 47 pts (7th)
			After 8 races: 59 pts (7th)
			Final race: 79 pts (8th)

Soling Class	Hayes, Matthew	12/22	After 2 races: 24 pts (13th)
	Jarvin, Steven		After 4 races: 43 pts (13th)
	McConaghy, Stephen		After 6 races: 72 pts (11th)
			After 8 races: 87 pts (9th)
			After 10 races: 116 pts (12th)
Star Class	Beashel, Colin	3/25	After 2 races: 12 pts (6th)
	Giles, David		After 4 races: 14 pts (1st)
			After 6 races: 25 pts (1st)
			After 8 races: 34 pts (1st)
			Final 2 races: 69 pts (3rd)
Laser Class	Blackburn, Michael	4/56	After 2 races: 10 pts (5th)
			After 4 races: 39 pts (6th)
			After 6 races: 70 pts (10th)
			After 8 races: 80 pts (7th)
			After 10 races: 91 pts (5th)
			Final race: 92 pts (4th)
Tornado Class	Booth, Mitchell	2/19	After 2 races: 6 pts (2nd)
	Landenberger, Andrew		After 4 races: 14 pts (1st)
			After 6 races: 45 pts (5th)
			After 8 races: 47 pts (2nd)
			After 10 races: 69 pts (2nd)
			Final race: 79 pts (2nd)

WOMEN

470 Class	Bucek, Addy	8/22	After 2 races: 16 pts (7th)
	Lidgett, Jennifer		After 4 races: 27 pts (8th)
			After 6 races: 62 pts (9th)
			After 8 races: 80 pts (8th)
			After 10 races: 94 pts (7th)
			Final race: 99 pts (8th)
Europe Class	Bridge, Christine	11/28	After 2 races: 26 pts (15th)
			After 4 races: 60 pts (17th)
			After 6 races: 69 pts (9th)
			After 8 races: 88 pts (7th)
			After 10 races: 113 pts (10th)
			Final race: 124 pts (11th)
Mistral Class	Sturges, Natasha	9/27	After 2 races: 21 pts (11th)
			After 4 races: 27 pts (4th)
			After 6 races: 43 pts (8th)
			After 8 races: 64 pts (9th)
			Final race: 71 pts (9th)

1998 Nagano, Japan

Chef de Mission: Ian Chesterman **Administration Director:** Craig Phillips **Team Attache:** Carole Yoshida
Media Services Manager: Barry White **Administration Manager:** Wendy Langton **Athlete Services Manager:**
Dr Peter Braun **Psychologist:** Jeffrey Bond **Physiotherapists:** Phillip Bedlington, Clare Walsh

Alpine Skiing
Section Manager: Helmut Spiegl **Coach:** Christopher Knight

WOMEN

Steggall, Zali	Slalom	3/27	1st run: 45.96
			2nd run: 46.71
			Total: 1:32.67 (3rd)

Biathlon
Coach/Manager: Cameron Morton

WOMEN

Rim, Kerryn	15 kilometres individual competition	43/64	1:01.38.1 (43rd)
	7.5 kilometres sprint competition	47/64	25:49.1 (47th)

Bobsleigh
Coach: Doru Francu-Cioclei **Technical Staff:** Justin McDonald

MEN

Two-man competition	Barclay, Adam	22/36	Heat 1: 55.56
	Giobbi, Jason		Heat 2: 55.47
			Heat 3: 55.26
			Heat 4: 55.31
			Total: 3:41.60 (22nd)
Four-man competition	Barclay, Adam	23/31	Heat 1: 54.72
	Giobbi, Jason		Heat 2: 54.93
	Polglaze, Ted		Heat 3: 55.23
	Walker, Scott		Total: 2:44.88 (23rd)

Cross-Country Skiing
Coach: Christer Skog

MEN

Evans, Anthony	Men's 30 kilometres classical	51/72	1:45.26.3 (51st)
	Men's 10 kilometres classical	66/97	31:12.7 (66th)
	Men's 15 kilometres free pursuit	55/74	1:15.07.4 (55th)
	Men's 50 kilometres free pursuit	48/75	2:21.44.4 (48th)
Gray, Paul	Men's 10 kilometres classical	88/97	34:45.1 (88th)
	Men's 15 kilometres free pursuit		DNF
	Men's 50 kilometres free pursuit	59/75	2:29.08.2 (59th)

Figure Skating
Coaches: Andrei Pachin, Sergei Shakhrai

MEN

Carr, Stephen	Pairs figure skating	13/20	Short program: 15
			Free skating: 13
			TFP: 20.5 pts (13th)
Lui, Anthony	Men's figure skating	25/29	Short program: 25
			Did not reach final

WOMEN

Carter, Joanne	Ladies figure skating	12/28	Short program: 11
			Free skating: 12
			TFP: 17.5 pts (12th)
McGrath, Danielle	Pairs figure skating	13/20	Short program: 15
			Free skating: 13
			TFP: 20.5 pts (13th)

Freestyle Skiing

Team Leader: Geoff Lipshut   **Coach:** Frank Bare (Aerials)   **Assistant Coach:** Christoph Jehle (Aerials)
Coaches: Charles Richards, Michael Kennedy (Moguls)

MEN

Costa, Adrian	Moguls	21/30	Qualification: 23.45 pts	Final: DNQ
Sweet, Jonathon	Aerials		DNC	

WOMEN

Cooper, Jacqueline	Aerials	23/24	Qualifying: 1st jump: 69.65 pts 2nd jump: 31.54 pts Total: 101.19 pts	Final: DNQ
Despas, Maria	Moguls	23/26	Qualifying: 18.94 pts	Final: DNQ
Marshall, Kirstie	Aerials	14/24	Qualifying: 1st jump: 66.46 pts 2nd jump: 82.53 pts Total: 148.99 pts	Final: DNQ

Short-track Speed Skating

Section Manager: Andrew Murtha   **Coach:** Ann Zhang   **Physiologist:** John Marsden

MEN

Bradbury, Steven	500 metres individual	19/30	Heat: 43.766 (3rd)
	1000 metres individual	21/30	Heat: 1:33.108 (3rd)
	5000 metres relay	8/8	Semifinal: 7:11.691 (3rd) B Final: 7:15.907 (4th)
Goerlitz, Richard	5000 metres relay	8/8	Semi Final: 7:11.691 (3rd) B Final: 7:15.907 (4th)
Hansen, Kieran	5000 metres relay	8/8	Semifinal: 7:11.691 (3rd) B Final: 7:15.907 (4th)
McNee, Andrew	5000 metres relay	8/8	Semi Final: 7:11.691 (3rd) B Final: 7:15.907 (4th)
Nizielski, Richard	5000 metres relay	8/8	Semifinal: 7:11.691 (3rd) B Final: 7:15.907 (4th)

WOMEN

Daly, Janet	500 metres individual	27/32	Heat: 49.158 (4th)
	1000 metres individual	29/30	Heat: 1:59.990 (4th)

Snowboarding

Coach: Freddie Moegul

MEN

Steggall, Zeke	Giant slalom	28/34	1st run: 1:08.10 2nd run: DSQ Total: 1:08.10 (28th)

2000 Sydney, Australia

Chef de Mission: John Coates **Assistant Chefs de Mission:** John Devitt, Peter Montgomery, Michael Wenden
Attaché: Dawn Fraser **Administration:** Craig McLatchey (Director), Mark Lockie (Assistant Director), Geoff Cohen
(Team Unit Administrator), Wendy Langton and Anne Vanden Hogen (Administration Coordinators), Pamela Harris
and Cheryl Ritchie (Administration Support), Damien Tickle (Finance Officer) **Operations:** Robert Thornton (Director),
Craig Phillips (Assistant Director), Peter Brockington and Kaye Hurn (Operations Coordinators), David Bonko and
Maree McArthur (Security Officers) **Athlete Services:** Herb Elliott (Director), Jodie Smith and Rosemary Towner
(Athlete Services Coordinators), Felicity Gadd, Chris Greenway and Megan Sissian (Athlete Services Support)
Athlete Liaison Officers: John Bertrand, Peter Brock, Laurie Lawrence, Robyn Maher, Megan Marcks
Media Services: Alex Hamill (Director), Mike Tancred (Assistant Director), Ian Heads (Main Press Centre),
Max Markson (Electronic Media Liaison), Colleen Richards (Media Support)
Media Liaison Officers: Rozanna Bozabalian, Greg Campbell, Alan Clarkson, Kevin Diggerson, John Gatfield,
Graeme Hannan, Ian Hanson, Stephen Lock, Megan Seton, Janene Mar, Tracie Spicer, Michael Stevens,
Michael Wilson **VIP/Protocol Services:** Marlene Mathews (Director), Ron Gray and David Morrison (VIP/Protocol
Services Coordinators) **Medical Services:** Dr Brian Sando (Director), Prof Peter Fricker (Assistant Director),
Graham Winter (Head of Psychology), Ross Smith (Head of Physiotherapy), Robert Granter (Head of Massage
Services), Louise Burke (Nutritionist), Denise Lickfold and Jill Young (Clinic Administrators)
Medical Support (Doctors): Dr Grace Bryant, Dr Mark Porter **Massage Therapists:** Bernd Adolph,
Howard Arbuthnot, Kristina Canavan, Bradley Hiskins, Tricia Jenkins, Max Metzker, Christine O'Connor
Physiotherapists: Elizabeth Austin, Peter Eckhardt, Stephen Evans, Peter Stanton, Denny Shearwood,
Patricia Wisbey-Roth **Psychologists:** Gayelene Clews, John Crampton, Vicki De Prazer

Archery

Section Manager: Stuart Atkins
Head Coach: Kisik Lee

MEN

Fairweather, Simon	Individual	1/64	Ranking round: 642 pts (8th)
			Round of 32: Defeated J. Stevens (CUB) 170–161
			Round of 16: Defeated J. Grandis (FRA) 161–150
			Round of 8: Defeated I. Arias (CUB) 167–163
			Quarter-final: Defeated B. Tsyrempilov (RUS) 113–104
			Semifinal: Defeated W. van Alten (NED) 112–110
			Final: Defeated V. Wunderle (USA) 113–106 (1st)
	Team	12/14	Ranking round: 1876 pts (10th)
			Round of 8: Defeated by Sweden 241–238 (12th)
Gray, Matthew	Individual	36/64	Ranking round: 631 pts (27th)
			Round of 32: Defeated by H. Tang (CHN) 163–161 (36th)
	Team	12/14	Ranking round: 1876 pts (10th)
			Round of 8: Defeated by Sweden 241–238 (12th)
Hunter-Russell, Scott	Individual	24/64	Ranking round: 603 pts (51st)
			Round of 32: Defeated O. Akbal (TUR) 154–146
			Round of 16: Defeated by M. Frangilli (ITA) 164–154 (24th)
	Team	12/14	Ranking round: 1876 pts (10th)
			Round of 8: Defeated by Sweden 241–238 (12th)

WOMEN

Fairweather, Kate	Individual	22/64	Ranking round: 630 pts (27th)
			Round of 32: Defeated K. Phutkaradze (GEO) 166–158
			Round of 16: Defeated by S. Kawauchi (JPN) 160–158 (22nd)
	Team	9/12	Ranking round: 1873 pts (10th)
			Round of 8: Defeated by Italy 237–236
			Final: DNQ (9th)
Jennison, Melissa	Individual	19/64	Ranking round: 628 pts (32nd)
			Round of 32: Defeated K. Lorigi (GEO) 160–151
			Round of 16: Defeated by S. Kim (KOR) 164–159 (19th)
	Team	9/12	Ranking round: 1873 pts (10th)
			Eighth round eliminator: Defeated by Italy 237–236
			Final: DNQ (9th)

Tremelling, Michelle	Individual	11/64	Ranking round: 615 pts (49th)
			Round of 32: Defeated J. Dykman (USA) 154–146
			Round of 16: Defeated K. Lewis (RSA) 162–147
			Eighth final: Defeated by S. Kim (KOR) 168–158 (11th)
	Team	9/12	Ranking round: 1873 pts (10th)
			Eighth round eliminator: Defeated by Italy 237–236
			Final: DNQ (9th)

Athletics

Section Manager: Dr Peter Brukner   **Assistant** Section Managers: Carol Grant, Geoff Rowe, Lawrie Woodman
Head Coach: Chris Wardlaw   **Coaches:** Jackie Byrnes, Keith Connor, Andrew Dawes, Peter Fortune, Craig Hilliard, Michael Khmel, John Quinn, Efim Shuravetsky, Rudolf Sopko, Ron Weigel   **Sports Scientist:** Dean Gathercole
Doctor: Chris Bradshaw   **Massage Therapists:** Anthony Bond, Malcolm Calcutt, Kyriacos Miritis, Bruno Rizzo
Physiotherapists: Kay Crossley, Dean Kenneally, Brent Kirkbride, Anne Lord   **Psychologist:** Jeffery Simons

MEN

A'Hern, Nicholas	20 kilometres walk	10/48	1:21:34.0 (10th)	
Anlezark, Justin	Shot-put	29/37	Qualifying: 18.59 metres	Final: DNQ
Batman, Daniel	400 metres	68/68	Heat 9: DNF	
	4 x 400 metres relay		DNC	
Beckenham, Matthew	400 metres hurdles	42/62	Heat 6: 51.27 (7th)	
Bezabeh, Sisay	10 000 metres	25/34	Heat 1: 28:21.63 (11th)	
Burge, Peter	Long jump	6/53	Qualifying: 8.06 metres	Final 8.15m (6th)
Burgess, Paul	Pole vault	16/37	Qualifying: 5.55 metres	Final: DNQ
Chistiakov, Victor	Pole vault	5/37	Qualifying: 5.70 metres	Final 5.80 metres (5th)
Cousins, Duane	50 kilometres walk	34/56	4:10:43.0 (34th)	
Creighton, Shaun	10 000 metres	29/34	Heat 1: 28:52.71 (14th)	
Cremer, Grant	800 metres	25/62	Heat 6: 1:45.86 (3rd)	Semifinal 2: 1:52.57 (8th)
Currey, Andrew	Javelin	22/36	Qualifying: 78.12 metres	Final: DNQ
De Highden, Roderic	Marathon	28/100	2:18:04.0 (28th)	
Deakes, Nathan	20 kilometres walk	8/48	1:21:03. (8th)	
	50 kilometres walk	6/56	3:47:29.0 (6th)	
Di Bella, Paul	100 metres	51/99	Heat 7: 10.52 (5th)	
	4 x 100 metres relay	16/40	Heat 4: 38.76 (2nd)	Semifinal 2: Disqualified
Dwyer, Patrick	400 metres	13/68	Heat 2: 45.82 (2nd)	Quarter-final 3: 45.38 (4th)
				Semifinal 1: 45.70 (7th)
	4 x 400 metres relay	8/34	Heat 3: 3:04.13 (3rd)	Semifinal 2: 3:01.91 (3rd)
				Final: 3:03.91 (8th)
Fearnley, Kurt	1500 metres wheelchair	4/8	3:08.27 (4th)	
Ferrier, Scott	Decathlon	29/38	3169 pts (11.11, 7.19 metres, 13.50 metres, 1.97 metres, DNS) DNF	
Forsyth, Timothy	High jump	14/36	Qualifying: 2.24 metres	Final: DNQ
Hatcher, Adrian	Javelin	21/36	Qualifying: 79.23 metres	Final: DNQ
Hazel, Michael	4 x 400 metres relay	8/34	Heat 3: 3:04.13 (3rd)	Semifinal 2: 3:01.91 (3rd)
				Final: 3:03.91 (8th)
Howarth, Nicholas	1500 metres	35/41	Heat 1: 3:45.46 (11th)	
Jamieson, Bradley	4 x 400 metres relay	8/34	Heat 3: 3:04.13 (3rd)	Semifinal 2: 3:01.91 (3rd)
				Final: 3:03.91 (8th)
				(ran final only)
Johnson, Patrick	100 metres	32/99	Heat 1: 10.31 (2nd)	Quarter-final 5: 10.44 (5th)
	200 metres	28/68	Heat 8: 20.88 (5th)	Quarter-final 3: 20.87 (7th)
	4 x 100 metres relay	16/40	Heat 4: 38.76 (2nd)	Semifinal 2: Disqualified
Markov, Dmitri	Pole vault	5/37	Qualifying: 5.70 metres	Final: 5.80 metres (5th)
Marsh, Damien	4 x 100 metres relay		DNC	
Martin, Andrew	Javelin	16/36	Qualifying: 81.31 metres	Final: DNQ
McCarthy, Kristopher	800 metres	46/62	Heat 8: 1:48.92 (4th)	
McLean, John	1500 metres wheelchair	8/8	DNF	
Mehari, Mizan	5000 metres	12/38	Heat 1: 13:24.56 (8th)	Final: 13:42.03 (12th)
Moneghetti, Stephen	Marathon	10/100	2:14:50.0 (10th)	
Mottram, Craig	5000 metres	17/38	Heat 2: 13:31.06 (8th)	
Murphy, Andrew	Triple jump	10/40	Qualifying: 17.12 metres	Final: 16.80 metres (10th)

Noonan, Kieran	4 x 100 metres relay		DNC	
Power, Michael	5000 metres	28/38	Heat 1: 13:51.00 (13th)	
Rendell, Stuart	Hammer-throw	28/44	Qualifying: 72.78 metres	Final: DNQ
Robinson, Rohan	400 metres hurdles	34/62	Heat 1: 50.80 (4th)	
Russell, Dion	20 kilometres walk	25/48	1:25:26.0 (25th)	
	50 kilometres walk	27/56	4:02:50.0 (27th)	
Shirvington, Matthew	100 metres	10/99	Heat 9: 10.35 (2nd)	Quarter-final 3: 10.13 (2nd)
				Semifinal 2: 10.26 (5th)
	200 metres	32/68	Heat 7: 20.91 (4th)	Quarter-final 4: Did not start
	4 x 100 metres relay	16/40	Heat 4: 38.76 (2nd)	Semifinal 2: Disqualified
Taurima, Jai	Long jump	2/53	Qualifying: 8.09 metres	Final 8.49m (2nd)
Troop, Lee	Marathon	66/100	2:29:32.0 (66th)	
Unthank, Christopher	3000 metres Steeplechase	36/40	Heat 1: 9:11.19 (12th)	
Vander-Kuyp, Kyle	110 metres hurdles	16/46	Heat 1: 13.67 (3rd)	Quarter-final 2: 13.62 (4th)
				Semifinal 1: 13.63 (8th)
Vincent, Casey	400 metres	11/68	Heat 1: 45.49 (3rd)	Quarter-final 1: 45.45 (4th)
				Semifinal 2: 45.61 (6th)
	4 x 400 metres relay	8/34	Heat 3: 3:04.13 (3rd)	Semifinal 2: 3:01.91 (3rd)
				Final: 3:03.91 (8th) (did not run final, injured)
Wohlsen, Daryl	200 metres	36/68	Heat 2: 20.98 (5th)	
	4 x 100 metres relay	16/40	Heat 4: 38.76 (2nd)	Semifinal 2: Disqualified
Young, Blair	400 metres hurdles	11/62	Heat 2: 49.75	Semifinal 2: 49.20 (4th)
	4 x 400 metres relay	8/34	Heat 3: 3:04.13 (3rd)	Semifinal 2: 3:01.91 (3rd)
				Final: 3:03.91 (8th)

WOMEN

Andrews, Susan	4 x 400 metres relay	5/23	Heat 3: 3:24.05 (2nd)	Final: 3:23.81 (5th) (ran heat only)
	800 metres	24/39	Heat 4: 2:03.31 (5th)	
Broadrick, Suzanne	4 x 100 metres relay	25/25	DNC	
Carroll, Nicole	Marathon	41/54	DNF	
Clarke, Georgina	1500 metres	20/43	Heat 2: 4:11.74 (8th)	Semifinal 2: 4:10.99 (10th)
Costian, Daniela	Discus	31/32	Qualifying: 51.96 metres	Final: DNQ
Cripps, Sharon	4 x 100 metres relay	25/25	Heat 1: DNF (missed 1st change)	
Cross, Anne	5000 metres	38/50	Heat 2: 16:07.18 (14th)	
Crowley, Margaret	800 metres		DNC	
	1500 metres	15/43	Heat 1: 4:08.85 (7th) Semifinal 1: 4:09.16 (8th)	
Currey, Louise	Javelin	31/35	Qualifying: 53.32 metres	Final: DNQ
Di Marco, Karyne	Hammer-throw	21/28	Qualifying: 59.49m	Final: DNQ
Edwards, Deborah	100 metres hurdles	28/38	Heat 1: 13.24 (5th)	
Fearnley, Clair	10 000 metres	29/44	Heat 1: 33:47.23 (15th)	
Freeman, Catherine	200 metres	7/54	Heat 2: 23.11 (3rd)	Quarter-final 1: 22.75 (2nd)
				Semifinal 2: 22.71(4th)
				Final: 22.53 (7th)
	400 metres	1/59	Heat 4: 51.63 (1st)	Quarter-final 4: 50.31 (1st)
				Semifinal 2: 50.01 (1st)
				Final: 49.11 (1st)
	4 x 400 metres relay	5/23	Heat 3: 3:24.05 (2nd)	Final: 3:23.81 (5th) (ran final only)
Gainsford Taylor, Melinda	100 metres	15/84	Heat 9: 11.34 (3rd)	Quarter-final 2: 11.24 (4th)
				Semifinal 1: 11.45 (8th)
	200 metres	6/54	Heat 4: 22.71 (1st)	Quarter-final 1: 22.75 (3rd)
				Semifinal 2: 22.61 (3rd)
				Final: 22.42 (6th)
	4 x 100 metres relay	25/25	Heat 1: DNF (missed 1st change)	
	4 x 400 metres relay	5/23	Heat 3: 3:24.05 (2nd)	Final: 3:23.81 (5th) (ran final only)
George, Emma	Pole vault	15/30	Qualifying: 4.25m	Final: DNQ

Grigorieva, Tatiana	Pole vault	2/30	Qualifying: 4.30 metres	Final: 4.55m (2nd)
Harvey, Natalie	10 000 metres	33/44	Heat 1: 34:12.90 (17th)	
Hewitt, Lauren	100 metres	25/84	Heat 4: 11.42 (4th)	Quarter-final 3: 11.54 (6th)
	200 metres	15/54	Heat 3: 23.07 (1st)	Quarter-final 4: 23.12 (3rd)
				Semifinal 1: 23.44 (7th)
	4 x 100 metres relay	25/25	Heat 1: DNF	
			(missed 1st change)	
Hobson, Susan	Marathon	35/54	2:38:44.0 (35th)	
Hutton, Elly	4 x 100 metres relay	25/25	Heat 1: DNF	
			(missed 1st change)	
Inverarity, Alison	High jump	32/38	Qualifying: 1.80 metres	Final: DNQ
Jamieson, Jane	Heptathlon	10/33	6104 pts (14.09, 181	
			metres, 13.59 metres,	
			25.27, 6.09 metres,	
			45.32 metres, 2:16.57)	
Jamieson, Sarah	1500 metres	30/ 43	Heat 3 4:12.90 (11th)	
Lever, Alison	Discus	16/32	Qualifying: 59.58m	Final: DNQ
Lewis, Tamsyn	800 metres	9/39	Heat 1: 2:00.23 (2nd)	Semifinal 1: 1:59.33 (4th)
	4 x 400 metres relay	5/23	Heat 3: 3:24.05 (2nd)	Final: 3:23.81 (5th)
McCann, Kerryn	Marathon	11/54	2:28:37.0 (11th)	
Medlicott, Melissa	4 x 100 metres relay		DNC	
Naylor, Lee	400 metres	32/59	Heat 2: 53.10 (5th)	Quarter-final 3: 53.83 (8th)
	4 x 400 metres relay		DNC	
Peris-Kneebone, Nova	400 metres	16/59	Heat 5: 52.51 (3rd)	Quarter-final 1: 51.28 (3rd)
				Semifinal 1: 52.49 (8th)
	4 x 400 metres relay	5/23	Heat 3: 3:24.05 (2nd)	Final: 3:23.81 (5th)
Pittman, Jana	400 metres hurdles	17/34	Heat 3: 56.76 (3rd)	
	4 x 400 metres relay	5/23	Heat 3: 3:24.05 (2nd)	Final: 3:23.81 (5th)
				(ran heat only)
Poetschka, Lauren	400 metres hurdles	26/34	Heat 4: 58.06 (6th)	
Price, Stephanie	400 metres hurdles	28/34	Heat 5: 58.81 (6th)	
Richardson, Kate	5000 metres	28/50	Heat 3:15:45.34 (9th)	
Risk, Kylie	10 000 metres	34/44	Heat 2: 34:30.91 (17th)	
Sauvage, Louise	800 metres wheelchair	1/8	1:56.07 (1st)	
Saville, Jane	20 kilometres walk	57/57	DSQ	
Saxby-Junna, Kerry	20 kilometres walk	7/57	1:32:02.0 (7th)	
Sheriden-Paolini, Elizabeth	20 kilometres walk	39/57	1:40:57.0 (39th)	
Sosimenko, Debbie	Hammer-throw	5/28	Qualifying: 64.01 metres	Final: 67.95 metres (5th)
Stone, Joanna	Javelin	17/35	Qualifying: 58.34 metres	Final: DNQ
Thompson, Bronwyn	Long jump	16/40	Qualifying: 6.55 metres	
Vizaniari, Lisa-Marie	Discus	8/32	Qualifying: 62.47 metres	Final: 62.57 metres (8th)
Willis, Benita	5000 metres	17/50	Heat 1: 15:21.37 (6th)	

Badminton

Section Manager: Peter Roberts **Head Coach:** Yvette Yun Luo

MEN

Bamford, David	Doubles	17/23	Round of 32: Defeated by Poland 15–5,16–17,15–6
	Mixed doubles	17/27	Round of 32: Defeated by Netherlands 15–10,15–3
Blackburn, Peter	Doubles	17/23	Round of 32: Defeated by Poland 15–5,16–17,15–6
	Mixed doubles	17/27	Round of 32: Defeated by Thailand 11–15,15–7, 17–16
Suryana, Rio	Singles	17/35	Round of 64: Bye
			Round of 32: Defeated by Svetoslav Stoyanov (BUL) 15–8,2–15,15–13
	Mixed doubles	17/27	Round of 32: Defeated by China 15–0,15–3

WOMEN

Cator, Rhonda	Singles	17/40	Round of 64: Bye
			Round of 32: Defeated by Nicole Grether (GER) 11–3,11–3
	Doubles	17/26	Round of 32: Defeated by Canada 15–13,15–6, 15–11
	Mixed doubles	17/27	Round of 32: Defeated by Thailand 11–15,15–7, 17–16
Hardy, Amanda	Doubles	17/26	Round of 32: Defeated by Canada 15–13,15–6, 15–11
	Mixed doubles	17/27	Round of 32: Defeated by Netherlands 15–10,15–3

Head, Rayoni	Singles	17/40	Round of 64: Defeated Robbyn Hermitage (CAN) 11–7,11–2
			Round of 32: Defeated by Ya Lin Chan (TPE) 11–1,11–1
	Doubles	17/26	Round of 32: Defeated by Thailand 15–7,15–4
Lucas, Kellie	Singles	33/40	Round of 64: Defeated by Nely Boteva (BUL) 11–5,11–6
	Doubles	17/26	Round of 32: Defeated by Thailand 15–7,15–4
	Mixed doubles	17/27	Round of 32: Defeated by China 15–0,15–3

Baseball

Section Manager: Bill O'Sullivan **Head Coach:** Jon Deeble **Coaches:** Philip Dale, Tony Harris, Greg Jelks
Technical Staff: Kylie Thomson **Physiotherapist:** Craig Allingham **Psychologist:** Philip Jauncey

MEN	Anderson, Craig	Gonzalez, Paul	Reeves, Glenn	7/8	Preliminary:
	Balfour, Grant	Hutton, Mark	Roneberg, Brett		Defeated by Netherlands 6–4
	Becker, Thomas	Johnson, Ronny	Snelling, Christopher		Defeated Korea 5–3
	Bennett, Shayne	McDonald, Grant	Thomas, Brad		Defeated by Japan 7–3
	Buckley, Mathew	Meagher, Adrian	Van Buizen, Rodney		Defeated South Africa 10–4
	Burton, Adam	Moyle, Michael	White, David		Defeated by Cuba 1–0
	Byrne, Clayton	Nakamura, Michael	White, Gary		Defeated by Italy 8–7
	Ettles, Mark	Nilsson, David	Williams, Glenn		Defeated by USA 12–1

Basketball (Men)

Section Manager: John Trivellion Scott **Head Coach:** Barry Barnes **Assistant Coaches:** Alan Black, Brett Brown
Doctor: Dr Peter Harcourt **Physiotherapist:** Craig Purdham

Anstey, Christopher	Longley, Luc	4/12	Preliminary:	Defeated by Canada 101–90
Bradtke, Mark	MacKinnon, Samuel			Defeated by Yugoslavia 80–66
Cattalini, Martin	Maher, Brett			Defeated Russia 75–71
Gaze, Andrew	Rogers, Paul			Defeated Angola 88–65
Grace, Ricky	Smith, Jason		Quarter-final:	Defeated Italy 65–62
Heal, Shane	Vlahov, Andrew		Semifinal:	Defeated by France 76–52
			Bronze final:	Defeated by Lithuania 89–71

Basketball (Women)

Section Manager: Marian Stewart **Head Coach:** Tom Maher **Assistant Coaches:** Jenny Cheesman, Carrie Graf
Doctor: Carolyn Broderick **Physiotherapist:** Jilliane Cook

Boyd, Carla	Hill, Joanne	2/12	Preliminary, Group A:	Defeated Canada 78–46
Brondello, Sandra	Jackson, Lauren			Defeated Brazil 81–70
Burgess, Annie	Sandie, Shelley			Defeated Slovakia 70–47
Fallon, Trisha	Sporn, Rachel			Defeated Senegal 96–39
Griffiths, Michelle	Timms, Michele			Defeated France 69–62
Harrower, Kristi	Whittle, Jennifer		Quarter-final:	Defeated Poland 76–48
			Semifinal:	Defeated Brazil 64–52
			Final:	Defeated by USA 76–54

Boxing

Section Manager: Peter Rogers **Head Coach:** Bodo Andreass **Coach:** Denis Hill

Collins, Henry	60 to 63.5 kilograms	9/28	Round 1: Defeated by Ricardo Williams (USA)
Geale, Daniel	63.5 to 67 kilograms	9/28	Round 1: Defeated by Leonard Bundu (ITA)
Green, Daniel	75 to 81 kilograms	9/28	Round 1: Defeated Laudelino Barros (BRA)
			Round 2: Defeated by Alexander Lebziak (RUS)
Hore, Bradley	Up to 48 kilograms		DNQ
Kane, Justin	51 to 54 kilograms	8/28	Round 1: Defeated Sontaya Wongprates (THA)
			Round 2: Defeated by Serguey Daniltchenko (UKR)
Katsidis, Michael	57 to 60 kilograms	9/28	Round 1: Defeated Agnaldo Magalhaes (BRA)
			Round 2: Defeated by Nurzhan Karimzhanov (KAZ)
Miller, Paul	71 to 75 kilograms	9/27	Round 1: Defeated Jerson Ravelo (DOM)
			Round 2: Defeated by Vugar Alekperov (AZE)
Rowles, Richard	67 to 71 kilograms	9/28	Round 1: Defeated Juan Jose Ubaldo Cabrera (DOM)
			Round 2: Defeated by Adnan Catic (GER)
Swan, James	54 to 57 kilograms	9/28	Round 1: Defeated by Vlademir Dos Santos Pereira (BRA)
Wiltshire, Erle	48 to 51 kilograms	9/28	Round 1: Defeated by Jerome Thomas (FRA)

Canoeing (Slalom)

Manager/Head Coach: Richard Fox   **Coach:** Mike Druce   **Physiotherapist:** Natalie McColl

MEN

C-1	Bell, Robin	9/16	Qualifying: 268.74 pts (5th)	Final: 244.48 pts (9th)
C-2	Farrance, Andrew	11/12	Qualifying: 347.33 pts (11th)	Final: DNQ
C-2	Swoboda, Kai	11/12	Qualifying: 347.33 pts (11th)	Final: DNQ
Slalom K-1	Wilkie, John	21/23	Qualifying: 320.84 pts (21st)	Final: DNQ

WOMEN

Slalom K-1	Woodward, Danielle	8/15	Qualifying: 313.80 pts (14th)	Final: 261.89 pts (8th)

Canoeing (Sprint)

Section Manager: Noel Harrod   **Head Coach:** Barry Kelly   **Coaches:** Ben Hutchings, Lynda Lehmann, Carsten Loemker, Ronald Robinson, John Sumegi   **Massage Therapist:** Samantha Couzin-Wood
Physiotherapist: Ivan Hooper

MEN

K-1 500 metres	Baggaley, Nathan	10/31	Heat 3: 1:41.854 (3rd)	Semifinal: 1:40.884 (4th) Final: DNQ
K-1 1000 metres	Robinson, Clint	10/31	Heat 3: 3:40.197 (4th)	Semifinal: 3:40.745 (5th) Final: DNQ
K-2 500 metres	Collins, Daniel Trim, Andrew	2/19	Heat 3: 1:30.393 (2nd)	Semifinal 1: 1:31.475 (1st) Final: 1:47.895 (2nd)
K-2 1000 metres	Morton, Brian Young, Luke	10/18	Heat 1: 3:20.934 (6th)	Semifinal: 3:25.046 (8th) Final: DNQ
K-4 1000 metres	Chaffer, Ross McFadzean, Cameron Scott, Peter Suska, Shane	10/13	Heat 2: 3:05.893 (6th)	Semifinal: 3:05.527 (7th) Final: DNQ

WOMEN

K-1 500 metres	Borchert, Katrin	3/17	Heat 2: 1:52.187 (4th)	Semifinal: 1:53.070 (1st) Final: 2:15.138 (3rd)
K-2 500 metres	Borchert, Katrin Wood, Anna	6/13	Heat 2: 1:45.250 (4th)	Semifinal: 1:44.682 (1st) Final: 2:01.472 (6th)
K-4 500 metres	Nossiter, Yanda Oates-Wilding, Shelley Randle, Kerri Simper, Amanda	10/10	Heat 2: 1:37.081 (4th)	Semifinal: 1:38.580 (4th) Final: DNQ

Cycling

Section Manager: Michael Flynn   **Head Coach (Track):** Charlie Walsh   **Coaches:** Shayne Bannan (Men's Road), Damian Grundy (Mountain-bike), James Victor (Women's Road), Gary West (Track, Sprint)
Mechanics: Jock Bullen (Track), Darrell McCulloch (Road), James Nitis (Mountain-bike)
Technical Staff: Paul Brosnan   **Doctor:** Dr Peter Barnes   **Massage Therapists:** James Green, Malcolm Morris
Physiotherapists: Emma Colson, Susan Everett, Victor Popov

MEN

Aitken, Brett	4000 metres team pursuit (track)	5/12	Qualifying: 4:06.361 (5th) Quarter-final: 4:03.209 (2nd)
	Madison (track)	1/14	Final: 26 pts (1st)
Brown, Graeme	4000 metres team pursuit (track)	5/12	Qualifying: 4:06.361 (5th) Quarter-final: 4:03.209 (2nd)
Eadie, Sean	Individual sprint (track)	7/19	Qualifying: 10.520 (8th) 1st round, heat 8: Relegated Repechage 3: 11.805 (1st) Eighth final, heat 1: Defeated by USA (2nd) Eighth final, repechage 1: 11.414 (1st) Final for 5–8th places: Defeated by Germany and Spain (3rd) Quarter-final: Heat 2: Defeated by France (2nd)
	Olympic sprint (track)	3/12	Qualifying: 44.719 (3rd) 2nd round, heat 2: 44.745 (3rd) Bronze final: 45.161 (1st)

Evans, Cadel	Cross-country (mountain bike)	7/49	Final: 2:13:31.65 (7th)
Hill, Darryn	Individual sprint (track)	12/19	Qualifying: 10.526 (9th)
			1st round, heat 9: 10.938 (1st)
			Eighth final: Defeated by Germany (2nd)
			Eighth final, repechage 1: Defeated by
			Sean Eadie (AUS) and CZE (3rd)
			Final for 9–12th places: DNS (12th)
	Olympic sprint (track)	3/12	Qualifying: 44.719 (3rd)
			2nd round, heat 2: 44.745 (3rd)
			Bronze final: 45.161 (1st)
Kelly, Shane	1 kilometre time trial (track)	3/16	Final: 1:02.818 (3rd)
Lancaster, Brett	4000 metres team pursuit (track)	5/12	Qualifying: 4:06.361 (5th)
			Quarter-final: 4:03.209 (2nd)
McEwen, Robert	Individual road race (road)	19/156	Final: 5:30:46 (19th)
McGee, Bradley	4000 metres individual pursuit (track)	3/17	Qualifying: 4:21.903 (4th)
			Semifinal, heat 2: 4:22.644 (2nd)
			Bronze final: 4:19.250 (1st)
	4000 metres team pursuit (track)	5/12	Qualifying: 4:06.361 (5th)
			Quarter-final: 4:03.209 (2nd)
McGrory, Scott	Madison (track)	1/14	Final: 26 pts (1st)
	Individual road race (road)		DNF
Neiwand, Gary	Olympic sprint (track)	3/12	Qualifying: 44.719 (3rd)
			2nd round, heat 2: 44.745 (3rd)
			Bronze final: 45.161 (1st)
	Keirin (track)	2/20	1st round, heat 1: (2nd)
			2nd round, heat 2: (2nd)
			Final: (2nd)
O'Grady, Stuart	Individual points race (track)	10/22	Final: 26 pts (10th)
	Individual road race (road)	77/156	Final: 5:36:14 (77th)
O'Neill, Nathan	Time trial (road)	19/37	Final: 1:00:32 (19th)
Roberts, Luke	4000 metres individual pursuit (track)	9/17	Qualifying: 4:31.162 (9th)
			Final: DNQ (9th)
Rogers, Michael	4000 metres team pursuit (track)	5/12	Qualifying: 4:06.361 (5th)
			Quarter-final: 4:03.209 (2nd)
Rowney, Paul	Cross-country (mountain bike)	10/49	Final: 2:14:22.44 (10th)
Vogels, Hendricus	Individual road race (road)	30/156	Final: 5:30:46 (30th)
White, Matthew	Individual road race (road)		DNF
Woods, Robert	Cross-country (mountain bike)	13/49	Final: 2:14:42.20 (13th)

WOMEN

Baylis, Anna	Cross-country (mountain bike)	21/30	Final: 2:00:53.20 (21st)
Burns, Alayna	3000 metres individual pursuit (track)	7/12	Qualifying: 3:38.223 (7th)
			Final: DNQ (7th)
	Individual points race (track)	9/18	Final: 7 pts (9th)
Feldhahn, Juanita	Individual road race (road)	28/58	Final: 3:06:37 (28th)
Ferris, Michelle	500 metres time trial (track)	2/17	Final: 34.696 (2nd)
	Individual sprint (track)	4/12	Qualifying: 11.512 (4th)
			Eighth final, heat 4: 12.078 (1st)
			Quarter-final, heat 4: 11.705 (1st)
			Semifinal: Defeated by France (2nd)
			Bronze final: Defeated by Ukraine (2nd)
Gaudry, Tracey	Individual road race (road)	23/58	Final: 3:06:31 (23rd)
	Time trial (road)	21/24	Final: 45.11 (21st)
Grigson, Mary	Cross-country (mountain bike)	6/30	Final: 1:53:22.57 (6th)
Higginson, Lyndelle	500 metres time trial (track)	14/17	Final: 35.859 (14th)
Wilson, Anna	Individual road race (road)	4/58	Final: 3:06:31 (4th)
	Time trial (road)	4/24	Final: 42.58 (4th)

Diving

Section Manager: Valerie Beddoe   **Coaches:** Wen Chen, Salvador Sobrino, Tong Xiang Wang

MEN

Helm, Mathew	10-metre platform	8/42	Preliminary: 455.37 (5th)	Semifinal: 198.03 (3rd)
				Final: 420.21 (11th)
	10-metre synchronised	5/8		Final: 333.24 pts (5th)
Newbery, Robert	10-metre platform	10/42	Preliminary: 434.70 (9th)	Semifinal: 185.28 (10th)
				Final: 428.70 (8th)
	10-metre synchronised	5/8		Final: 333.24 pts (5th)
	3-metre springboard	15/49	Preliminary: 402.03 (9th)	Semifinal: 192.87 (18th)
	3-metre synchronised	3/8		Final: 322.86 pts (3rd)
Pullar, Dean	3-metre springboard	5/49	Preliminary: 406.65 (8th)	Semifinal: 222.78 (9th)
				Final: 424.62 (5th)
	3-metre synchronised	3/8		Final: 322.86 pts (3rd)

WOMEN

Gilmore, Rebecca	10-metre platform	11/40	Preliminary: 288.99 (12th)	Semifinal: 175.92 (6th)
				Final: 273.03 (10th)
	10-metre synchronised	3/8		Final: 301.50 pts (3rd)
	3-metre springboard	17/43	Preliminary: 259.74 (18th)	Semifinal: 215.55 (14th)
Michell, Chantelle	3-metre springboard	7/43	Preliminary: 270.75 (13th)	Semifinal: 228.84 (7th)
				Final: 321.84 (6th)
	3-metre synchronised	4/8		Final: 283.05 pts (4th)
Tourky, Loudy	10-metre platform	24/40	Preliminary: 257.40 (24th)	Final: DNQ
	10-metre synchronised	3/8		Final: 301.50 pts (3rd)
	3-metre synchronised	4/8		Final: 283.05 pts (4th)

Equestrian

Section Manager: Gareth McKeen   **Head Coach:** Wayne Roycroft   **Coaches:** Alexa Bell, Clemens Dierks
Assistant Coach: Heath Ryan   **Chefs D'Equipe:** Kerry Brydon, Jim Dunn, Stephen Lamb
Technical Staff: Bob Sim   **Veterinarian:** Denis Goulding

MEN

Bloomfield, Geoffrey (riding Money Talks)		Showjumping individual	20/74	Qualifying: 36.50
				Round A: 12.00
				Round B: 08.00
		Showjumping team	10/14	Round 1: 20.00 (8th)
				Round 2: 36.00 (10th)
Chester, Gavin	(riding Another Flood)	Showjumping team	10/14	Round 1: 20.00 (8th)
				Round 2: 36.00 (10th)
Coman, James	(riding Zazu)	Showjumping team	10/14	Round 1: 20.00 (8th)
				Round 2: 36.00 (10th)
Dutton, Phillip	(riding House Doctor)	Three-day event team	1/12	Final: 146.80 pts (1st)
Easey, Ronald	(riding Rolling Thunder)	Showjumping team	10/14	Round 1: 20.00 (8th)
				Round 2: 36.00 (10th)
Hoy, Andrew	(riding Swizzle In)	Three-day event individual	2/38	Final: 39.80 pts (2nd)
	(riding Darien Powers)	Three-day event team	1/12	Final: 146.80 pts (1st)
Ryan, Matthew	(riding Kibah Sandstone)	Three-day event team	1/12	Final: 146.80 pts (1st)
Staples, Brook	(riding Master Monarch)	Three-day event individual	16/38	Final: 96.40 pts (16th)
Tinney, Stuart	(riding Jeepster)	Three-day event team	1/12	Final: 146.80 pts (1st)

WOMEN

Bunn, Olivia			DNC	
Downs, Rachael	(riding Aphrodite)	Dressage individual	33/48	Final: 64.52% (33rd)
		Dressage team	6/9	Final: 4925 pts (6th)
Hanna, Mary	(riding Limbo)	Dressage individual	34/48	Final: 64.32% (34th)
		Dressage team	6/9	Final: 4925 pts (6th)
MacMillan, Erica	(riding Crisp)	Dressage individual	35/48	Final: 64.08% (35th)
		Dressage team	6/9	Final: 4925 pts (6th)
Oatley-Nist, Kristy	(riding Wall Street)	Dressage individual	9/48	Final: 210.79% (9th)
		Dressage team	6/9	Final: 4925 pts (6th)
Ross, Amanda	(riding Otto Schumaker)	Three-day event individual	20/38	Final: 149 pts (20th)

Fencing

Section Manager: Helen Smith   **Head Coach:** Vladimir Sher   **Coach:** Alwyn Wardle

MEN

Adamo, Gerard	Epee team	8/11	Round of 16: Defeated China 45-38
			Quarter-final: Defeated by Italy 45-34
			Final for 5-8 Place: Defeated by Belarus 45-34
	Epee individual	15/42	Round of 64: Defeated Carlos Pedroso (CUB) 15-13
			Round of 32: Defeated Ivan Kovacs (HUN) 15-14
			Round of 16: Defeated by Hugues Obry (FRA) 15-5
Cartillier, Luc	Epee team	8/11	Round of 16: Defeated China 45-38
			Quarter-final: Defeated by Italy 45-34
			Final for 5-8 Place: Defeated by Belarus 45-34
Heffernan, Nick	Epee team	8/11	Round of 16: Defeated China 45-38
			Quarter-final: Defeated by Italy 45-34
			Final for 5-8 Place: Defeated by Belarus 45-34
	Epee individual	39/42	Round of 64: Defeated by Mauricio Rivas (COL) 15-10
McMahon, Gerald	Foil	35/40	Round of 64: Defeated by Haibin Wang (CHN) 15-9
Nathan, David	Epee individual	41/42	Round of 64: Defeated by Laurie Shong (CAN) 15-8

WOMEN

Halls, Evelyn	Epee individual	20/39	Round of 64: BYE
			Round of 32: Defeated by Andrea Rentmeister (AUT) 15-14
Halls, Jo	Foil	37/40	Round of 64: Defeated by Eloise Smith (GBR) 15-8

Football (Men)

Section Manager: Peter Kelly   **Head Coach:** Raul Blanco   **Coaches:** Adrian Santrac, Les Scheinflug
Gear Steward: Nelson Delasio   **Doctor:** Dr Trevor Law   **Massage Therapist:** Mathew Baker
Physiotherapist: Peter Georgilopoulos

Blatsis, Con	Foxe, Hayden	Rizzo, Nick	15/16	Preliminary, Group A:
Bresciano, Mark	Grella, Vincenzo	Skoko, Josip		Defeated by Italy 1-0
Colosimo, Simon	Laybutt, Stephen	Turnbull, Michael		Defeated by Nigeria 2-3
Culina, Jason	Lazaridis, Stan	Viduka, Mark		Defeated by Honduras 2-1
Curcija, Michael	Milosevic, Dejan	Wehman, Kasey		
Emerton, Brett	Neill, Lucas	Zane, Clayton		

Football (Women)

Section Manager: Lesley Mann   **Head Coach:** Chris Tanzey   **Coach:** Ian Murray   **Technical Staff:** Karly Pumpa
Doctor: Dr Kieran Fallon   **Physiotherapist:** Edward Hollis   **Psychologist:** Rachel Harrigan

Alagich, Dianne	Golebiowski, Kelly	Starr, Bridgette	7/16	Preliminary, Group E:
Black, Sharon	Hepperlin, Peita-Claire	Tann-Darby, Anissa		Defeated by Germany 3-0
Duus, Bryony	Hughes, Sunni	Trimboli, Leanne		Drew with Sweden 1-1
Ferguson, Alicia	McShea, Kate	Wainwright, Sacha		Defeated by Brazil 2-1
Forman, Alison	Murray, Julie	Wheeler, Tracey		
Garriock, Heather	Salisbury, Cheryl	Wilson, Amy		

Gymnastics

Section Manager: Ken Williamson   **Head Coaches:** Peggy Liddick (Women's Artistic), Warrick Forbes (Men's Artistic)
Coaches: Mark Carlton (Women's Artistic), Katie Mitchell (Rhythmic), Joanne Richards (Women's Artistic),
Nikolay Zhuravlev (Trampoline)   **Physiotherapist:** Leanne Taig

MEN

Istria, Damian	Individual all-round	47/97	Qualifying:	Parallel bars: 8.937 pts (66th)
			Floor: 9.012 pts (52nd)	Horizontal bar: 9.112 pts (67th)
			Pommel horse: 8.175 pts (77th)	Total: 53.973 pts (47th)
			Rings: 9.462 pts (42nd)	
			Vault: 9.275 pts (52nd)	Final: DNQ

			Qualifying:	Final:
Rizzo, Philippe	Individual all-round	29/97	Floor: 9.312 pts (33rd)	Floor: 9.350 pts (17th)
			Pommel horse: 9.225 pts (58th)	Pommel horse: 9.637 pts (14th)
			Rings: 8.837 pts (68th)	Rings: 8.775 pts (34th)
			Vault: 9.037 pts (67th)	Vault: 9.087 pts (31st)
			Parallel bars: 9.237 pts (51st)	Parallel bars: 9.187 pts (31st)
			Horizontal Bar: 8.475 pts (76th)	Horizontal bar: 9.750 pts (6th)
			Total: 54.123 pts (44th)	Total: 55.675 pts (29th)
Wallace, Ji	Trampoline	2/16	Qualifying: 67.40 pts (4th)	Final: 39.30 pts (2nd)

WOMEN

			Qualifying:	Floor: 38.337
Cleland, Melinda	Teams–Artistic	7/12	Vault: 36.423	Total: 151.057
			Uneven bars: 38.561	
			Beam: 37.736	Final: DNQ
	Individual all-round	82/97	Qualifying:	Floor: DNC
			Vault: 9.393 pts (21st)	Total: 19.030 pts (82nd)
			Uneven bars: 9.637 pts (23rd)	
			Beam: DNC	Final: DNQ
Croak, Alexandra	Teams–Artistic	7/12	Qualifying:	Floor: 38.337
			Vault: 36.423	Total: 151.057
			Uneven Bars: 38.561	
			Beam: 37.736	Final: DNQ
	Individual all-round	70/97	Qualifying:	Floor: 9.250 pts (44th)
			Vault: DNC	Total: 28.087 pts (70th)
			Uneven bars: 9.275 pts (56th)	
			Beam: 9.562 pts (22nd)	Final: DNQ
Forbes, Robyn	Trampoline	10/16	Qualifying: 60.70 pts (10th)	
Leray, Danielle	Individual rhythmic	19/24	Rope: 9.575 pts (16th)	Ribbon: 9.483 pts (21st)
			Hoop: 9.591 pts (18th)	Total: 38.215 pts (19th)
			Ball: 9.566 pts (19th)	Final: DNQ
McIntosh, Trudy	Teams–Artistic	7/12	Qualifying:	
			Vault: 36.423	Floor: 38.337
			Uneven bars: 38.561	Total: 151.057
			Beam: 37.736	Final: DNQ
	Individual all-round	66/97	Qualifying:	Floor: 9.612 pts (11th)
			Vault: 9.506 pts (12th)	Total: 28.730 pts (66th)
			Uneven bars: DNC	
			Beam: 9.612 pts (19th)	Final: DNQ
Skinner, Lisa	Floor exercise	8/91	Qualifying: 9.725 pts (4th)	Final: 9.012 pts (8th)
	Individual all-round	8/97	Qualifying:	Final:
			Vault: 9.156 pts (47th)	Vault: 9.168 pts (29th)
			Uneven bars: 9.687 pts (12th)	Uneven Bars: 9.650 pts (12th)
			Beam: 9.162 pts (59th)	Beam: 9.625 pts (9th)
			Floor: 9.725 pts (4th)	Floor: 9.750 pts (4th)
			Total: 37.730 pts (18th)	Total: 38.193 pts (9th)
	Teams–Artistic	7/12	Qualifying:	Floor: 38.337
			Vault: 36.423	Total: 151.057
			Uneven bars: 38.561	
			Beam: 37.736	Final: DNQ
Slater, Allana	Individual all-round	16/97	Qualifying:	Final:
			Vault: 8.268 pts (82nd)	Vault: 9.025 pts (34th)
			Uneven bars: 9.675 pts (17th)	Uneven bars: 9.712 pts (8th)
			Beam: 9.387 pts (37th)	Beam: 9.112 pts (25th)
			Floor: 9.625 pts (10th)	Floor: 9.662 pts (8th)
			Total: 36.955 pts (39th)	Total: 37.511 pts (17th)
	Teams–Artistic	7/12	Qualifying:	Floor: 38.337
			Vault: 36.423	Total: 151.057
			Uneven bars: 38.561	
			Beam: 37.736	Final: DNQ

| Walker, Brooke | Teams–Artistic | 7/12 | Qualifying:
Vault: 36.423
Uneven Bars: 38.561
Beam: 37.736 | Floor: 38.337
Total: 151.057 |
| | Individual all-round | 44/97 | Qualifying:
Vault: 8.368 pts (81st)
Uneven bars: 9.562 pts (35th)
Beam: 9.175 pts (57th) | Final: DNQ
Floor: 9.375 pts (28th)
Total: 36.480 pts (44th) |

Handball (Men)

Section Manager: Tom York   **Head Coach:** Zoltan Marczinka   **Coach:** Janos Olah   **Technical Staff:** Dr Ilan Kogus
Massage Therapist: Krzysztof Frankowski

Bach, Peter	Ramadani, Taip	12/12	Preliminary, Pool B:	Final for 11/12th place:
Bajan, Cristian	Schofield, Lee		Defeated by Sweden 44–23	Defeated by Cuba 26–24
Cheung, Vernon	Sestic, Dragan		Defeated by Spain 39–23	
Garnett, Russell	Sestic, Sasa		Defeated by Slovenia 33–20	
Gonzalez, David	Shehab, Karim		Defeated by Tunisia 34–24	
Groenintwoud, Kristian	Slavujevic, Milan		Defeated by France 28–16	
McCormack, Darryl	Taylor, Brendon			
Pavlovic, Rajan				

Handball (Women)

Section Manager: Patricia Bell-Bartels   **Head Coach:** Christoph Mecker   **Coach:** Ozgen Oztorun
Technical Staff: Lutz Bartels   **Physiotherapist:** Andrew Harper

Bach, Janni	Ignjatovic, Vera	10/10	Preliminary, Pool B:	Final for 9/10th place:
Besta, Petra	Jamnicky, Jana		Defeated by Brazil 32–19	Defeated by Angola 26–18
Bjarnason, Rina	Kahmke, Lydia		Defeated by Norway 28–18	
Boulton, Raelene	Kopcalic, Marina		Defeated by Denmark 38–12	
Briggs, Kim	Milosevic, Jovana		Defeated by Austria 39–10	
Edland, Mari	Ormes, Shelley			
Hammond, Sarah	Shinfield, Katrina			
Hannan, Fiona				

Hockey (Men)

Section Manager: David Coldrey   **Head Coach:** Terry Walsh   **Coach:** Jim Irvine   **Technical Staff:** Gordon Clarke
Doctor: Dr Peter Bacqui   **Massage Therapist:** Noel McRoberts   **Physiotherapist:** Graham Reid
Psychologist: Patrick Farrell

Brennan, Michael	Gaudoin, Paul	3/12	Preliminary, Pool B:	Bronze final:
Commens, Adam	Holt, Stephen		Defeated Poland 4-0	Defeated Pakistan 6–3
Davies, Stephen	Livermore, Brent		Drew with India 2–2	
Diletti, Damon	Sproule, Daniel		Drew with Spain 2–2	
Dreher, Lachlan	Stacy, Jason		Defeated Argentina 2–1	
Duff, Jason	Victory, Craig		Defeated Korea 2–1	
Elder, Troy	Wells, Matthew		Semifinal:	
Elmer, James	York, Michael		Drew with Netherlands 0–0	

Hockey (Women)

Section Manager: Wendy Pritchard   **Head Coach:** Ric Charlesworth   **Coaches:** Herb Haigh, Frank Murray
Technical Staff: Tricia Heberle   **Doctor:** Dr Andrew Potter   **Physiotherapist:** Dean Whittington
Psychologist: Corinne Reid

Allen, Katie	Maitland, Clover	1/10	Preliminary, Pool C:	Medal pool:
Annan, Alyson	Mitchell-Taverner, Claire		Defeated Great Britain 2–1	Defeated New Zealand 3–0
Carruthers, Lisa	Morris, Jennifer		Drew with Spain 1–1	Defeated Netherlands 5–0
Garard, Renita	Peek, Alison		Defeated Argentina 3–1	Defeated China 5–1
Haslam, Juliet	Powell, Katrina		Defeated Korea 3–0	
Hawkes, Rechelle	Skirving, Angela			Gold final:
Hudson, Nicole	Starre, Kate			Defeated Argentina 3–1
Imison, Rachel	Towers, Julie			

Judo

Section Manager: Colin Hill **Head Coach:** Peter Herrmann **Coaches:** Steven Hill, Gabor Szabo

MEN

Ball, Robert	Over 100 kilograms	25/33	1st round: Defeated by A. Tangriev (UZB)
Collett, Andrew	60 to 66 kilograms	17/35	1st round: Defeated J. Wanga (ARU)
			2nd round: Defeated by G. Zhang (CHN)
Hill, Tom	66 to 73 kilograms	25/34	1st round: Defeated by G. Velazco (PER)
Ivers, Robert	81 to 90 kilograms	25/32	1st round: Defeated by K. Morgan (CAN)
			2nd round: Defeated by R. Salimov (AZE)
Kelly, Daniel	73 to 81 kilograms	9/37	1st round: Defeated J. Morris (USA)
			2nd round: Defeated by N. Delgado (POR)
			3rd round: Defeated F. Lepre (ITA)
			4th round: Defeated by K. Sarikhani (IRI)
Robertson, Adrian	Up to 60 kilograms	25/34	1st round: Defeated by M. Ayed (TUN)
Rusitovic, Daniel	90 to 100 kilograms	25/33	1st round: Defeated by S.Khalki (TUN)

WOMEN

Arlove, Catherine	63 to 70 kilograms	13/23	1st round: Defeated by S. Bacher (USA)
Curren, Caroline	Over 78 kilograms	13/24	1st round: Defeated by D.M. Beltran (CUB)
Dixon, Carly	57 to 63 kilograms	18/22	1st round: Defeated by O. Artamonova (KGZ)
Hill, Jennifer	Up to 48 kilograms	13/23	1st round: Defeated by A. Simons (BEL)
Jenkinson, Natalie	70 to 78 kilograms	13/23	1st round: Defeated by E. Silva (BRA)
Pekli, Maria	52 to 57 kilograms	3/23	1st round: Defeated Z. Huseynova (AZE)
			2nd round: Defeated F.M. Nguele (CMR)
			Quarter-final: Defeated P. Andersson (SWE)
			Semifinal: Defeated by I. Fernandez (ESP)
			Bronze final: Defeated by M. Lomba (BEL)
Sullivan, Rebecca	48 to 52 kilograms	9/24	1st round: Defeated L. Tignola (FRA)
			2nd round: Defeated by S.H. Kye (PRK)
			3rd round: Defeated by D. Gravenstijn (NED)

Modern Pentathlon

Section Manager/Coach: Tim Mahon

MEN

McGregor, Robert	Shooting	11/24	1072 pts (11th)
	Fencing	22/24	640 pts (22nd)
	Swimming	24/24	1119 pts (24th)
	Riding	17/24	905 pts (17th)
	Running	17/24	1048 pts (17th)
		20/24	Final: 4784 pts (20th)

WOMEN

Chiller, Kitty	Shooting	16/24	1000 pts (16th)
	Fencing	18/24	760 pts (18th)
	Swimming	10/24	1142 pts (10th)
	Riding	2/24	1040 pts (2nd)
	Running	14/24	944 pts (14th)
		14/24	Final: 4886 pts (14th)

Rowing

Section Manager: Michael Eastaughffe **Assistant Section Manager:** Paul Sloan **Head Coach:** Reinhold Batschi
Coaches: Uwe Bender, Bob Bleakley, Noel Donaldson, Nick Garrett, Harald Jahrling, Peter Le Compte,
Lyall McCarthy, Tim McLaren, Ellen Randell, Brian Richardson, Paul Thompson **Doctor:** Dr William Webb
Massage Therapist: Luke Atwell Physiotherapists: Allan Bourke, Fiona Gutschlag **Psychologist:** Jeffery Bond

MEN

Lightweight double sculls	Hick, Bruce	7/19	Heat 2: 6:33.48 (1st)
	Karrasch, Haimish		Semifinal A/B 1: 6:25.20 (4th)
			Final B: 6:26.21 (1st)
Coxless pair	Long, Matthew	3/15	Heat 3: 6:46.99 (2nd)
	Tomkins, James		Semifinal A/B 2: 6:34.42 (1st)
			Final A: 6:34.26 (3rd)

Lightweight coxless four	Balmforth, Darren Burgess, Simon	Edwards, Anthony Richards, Robert	2/14	Heat 2: 6:11.42 (1st) Semifinal A/B 1: 6:00.82 (1st) Final A: 6:02.90 (2nd)
Quad sculls	Day, Jason Free, Duncan	Hardcastle, Peter Reside, Stuart	4/13	Heat 2: 5:52.09 (1st) Semifinal A/B 1: 5:50.26 (2nd) Final A: 5:50.32 (4th)
Coxless four	Dodwell, Benjamin Hanson, Boden	Stewart, Geoffrey Stewart, James	3/13	Heat 1: 6:05.03 (2nd) Semifinal A/B 2: 6:02.03 (1st) Final A: 5:57.61 (3rd)
Coxed eight	Burke, Daniel Fernandez, Jaime Gordon, Alistair Hayman, Brett (cox) Jahrling, Robert	McKay, Michael Porzig, Nicholas Ryan, Christian Welch, Stuart	2/9	Heat 2: 5:32.85 (1st) Final A: 5:33.88 (2nd)

WOMEN

Single sculls	Douglas, Georgina		5/19	Heat 1: 7:43.48 (2nd) Repechage 4: 7:42.67 (1st) Semifinal A/B 1: 7:32.34 (2nd) Final A: 7:37.88 (5th)
Double sculls	Hatzakis, Marina Roye, Bronwyn		6/10	Heat 1: 7:18.40 (4th) Repechage 1: 7:10.09 (2nd) Final A: 7:05.35 (6th)
Lightweight double sculls	Lee, Virginia Newmarch, Sally		4/18	Heat 2: 7:11.11 (2nd) Repechage 2: 7:14.08 (1st) Semifinal A/B 1: 7:06.58 (3rd) Final A: 7:12.04 (4th)
Coxless pair	Slatter, Kate Taylor, Rachael		2/10	Heat 2: 7:20.69 (2nd) Repechage 2: 7:20.12 (2nd) Final A: 7:12.56 (2nd)
Quad sculls	Heinke, Monique Knowler, Kerry	Robbins, Sally Wilson, Julia	7/9	Heat 2: 6:47.01 (4th) Repechage 2: 6:42.22 (3rd) Final B: 6:37.22 (1st)
Coxed eight	Davies, Alison Foulkes, Katie Kininmonth, Rachael Larsen, Kristina Martin, Emily	Roberts, Victoria Robinson, Jane Thompson, Bronwyn Winter, Jodi	5/7	Heat 1: 6:17.44 (2nd) Repechage: 6:17.72 (3rd) Final A: 6:15.16 (5th)

Sailing

Section Manager: John Harrison **Coaches:** Ian Brown, Mike Fletcher, Victor Kovalenko, Dayne Sharp, Erik Stibbe, Brendan Todd **Technical Staff:** Graeme Owens **Physiotherapist:** Catriona Owens **Psychologist:** Patricia Leahy

MEN

Star Class	Beashal, Colin Giles, David	7/16	Final: 51 pts (7th)
Laser	Blackburn, Michael	3/43	Final: 60 pts (3rd)
Tornado Class	Bundock, Darren Forbes, John	2/16	Final: 25 pts (2nd)
Soling Fleet	Edwards, David Grace, Joshua Wittey, Neville	8/16	Fleet race 1: 1:56 (8th) Fleet race 2: 1:40 (11th) Fleet race 3: 5:13 (6th) Fleet race 4: 0:00 (1st) Fleet race 5: 2:05 (9th) Fleet race 6: 4:11 (14th) Round robin 2, Flight 1, Match 2: Defeated USA Round robin 2, Flight 2, Match 1: Defeated by Sweden Round robin 2, Flight 3, Match 1: Defeated by Russia Round robin 2, Flight 4, Match 4: Defeated by Denmark Round robin 2, Flight 5, Match 3: Defeated by Germany Final: DNQ (8th)
470 Class	King, Thomas Turnbull, Mark	1/29	Final: 38 pts (1st)

Mistral	Kleppich, Lars	4/36	Final: 61 pts (4th)	
49er	Nicholson, Christopher	6/17	Final: 86 pts (6th)	
	Phillips, Daniel			
Finn Class	Nossiter, Anthony	13/25	Final: 94 pts (13th)	

WOMEN

470 Class	Armstrong, Jennifer	1/19	Final: 33 pts (1st)	
	Stowell, Belinda			
Mistral	Crisp, Jessica	5/29	Final: 59 pts (5th)	
Europe	Dennison, Melanie	15/27	Final: 102 pts (15th)	

Shooting

Section Manager: Yvonne Hill **Head Coach:** Bill Murray **Coaches:** Anatoli Aktov, Greg Chan, John Gillman, Luca Scribani Rossi, Miro Sipek **Gunsmith:** Sergei Eglevski Massage Therapist: Darien Roach

MEN

Barton, Clive	Skeet	14/49	Qualifying: 121 pts (14th)	Final: DNQ
Chapman, David	Rapid-fire pistol	20/21	Qualifying: 557 pts (20th)	Final: DNQ
Cunningham, David	Skeet	39/49	Qualifying: 116 pts (39th)	Final: DNQ
Diamond, Michael	Double trap	9/25	Qualifying: 135 pts (9th)	Final: DNQ
	Trap	1/41	Qualifying: 122 pts	Final: 147 pts (1st)
Gitsham, Adam	10 metres running target	17/18	Qualifying: 556 pts (17th)	Final: DNQ
Jones, David	10 metres running target	16/18	Qualifying: 562 pts (16th)	Final: DNQ
Lowndes, Timothy	50 metres free rifle (60 shots)	19/54	Qualifying: 593 pts (19th)	Final: DNQ
	50 metres free rifle (3 x 40 shots)	20/44	Qualifying: 1159 pts (20th)	Final: DNQ
	10 metres air rifle (60 shots)	41/48	Qualifying: 582 pts (41st)	Final: DNQ
Mark, Russell	Double trap	2/25	Qualifying: 143 pts	Final: 187 pts (2nd)
	Trap	13/41	Qualifying: 113 pts (13th)	Final: DNQ
Moore, David	10 metres air pistol	32/43	Qualifying: 567 pts (32nd)	Final: DNQ
	50 metres free pistol	18/36	Qualifying: 556 pts (18th)	Final: DNQ
Porter, David	10 metres air pistol	38/43	Qualifying: 561 pts (38th)	Final: DNQ
	50 metres free pistol	20/31	Qualifying: 553 pts (20th)	Final: DNQ
Potent, Warren	50 metres free rifle (60 shots)	19/54	Qualifying: 593 pts (19th)	Final: DNQ
Wieland, Robert	10 metres air rifle (60 shots)	27/48	Qualifying: 587 pts (27th)	Final: DNQ
Wieland, Samuel	50 metres free rifle (3 x 40 shots)	22/44	Qualifying: 1158 pts (22nd)	Final: DNQ

WOMEN

Baynes, Deserie	Double trap	9/17	Qualifying: 98 pts (9th) 5	Final: DNQ
	Trap	12/17	Qualifying: 61 pts (12th)	Final: DNQ
Forder, Annemarie	10 metres air pistol	3/45	Qualifying: 385 pts	Final: 484 pts (3rd)
Imgrund, Belinda	10 metres air rifle (40 shots)	41/49	Qualifying: 387 pts (41st)	Final: DNQ
Lonsdale, Natasha	Skeet	4/13	Qualifying: 70 pts	Final: 98 pts (4th)
McCready, Susan	50 metres sport rifle	20/42	Qualifying: 574 pts (20th)	Final: DNQ
	10 metres air rifle (40 shots)	15/49	Qualifying: 392 pts (15th)	Final: DNQ
Quigley, Carolyn	50 metres sport rifle	39/42	Qualifying: 551 pts (39th)	Final: DNQ
Roberts, Annmaree	Double trap	9/17	Qualifying: 98 pts (9th)	Final: DNQ
Ryan, Linda	10 metres air pistol	28/45	Qualifying: 375 pts (28th)	Final: DNQ
	25 metres sport pistol	11/42	Qualifying: 579 pts (11th)	Final: DNQ
Smith, Lisa-Anne	Trap	10/17	Qualifying: 62 pts (10th)	
Trefry, Christine	25 metres sport pistol	15/42	Qualifying: 578 pts (15th)	Final: DNQ

Softball

Section Manager: Faye Bourne **Head Coach:** Bob Crudgington **Coach:** Barry Blanchard, Simon Roskvist
Sport Scientist: Lachlan Penfold **Technical Staff:** Graeme Rose **Physiotherapist:** Wendy Braybon

WOMEN	Allen, Sandra	Harding, Tanya	3/8	Preliminaries:	Semifinal:
	Brown, Joanne	McCreedy, Sally		Defeated New Zealand 3-2	Defeated by Japan 1–0
	Dienelt, Kerry	Morrow, Simmone		Defeated Italy 7–0	Final:
	Edebone, Peta	Roche, Melanie		Defeated Canada 1–0	Defeated by USA 1–0
	Fairhurst, Sue	Titcume, Natalie		Defeated by Japan 1–0	
	Follas, Selina	Ward, Natalie		Defeated USA 2–1	
	Hanes, Fiona	Wilkins, Brooke		Defeated China 1–0	
	Hardie, Kelly			Defeated Cuba 8–1	

Swimming

Section Manager: Alan Thompson **Head Coach:** Donald Talbot **Coaches:** John Carew, Denis Cotterell,
Douglas Frost, Ian Pope, Mark Regan, Greg Salter, Brian Sutton, Guennadi Touretski, Scott Volkers, Kenneth Wood
Assistant Manager: Lynn Fowlie Sport Scientists: Graeme Maw, David Pyne, Robert Treffene
Technical Staff: Bruce Steed, Janet Talbot Massage Therapist/Chiropractor: George Dragasevich
Massage Therapists: Nicole Massaro, Anthony Scown, Jo-Anne Yeoman-Hare
Physiotherapists: Peter Blanch, Roger Fitzgerald **Psychologist:** Clark Perry

MEN

Name	Event		Heat	Semifinal / Final
Callus, Ashley	4 x 100 metres freestyle relay	1/23	Heat 2: 3:17.37 (1st)	Final: 3:13.67 (1st)
Delaney, Cameron	200 metres backstroke	11/46	Heat 6: 1:59.61 (2nd)	Semifinal 2: 2:00.39 (5th)
Dunn, Matthew	200 metres individual medley	9/56	Heat 6: 2:02.44 (2nd)	Semifinal 1: 2:01.95 (5th)
	400 metres individual medley	12/45	Heat 4: 4:20.31 (4th)	
Fydler, Christopher	50 metres freestyle	10/80	Heat 10: 22.80 (5th)	Semifinal 1: 22.41 (5th)
	100 metres freestyle	8/74	Heat 8: 49.45 (2nd)	Semifinal 2: 49.55 (5th)
				Final: 49.44 (8th)
	4 x 100 metres freestyle relay	1/23	Heat 2: 3:17.37 (1st)	Final: 3:13.67 (1st)
Hackett, Grant	200 metres freestyle	8/53	Heat 6: 1:49.23 (3rd)	Semifinal 2: 1:48.76 (4th)
				Final: 1:49.46 (8th)
	400 metres freestyle	7/46	Heat 5: 3:48.91 (3rd)	Final: 3:48.22 (7th)
	1500 metres freestyle	1/41	Heat 6: 15:07.50 (1st)	Final: 14:48.33 (1st)
	4 x 200 metres freestyle relay	1/16	Heat 2: 7:14.27 (1st)	Final: DNC
Harrison, Regan	200 metres breaststroke	4/49	Heat 7: 2:14.85 (4th)	Semifinal 2: 2:13.75 (3rd)
				Final: 2:12.88 (4th)
	4 x 100 metres medley relay	2/24	Heat 2: DNC	Final: 3:35.27 (2nd)
Hawke, Brett	50 metres freestyle	13/80	Heat 10: 22.45 (3rd)	Semifinal: 2: 22.49 (7th)
Huegill, Geoff	100 metres butterfly	3/63	Heat 8: 52.79 (1st)	Semifinal 1: 51.96 (1st)
			Final: 52.22 (3rd)	
	4 x 100 metres medley relay	2/24	Heat 2: DNC	Final: 3:35.27 (2nd)
Klim, Michael	100 metres freestyle	4/74	Heat 10: 49.09 (1st)	Semifinal 1: 48.80 (1st)
			Final: 48.74 (4th)	
	100 metres butterfly	2/63	Heat 7: 52.73 (1st)	Semifinal 2: 52.63 (1st)
				Final: 52.18 (2nd)
	4 x 100 metres freestyle relay	1/23	Heat 2: DNC	Final: 3:13.67 (1st)
	4 x 200 metres freestyle relay	1/16	Heat 2: DNC	Final: 7:07.05 (1st)
	4 x 100 metres medley relay	2/24	Heat 2: DNC	Final: 3:35.27 (2nd)
Kirby, William	4 x 200 metres freestyle relay	1/16	Heat 2: 7:14.27 (1st)	Final: 7:07.05 (1st)
Kowalski, Daniel	4 x 200 metres freestyle relay	1/16	Heat 2: 7:14.27 (1st)	Final: DNC
Mitchell, Ryan	200 metres breaststroke	8/49	Heat 5: 2:14.69 (1st)	Semifinal 2: 2:13.87 (4th)
				Final: 2:14.00 (8th)
	4 x 100 metres medley relay	2/24	Heat 2: 3:39.38 (1st)	Final DNC
Norris, Justin	200 metres butterfly	3/46	Heat 6: 1:57.60 (2nd)	Semifinal 1: 1:57.10 (2nd)
				Final: 1:56.17 (3rd
	400 metres individual medley	6/45	Heat 5: 4:17.36 (3rd)	Final: 4:17.87 (6th)
Pearson, Todd	4 x 100 metres freestyle relay	1/23	Heat 2: 3:17.37 (1st)	Final: DNC
	4 x 200 metres freestyle relay	1/16	Heat 2: 7:14.27 (1st)	Final: 7:07.05 (1st)
Perkins, Kieren	1500 metres freestyle	2/41	Heat 4: 14:58.34 (1st)	Final: 14:53.59 (2nd)
Pine, Adam	4 x 100 metres freestyle relay	1/23	Heat 2: 3:17.37 (1st)	Final: DNC
	4 x 100 metres medley relay	2/24	Heat 2: 3:39.38 (1st)	Final: DNC
Ramsay, Heath	200 metres butterfly	11/46	Heat 4: 1:58.82 (3rd)	Semifinal 1: 1:57.90 (6th)
Rogers, Philip	100 metres breaststroke	17/66	Heat 6: 1:02.77 (1st)	
Thorpe, Ian	200 metres freestyle	2/53	Heat 7: 1:46.56 (1st)	Semifinal 2: 1:45.37 (1st)
				Final: 1:45.35 (2nd)
	400 metres freestyle	1/46	Heat 6: 3:44.65 (1st)	Final: 3:40.59 (1st)
	4 x 100 metres freestyle relay	1/23	Heat 2: DNC	Final: 3:13.67 (1st)
	4 x 200 metres freestyle relay	1/16	Heat 2: DNC	Final: 7:07.05 (1st)
	4 x 100 metres medley relay	2/24	Heat 2: 3:39.38 (1st)	Final: DNC
van der Zant, Robert	200 metres individual medley	14/56	Heat 7: 2:02.77 (3rd)	Semifinal 2: 2:02.91 (7th)
Watson, Josh	100 metres backstroke	4/55	Heat 7: 55.09 (2nd)	Semifinal 1: 54.93 (2nd)
			Final: 55.01 (4th)	
	4 x 100 metres medley relay	2/24	Heat 2: 3:39.38 (1st)	Final: DNC
Welsh, Matthew	100 metres backstroke	2/55	Heat 6: 54.70 (1st)	Semifinal 1: 54.52 (1st)
				Final: 54.07 (2nd)

	200 metres backstroke	3/46	Heat 6: 1:59.76 (3rd)	Semifinal 1: 1:58.57 (2nd) Final: 1:57.59 (3rd)
	4 x 100 metres medley relay	2/24	Heat 2: 3:39.38 (1st)	Final: 3:35.27 (2nd)
WOMEN				
Brown, Rebecca	200 metres breaststroke	14/36	Heat 4: 2:28.24 (7th)	Semifinal 2: 2:29.90 (7th)
Calub, Dyana	100 metres backstroke	7/47	Heat 4: 1:02.46 (4th)	Semifinal 1: 1:01.86 (4th) Final: 1:01.61 (7th)
	200 metres backstroke	24/36	Heat 4: 2:17.05 (8th)	
	4 x 100 metres medley relay	2/18	Heat 2: 4:04.75 (1st)	Final: 4:01.59 (2nd)
D'Arcy, Sarah	400 metres freestyle	27/39	Heat 5: 4:18.05 (8th)	Final: DNQ
Dodd, Melanie	4 x 100 metres freestyle relay	6/13	Heat 2: 3:43.56 (4th)	Final: DNC
Giteau, Kasey	400 metres freestyle	18/39	Heat 4: 4:15.54 (6th)	Final: DNQ
Graham, Elka	4 x 100 metres freestyle relay	6/13	Heat 2: 3:43.56 (4th)	Final: 3:40.91 (6th)
	4 x 200 metres freestyle relay	2/15	Heat 1: 8:03.26 (1st)	Final: DNC
Harris, Rachel	800 metres freestyle	12/28	Heat 4: 8:36.94 (5th)	
	400 metres individual medley	12/28	Heat 2: 4:46.02 (5th)	
Hildreth, Caroline	200 metres breaststroke	10/36	Heat 4: 2: 27.60 (5th)	Semifinal 1: 2:28.30 (5th)
Jones, Leisel	100 metres breaststroke	2/44	Heat 6: 1:07.92 (2nd)	Semifinal 2: 1:08.03 (2nd) Final: 1:07.49 (2nd)
	4 x 100 metres medley relay	2/18	Heat 2: DNC	Final: 4:01.59 (2nd)
Lewis, Hayley	800 metres freestyle	13/28	Heat 2: 8:38.75 (3rd)	
O'Neill, Susan	50 metres freestyle	12/74	Heat 8: 25.73 (3rd)	Semifinal 1: 25.74 (6th)
	100 metres freestyle	31/56	Heat 7: 57.78 (7th)	
	200 metres freestyle	1/41	Heat 6: 1:59.14 (1st)	Semifinal 2: 1:59.37 (1st) Final: 1: 1:58.24 (1st)
	100 metres butterfly	7/50	Heat 5: 59.49 (3rd)	Semifinal 2: 59.05 (5th) Final: 59.27 (7th)
	200 metres butterfly	2/36	Heat 5: 2:07.97 (1st)	Semifinal 1: 2:07.57 (1st) Final: 2:06.58 (2nd)
	4 x 100 metres freestyle relay	6/13	Heat 2: 3:43.56 (4th)	Final: 3:40.91 (6th)
	4 x 200 metres freestyle relay	2/15	Heat 1: DNC	Final: 7:58.52 (2nd)
	4 x 100 metres medley relay	2/18	Heat 2: DNC	Final: 4:01.59 (2nd)
Overton, Elli	200 metres individual medley	11/36	Heat 5: 2:16.76 (5th)	Semifinal 1: 2:15.74 (6th)
Reilly, Jennifer	400 metres individual medley	8/28	Heat 4: 4:41.51 (3rd)	Final: 4:45.99 (8th)
Rooney, Giaan	200 metres freestyle	14/41	Heat 5: 2:00.99 (4th)	Semifinal 2: 2:00.84 (6th)
	100 metres backstroke	19/47	Heat 6: 1:03.20 (6th)	
	4 x 100 metres freestyle relay	6/13	Heat 2: 3:43.56 (4th)	Final: 3:40.91 (6th)
	4 x 200 metres freestyle relay	2/15	Heat 1: 8:03.26 (1st)	Final: 7:58.52 (2nd)
	4 x 100 metres medley relay	2/18	Heat 2: 4:04.75 (1st)	Final: DNC
Ryan, Sarah	50 metres freestyle	23/74	Heat 8: 26.05 (8th)	
	100 metres freestyle	12/56	Heat 6: 56.05 (5th)	Semifinal 1: 55.93 (6th)
	4 x 100 metres freestyle relay	6/13	Heat 2: 3:43.56 (4th)	Final: 3:40.91 (6th)
	4 x 100 metres medley relay	2/18	Heat 2: 4:04.75 (1st)	Final: DNC
Stoney, Clementine	200 metres backstroke	13/36	Heat 3: 2:14.61 (5th)	Semifinal 1: 2:14.25 (6th)
Thomas, Petria	100 metres butterfly	4/50	Heat 7: 58.52 (2nd)	Semifinal 2: 58.11 (2nd) Final: 58.49 (4th)
	200 metres butterfly	3/36	Heat 4: 2:08.70 (1st)	Semifinal 1: 2:07.63 (2nd) Final: 2:07.12 (3rd)
	4 x 200 metres freestyle relay	2/15	Heat 1: DNC	Final: 7:58.52 (2nd)
	4 x 100 metres medley relay	2/18	Heat 2: 4:04.75 (1st)	Final: 4:01.59 (2nd)
Thomson, Kirsten	4 x 200 metres freestyle relay	2/15	Heat 1: 8:03.26 (1st)	Final: 7:58.52 (2nd)
Van Lint, Jacinta	4 x 200 metres freestyle relay	2/15	Heat 1: 8:03.26 (1st)	Final: DNC
White, Tarnee	100 metres breaststroke	7/44	Heat 4: 1:08.35 (2nd)	Final: 1:09.09 (7th) Semifinal 2: 1:08.61 (3rd)
	4 x 100 metres medley relay	2/18	Heat 2: 4:04.75 (1st)	Final: DNC
Windsor, Anna	200 metres individual medley	25/36	Heat 4: 2:19.44 (8th)	

Synchronised Swimming
Section Manager: Laurel Glancy   **Head Coach:** Deborah Muir   **Coach:** Candice Ashman

Davis, Tracey	Team routine	8/24	Technical: 31.383 pts (8th) Free: 58.110 pts (8th) Final: 89.493 pts (8th)
Geraghty, Kelly	Team routine	8/24	Technical: 31.383 pts (8th) Free: 58.110 pts (8th) Final: 89.493 pts (8th)
Laird, Amanda	Team routine	8/24	Technical: 31.383 pts (8th) Free: 58.110 pts (8th) Final: 89.493 pts (8th)
Liesch, Dannielle	Team routine	8/24	Technical: 31.383 pts (8th) Free: 58.110 pts (8th) Final: 89.493 pts (8th)
Olevsky, Irena	Team routine	8/24	Technical: 31.383 pts (8th) Free: 58.110 pts (8th) Final: 89.493 pts (8th)
	Duet routine	16/24	Preliminary: Technical: 30.543 pts Free: 56.464 pts Total: 87.007 pts (16th)
Orpwood, Katrina	Team routine	8/24	Technical: 31.383 pts (8th) Free: 58.110 pts (8th) Final: 89.493 pts (8th)
Ren, Rachel	Team routine	8/24	Technical: 31.383 pts (8th) Free: 58.110 pts (8th) Final: 89.493 pts (8th)
Wightman, Cathryn	Team routine	8/24	Technical: 31.383 pts (8th) Free: 58.110 pts (8th) Final: 89.493 pts (8th)
Young, Naomi	Team routine	8/24	Technical: 31.383 pts (8th) Free: 58.110 pts (8th) Final: 89.493 pts (8th)
	Duet routine	16/24	Preliminary: Technical: 30.543 pts Free: 56.464 pts Total: 87.007 pts (16th)

Table Tennis
Section Manager: Aleksander Jakubczak   **Head Coach:** Robert Tuckett   **Coach:** Peng Quach

MEN

Clarke, Brett	Men's doubles	17/39	Qualifying, Group H: Defeated by Yugoslavia 2-0 Defeated by Germany 2-0	Final DNQ: (17th)
Gerada, Simon	Men's singles	33/64	Qualifying, Group E: Defeated by Adrian Crisan (ROM) 3-0 Defeated by Lucjan Blaszczyk (POL) 3-0	Final: DNQ (33rd)
	Men's doubles	17/39	Qualifying, Group C: Defeated by Greece 2-0 Defeated by Hong Kong 2-0	Final: DNQ (17th)
Lavale, Russell	Men's singles	33/64	Qualifying, Group K: Defeated by Tomasz Krzeszewski (POL) 3-0 Defeated by Danny Heister (NED) 3-0	Final: DNQ (33rd)
Plumb, Jeffrey	Men's doubles	17/39	Qualifying, Group H: Defeated by Yugoslavia 2-0 Defeated by Germany 2-0	Final DNQ: (17th)
Smythe, Mark	Men's singles	33/64	Qualifying, Group I: Defeated by Chu Yan Leung (HKG) 3-2 Defeated by Seung-Min Yoo (KOR) 3-0 (33rd)	
	Men's doubles	17/39	Qualifying, Group C: Defeated by Greece 2-0 Defeated by Hong Kong 2-0	Final: DNQ (17th)

WOMEN

Lay, Jian	Women's doubles	17/34	Qualifying, Group B: Defeated by Japan 2-1 Defeated by Lithuania 2-0	Final: DNQ (17th)
Miao, Miao	Women's singles	33/64	Qualifying, Group F: Defeated by Rinko Sakata (JPN) 3-0 Defeated Funke Osonaike (NGR) 3-0	Final: DNQ (33rd)
	Women's doubles	5/34	Qualifying, Group A: Defeated Austria 2-1 Defeated Canada 2-1 Round of 16: Defeated Luxembourg 3-2	Quarter-final: Defeated by China 3-0 (5th)

Zhou, Shirley	Women's singles	33/64	Qualifying, Group A: Defeated by Lijuan Geng (CAN) 3–0 Defeated Nanthana Komwong (THA) 3–1	Final: DNQ (33rd)
	Women's doubles	5/34	Qualifying, Group A: Defeated Austria 2–1 Defeated Canada 2–1 Round of 16: Defeated Luxembourg 3–2	Quarter-final: Defeated by China 3–0 (5th)
Zhou, Xi Tao	Women's singles	33/64	Qualifying, Group D: Defeated by Andrea Bakula (CRO) 3–2 Defeated by Jun Gao Chang (USA) 3–0	Final: DNQ (33rd)
	Women's doubles	17/34	Qualifying, Group B: Defeated by Japan 2–1 Defeated by Lithuania 2–0	Final: DNQ (17th)

Taekwondo

Section Manager: John Kotsifas   **Head Coach:** Ross Hartnett   **Coaches:** Martin Hall, Jin Tae Jong

MEN

Hansen, Warren	Under 80 kilograms	5/13	Preliminary 1, Pool B: Defeated Muhammed Dahmani (DEN) 6–5 Preliminary 2, Pool B: Defeated by Faissal Ebnoutalib (GER) 2–1 Repechage 1: Defeated Mohammed Alfararjeh (JOR) 5–4 Repechage 2: Defeated by Roman Livaja (SWE) 1–0 (5th)
Lyons, Paul	Under 58 kilograms	9/14	Preliminary 1, Pool B: Defeated by Younes Sekkat (MAR) 4–4 Final: DNQ (9th)
Massimino, Carlo	Under 68 kilograms	5/14	Preliminary 1, Pool B: Defeated Francisco Zas (ESP) 3–3 Preliminary 2: Defeated by Steven Lopez (USA) 1–1 (5th)
Trenton, Daniel	Over 80 kilograms	2/14	Preliminary 1, Pool A: Defeated Marcus Thoren (SWE) 6–3 Preliminary 2, Pool A: Defeated Colin Daley (GBR) 8–4 Preliminary 3: Defeated Milton Castro (COL) 8–2 Final: Defeated by Kyong-Hun Kim (KOR) 6–2 (2nd)

WOMEN

Burns, Lauren	Under 49 kilograms	1/12	Preliminary 1, Pool B: Defeated Shu-Ju Chi (TPE) 3–3 Preliminary 2, Pool B: Defeated Hanne Poulsen (DEN) 1–0 Final: Defeated Urbia Melendez-Rodriguez (CUB) 4–2 (1st)
Cameron, Cynthia	Under 57 kilograms	9/12	Preliminary 1, Pool A: Defeated by Chih-Ling Hsu (TPE) 6–0 Final: DNQ (9th)
O'Keefe, Lisa	Under 67 kilograms	9/12	Preliminary 1, Pool A: Defeated by Mirjam Mueskens (NED) 8–6 Final: DNQ (9th)
White, Tanya	Over 67 kilograms	9/12	Preliminary 1, Pool A: Defeated by Zhong Chen (CHN) 6–0 Repechage 1: Defeated by Mounia Bourguigue (MAR) 3–1 (9th)

Tennis

Section Manager: Fenton Coull   **Coaches:** Lesley Bowrey (women), Tony Roche (men)   **Chiropractor:** Andrea Bisaz
Physiotherapist: Kathryn Martin

MEN

Hewitt, Lleyton	Men's singles	33/64	1st round: Defeated by Max Mirnyi (BLR) 6–3,6–3
Ilie, Andrew	Men's singles	33/64	1st round: Defeated by Fernando Vicente (ESP) 6–3,6–3
Philippoussis, Mark	Men's singles	9/64	1st round: Defeated Thomas Johansson (SWE) 7–6(6),6–4 2nd round: Defeated Kristian Pless (ARM) 6–4,6–4 3rd round: Defeated by Yevgeny Kafelnikov (RUS) 7–6(4),6–3
Rafter, Patrick	Men's singles	17/64	1st round: Defeated Vincent Spadea (USA) 6–4,6–3 2nd round: Defeated by Daniel Nestor (CAN) 7–5,7–6(4)
Woodbridge, Todd	Men's doubles	2/29	1st round: Bye 2nd round: Defeated India 6–3,7–6(1) Quarter-final: Defeated Slovakia 7–6(5),6–4 Semifinal: Defeated Spain 6–3,7–6(5) Final: Defeated by Canada 5–7,6–3,6–4,7–6(2)

Woodforde, Mark	Men's doubles	2/29	1st round: Bye 2nd round: Defeated India 6–3,7–6(1) Quarter-final: Defeated Slovakia 7–6(5),6–4 Semifinal: Defeated Spain 6–3,7–6(5) Final: Defeated by Canada 5–7,6–3,6–4,7–6(2)

WOMEN

Dokic, Jelena	Women's singles	4/64	1st round: Defeated Ai Sugiyama (JPN) 6–0,7–6(1) 2nd round. Defeated Rita Grande (ITA) 5–7,6–3,6–3 3rd round: Defeated Rossana de los Rios (PAR) 7–6(5),7–5 Quarter-final: Defeated Amanda Coetzer (RSA) 6–1,1–6,6–1 Semifinal: Defeated by Elena Dementieva (RUS) 2–6,6–4,6–4
	Women's doubles	9/31	1st round: Defeated India 6–0,6–0 2nd round: Defeated by Netherlands 6–2,6–1
Molik, Alicia	Women's singles	33/64	1st round: Defeated by Barbara Schett (AUT) 7–6(7),6–2
Pratt, Nicole	Women's singles	17/64	1st round: Defeated Ruxandra Dragomir (ROM) 6–3,6–3 2nd round: Defeated by Nathalie Dechy (FRA) 6–3,6–1
Stubbs, Rennae	Women's doubles	9/31	1st round: Defeated India 6–0,6–0 2nd round: Defeated by Netherlands 6–2,6–1

Triathlon

Section Manager: Emery Holmik   **Coach:** Kieran Barry, Peter Coulson, Bill Davoren, Colin Stewart
Physiotherapist: Peter Stanton

MEN

Stewart, Miles	Triathlon	6/52	Swim 1.5 kilometres: 17:55.49 (26th) Bike 40 kilometres: 1:17:01.99 (4th) Run 10 kilometres: 31:54.43 (8th) Total: 1:49:14.52 (6th)
Walton, Craig	Triathlon	27/52	Swim 1.5 kilometres: 17:17.69 (1st) Bike 40 kilometres: 1:17:01.09 (3rd) Run 10 kilometres: 33:36.97 (32nd) Total: 1:50:57.66 (27th)
Robertson, Peter	Triathlon	34/52	Swim 1.5 kilometres: 18:26.99 (46th) Bike 40 kilometres: 1:17:10.99 (24th) Run 10 kilometres: 34:10.65 (38th) Total:1:51:39.04 (34th)

WOMEN

Jones, Michellie	Triathlon	2/48	Swim 1.5 kilometres: 19:21.68 (8th) Bike 40 kilometres: 1:24:57.08 (5th) Run 10 kilometres: 35:25.77 (3rd) Total: 2:00:42.55 (2nd)
Harrop, Loretta	Triathlon	5/48	Swim 1.5 kilometres: 19:13.58 (4th) Bike 40 kilometres: 1:24:58.38 (9th) Run 10 kilometres: 36:24.14 (7th) Total: 2:01:42.82 (5th)
Hackett, Nicole	Triathlon	9/48	Swim 1.5 kilometres: 19:12.98 (3rd) Bike 40 kilometres: 1:24:57.68 (6th) Run 10 kilometres: 37:52.63 (19th) Total: 2:03:10.81 (9th)

Volleyball, Beach

Section Manager: Ben Jones   **Head Coach:** Steve Tutton
Coaches: Steve Anderson, Russell Borgeaud, Alexis Lebedew, Craig Marshall, Indra Reinpuu

MEN

Pairs (with Joshua Slack)	Grinlaubs, Matthew	17/24	Elimination round 1: Defeated by Emanuel/Loiola (BRA) 15–3 Elimination round 2: Defeated Baracetti/Salema (ARG) 15–2 Elimination round 3: Defeated by Stamm/Berger (AUT) 15–10
Pairs (with Lee Zahner)	Prosser, Julien	9/24	Elimination round 1: Defeated by Sotelo/Ibarra (MEX) 15–12 Elimination round 2: Defeated Kvalheim/Maaseide (NOR) 15–12 Elimination round 3: Defeated Wong/Heidger (USA) 15–11 Eighth final: Defeated by Laciga P./Laciga M. (SUI) 15–8
Pairs (with Matthew Grinlaubs)	Slack, Joshua	17/24	Elimination round 1: Defeated by Emanuel/Loiola (BRA) 15–3 Elimination round 2: Defeated Baracetti/Salema (ARG) 15–2 Elimination round 3: Defeated by Stamm/Berger (AUT) 15–10
Pairs (with Julien Prosser)	Zahner, Lee	9/24	Elimination round 1: Defeated by Sotelo/Ibarra (MEX) 15–12 Elimination round 2: Defeated Kvalheim/Maaseide (NOR) 15–12 Elimination round 3: Defeated Wong/Heidger (USA) 15–11 Eighth final: Defeated by Laciga, P./Laciga, M. (SUI) 15–8

WOMEN

Pairs (with Kerri Pottharst)	Cook, Natalie	1/24	Elimination round: Defeated Gaxiola/Galindo (MEX) 15–11 Eighth final: Defeated Xiong/Chi (CHN) 15–2 Quarter-final: Defeated Bruschini/Solazzi (ITA) 15–11 Semifinal: Defeated Sandra/Adriana (BRA) 15–6 Final: Defeated Adriana Behar/Shelda (BRA) 12–11, 12–10
Pairs (with Pauline Manser)	Gooley, Tania	5/24	Elimination round: Defeated Gattelli/Perrotta (ITA) 15–9 Eighth final: Defeated Prawerman/Rigaux (FRA) 15–3 Quarter-final: Defeated by Adriana Behar/Shelda (BRA) 15–7
Pairs (with Sarah Straton)	Huygens Tholen, Annette	19/24	Elimination round 1: Defeated by Jordan/Davis (USA) 15–13 Elimination round 2: Defeated by Friedrichsen/Musch (GER) 15–9
Pairs (with Tania Gooley)	Manser, Pauline	5/24	Elimination round: Defeated Gattelli/Perrotta (ITA) 15–9 Eighth final: Defeated Prawerman/Rigaux (FRA) 15–3 Quarter-final: Defeated by Adriana Behar/Shelda (BRA) 15–7
Pairs (with Natalie Cook)	Pottharst, Kerri	1/24	Elimination round: Defeated Gaxiola/Galindo (MEX) 15–11 Eighth final: Defeated Xiong/Chi (CHN) 15–2 Quarter-final: Defeated Bruschini/Solazzi (ITA) 15–11 Semifinal: Defeated Sandra/Adriana (BRA) 15–6 Final: Defeated Adriana Behar/Shelda (BRA) 12–11, 12–10
Pairs (with Annette Huygens Tholen)	Straton, Sarah	19/24	Elimination round 1: Defeated by Jordan/Davis (USA) 15–13 Elimination round 2: Defeated by Friedrichsen/Musch (GER) 15–9

Volleyball (Men)

Section Manager: Phil Borgeaud   **Head Coach:** Stelio De Rocco   **Coach:** Mark Lebedew   **Doctor:** Dr Stuart Watson

Beard, David	Marazios, Spiros	8/12	Preliminary rounds, Pool A:
Hardy, Benjamin	Newcomb, Scott		Defeated by Brazil 3–0 (25–13, 25–14, 25–21)
Howard, Daniel	Ronan, Daniel		Defeated by Netherlands 3–0 (25–19, 25–17, 25–15)
Jakavicius, Nathan	Van Beest, Hidde		Defeated Spain 3–1 (23–25, 25–20, 25–23, 25–19)
Keir, Steven	Wentworth, Russell		Defeated by Cuba 3–0 (25–17, 25–20, 25–18)
Loft, Benjamin	Williams, Mark		Defeated Egypt (3–0 (25–17, 25–23, 25–22)
			Classifications 5–8:
			Defeated by Netherlands 3–0 (25–20, 25–15, 25–21)
			Classifications 7–8:
			Defeated by Cuba 3–0 (25–23, 25–11, 25–15)

Volleyball (Women)

Section Manager: Wanda Sipa   **Head Coach:** Brad Saindon   **Coach:** Mark Barnard
Physiotherapist: Andrew Hughes

Barnett, Tamsin	Daly, Beatrice	11/12	Preliminary, Pool A:
Bawden, Louise	Maycock, Renae		Defeated by Croatia 3–1 (25–21, 22–25, 25–14, 25–16)
Bowen, Sandra	Mokotupu, Christie		Defeated by Brazil 3–0 (25–13, 25–18, 25–17)
Brett, Elizabeth	Ruddle, Priscilla (capt.)		Defeated Kenya 3–1 (16–25, 25–20, 25–15, 28–26)
Brown, Majella	Scoble, Selina		Defeated by USA 3–0 (25–11, 25–17, 25–10)
Clarke, Angela	White, Rachel		Defeated by China 3–0 (25–18, 25–14, 25–15)

Water Polo (Men)

Section Manager: Christopher Harrison   **Head Coach:** Donald Cameron   **Coach:** Denes Poksic
Psychologist: Christopher Horsley   **Doctor:** Warren McDonald

Boyd, Sean	Owen-Jones, Hugh	8/12	Preliminary, Group A:	Quarter-final:
Denis, Edward	Sterk, Rafael		Defeated by Russia 6–4	Defeated by Yugoslavia 7–3
Kovalenko, Andrei	Thomas, Nathan		Drew with Kazakhstan 11–11	Final for 5th–8th places:
Marsden, Daniel	Waterman, Grant		Defeated Slovakia 11–6	Defeated by Italy 8–4
Miller, Craig	Whalan, Thomas		Defeated by Italy 6–5	Final for 7th–8th places:
Neesham, Timothy	Woods, Gavin		Drew with Spain 7–7	Defeated by Croatia 10–8
Oberman, Mark				

Water Polo (Women)

Section Manager: Jeanette Gunn   **Head Coach:** Istvan Gorgenyi
Coach: Sharyn Gist, Jacqueline Northam, Gary Roberts   **Physiotherapist:** Andrea Mosler

Castle, Naomi	Miller, Gail	1/6	Preliminary, Group A:	Semifinal:
Fox, Joanne	Mills, Melissa		Defeated Kazakhstan 9–2	Defeated Russia 7–6
Gusterson, Bridgette	Watson, Deborah		Defeated Russia 6–3	Final:
Hankin, Simone	Weekes, Elizabeth		Defeated by Netherlands 5–4	Defeated USA 4–3 (1st)
Higgins, Yvette	Woodhouse, Danielle		Defeated USA 7–6	
Hooper, Kate	Woods, Taryn		Defeated Canada 9–4	
Mayer, Bronwyn				

Weightlifting

Section Manager: Robert Kabbas   **Head Coach:** Luke Borreggine   **Coaches:** Martin Leach, Jack Walls

MEN

Brown, Damian	Up to 77 kilograms	14/18	Final:320.0 pts (14th)
Chakhoyan, Sergo	Up to 85 kilograms	6/20	Final: 377.5 pts (6th)
Karapetyn, Aleksan	Up to 94 kilograms	10/19	Final: 382.5 pts (10th)
Kounev, Kiril	Up to 94 kilograms	14/19	Final: 375.0 pts (14th)
Martin, Anthony	Over 105 kilograms	19/24	Final: 370.0 pts (19th)
Rae, Christopher	Over 105 kilograms	20/24	Final: 360.0 pts (20th)
Sarkisian, Yourik	Up to 62 kilograms	9/21	Final: 290.0 pts (9th)
Yagci, Mehmet	Up to 56 kilograms	17/22	Final: 235.0 pts (17th)

WOMEN

Barker, Natasha	Up to 58 kilograms	10/12	Final: 180.0 pts (10th)
Kettner, Michelle	Up to 69 kilograms	9/15	Final: 222.5 pts (9th)
Phillips, Amanda	Up to 63 kilograms	6/9	Final: 190.0 pts (6th)
Warthold, Meagan	Up to 58 kilograms	12/17	Final: 175.0 pts (12th)

Wrestling

Section Manager: James Sinclair   **Coaches:** Samuel Parker, Arnold Sher

FREESTYLE

Abdullah, Mushtaq		DNC	
Ilhan, Musa	Up to 63 kilograms	18/19	1st round, Pool 6: Defeated by J. Jang (KOR)
			2nd round, Pool 6: Defeated by S. Afandiyev (AZE)
			3rd round, Pool 6: Defeated by S. Fernyak (SVK)
Johnston, Cameron	Up to 69 kilograms	13/20	1st round, Pool 6: Defeated by S. Demchenko (BLR)
			2nd round, Pool 6: Defeated by R. Veliyev (KAZ)
			3rd round, Pool 6: Defeated by A. Askarov (KGZ)
O'Brien, Cory	Up to 58 kilograms	18/20	1st round, Pool 2: Defeated by O. Purevbaatar (MGL)
			2nd round, Pool 2: Defeated by A. Guzov (BLR)
Ozoline, Reinold	Up to 76 kilograms	18/20	1st round, Pool 5: Defeated by M. Jurecki (POL)
			2nd round, Pool 5: Defeated E. Moon (KOR)
			3rd round, Pool 5: Defeated by A. Muzayev (UKR)
Praporshchikov, Igor	Up to 85 kilograms	19/20	1st round, Pool 3: Defeated by A.Saitiev (RUS)
			2nd round, Pool 3: Defeated B. Musaev (BLR)
Szerda, Gabriel	Up to 97 kilograms	12/19	1st round, Pool 6: Defeated by A. Shermarov (BLR)
			2nd round, Pool 6: Defeated by M. Garmulewicz (POL)
			3rd round: Defeated D. Schmeichel (CAN)

GRECO-ROMAN

Abdo, Ali	Up to 69 kilograms	19/19	2nd round, Pool 2: Defeated by Ender Memet (ROM)
Cash, Brett	Up to 58 kilograms	17/20	1st round, Pool 5: Defeated by Nepes Gukulov (TKM)
			2nd round, Pool 5: Defeated by Armen Nazarian (BUL)
Kovacs, Laszlo	97 to 130 kilograms	18/20	2nd round, Pool 3: Defeated by Rafael Barreno (VEN)
Olczak, Arkadiusz	Up to 85 kilograms	18/19	1st round, Pool 5: Defeated by Eddy Bartolozzi (VEN)
			2nd round, Pool 5: Defeated by Sandor Bardosi (HUN)
			3rd round, Pool 5: Defeated by Martin Lidberg (SWE)
Vincent, Benjamin	Up to 97 kilograms	20/20	1st round, Pool 5: Defeated by Urs Buergler (SUI)
			Final: DNQ

2002 Salt Lake City, USA

Chef de Mission: Ian Chesterman   **Administration and Operations Director:** Craig Phillips
Technical Director: Geoff Lipshut   **Team Attaché:** Michelle Demschar   **Athlete Liaison Officers:** Nick Green,
Susie O'Neill   **Administration Officers:** Peter Brockington, Anne Vanden Hogen   **Medical Director:** Dr Peter Braun
Physiotherapists: Peter Hogg, Bianca Matheson, Clare Walsh

Alpine Skiing

Head Coach: Helmut Spiegl   **Coaches:** Michael Branch, Caterina Dietschi, Richard Lepage, Euan Patterson,
Scott Sanderson, Robert Zallmann

MEN

Bear, Aaron	Downhill	37/54	1:43.19
	Super-G		DSQ
	Combined	/47	Combined downhill: 1:41.02
			Combined slalom:
			1st run: DSQ Gate 39
			2nd run: DSQ Rule 629.3
Branch, Craig	Downhill	45/54	1:45.34
	Super-G	27/34	1:27.15
	Combined	/47	Combined slalom: DNC
			Combined downhill: DSQ Rule 627.2
Dickson, Michael	Slalom	/78	1st run: 56.88 (42nd)
			2nd run: DNF
Wall, Bradley	Giant slalom	33/78	1st run: 1:15.69 (37th)
			2nd run: 1:14.59
			Total: 2:30.28 (33rd)

WOMEN

Bright, Rowena	Combined	24/29	Downhill: 1:19.46
			Slalom: 1:51.22
	Slalom	/70	1st run: 1:00.22
			2nd run: DNF
			2nd run: DNF
Jones, Alice	Downhill	27/39	1:43.07 (45.13 pts) (27th)
	Super-G	/43	DNF
	Combined	12/29	Combined downhill: 1:17.83 (15th)
			Combined slalom: 1:32.39 (13th)
			Combined total: 2:50.22 (12th)
Korten, Jeannette	Slalom	25/70	1st run: 57.85
			2nd run: 58.25
			Total: 1:56.10 (25th)
	Giant slalom	/69	1st run: 1:19.00
			2nd run: DSQ (Gate 19)
Nikolussi, Kathrin	Slalom	/70	1st run: DNF
Owens, Jenny	Downhill	29/35	1:44.15
	Super-G	29/43	1:17.84
	Combined	9/29	Combined downhill: 1:16.96 (9th)
			Combined slalom: 1:32.35 (12th)
			Combined total: 2:49.31 (9th)
	Giant slalom	/69	1st run: DNF
Steggall, Zali	Slalom	/70	1st run: DNF

Figure Skating

Coach: Evelyn Kramer

MEN

Liu, Anthony	Individual	10/28	Short program: 5 pts (10th)	Total: 15.0 pts
			Free skating: 10 pts (10th)	

WOMEN

Zhang, Stephanie	Individual	25/27	Short program: 12.5 pts (25th)
			Free skating: Did not reach final

Freestyle Skiing

Coaches: Steve Desovich (Moguls), Peter Judge (Aerials), Michael Kennedy, Todd Ossian (Aerials)

MEN

Costa, Adrian	Moguls	18/30	Qualification: 24.13 pts (18th)	Final: DNQ
Paynter, Trennon	Moguls	23/30	Qualification: 22.53 pts (23rd)	Final: DNQ

WOMEN

Berchtold, Manuela	Moguls	27/29	Qualification: 19.59 pts (27th)	Final: DNQ
Camplin, Alisa	Aerials	1/21	Qualification:	Final:
			1st jump: 93.89 pts	1st jump: 93.72 pts
			2nd jump: 89.77 pts	2nd jump: 99.75 pts
			Total: 183.66 pts (2nd)	Total: 193.47 pts (1st)
Cooper, Jacqueline	Aerials		DNC (injured)	
Despas, Maria	Moguls	21/29	Qualification: 21.19 pts (21st)	Final: DNQ
Ierodiaconou, Lydia	Aerials	8/21	Qualification:	Final:
			1st jump: 82.21 pts	1st jump: 84.49 pts
			2nd jump: 83.85 pts	2nd jump: 84.89 pts
			Total: 166.06 pts (10th)	Total: 169.38 pts (8th)
Sexton, Jane	Moguls	25/29	Qualification: 20.47 pts (25th)	Final: DNQ

Short-track Speed Skating

Coach: Ann Zhang

MEN

Bradbury, Steven	500 metres individual	14/31	Heat: 43.226 (2nd)	Quarter-final: 44.982 (3rd)
				Semifinal: DNQ
	1000 metres individual	1/29	Heat: 1:30.956 (1st)	Semifinal: 1:29.189 (1st)
			Quarter-final: 1:29.265 (2nd)	Final: 1:29.109 (1st)
	1500 metres individual	10/29	Heat: 2:22.632 (3rd)	Semifinal: 2:25.457 (4th)
				B final: 2:28.604 (5th)
	5000 metres relay	6/7	Semifinal: 7:19.177 (3rd)	B final: 7:45.271 (2nd)
Lee, Steven	5000 metres relay	6/7	Semifinal: 7:19.177 (3rd)	B final: 7:45.271 (2nd)
McEwan, Alex	5000 metres relay	6/7	Semifinal: 7:19.177 (3rd)	B final: 7:45.271 (2nd)
McNee, Andrew	500 metres individual	28/31	Heat: 44.289 (4th)	Quarter-final: DNQ
	5000 metres relay	6/7	Semifinal: 7:19.177 (3rd)	B final: 7:45.271 (2nd)
McNee, Mark	1000 metres individual	15/29	Heat: 1:39.325 (2nd)	Quarter-final: 1:46.701 (4th)
				Semifinal: DNQ
	1500 metres individual	28/29	Heat: 2:27.840 (5th)	Quarter-final: DNQ
Goerlitz, Richard		DNC		

Snowboard

MEN

Steggall, Zeke	Parallel giant slalom	26/32	Qualification: 38.69

Australian Olympic medal winners 1996–2002

1996: Atlanta, USA

Gold medals (9)

(Equestrian) Three-day event team (Phillip Dutton, Andrew Hoy, Gillian Rolton, Wendy Schaeffer)

Hockey (Women) (Michelle Andrews, Alyson Annan, Louise Dobson, Renita Farrell, Juliet Haslam, Rechelle Hawkes, Clover Maitland, Karen Marsden, Jennifer Morris, Jacqueline Pereira, Nova Peris, Katrina Powell, Lisa Powell, Danielle Roche, Kate Starre, Liane Tooth)

(Rowing) (Men's) Coxless four (Drew Ginn, Nicholas Green, Michael McKay, James Tomkins)

(Rowing) (Women's) Coxless pair (Kate Slatter, Megan Still)

Diamond, Michael (Shooting) Trap

Mark, Russell (Shooting) Double trap

O'Neill, Susan (Swimming) 200 metres butterfly

Perkins, Kieren (Swimming) 1500 metres freestyle

(Tennis) Men's doubles (Todd Woodbridge, Mark Woodforde)

Silver medals (9)

Freeman, Cathy (Athletics) 400 metres

McPaul, Louise (Athletics) Javelin

Ferris, Michelle (Cycling) Individual sprint

(Rowing) Coxless pair (Robert Scott, David Weightman)

Kowalski, Daniel (Swimming) 1500 metres freestyle

Miller, Scott (Swimming) 100 metres butterfly

Thomas, Petria (Swimming) 200 metres butterfly

(Swimming) (Women's) 4 × 100 metres medley relay (Helen Denman, Angela Kennedy, Susan O'Neill, Samantha Riley, Sarah Ryan, Nicole Stevenson)

(Yachting) Tornado Class (Mitchell Booth, Andrew Landenberger)

Bronze medals (23)

Basketball (Women) (Carla Boyd, Michelle Brogan, Sandra Brondello, Michelle Chandler, Allison Cook, Trisha Fallon, Robyn Maher, Fiona Robinson, Shelley Sandie, Rachael Sporn, Michele Timms, Jennifer Whittle)

Robinson, Clint (Canoeing) K1, 1000 metres

(Canoeing) (Women) K2, 500 metres (Katrin Borchert, Anna Wood)

(Canoeing) (Men) K2, 500 metres (Daniel Collins, Andrew Trim)

McGee, Bradley (Cycling) 4000 metres individual pursuit

O'Grady, Stuart (Cycling) Individual points race

Tyler-Sharman, Lucy (Cycling) Individual points race

(Cycling) 400 metres team pursuit (Brett Aitken, Bradley McGee, Stuart O'Grady, Timothy O'Shannessey, Dean Woods)

Hockey (Men) (Stuart Carruthers, Baeden Choppy, Stephen Davies, Damon Diletti, Lachlan Dreher, Lachlan Elmer, Brendan Garard, Paul Gaudoin, Mark Hager, Paul Lewis, Matthew Smith, Daniel Sproule, Jason Stacy, Kenneth Wark, Michael York)

(Rowing) Men's lightweight double sculls (Anthony Edwards, Bruce Hick)

(Rowing) Quad sculls (Duncan Free, Boden Hanson, Janusz Hooker, Ronald Snook)

(Rowing) Women's lightweight double sculls (Rebecca Joyce, Virginia Lee)

Huddleston, Deserie (Shooting) Double trap

Softball (Women) (Joanne Brown, Kim Cooper, Carolyn Crudgington, Kerry Dienelt, Peta Edebone,
    Tanya Harding, Jennifer Holliday, Jocelyn Lester, Sally McDermid, Francine McRae, Haylea Petria, Nicole
    Richardson, Melanie Roche, Natalie Ward, Brooke Wilkins)
Goodman, Scott (Swimming) 200 metres butterfly
Kowalski, Daniel (Swimming) 200 metres freestyle
Kowalski, Daniel (Swimming) 400 metres freestyle
Riley, Samantha (Swimming) 100 metres breaststroke
(Swimming) (Men) 4 × 100 metres medley relay (Steven Dewick, Toby Haenen, Michael Klim, Scott Miller,
    Philip Rogers)
(Swimming) Women 4 × 200 metres freestyle relay (Julia Greville, Emma Johnson, Lisa Mackie,
    Susan O'Neill, Nicole Stevenson)
Volleyball, Beach (Women) (Natalie Cook, Kerri-Ann Pottharst)
Botev, Stefan (Weightlifting) Over 108 kilograms
(Yachting) Star Class (Colin Beashel, David Giles)

1998: Nagano, Japan
Bronze medals (1)
Steggall, Zali (Alpine Skiing) (Women) Slalom

2000: Sydney, Australia
Gold medals (16)
Fairweather, Simon (Archery) Individual
Freeman, Cathy (Athletics) 400 metres
(Cycling) Madison — track (Brett Aitken, Scott McGrory)
(Equestrian) Three-day event team (Phillip Dutton, Andrew Hoy, Matthew Ryan, Stuart Tinney)
Hockey (Women) (Katie Allen, Alyson Annan, Lisa Carruthers, Renita Garard, Juliet Haslam, Rechelle Hawkes,
    Nicole Hudson, Rachel Imison, Clover Maitland, Claire Mitchell-Taverner, Jennifer Morris, Alison Peek,
    Katrina Powell, Angela Skirving, Kate Starre, Julie Towers)
(Sailing) 470 Class (Men) (Thomas King, Mark Turnbull)
(Sailing) 470 Class (Women) (Jennifer Armstrong, Belinda Stowell)
Diamond, Michael (Shooting) Trap
Hackett, Grant (Swimming) 1500 metres freestyle
O'Neill, Susan (Swimming) 200 metres freestyle
Thorpe, Ian (Swimming) 400 metres freestyle
(Swimming) 4 × 100 metres freestyle relay (Ashley Callus, Chris Fydler, Michael Klim, Todd Pearson, Adam Pine,
    Ian Thorpe)
(Swimming) 4 × 200 metres freestyle relay (Grant Hackett, William Kirby, Michael Klim, Daniel Kowalski,
    Todd Pearson, Ian Thorpe)
Burns, Lauren (Taekwondo) Under 49 kilograms
Volleyball, Beach (Women) (Natalie Cook, Kerri-Ann Pottharst)
Water Polo (Women) (Naomi Castle, Joanne Fox, Brigette Gusterson, Simone Hankin, Yvette Higgins,
    Kate Hooper, Bronwyn Mayer, Gail Miller, Melissa Mills, Deborah Watson, Elizabeth Weekes,
    Danielle Woodhouse, Taryn Woods)

Silver medals (25)
Grigorieva, Tatiana (Athletics) Pole vault
Taurima, Jai (Athletics) Long jump
Basketball (Women) (Carla Boyd, Sandra Brondello, Annie Burgess, Trish Fallon, Michelle Griffiths,
    Kristi Harrower, Joanne Hill, Lauren Jackson, Shelley Sandie, Rachel Sporn, Michele Timms,
    Jennifer Whittle)
(Canoeing) K2, 500 metres (Daniel Collins, Andrew Trim)
Ferris, Michelle (Cycling—track) 500 metres time trial

Neiwand, Gary (Cycling — track) Keirin
Hoy, Andrew (Equestrian) Three-day event individual
Wallace, Ji (Gymnastics) Trampoline
(Rowing) (Men) Coxed eight (Daniel Burke, Jaime Fernandez, Alistair Gordon, Robert Jahrling, Michael McKay,
        Nicholas Porzig, Christian Ryan, Stuart Welch)
(Rowing) (Women) Coxless pair (Kate Slatter, Rachael Taylor)
(Rowing) (Men) Lightweight coxless fours (Darren Balmforth, Simon Burgess, Anthony Edwards,
        Robert Richards)
(Sailing) Tornado Class (Darren Bundock, John Forbes)
Mark, Russell (Shooting) Double trap
Jones, Leisel (Swimming) 100 metres breaststroke
Klim, Michael (Swimming) 100 metres butterfly
O'Neill, Susan (Swimming) 200 metres butterfly
Perkins, Kieren (Swimming) 1500 metres freestyle
Thorpe, Ian (Swimming) 200 metres freestyle
Welsh, Matthew (Swimming) 100 metres backstroke
(Swimming) (Women) 4 × 200 metres freestyle relay (Elka Graham, Susan O'Neill, Giaan Rooney,
        Petria Thomas, Kirsten Thomson, Jacinta van Lint)
(Swimming) (Men) 4 × 100 metres medley relay (Regan Harrison, Geoff Huegill, Michael Klim, Ryan Mitchell,
        Adam Pine, Ian Thorpe, Josh Watson, Matthew Welsh)
(Swimming) (Women) 4 × 100 metres medley relay (Dyana Calub, Leisel Jones, Susan O'Neill, Giaan Rooney,
        Sarah Ryan, Petria Thomas, Tarnee White)
Trenton, Daniel (Taekwondo) Over 80 kilograms
(Tennis) Men's doubles (Todd Woodbridge, Mark Woodforde)
Jones, Michellie (Triathlon) (Women)

Bronze medals (17)
Borchert, Katrin (Canoeing) K1, 500 metres
Kelly, Shane (Cycling) 1 kilometre time trial — track
McGee, Bradley (Cycling) 4000 metres individual pursuit — track
(Cycling) Olympic sprint — track (Sean Eadie, Darryn Hill, Gary Neiwand)
(Diving) (Men) 3-metres synchronised (Robert Newbery, Dean Pullar)
(Diving) (Women) 10-metres synchronised (Rebecca Gilmore, Loudy Tourky)
Hockey (Men) (Michael Brennan, Adam Commens, Stephen Davies, Damon Diletti, Lachlan Dreher, Jason Duff,
        Troy Elder, Paul Gaudoin, Stephen Holt, Brent Livermore, Daniel Sproule, Jason Stacy, Craig Victory,
        Matthew Wells, Michael York)
Pekli, Maria (Judo) 52–57 kilograms
(Rowing) (Men) Coxless pair (Matthew Long, James Tomkins)
(Rowing) (Men) Coxless four (Benjamin Dodwell, Boden Hanson, Geoffrey Stewart, James Stewart)
Blackburn, Michael (Sailing) Laser
Forder, Annemarie (Shooting) 10 metres air pistol
Softball (Women) (Sandra Allen, Joanne Brown, Kerry Dienelt, Peta Edebone, Sue Fairhurst, Selina Follas,
        Fiona Hanes, Kelly Hardie, Tanya Harding, Sally McCreedy, Simmone Morrow, Melanie Roche,
        Natalie Tacume,
        Natalie Ward, Brooke Wilkins)
Huegill, Geoffrey (Swimming) 100 metres butterfly
Norris, Justin (Swimming) 200 metres butterfly
Thomas, Petria (Swimming) 200 metres butterfly
Welsh, Matthew (Swimming) 200 metres backstroke

2002: Salt Lake City, USA
Gold medals (2)
Camplin, Alisa (Freestyle Skiing) Aerials
Bradbury, Steven (Short-track Speed Skating) 1000 metres individual

Index